INDEPENDENTS

ALLAN   FULLER   I. DUNCAN

ENTERS   KINCH   DUNHAM   STRAWBRIDGE

BEATTY

HOLM

NIKOLAIS
LAMHUT
LOUIS
PILOBOLUS
SCHMIDT
WODYNSKI
ZAMIR

ANTHONY   BETTIS   REDLICH   TETLEY

TAMIRIS

NAGRIN   SCOTT

DUNAS   FOREMAN   KEEN

K. KING   KEUTER

NEVILLE

HORTON

AILEY

FAISON

LEWITZKY   TRISLER   TRUITTE

Other Books by Don McDonagh:

MARTHA GRAHAM
THE RISE AND FALL AND RISE OF MODERN DANCE
BALLET FOR ALL (Contributor)

THE COMPLETE GUIDE TO MODERN DANCE

The Complete Guide to Modern Dance

DON McDONAGH

DOUBLEDAY & COMPANY, INC., GARDEN CITY, NEW YORK, 1976

FIRST PERFORMANCE CREDITS AND CHOREOCHRONICLES
ASSEMBLED BY ANDREW MARK WENTINK.

PHOTOGRAPHS OF MAUD ALLAN, LOIE FULLER, ISADORA DUNCAN
(IRMA DUNCAN COLLECTION), TED SHAWN AND RUTH ST. DENIS,
HELEN TAMIRIS, CHARLES WEIDMAN AND DORIS HUMPHREY, ALVIN
AILEY, KATHERINE DUNHAM, AND ANNA SOKOLOW ARE REPRODUCED
BY COURTESY OF THE DANCE COLLECTION, PERFORMING ARTS
RESEARCH CENTER, NEW YORK PUBLIC LIBRARY AT LINCOLN
CENTER, ASTOR, LENOX AND TILDEN FOUNDATIONS.

LIBRARY OF CONGRESS CATALOGING IN PUBLICATION DATA
MCDONAGH, DON.
THE COMPLETE GUIDE TO MODERN DANCE.
BIBLIOGRAPHY: P. 509.
INCLUDES INDEX.
I. MODERN DANCE.   I. TITLE.
GV1783.M26   793.3'2
ISBN 0-385-05055-0
LIBRARY OF CONGRESS CATALOG CARD NUMBER 75–21235

BOOK DESIGN BY BEVERLEY GALLEGOS

Contents

FREEDOM AND NEW FORMALISM (SECOND GENERATION)

List of Illustrations

To the artists whose dedication and work made this book possible.

Foreword

The awesome first step in compiling a one-volume sampler of modern dance creativity is to select the choreographers and to choose from their works those which most merit attention. To include all of those who have choreographed dances in the history of modern dance was impossible, and it was equally impossible to describe all of the dances created by those individuals who were included. The selection offered is a representative anthology and was governed by the desire to include all choreographers who have demonstrated some personal creative statement which was significant.

Those artists who have worked with their own companies or who have presented their works as solo artists for at least five years, or whose work has been maintained by other companies for a like period of time, comprised the basic pool of committed professionals. Selecting individual works to describe was mandated in certain cases, e.g., Isadora Duncan's *La Marseillaise,* Martha Graham's *Appalachian Spring,* Doris Humphrey's trilogy *New Dance,* or Charles Weidman's *Fables for Our Times.* Others were picked because they represented the artist at peak creative power shaping mainstream emotional themes or evolving innovative form.

The brief biographical sketch for each of the choreographers touches merely the outlines of their careers, and the selection of works is likewise restricted to special high points. So that the reader may be aware of the volume of creative work represented by the descriptions, a choreochronicle is appended for each artist, showing all the known works. The dedication and diligence of my research assistant, Andrew Wentink, to assembling this material has been exceptional, and in most cases these choreochronicles represent the first such compilation. A special thanks is due to those choreographers who set aside time to answer queries and furnish lists and programs of their work. I would also like to thank Cyrus Rogers for his invaluable reading of the text and Beverley Gallegos, who designed the book.

Once again, the Dance Collection, New York Public Library at Lincoln Center, proved an inexhaustible font of information. Its collection of programs, flyers, photographs, clippings, films, and books were generously put at my disposal by Genevieve Oswald and her helpful staff. The asterisk (*) preceding a work indicates one described in detail, (p) is a play, (mc) a musical comedy, (tv) a television production, and (mp) is a motion picture.

D.McD.

Introducing Modern Dance

Despite the fact that there were established modern dance companies in the United States prior to the founding of our present national ballet companies, there has always lurked about modern dance something of newness and a feeling of revolutionary activity. The reputation is deserved but does not reflect the whole story. The first of the large modern dance companies was the Denishawn company, which began in 1915 and was founded by Ruth St. Denis and Edwin Meyers (Ted) Shawn, both of whom were pioneers of serious concert dance in the United States. The first native American ballet companies were not founded until the 1930s, and by that time Denishawn had completed several national and international tours and had founded Denishawn licensed schools across the United States.

The most obvious differences between modern dance, as it was practiced by Denishawn and its pupils who considerably modified it, and the ballet are to be observed in the basic techniques of movement. The balletic movement is by and large broadly conceived with the largeness of an opera house audience in mind. It is movement which strives for and attains lightness by stressing the dancer's ability to rise from the floor in defiance of gravity. It is movement which has been modified through three hundred years of work by teachers and dancers contributing to its possibilities.

The attitude of the ballet dancer's body is one of formal correctness in a way which owes much to the aristocratic court dance of Western Europe from which it developed. Ballet dancing is the most dramatic and technically accomplished offshoot of court dancing that is extant. The only other tributary of court dance which can still be seen is formal horseback riding, the art of dressage. The rider positions his body and aligns his head and torso in much the same way that the court dancer did, and leads his mount through patterns of movement in rhythmic measures that derive in large measure from court dance as it was practiced in the seventeenth century at the court of Louis XIV. The claim has been made that the Spanish Riding School of Vienna, home of the famed white Lipizzaner horses, should be counted among the world's great ballet companies. The enthusiam is understandable and makes a point that might otherwise be lost.

Modern dance does not look to European dance models for the primary sources of its movement techniques. Modern dance in its strongest impulses looks within the individual, whose expressive needs then determine the types of gesture that will emerge when the dancer starts to move. The ballet is a formal classical style of dance, and modern dance is expressionistic in its thrust. Where ballet movement begins and ends in one of the five positions of the feet which have become the basis of ballet dancing, modern dance does not recognize the convention of only five positions. It asserts that there are as many positions as are needed by the artist to create his effects. In this sense modern dance is revolutionary by definition. It would claim that there is no set number of positions or movements any more than there is a single arithmetic number which represents the largest conceivable magnitude, one only has to add "1" to it and a whole new series has begun. Modern dance is more receptive to the possibilities of unorthodox movement because of this basic attitude and in the course of the seventy-odd years of its existence has witnessed and incorporated a great number of changes in specific movement. One thing, however, has remained constant, no matter which modification of dance technique was used, and that is, that the approach was determined by creative needs. The technique did not exist completely formed before the dance designer began to create a dance. Each of the great modern dance choreographers has shaped the human body in a distinctly personal way to frame those creative ideas that he or she wanted to express, so that one can speak of Denishawn or Isadora Duncan styles of movement as well as those of Martha Graham, Doris Humphrey, Merce Cunningham, Alwin Nikolais, or most recently Twyla Tharp. Their styles are as recognizable as those of writers or painters. Modern dance differs from classic ballet in many of the ways that modernist painting differs from the classical; both allow expressive needs to determine the form of expression rather than restrict the expressive range because of the dictates of the form.

In concrete terms the modern dancer regarded the formalism of ballet as a stultifying rather than a useful device. The first modern dancers saw no need to attempt to rise from the floor to defy gravity. The ground in the oldest societies was thought of as a source of stability and strength. To come in greater contact with the floor, the modern dancers removed their shoes and danced with bare feet to emphasize their sympathy and closeness with the energy to be derived from the floor. They could leap away from it, but they also could bend and prostrate their bodies on the floor to develop dance movement needing such an impetus. The torso, which in ballet dancing is strongly controlled with a high arch to the spine, found a counterdesire among modern dancers, and that was to introduce a supple strength into the spine. The legs, which in ballet are rotated outward so that they are seen in profile, were kept in their normal walking stance in modern dance.

There are other differences, but these are the main ones observable in regular concertgoing, and of course both the ballet and modern dance have had an effect on one another so that neither is quite as different as it once was. Modern dance's doctrinaire insistence that the toes be pointed forward, as opposed to being pointed to the side when standing, has been changed so that the feet are now customarily half turned out in the manner that can be observed in Balinese dance. Ballet, on its part, while holding strongly to the necessity of its five positions of the feet and the turn out of the leg, has found that a more supple torso is an addition to the expressive possibilities of the human body. Neither form of dancing has by any means abandoned its roots, but each has come to recognize advantageous techniques which can be incorporated into its own way of moving. There is no reason to think that there ever will be a single all-encompassing technique of theatrical dancing that will supersede these two major styles. There will be a give and take between them with influences on both from contemporary social dance or even newly examined folk dances from other parts of the globe, but each will remain faithful to its origins. In classical antiquity it was always recognized that there were two basic modes of expression, which were designated the Apollonian and Dionysiac, that is, the style which was happiest in structured restraint and the other more emotionally driven in its expression and less bound by a pre-existent set of rules. The alternation between the two has been an observable pattern in artistic expression throughout the ages.

Aside from the differences in the manner of moving there are some other substantial differences between modern dance and ballet, and that is in their subject matter. Romantic ballet found it congenial to select subject matter from European fairy tales and folk stories, which modern dance for the most part has not. Modern dance, when it has used such stories for the bases of dances, has generally sought out tales from antiquity, Middle Eastern or Indian sources, or the stories of the peoples of the Western Hemisphere. *Giselle,* perhaps the most perfect of the romantic ballets, is based on an old Germanic legend, while Martha Graham's *Clytemnestra* draws upon classical antiquity for its story of torment and redemption. In addition, modern dance has always shown a special sympathy to the social concerns of its particular age. This sensitivity could be expressed in obvious dances about political or economic crises, such as were produced by the generation of the 1930s, but it could also find a way to the dance stage in the work of a choreographer like Merce Cunningham, who realized that stories no longer reflected the myriad of impressions that people received from life. Experience was not arranged in a neat straight line but was a jumble, a tangle of incident, and in his methods of creating a dance Cunningham attempted to be true to this fact by letting chance play a part in his method of composition and in ordering the parts of a dance. Thus within a few broad rules a variety of sequences and impressions were possible, each having the basic tone of the work as it was made but expressing it in a slightly different manner. In a way it was like a sports contest played under identical rules each time. The outline was the same but the specific game was different.

Modern dance has traditionally treated each of the members of a particular company as being equal and liable to be given individual variations to dance in the course of a piece. The company was considered an ensemble basically, contrasted to the traditional ballet company, which was as hierarchically arranged as an army or a king's court. The dancers who form the corps de ballet are the lowest rung of this hierarchy and dance in ensembles and in traditionally less complex dance passages than those who are more advanced. The coryphees, who are the next rank up, are given the opportunity to dance quartets or trios and occasionally a duo, which are a little more complex and given greater attention than the corps movements. Soloists dance individual variations but are not given the leading roles in a dance. These are reserved for the first dancers in the company, the principals; the female being designated a ballerina and the male a danseur noble. The gradations do not exist so formally in modern dance, but careful examination of any modern dance company shows that there are "stars" even in its basically egalitarian organization. One easily observed rule is that the name of a modern dance company usually denotes both the choreographer of the dances and the chief dancer. It is not infallible but is a good rule of thumb. The exact opposite is true of ballet companies. The name of the New York City Ballet, for instance, does not give any indication of the finest dancers in the company, and one must rely on program designation of principal, soloist, and so forth for that information. In a modern dance theater program one would seek in vain for such information. Only the frequency with which a dancer's name appears in several works or the assignment of solo variations indicates the hierarchy of accomplishment.

Modern dance's emphasis on the individual has resulted in a situation where there are few companies which approach the size of a major ballet company. But what modern dance lacks in ensemble size is more than made up for in the numbers of companies. At present there is a myriad of companies ranging from the smallest, i.e., two dancers, to the largest, about thirty. Most of these companies take their creative direction from a single choreographer who at one time danced with another modern dancer and then decided to create dances to express his or her own ideas about dance structure. The choreographer creates not only most of the dances that the company performs but also teaches his dancers the style which he feels is most perfectly designed for the realization of those creative ideas.

It is this breaking off of one choreographer from another which lends modern dance the variety of personal movement styles which can be observed in the course of a season of viewing. It is not to say that any one style is better than any other but that for a particular choreographer's work it is definitely preferable. There is no doubt that a fine dancer from any of the modern dance companies could dance a role that was created with the particular choreographic accents of another company. The dancer would perform it with great fidelity to the original choreographer's intent but would not capture all of the small nuances of the role which were put into it at the beginning. It is a situation which exists in all dancing, including ballet. There is simply no way for a contemporary trained ballet dancer to perform any of the nineteenth-century classics such as *Swan Lake* or *Sleeping Beauty* or *Giselle,* in a completely accurate nineteenth-century style. These pieces were created for the dancers as they existed at that time, and subsequent generations have not been trained in precisely the same manner. Despite this they are able to project the bulk of the roles which they inherit, although there are undoubtedly gestural niceties lacking. In a way it is similar to the problem of contemporary musicians who despite the notations on an orchestral score do not know precisely the rhythmic values of pieces from other centuries and simply play a "presto" as they have learned to play it during their training, although it may be slower than the presto that the composer originally intended. There is undoubtedly some artistic loss, but the gain of hearing the piece, even imperfectly, far outweighs that loss.

In brief, there are differences between modern dance and ballet in approach to movement, but these are not so much antagonistic as simply different ways of presenting serious theatrical dance. When one thinks of popular dancing in the movies one thinks of the great figures of Fred Astaire and Gene Kelly as the two most outstanding male dancers of the screen. In an analogy that shouldn't be pushed too far one might think of Astaire as representing classic ballet and Kelly modern dance. Although each has played in many roles, one tends to see Astaire in white tie and tails, his feet neatly laced into shiny pumps, dancing in a formally organized space such as the ballroom floor of a large night club. He handles his partner deftly, indicating changes of direction with a light touch hardly seeming to exercise any obvious control at all. The dancing is elegant. One equally easily imagines Kelly in a casual shirt, probably open at the neck, with his feet tucked into a pair of loafers sauntering down a street. He incorporates anything he encounters into his dance, a street lamp to swing around, a fire hydrant to vault across in order to meet his partner, who is equally casually and attractively attired. Their duet has a sportive energy and less formal restraint. In both cases the dancing has been beautiful, but the approach is different. Neither one is to be enjoyed at the expense of ignoring the other. Both elicit our admiration and show us some creative possibilities.

In the following pages are to be found descriptions of over two hundred dances which have been created by modern dance choreographers dating from the last decade of the nineteenth century right up to the present time. For the sake of clarity they have been classified into five broad groupings within which the artistic climate was shared by those working at the time. They all did not do precisely the same thing, as a matter of fact far from it, but they were all linked by some basic similarities in their attitudes toward the use of theatrical space.

Within each of the large sections there are listed the works of the individuals spoken of, and a brief biographical sketch of each artist has been included. With so many dances to include it is obvious that selections had to be made. These were made first on the worth of the individual pieces and secondly to show the variety of dance approaches that existed side by side. There is no easy formula to indicate which dances should be included from the work of any individual's output, but generally that which was considered the best exemplar of a particular series was included or a piece which has received wide acclaim.

The Forerunners

Among those dancers who comprise the first generation of modern dance the most vital names are those of Isadora Duncan, Ruth St. Denis, Ted Shawn, Maud Allan, and Loie Fuller. These dancers all creatively shared the period beginning roughly at the end of the nineteenth century and continuing up through the first thirty years of the twentieth. They were all pioneers of a dance form which was later to be called modern dance, but in their own time they were individuals who did not have a sense of themselves as being part of a movement but simply artists who were devising suitable ways to dance. Critics referred to them as "aesthetic," "barefoot," or "dramatic" dancers.

In the United States at the time there were few ballet teachers of any skill, and ballet was presented as a specialty act in the theater along with other types of dance loosely called show dancing. This latter form of dance stuck pretty firmly to the idea that a group of pretty girls doing a simple step repeatedly was about as much dance as the public wanted to see. It was, in its way, modestly successful. The public did not demand much more than occasional glimpses of an exotic dancer from the Far East or the Middle East. Some of the native American dancers who went into the theater attempted to imitate these performers and their sensual daring. The most famous of these billed herself as "Little Egypt" and was the scandalous hit of the Chicago World's Fair, held in 1893.

The more serious dancers of the pioneer generation were not immune to this spirit of daring and in creating their own dances relied quite often on sexy allure. But before any of these dancers struck out on an individual career, each began dancing in what was then the popular theater of the day. None of them stayed at it for very long but each of them received his or her initial experience of the theater in what was then the equivalent of Broadway. None of them began as rebels and none of them had any models to imitate, except perhaps the solo "exotics," as each began to move further and further away from conventional entertainment.

In all cases they were driven by a desire to dance in pieces that had a more serious content than those connected with the popular theater. These were dance vehicles which were created according to a fairly standard formula which varied little from one show to another. The pioneers felt that dance was capable of creating more than a momentary diversion in the attention of an audience and was in fact capable of moving people deeply and seriously. The thought was revolutionary. The only existing form of serious theatrical dance that was then recognized was ballet, and it was concentrated mainly in Europe.

The pioneers began when the nineteenth century was beginning to change into what we would recognize as the twentieth. The settled and established order of life was going to change because the world had changed. By the time of the cataclysm of World War I the change was well on its way, and the dancers were exploring the expressive possibilities of their individual styles of movement. They struggled against the conventions that relegated women's dance presentations to matinee performances only and against the theatrical wisdom which held that no dancer could possibly have a week-long season without any other supporting "acts." They introduced new types of characters on the stage by turning to ancient India and presenting gods or goddesses of that culture or from Middle Eastern legend and ritual or from the stories of the Indians of the Americas. They sought out and cherished mythical tales and legends to translate into dance, and they also created simple mood dances in imitation of birds, insects or even a flickering flame. They were trying to make a place for a new art form in the most commercial of all atmospheres, the musical theater.

It is one thing to effect a revolution with a monarch's patronage or in an academic setting but quite another under the watchful eyes of professional theater managements, so that of necessity their art, such as it was, had to be accessible to the audiences of the day. They could not afford to be unpopular to the extent of ignoring audiences, for they had to strive to attract an audience so as to be able to afford to form their emerging art. It was a difficult and frustrating experience. The pioneers did not by any means despise audience enthusiasm; they were all products of the theater world no matter how much they wished to change it, and as a result made compromises to popular taste. They made compromises in order to survive. There was at the time no alternative to the popular theater if one wished to perform in public. There was no off-Broadway; there were no universities with dance programs to be host to such dance companies. The first generation had to make its way in the market place.

One of the things which characterized this generation was its use of the theatrical elements of costume, lighting, and décor. When they came on stage it was obvious that their training had been put to canny use. They might have been exotic but they were theatrically correct in the impression that they made. Good materials were customarily used for costumes and décor and in some cases lighting designs unequaled until our own time for their freshness and imagination. Technically the dancers were not much beyond their contemporaries in the commercial theater; after all they had received the same training. What distinguished them was a seriousness of purpose and the projection of personality or beauty dedicated to some lofty or mysterious purpose. They could entertain but they could also stimulate the imagination to speculate on the purpose of the dance; why it was designed in a particular way and what its intent was. Even if one were not drawn into speculation, one was aware of a talented dancer, fully the equal of others of less import, who could be beguiling at the very least.

Of the five pioneers only Ted Shawn made his career almost exclusively within the United States. The four others—Maud Allen, Isadora Duncan, Ruth St. Denis, and Loie Fuller—each went abroad for extended periods of time to dance to generally greater acclaim than they ever received in the United States. It was ironic that the first great successes that these artists had were experienced in Europe. Only after such acclaim were they able to do successful touring in the United States. For all of them financial stability was the same as it was for any other member of the theater at the time. It was insecure for all but the very few who were at the top of the profession. The pioneers were successful eventually but never occupied the assured place that would guarantee them financial security. They created the climate for an art form while struggling for their own existence.

MAUD ALLAN

She was the daughter of two practicing physicians and was born in Toronto, Canada. She was brought up for the most part in San Francisco and thought of herself as an American. As a young girl, she studied music in Berlin and spent much time visiting art galleries. The combination of her musical and artistic interests led her to conceive of a career in dancing as the logical expression of both interests, and she made her first public appearances in Austria.

She was self-taught as a dancer and was influenced by the work of Isadora Duncan. Her first great success came in London, and England remained a special place for her to the end of her life. Long after she had stopped dancing she returned to England during World War II to volunteer as an ambulance driver.

Just as Duncan was sensitive to music, many of Allan's strongest works arose from a deep appreciation of first-rate music. Composers such as Bach, Schubert, and Mendelssohn furnished her with scores to dance to. She found herself in conflict with Duncan, who accused her of imitating her (Duncan's) art, but the furor passed almost as soon as it arose. The dancers obviously did influence one another in the way that any artist influences another, but only the second-rate plagiarists add nothing of themselves to the model they imitate.

In any case Allan found that she created imitators of her *Vision of Salomé*, but none were able to do anything memorable with the theft. Allan continued to work through the 1920s and 1930s but achieved her greatest fame during the years prior to World War I. She called her style dramatic dancing and loathed being referred to as an "aesthetic" or "barefoot" dancer.

SPRING SONG

Choreography by Maud Allan. Music by Felix Mendelssohn. First performed at Theatre Hall, Royal Conservatory of Music, Vienna, Austria, 1903, by Maud Allan.

The music of Mendelssohn and the painting of Botticelli were the strongest influences on Allan when she created this dance. She was familiar with the music from her own studies and, when in rapid succession she first saw Botticelli's *The Return of Spring* and later *Birth of Venus,* the dance began to take shape.

For this work she chose a Grecian tunic as her costume and created a joyful and flowing dance that was favorably received even by some who were not especially admiring of her other works. The combination of Mendelssohn's lilting melody and a flow of gesture miming the gathering of flowers produced a harmonious spectacle. From time to time during the piece Allan hopped lightly on one foot drawing her knee high in the air like the skipping motion of a frolicking creature. To one reviewer she was the embodiment of all things Grecian and the "interpreter of strange, half remembered thoughts."

For the most part Allan's repertory of dance consisted of solo variations, such as this one, to recognized and attractive music. She was not drawn to music of symphonic length and was most effective in creating mood in shorter pieces. She admired the lyricism of the figures she observed on Grecian vases and in this work created an homage to the civilization that meant so much to her.

VISION OF SALOMÉ

Choreography by Maud Allan. Costumed by Marcel Remy. First performed in Munich, Germany, April 1907, by Maud Allan.

Of all the legendary women of history it was almost inevitable that Allan would have selected Salomé as the subject of her dance. She enjoyed her greatest successes in England, where Wilde's play *Salomé* had a scandalous popularity. The calculated decadence of Beardsley's drawings contributed to the titillation, and Richard Strauss based his sensuous opera on the German translation of Wilde's play. The subject was in the air. Allan, though not particularly beautiful, possessed an attractive figure and, clothed in an abbreviated costume, she was shockingly spectacular. Her *Salomé* elevated her to fame in the years before the outbreak of World War I.

The dance was performed with dramatic lighting so as to heighten the effect of her seductively persuasive movement. When first seen she is standing alone in the garden of an oriental palace. She wears a halter of beads above the waist, and a dark transparent skirt extends from the hips to her feet, which are unclad. At first her movements are confined to gestures of the arms and highly expressive fingers. Only the columns of the palace garden enclosure frame her. Suddenly the head of John the Baptist is seen on a pedestal to her left. Her body convulses and she recoils from it, but the attraction that she feels draws her and she creeps toward it with long, low strides.

She pauses, hesitates, and her body throbs with hidden feelings as she averts her gaze from it. But she turns again and approaches the pedestal. Quickly she grasps the head and holds it at arm's length, swinging it above her head as she stretches her body to its full height. She draws the head toward her face and then tips the dead lips of the prophet to her own as if to drink obscene kisses from the brim of a cup. Her body contorts once more with an anguish that sends her writhing. She places the head down and retreats away toward the pedestal, where she falls shuddering on her knees. The compulsion to return to the head draws her slowly upward. Her body quivers and she stretches and writhes as she approaches the fallen head. She fills the air with gesture from her arms and gleaming body. She staggers, reels, and collapses as a shining mass in the pallid moonlight.

In some performances she only mimed caressing the head, but in others she actually had a stage property head which she stroked, but in every case the impression of an abandoned half-nude woman in the throes of lust made *Salomé* a great audience favorite. As she sprang, glimpses of her bare legs could be seen beneath the black skirt, and her bare back gave the impression of wanton nudity. Many in her audience were attracted by the scandalous costuming, which today would be accepted as entirely appropriate, but Allan was serious in her attempt to create this portrait of the sensuous dancing girl and felt that the costume she designed was suitable. In later years she fought against being known as the Salomé dancer, since it was the only work in her entire repertory that was so daring, but the impression that she created stayed with her throughout her career.

CHOREOCHRONICLE
OF MAUD ALLAN

1903

Dances to the music of Bach,
   Beethoven, Schubert, Schumann
*Spring Song

1907

*Vision of Salomé

1908

Nair, the Slave
Melody in F (Rubinstein)
Valse Caprice (Rubinstein)

1910

Orfeo

Dates Uncertain

Am Meer (Schubert)
Barcarolle, from Tales of
   Hoffmann (Offenbach)
Blue Danube Waltz (Strauss)
Eight Preludes, Mazurka in B flat,
   Mazurka in G sharp minor
   (Chopin)
Moment Musical (Schubert)
Nutcracker Suite (Tchaikovsky)
Passepied (Le Roi s'amuse,
   Delibes)
Peer Gynt Suite
Sarabande and Gavotte (Bach)

ISADORA DUNCAN

The legend of Isadora almost totally obscures the creative genius of Duncan. She was not the first of the pioneering generation who tried to create serious truth through the beauty of expressive movement, but her name and its scandalous overtones have become part of the mythical mist from which modern dance emerged. She was born in 1878 in San Francisco to a father who faded early from the family hearth and a strong-willed mother with a great sensitivity for music. Duncan subsequently appropriated concert level music for the dance stage and displayed daring taste in her selection of composers to the end of her career.

She began modestly as a show dancer in Chicago, but her restless nature drove her to New York, where she did interpretive dancing for social salons and later transferred her activity to London. She had a modest success as a concert dancer but went to Paris to join the company organized by Loie Fuller, with whom she toured. Despite her antipathy to dance other than that of her own devising she admired Fuller's skill and deplored that of Fuller's imitators. When she launched her own independent career, it was to celebrate the dance energy she felt that ancient Grecian civilization possessed. She adored Grecian ruins, so far as to design a house in Greece for herself and her brothers and sister, and frequently danced in classical tunics.

Her art consisted in her sensitive visual realization of the deep rhythms of the concert level music she selected. She was exceptionally receptive to the subtleties of great music and created gestural equivalents to its tones that enchanted audiences. She did not bequeath a systematized vocabulary of movement to her students but attempted to arouse in them the receptivity to musical impulse that she herself felt. Her art was intensely personal and no one has ever adequately succeeded in projecting the intensity of her own personal vision, although substantially successful revivals of her dances have been made.

Her private life was violently unconventional. She had three children out of wedlock by two different men; Paris Singer, who was enormously rich, and Gordon Craig, who was an enormously talented man of the theater. One of the children died shortly after being born and the two others were drowned in a ghastly auto accident that plunged their car into the Seine. She drank heavily in her later years and married Sergei Essenin, a Russian poet twenty years her junior. She founded schools in Germany, France, and Russia, but none ever produced that race of superchildren that she hoped would emerge. Her husband committed suicide, and she was killed in a bizarre auto accident when her scarf became tangled in the spokes of an automobile wheel and she was choked to death. But what is remembered is the integrity of her vision of great music matched by natural but expressive movement. She has had her imitators but none that showed the gift for translating abstract sound into striking movement with her special sensitivity.

IPHIGENIA IN AULIS

Choreography by Isadora Duncan. Music by Christoph Willibald Gluck. First performed at the Krystall-Palast, Berlin, Germany, November 24, 1905, by Isadora Duncan.

Gluck's opera was a turning point in opera history and was exactly the sort of concert level music that Duncan was interested in performing. She had a suite made for orchestra that contained twelve parts, and she danced in seven of them. The dance was arranged in three large sections of which the second was purely orchestral. When Gluck created the opera, he was congratulated for having immersed himself in the Grecian style and not just creating a surface imitation of its mode. Duncan did precisely the same and further penetrated to the rhythmic heart of the music to create her characterization of the daughter of Agamemnon, by whom she was to be sacrificed for favorable winds. (According to the legend the Greek fleet was becalmed and unable to sail for Troy and pursue its war with the Trojans.) The commentary offered by Marie-Thérèse, a Duncan dancer, evokes the special performing qualities of the choreographer in this work.

Again I see her now as she danced with infinite grace the serene happy dances of the Thessalian maiden, Iphigenia, followed by the grief and austerity of the classical dance of her sacrifice. Gliding, swaying she achieved an almost unearthly lightness. At times her movements had the quasi, unreal flowing continuity of dissolving into endless horizons as she danced the imperceptible transitions of a dream like calando, seemingly lifted on the rosy cloud of a zephyr, sempre legatissime vanishing into the periphery of unheard sounds and unseen movements suspendent, dissolving with infiniter gentleness . . . beyond the sphere of musical imagination.

It was one of Duncan's most warmly received works, but it also required the services of a full orchestra, which was an expense that she could not always afford, so that *Iphigenia* received fewer performances than others of her works which demanded only piano accompaniment. It did, however, effectively demonstrate her performing power in that she was able to command audience attention pitted against the resources of a great score and a symphonic ensemble.

MARSEILLAISE

Choreography by Isadora Duncan. Music by Rouget de Lisle (Marseillaise). *First performed at the Trocadéro, Paris, France, 1915, by Isadora Duncan. First United States performance at the Metropolitan Opera House, New York, N.Y., 1915, by Isadora Duncan.*

This, one of Duncan's most successful dances, was again born of her natural sympathy for those attempting to overthrow the established order. The tune which was to become the French national anthem was heard being sung by crowds of revolutionaries marching to Paris from Marseille, hence its name. Both in France and elsewhere, Duncan literally brought audiences shouting to their feet at the conclusion of her pantomimic interpretation of the stirring anthem.

She stands enfolded in a crimson robe that extends to the ground. Then she reacts as if observing an advancing enemy. The assault almost crushes her, her throat is seized, but she kisses her flag for sustenance, she has tasted blood but she rises sweeping her arm over her head. Her mouth is opened in a silent cry and the great cloak hangs from her clenched fists like an awful banner. Her anguished outburst is also a summons to arms to her comrades. She makes no sound, but the effect of her attitude seems to make the words echo through everyone's ears.

Her body has a heroic grandeur, her gestures are imperious, she will triumph! And then the strife is followed by a majestic calm and she has the epic look of great statuary.

The final pose reminded one viewer of the *Winged Victory of Samothrace* and inspired several artists to do sketches of her. It was one of Duncan's great solo dances and one which she performed all over Europe and the United States with acclaim. Unlike her imitators she was able to sense the broad rhythmic thrust of any piece of music and dance to its long phrasing rather than simply mime individual passages.

MARCHE SLAVE

Choreography by Isadora Duncan. Music by Peter Ilyich Tchaikovsky. First United States performance at the Metropolitan Opera House, New York, N.Y., April 26, 1917, by Isadora Duncan.

Duncan, whose life was spent struggling for artistic recognition, had a natural sympathy for anyone struggling against the established order. The subject of the Russian peasants' struggle for freedom elicited a deeply emotional response from her.

The dance begins with Duncan standing alone and her hands drawn behind her back as if bound. She moves forward slowly with difficulty, feeling her way tentatively, bent slightly. She darts her eyes upward, fearfully anticipating what she might see looming ahead of her. Suddenly her knees, already bent, buckle and she falls. Her body trembles from unseen blows. But then the bonds that confine her are loosened and she hauls hers arms forward slowly and they are seen to be almost useless from their long period of confinement. They are not the supple hands of the free man but appendages withered from long disuse. But they are free at last and she gives an expression of apprehensive but genuine joy at her release.

As with others of her great dances, Duncan concentrates attention on small details of dramatic mime rather than on light or tripping movement. She was capable of such movement, but her dramatic range was greater than that of any of her contemporaries. Ironically, when she was teaching and performing in the Soviet Union she was criticized for *Marche Slave* because it contained the melody of *God Save the Czar*. Her critics obviously did not note that the introduction of that melody coincided with the severest beatings that she absorbed as the downtrodden peasant.

CHOREOCHRONICLE OF
ISADORA DUNCAN

1902

Orpheus (3 parts)

1901–4

Dance Idylls—included variously:
Bacchus et Ariadne
Primavera
Pan et Echo
Musette
Tambourin
Musette
Ange avec violon
Musette
Das Mädchen und der Tod
Orpheus
Menuet
Romanesca (danced by
  children)
Entre acte (danced by children)
Rondo (danced by children)

1904

Beethoven Program:
*Sonate quasifantasia, Op. 27,
  No. 2*
*Studien zur siebenten
  Symphonie, Op. 92*
*Presto aus der Sonate, Op. 10,
  No. 1*
Menuet (arr. by Hans von
  Bülow)
Sonate Pathétique, Op. 13

1905

Brahms Waltzes:
Op. 52, No. 6
Op. 39, No. 15
Chopin Waltzes:
Op. 64, No. 2
Op. 70, No. 1
Op. 69, No. 1
Op. 64, No. 1
Chopin Mazurkas:
Op. 33, No. 3
*Introduktion und sieben deutsche
  Tänze*
An der schöne blaue Donau
*Iphigenia in Aulis
Orpheus (4 parts)

1908

Seventh Symphony (Beethoven)
Three National Dances:
Norwegian Dance
Slavonic Dance
Spanish Dance

1909

Marche Militaire
Six German Dances

1911

Gigue
Two Gavottes
Bacchanale, from *Tannhäuser*

Dance of the Flower Maidens,
   from Parsifal, Act III
Dance of the Apprentices, from
   Die Meistersinger, Act III
Orpheus (23 selections including
   scenes with vocal soloist and
   chorus)

1914

Ave Maria
Marche héroïque
King Stephen
Unfinished Symphony
Waltzes (Reflet d'Allemagne)

1915

Chopin Program:
   Preludes [1]
   Preludes [2]
   Étude
   Impromptu
   Nocturnes
   Polonaise
   Mazurkas
   Waltzes
Oedipus
Fifth Symphony (Beethoven)
*Marseillaise

1916

Iphigenia in Tauris
Morceau symphonique de la
   rédemption
Sixth Symphony (Tchaikovsky)

1917

Marche Lorraine
*Marche Slave

1919

Marche funèbre

("Moonlight") Sonate
Trois poèmes

1920

Prelude to Parsifal
Régénération de Kundry, from
   Parsifal

1921

Seventh Symphony (Schubert)

1922

Internationale
Bénédiction de Dieu
Funérailles
Scriabin Program:
   Scherzo from First Symphony
   Idyll from Second Symphony
   Sonata No. 4
   Three Études
Funeral March, from
   Götterdämmerung
Prelude and Death of Isolde, from
   Tristan und Isolde

1923

Une Nuit sur le Mont Chauve
Southern Roses Waltz
Entrance of the Gods into
   Valhalla, from Das Rheingold

1926–29*

Impressions of Revolutionary
   Russia (included Marche Slave)

1928

Mazurka
Slow March
The Three Graces

* Complete work first performed posthumously by Irma Duncan and dancers in Paris, 1929.

LOIE FULLER

Marie Louise (Loie) Fuller was the child of a theatrical family and made her first professional appearance when at the age of two and a half she leaped onto the stage and recited inspirational religious verses. She grew up touring in minor dramatic roles and variety entertainment "turns," and had little or no formal dance training. It was while improvising delirium-induced movements in a play that she made her first dance impression of any note. She manipulated a filmy silk dress into rippling, almost magical shapes as she moved around the stage. She presented a solo program of dance which was modestly successful and traveled to Germany, then France to further her career. She attempted to secure an engagement at the Opéra but was refused and went to audition for the Folies-Bergère, where she was accepted. Her three-quarter-hour program of dances was acclaimed for its originality and exceptional use of lighting, and France became her spiritual home for the rest of her life.

Her discovery of lighting effects and the airy sculptural designs to be achieved with lightweight cloth was her contribution to the art of dance. Her own technique was exceptionally modest and her shape full to the point of corpulence, but all was forgotten when she created her *Fire Dance* or *Serpentine* under the glare of her carefully designed light plots.

She spawned a host of imitators almost immediately, but Isadora Duncan, who was a member of her company for a time, testified that none of them ever approached Fuller in skill. She was highly interested in the possibilities of theatrical lighting, and she put her brother in charge of her electricians to ensure their loyalty. At the time that radium was discovered by the Curies, she was prompted to experiment with phosphorescent salts to further develop the magic of her presentations.

Skilled lighting has been a tool of the modern dancers almost more than any other production technique, and Fuller was the first to extend its scope well beyond the range that she encountered in traditional theatrical practice. She was highly secretive about the exact means she used to achieve her effects, but it is known that among other innovations she introduced indirect lighting from beneath a floor panel of clear glass and that she mixed colors with great skill. In the beginning of her career she worked with simple unmixed lights and danced to popular music, but before she retired she was using colors of enormously subtle gradations and concert level music. She numbered among her friends Flammarion the astronomer, and Anatole France the writer. Her art was esteemed by William Butler Yeats, who commented on her in his poem "Nineteen Hundred Nineteen," and she drew crowds of intellectuals to the Folies-Bergère. She left no technique to learn and founded no school but set an example of theater magic arrived at through the use of lighting and deft manipulation of material.

SERPENTINE

Choreography by Loie Fuller. Music by Gillet ("Loin du bal"). First performed at the Casino Theater, New York, N.Y., 1891, by Loie Fuller.

This was Fuller's debut as a dancer, and it is ironic that she did not even title the dance. That was done by the director of the Casino Theater in New York, who auditioned her and then even added the music that he thought appropriate; a popular tune, "Loin du Bal." Her modest success was still enough to satisfy her ambition for a career beyond that of a bit player in melodramas such as *Quack M.D.*, where she had first excited her audience with the swirling and twirling of her skirt.

The dancer appears on a darkened stage in a long silken dress that is cinched at the waist and falls to the floor. A wavy line circles the garment at the hem, and a similar wavy line undulates across the circle-cut neckline. Suddenly the folds of the dress begin to ripple and seethe and light beams out from the dancer. She holds the hem at shoulder height and with rapid "rowing" motions creates cascades of folds in it. It becomes a swirling, billowing mass of motion.

She moves from side to side, always bathed in lights, and then, turning her back, she dips her head toward her audience and the skirt now becomes like a flower circling her torso, when a moment before it had been like some enchanted butterfly. The dance ended with the filmy folds collapsing around her in light-stained glory.

Serpentine was only the first of dozens of dances that Fuller created using masses of lightweight material and the most imaginative lighting designs that had been seen on the stage at the time. She never attempted to tell a story in the narrative sense but created dances of lyric mood. She imitated physical phenomena, most notably flowers, insects, and atmospheric illuminations, and remained always one step ahead of her many imitators. She was called a creature of light; it is an apt summation of her special quality.

FIRE DANCE
(FLAME)

Choreography by Loie Fuller, first performed at the Folies-Bergère, Paris, France, 1895, by Loie Fuller.

Throughout her career Fuller made technical innovations in the use of light and the development of lightweight cloth fabric. For this dance she made one of her most exciting: she set a strong plate-glass sheet in the floor of the stage and had herself illuminated with two powerful lights from beneath. The effect on those who saw her first was indelible, for it seemed to them that she became engulfed in a rising flush of flame-colored light so that her whole costume became ignited.

At the start of the dance Fuller springs up and spreads her broad dress as widely as possible with the aid of supports hidden inside so that she takes on the configuration of a broad, flat gas flame. She moves forward, sweeping her voluminous dress in the shape of large figure eights, first to the side and then overhead to simulate the flickering of the flames. As she slowly turns she moves her arms with their extensions inside the dress in an up and down rippling motion so that it assumes a pattern such as can be observed in the ripples of an ice skater's short skirt as she revolves rapidly. The curious thing is that her torso and head are absolutely calm at the vortex of the agitated moving of the dress, which glows hotly and flickers out and back. She faces the audience at first and then turns away from it while continuing the restless movement of the dress, giving the impression of perpetual activity which subsides only at the end of the dance.

Like most of Fuller's early dances, *Fire Dance* was relatively short, approximately six or seven minutes, but within that time she created the mood she was striving for. The work was eventually filmed, and the device chosen to open the movie was that of a bat flying erratically around the stage. When the creature finally settled, it vanished, to be replaced by Fuller, who rose as if propelled upward like a jet of flame.

CHOREOCHRONICLE OF
LOIE FULLER*

1891

*Serpentine

1892

Violet
Butterfly
Danse blanche

1893

Widow
Mirror
Good Night Dances
La Danse des nuages
The Flower
The Rainbow

1895

Salomé (Salute of the Sun, Les
    Éclairs, L'Orage)
La Nuit
Le Firmament
The Lily Dance
*Fire Dance (Flame)

1898

The Bird
Une Pluie de Fleurs

1899

Les Sylphes
Lumière et ténèbrè

Danse de l'or
L'Archange

1901

Danse flourescent
La Tempête

1902

La Danse funèbre
La Danse religion
La Danse de peur
La Danse d'aveugle
La Danse inspirée par le nocturne
    de Chopin

1903

The Grottoes
Danse mystérieuses
Les Petites femmes
Chez les papillons
L'Eau
Danse l'espèce

1904

Radium Dance

1905

Flight of the Butterflies
Dance of 1000 Veils (Storm at
    Sea, Wrecked, Lost, River of
    Death, The Fire of Life, Ave
    Maria, The Land of Vision)

* Compiled by Margaret H. Harris and Sally R. Sommer. This represents work in progress and new amendments are continually added.

1906

Bottom of the Sea
Egyptian Dance from Aïda
Gypsy Dance from The Huguenots
Spanish Dance from Carmen

1907

India Pantomime (Les Ames
  errantes, Les Nuages qui
  passent, Les Feux de l'enfer)
Salomé (d'Humieres-Schmitt)
  (Danse des perles, Danse du
  paon, Danse des serpents, Danse
  de l'acier, Danse de l'argent,
  Danse de la peur)

1908

Ballet of Light (Open Sea,
  Snowstorm, Unfolding Spirit)

1909

Butterflies (Massenet)
Marche turque
Elfin Dance
Spring Song
Ophelia
Tragedy Dance
Diana the Huntress
Dance des sylphes
Dance of The Hands
Peer Gynt (Ase's Death, Dance of
  Anitra, The Arab Dance,
  Solveig's Song and Mourning)
Ave Maria
Prelude No. 4 (Chopin)
Valse, Rosen aus Dem Süden
Chaconne (Durnad)
Bacchanal
Tarantella
Scherzo (Schumann)
Das Mädchen und der Tod
Suite (Rameau)

Studies, Op. 25 (Chopin)
Serenade (Schubert)
Shadow Dance (Meyerbeer)
Midsummer Night's Dream
Lied
Intermezzo
Nocturne (Griffin)
Finale
Wedding March

1910

Volcanic Eruptions
Sweeping Fires

1911

Dance of Miriam
Danse Macabre
La Danse de martyrs
Danse de l'offrande
Danse de coquetterie
Dance of the Eyes
Numéro fantastique (Un Grand
  voile)
L'Oiseau noir
Danse ultra violette

1912

Cycles de danses
Les Petits riens (Mozart)
Water Music (Handel)
Points of Light
Nell Gwyn Dance
Dance for Music from Diocletian
Danse des sylphes (from The
  Damnation of Faust)

1913

Mille et une nuits (Fêtes, Sirènes,
  Pelleas et Mélisande, Dans
  l'oasis, Orgie de lumière)
Children's Corner (Dr. Gradus ad
  Parnassum, Jimbo's Lullaby,
  Serenade a la Poupée, La Neige
  Danse, Le Petit berger,
  Gollywog's Cakewalk)

1914

Hall of the Mountain King (Peer
  Gynt)
Orchestration de Coulerus sur
  deux préludes
Prométhée
Pastorale
La Forêt Hantée
La Feu d'artifice
Egyptian Sun Dance

1915

Ballet of Serpents
Ballet d'opal noire
Black Flame
Marche militaire
School of Imagination Dances
  (The crowd in succession:
  Hatred, Joy, Sorrow,
  Indignation, Sacrifice, Waiting,
  Longing, Suspense, Despair,
  Tears, Laughter, Fear,
  Indifference, Emotion, Calm,
  Anxiety, Ecstasy, Faith,
  Abondonment)
Clown Dance
Battle of the Flowers

Emptying the Bobbin of Its
  Thread
The Wind
Thunder
Water
The Grinding Mill
Tearing of the Rose
Till She Falls
Butterfly and Birds
St. Jean Preaching to the Birds
St. Jean Walking on the Water
Little Witches

1920

Le Lys de la vie

1921

Chimères
Chant de Nigamon
Saudades de Brazil

1922

Ballet fantastique
Les Ombres
Sorcières gigantiques
Ombres partes (Gennes Feériques,
  Point, Feu, Lys)
Bal de neige

1924

Temptation du feu
Le Deluge

1925

L'Escalier monumental

RUTH ST. DENIS

"Miss Ruth" was the affectionate form of address for Ruth St. Denis and acknowledged her position as first lady of American dance. As a young woman, however, she struggled along in minor roles in musical plays until the poster of the goddess Isis advertising Egyptian Deities cigarettes turned her definitely to the world of serious dance exploration. Her training had been in popular physical exercises at home, followed by study with local teachers in her home town in New Jersey. For her own career she evolved movement based on Eastern dance.

She frequented shows at New York's Coney Island Amusement Park, where she studied Eastern dancers, and when she presented her first program it was of five works modeled on such dancing. The dances, however, were not authentic in the sense that they exactly replicated the originals. They were individual adaptations that were greeted with great enthusiasm.

She appeared in both London and Paris but enjoyed her greatest success in Berlin, where she encountered poet Hugo von Hofmannsthal, who was a particular admirer of her work. She was offered a five-year contract and a theater built to her own specifications if she would remain in Germany. She declined and returned to the United States and a career in vaudeville. Her solo appearances were at first successful, but increasingly the public demanded a dancing couple rather than a female solo artist. When the enthusiastic young Ted Shawn presented himself at her New York home, she saw the possibility of sustaining her career. They became dance partners and then marriage partners and, though estranged from one another artistically for periods of time, danced together on their fiftieth wedding anniversary.

St. Denis's particular interest in dance was the expression of religious and mystical themes. She herself was influenced both by Eastern philosophy and the teachings of Mary Baker Eddy. She was a strikingly beautiful woman and was sketched by Rodin and modeled by Gaston Lachaise. She possessed an extraordinary fluidity in her arm movements, so much so that a team of German doctors examined her to see whether she was anatomically the same as everyone else.

Though she had a long and productive career, she never exceeded the artistry of the first dances that she created for herself. She was inspiring as a dancer to a generation of young girls among whom was Martha Graham. St. Denis was not a particularly good teacher and so left most of that work to her husband Shawn. She was a muse and a particularly effective one for the history of modern dance.

COBRAS

Choreography by Ruth St. Denis. Music by Léo Delibes (from Lakmé). First performed at the Hudson Theatre, New York, N.Y., March 26, 1906, by Ruth St. Denis.

Traders haggle in a village square with strollers, and the setting is reminiscent of a bazaar in a small Mid-Eastern town. Into the group the dancer enters in the tattered garments of a snake charmer. She is obviously an occasional visitor to the place as she takes her folded leg position on a platform.

There is a wig low on her forehead, and her arms are sheathed in greenish sleeves, and on the first and fourth fingers of each hand she wears large emerald rings which glitter evilly and represent the eyes of the snakes. As she enters her arms are wrapped around her neck, and then to the melody of a flute she unwinds the cobras from her neck and makes them dance to the reedy tune. The "snakes" crawl all over her body, rising over her head and then slithering along the length of her body again. Because of her great suppleness St. Denis could actually create a believable illusion of live snakes. When at the conclusion her hands with the massive green rings are raised above her head, the illusion of weaving cobras ready to strike is unmistakable. She asks for coins but the people in the square go back to what they were doing before they started watching. Contemptuously, she leaves.

In this dance St. Denis created a work that employed very little in the way of conventional dance movement. Her skill at mime was so strong she did fashion compelling dances out of the smallest bits of material. As an ironic sidelight to her performance, cartoonists became attracted to her work as an example of a new dance trend and caricatured her frequently in her role as the snake charmer.

INCENSE

Choreography by Ruth St. Denis. Music by Harvey Worthington Loomis. First performed at the Hudson Theatre, New York, N.Y., March 26, 1906, by Ruth St. Denis.

A woman in voluminous robes moves toward the audience with a bowl of incense grains. She circles to the right and then in the opposite direction to the left, holding the bowl like a tray before her. On either side of the stage stands a brazier and she sifts a few grains of the aromatic powder in each and places the bowl on the stage. Thin curling lines of smoke arise from the braziers, and she begins to reflect the undulations of these vaporous columns in her torso. The movement spreads out through the arms and into the sensitively articulated fingers as she makes filigrees of small gestures which finally fade away, as do the light streams of smoke rising from the small pinches of burning incense. Again she bears the bowl around the stage in circles before placing small quantities of the powder on the coals. Once more she comes under the spell of the idly drifting smoke and her body takes up a sympathetic movement, and finally she presses the backs of her hands together over her head in a gesture of pious finale.

Incense, like *Radha, Nautch, Cobras,* and *The Yogi,* was one of her East Indian cycle of dances which brought her early fame and which she performed extensively during 1906–10 before joining with Ted Shawn to form the Denishawn company, for which she began to create other, larger-scaled works. But in these early dances we are able to see clearly those elements that so sensitively and clearly presented her great physical beauty to audiences in the United States and abroad. Her costuming was exotically seductive, and the dance materials she chose were based on remote and little known models that created an aura of mysterious excitement.

RADHA

Choreography by Ruth St. Denis. Music by Léo Delibes (later version with music by Jess Meeker). First performed at the New York Theatre, New York, N.Y., January 28, 1906, by Ruth St. Denis.

The dance takes place in a setting reminiscent of an Indian temple with decorated columns and arches in several rows and an altar upon which sits the immobile Radha. Two files of priests enter, and the chief priests salute Radha as the others seat themselves at either side of the stage. As the music begins Radha opens her eyes for "The Awakening" section, her body begins to surge with life, and her breathing is deep and controlled, and she then cups her hands in the shape of a lotus beneath her chin. Her slow swaying takes her from the altar and she descends to salute the priests who await her. After the greeting she is ready to do the dances of the five senses.

She begins with "The Dance of Touch" by affixing beaded amulets to her wrists and then starting to clash finger cymbals. Her arms arch over her head, dramatically she brings them straight down. One arm in front has the hand flexed and points to the left, and the other in back points in the opposite direction in the manner of a two dimensional wall painting. In this pose she walks slowly down between the lines of the priests and then returns to the altar. Her costume is a richly woven halter and shorts of a similar opulence. The effect is almost cloyingly exotic except for the spectacular grace of the arm movements, which exhibit the refinement and delicacy that give this dance drama its chief interest. The movements of the legs and feet do not have any great rhythmic subtlety, but the expressiveness of the upper body carries the presentation along through the various developments of the senses. Between each section there is silence and then a simple drumbeat as she takes off the bits of costume ornament that characterize each sense, and dons those that mark the succeeding portion.

In the sense of smell she entwines her body with garlands of flowers, at times gathering them in clusters in each hand and then drawing them languorously across her body. Finally she frames her face with them and allows them to fall in a long line across her to the floor. In "The Dance of Taste" she deftly manipulates a bowl, and finally in "The Delirium of the Senses" she arranges a cloak across her shoulders and a skirt around her waist. She begins her dance of possession as she slowly runs one hand caressingly along her arm while seated and then rises to outline her body with both hands, dipping in and rounding out to emphasize her womanliness. Her hips begin to sway softly and then with more pronounced vigor to send her skirt whirling as the full power of the self-intoxication flows through her. Her extended arms ripple as if devoid of their bone core, and she throws her head back and turns ever more rapidly until finally the power departs and she sinks backward.

She returns to her normal state of possession and slips out of the skirt and clasps her hands in a prayerful attitude of contrition. Again she frames her face with her cupped hands and returns to the throne after bowing and extending her prayerful gesture to the priests. The priests salute her once more and she is immobile as at the start of the ceremony.

St. Denis considered *Radha* to be her masterpiece. It was the first dance that she achieved general success with, and it brought her great popularity both in the United States and in Europe before the outbreak of World War I. She kept it in her repertory almost continuously and as late as 1940, when she was in her sixties, St. Denis still performed *Radha*.

NAUTCH [1908]

Choreography by Ruth St. Denis. First performed at the Ronacher Theatre, Vienna, Austria, February 5, 1908, by Ruth St. Denis.

The nautch dancers were entertainers who were originally imported into India from Persia. They did not have a religious base to their dances but conceived movement with an eye toward its seductive appeal. St. Denis included her conception of a typical nautch dance as one of the five works she created for her solo program, collecting them under the heading of a Suite of East Indian Dances.

Her costuming was alluring in the richness and colorations of the fabric and also in that it was a bit revealing according to the standards of the day. The voluminous emerald green skirt became like "the cup of a strange exotic flower" as she whirled. The setting was an entertainment arranged by a rajah for a guest, and St. Denis enters to the accompaniment of singing and music. She is wreathed in a gold-fringed sari that is transparent and that she alternately uses to partially conceal and partially reveal herself.

The basic movements of the dance are a turning step, stamping of the feet, which are adorned with small bells, and back bends. Arms open and close as they manipulate the light sari. The dance begins with an impulsive joyousness and lyrical caressing movements, and the pace gradually increases as the movements become more sensual and arousing, but concludes before reaching an orgiastic level.

Commentators in the English press who had seen nautch girls in India mentioned that the dance was more energetic than they had seen in India but that it was free from "indecent exposure." St. Denis had selected those elements of the dance that suited her own somewhat prudish temperament and created what might be thought of as a flirtatious but not voluptuous dance. It was enormously popular, especially, thought St. Denis, among the lower-priced seats.

THE YOGI

Choreography by Ruth St. Denis. Music by Meyrowitz. First performed at the Ronacher Theatre, Vienna, Austria, February 9, 1908, by Ruth St. Denis.

Among the suite of five East Indian dances that St. Denis created for her first major appearence, *The Yogi* retained a special place in her own esteem. She had displayed an interest in religious things from her childhood, and in *The Yogi* she was able to combine mystical speculation with her developing dance style.

The setting for the piece is a clearing in the forest where the holy man comes to meditate. St. Denis enters with an easy swinging stride carrying a begging bowl and a necklace of prayer beads. She circles the prayer rug and then slowly sinks into a cross-legged pose. Her body is calm and her lowered eyes suggest the beginning of religious concentration. She breathes deeply and extends one arm with palm out and then the other. It is the beginning of her spiritual exercises. In a moment she rises slowly and again circles the tiger rug upon which she had been seated. When she resumes her place in the center of the rug, she balances carefully, bringing her body into conformation with directions of the compass. She is at the apex where all forces converge. Physically she has located herself in a receptive position symbolizing the openness of her being to divine influence.

Then slowly she settles onto the rug once again with head bowed forward to nestle near the ground between her ankles. The attitude of the body is one of repose and acceptance. All is calm and then with infinite care she begins to rise once again to her full height in a confident balance. In the background is heard a light voice chanting to the deity Shiva. As the chant continues she raises her arms straight over her head, pressing the backs of the hands together, and then slowly brings them downward in two wide half-circles. When they are both down she allows the prayer beads to drop from her left hand and their soft clatter is heard just before the curtain descends.

For St. Denis the dance was a risk. She doubted whether she could keep an audience attentive through what was in effect a dance that had little "normal" dance movement. When the dance was over and she received only a light smattering of applause, she felt that she had failed, and ran to her dressing room bitterly disappointed. The warm praise she read in the next day's newspapers soon told her that the dance had been a success. She had worked very hard to evoke the meditative quiet of the holy man but was forced to take the risk of a minimum amount of movement. As she observed later, *Nautch* and *Radha* were more popular with audiences, but *The Yogi* was "rarely received with enthusiasm except by the elect."

CHOREOCHRONICLE
OF RUTH ST. DENIS

1906

Cobras
Incense
Radha

1908

Nautch [1908]
 A Shirabyoshi
The Yogi

1910

 Egypta
 The Lotus Pond

1913

Dance of Rosebuds
Bakawali
The Impromptu
O-Mika

1914

Champagne Dance
Chitra Hunting
Danse impromptu
La Marquise
The Peacock
The Scherzo Waltz

1915

The Garden of Kama
A Lady of the Genvoko Period
O-Mika Arranges Her Flowers
  and Starts for a Picnic
The Spirit of the Sea (solo)

1916

Dance with Scarf
Review of Dance Pageant of
  India, Greece, and Egypt (with
  Ted Shawn)

1918

Dance of Tahoma
Dance of Theodora
Dance of the Royal Ballet of
  Siam
Danse Siamese
Greek Scene
An Indian Temple Scene
Jeptha's Daughter
Nautch [1918]
The Spirit of Democracy
Syrian Sword Dance
Vision of Yashodhara
Rosamund

1919

At Evening
Dance of Devidassis
Coolan Dhu
Dancer from the Court of King
  Ahasuerus
Danse
First Arabesque
Egyptian Suite (with Ted
  Shawn)
Floods of Spring
Gavotte
Hungarian Dance No. 6
Impromptu

Intermezzo No. 1, Op. 119
Intermezzo No. 3
J'ai pleuré en rêve
Juggleress
Kuan Yin
Little Banzo
Orientale
Phryne
Polonaise
Prelude No. 4
Première valse oubliée
Rigaudon
Romance
Schottische
Second Arabesque
Soaring (with Doris Humphrey)
Sonata Pathétique
The Spirit of the Rose
Street Nautch Dance
The Street of the Dancers
Suite of Lyric Pieces
Three Ladies of the East
Two Waltzes
Valse brillante
Vizione veneziana
Waltz No. 15
Why

1921

The Beloved and the Sufi
Hymn to the Sun
Impressions of a Japanese
  Tragedy
The Poet and the Dancer
Poetess of the Thirteenth Century
The Salutation
Sappho
When I Go Alone at Night . . .

1922

East Indian Suite
Japanese Suite
Liebestraum
Street Nautch
The Three Apsarases
Waltz, Op. 33, No. 15

1923

Cupid and Psyche
Dance, O Dance, Maidens Gay
Impressions of a Japanese Story
    Teller
Ishtar of the Seven Gates
Sonata Tragica (with Doris
    Humphrey)
The Spirit of the Sea (group)

1924

Allegro risoluto
Valse à la Loïe
Vision of the Aissoua
Waltzes [Schubert]

1925

American Sketches I (with Ted
    Shawn)
Dance of the Volcano Goddess
Garland Plastique
Queen of Heaven
Love Crucified

1926

A Burmese Yien Pwe
Festival of Saraswati
In the Bunnia Bazaar
Invocation to the Buddha
Javanese Court Dancer
The Singer
The Soul of India
Suite for Violin and Piano

White Jade
A Yien Pwe (with Doris
    Humphrey)

1927

Dance of the Red and Gold Saree

1928

The Batik Vender
Black and Gold Sari
The Lamp
Three Coolie Girls

1929

Burmese Dance
Daughter of Desire
Dojoji
A Figure from Angkor Vat
Kwannon
Prophet Bird
Scarf Dance
A Tagore Poem
Waltz [Rubinstein]

1930

Angkor Vat
A Buddhist Festival
Nautch Dance Ensemble

1931

Dance Balinese
Modern Nautch
The Prophetess
Salome
Unfinished Symphony (with
    Klarna Pinska)

1933

Balinese

1934

Masque of Mary

1941

  Adventures of Marco Polo

1946

  Color Study of the Madonna

1949

  Buddhist Nun

1950

  Gregorian Chant

1951

  Three Poems in Rhythm

1955

  Freedom

1957

  To a Chinese Flute

TED SHAWN

Edwin Meyers (Ted) Shawn became a dancer through courses he took as therapy to strengthen his legs. He had been partially paralyzed because of an overdose of medication given during a bout of diphtheria. He abandoned his studies for the ministry and became a professional performer, starting with Norma Gould doing *Tango Teas*. He saw Ruth St. Denis, who was to become his partner and wife, first in 1911 while she was on tour, and subsequently in New York he persuaded her that together they would make a marvelous team.

They joined forces and toured extensively. Shawn felt that a school was needed to supply them with dancers, an assured income, and a base where they could create new productions and store scenery and props. The first Denishawn school opened in Los Angeles in 1915 and immediately attracted students. Within a few years Martha Graham, Doris Humphrey, and Charles Weidman all had studied there and had joined the Denishawn company.

During World War I, Shawn entered the Army and did not resume his career until 1919. St. Denis had been touring with an all-girl company, but they reunited in 1921 and under the management of Daniel Mayer for the next four years became the highest paid and most talked about dance company in the country.

Shawn taught tirelessly and franchised Denishawn schools throughout the country. When they closed down the Los Angeles school, he established a new school for himself and St. Denis in New York on a tract of land near

Van Cortlandt Park. The company toured nearly all the year during the 1920's both in the United States and in the Far East. Everywhere Shawn sought out ethnic dances which he could include in the Denishawn repertory.

By the beginning of the 1930s Shawn decided to establish an all-made company to show the public that dancing was a man's business and not the exclusive property of women. St. Denis continued with an all-girl troupe and followed her religious instincts by creating dancing choirs. Shawn continued his men's company from 1933–40 and used a farm in Becket, Massachusetts, as its base. It was called Jacobs Pillow because of a rock formation that suggested the biblical story, and with the final appearence of the men's group he established the Jacobs Pillow Dance Festival and school. His tastes in dance were all inclusive, and he insisted that each performance contain ethnic and modern dance and ballet, and all three disciplines were taught in the school, which operated during the summers.

Through the festival Shawn introduced many dancers of note to American audiences, and for his labors on behalf of the Royal Danish Ballet was awarded the Order of Dannebrog. Among the books he wrote were *Ruth St. Denis: Pioneer and Prophet, Gods Who Dance, Every Little Movement,* and his autobiography, *One Thousand and One Night Stands.* He collected film records of many artists who appeared at Jacobs Pillow and left his extensive collection to the Dance Collection of the New York Public Library. His organizational genius provided the steppingstone for the major developments of modern dance.

DEATH OF ADONIS

Choreography by Ted Shawn. Music by Benjamin Godard (Adagio pathétique). *First performed at the Academy of Music, Newburgh, N.Y., October 6, 1924, by Ted Shawn.*

Adonis, a Phoenician god who was wounded while hunting wild boar, was regarded as an example of great physical beauty and in classical sculpture was presented nude except for a fig leaf. Shawn daringly chose to present himself on stage similarly. After studying pictures of classical statuary he created a powdered white wig of closely grouped curls, powdered his body dead white, and, wearing only a *cache-sexe,* presented a solo dance that consisted of a series of plastique poses which melted into one another. The dance begins with a presentation of the young god in his strength and beauty rising on the balls of his feet, stretching out his arms, and then slowly, gracefully turning in profile to extend one leg behind him and his arm forward. After presenting himself in a series of sculpturally sensuous poses he is gradually drained of the strength and vitality that he has shown and sinks slowly toward the earth.

Since he had continually and systematically fought for greater freedom of expression for dancers, it was logical for Shawn to be the first male concert dancer to attempt to appear on stage nearly nude. He chose the third of Denishawn's very successful cross-country tours for the occasion and presented *Death of Adonis,* at times under the title *Adagio pathétique* on the first part of his programs, sometimes alternating it with *Étude,* another solo for himself. Because of the conservative restrictions of the day it was not given in all of the cities in which the company played but was shown selectively. Even so it was an innovative dance that explored the beauty of the male form and was a first for concert level dance.

MEVLEVI DERVISH

Choreography by Ted Shawn. Music by Anis Fuleihan. First performed at Carnegie Hall, New York, N.Y., April 15, 1929, by Ted Shawn.

In the spring of 1929 Shawn and Ruth St. Denis temporarily disbanded their company and each was working separately. Shawn decided to give a program of solo dances at Carnegie Hall in New York. Strictly speaking, it was not a solo program, since he created a few small supporting roles for the women who danced with him, but the bulk of the evening was carried by Shawn. It was a combination of revivals and one completely new work, *Mevlevi Dervish.*

Shawn had learned the technique of dervish turning, which demands great concentration while whirling continuously. The technique is used as a religious aid to meditation, and he decided to do the turning while the other dancers created small episodes, like *tableaux vivants,* to represent the visions of the dervish.

Standing at the center of the stage, a brightly illuminated Shawn slowly starts his turning. The long skirt that reaches nearly to the ground begins to rise up and outward in rippling waves. His head is covered with a soft, high-crowned tapering fez that is flat on top. The other dancers begin to appear but only in silhouette, due to the lighting design, and create incidents that depict loving encounter, merry reveling, mourning, and inevitably death. It is a cycle of thoughts such as anyone might have and through it all the central figure of Shawn is seen turning, turning, and turning to the end.

The dance received a mixed reception when it was first performed, though all admitted that it was a tour de force. Shawn liked the piece and kept it as part of his repertory for many years. It was a direct result of his insatiable curiosity about ethnic dance. Wherever he went on his considerable travels, he sought out local dances and learned them. He was eclectic, sometimes to a fault, but his open enthusiasm was a breath of fresh air in the sometimes monomaniacal world of emerging modern dance.

PROMETHEUS BOUND

Choreography by Ted Shawn. Music by Alexander Scriabin. First performed at Lewisohn Stadium, New York, N.Y., August 6, 1929, by Ted Shawn.

During a tour in Europe, Shawn was invited to perform in Greece, and he adapted this dance pantomime on a famous Greek legend for the theater. In its open-air setting with the valleys and hills of Greece visible in the background it was spectacular. It was based on the Aeschylus play recounting the punishment of Prometheus by Zeus for stealing the sacred fire from Mount Olympus and bringing it back to all men.

It begins with a procession of four figures in long robes ascending a staircase cut into the rock of a peak overlooking a valley. The climb is difficult, but once at the summit Prometheus is chained to the rock and secured with spikes driven into the stone. The daughters of the ocean, hearing of his plight, gather at the base of the peak to offer a dance expressing mankind's gratitude. It is a slow and stately procession consisting of four files of women in light-colored tunics, resting one hand lightly on the shoulder of the dancer immediately in front of herself to form moving human chains. As they walk in arcs they gratefully extend an arm with palm up to the imprisoned Prometheus, who watches.

While the two leaders of the chorus speak the feelings of all, the women gather to kneel, stand, extend an arm or brush a hand across the brow in a pantomime of gesture strongly suggestive of figures on ancient Greek vases. Their unison bow ends the first part of the dance.

The sea god Poseidon enters and expresses sympathy, and Io, who had displeased Zeus's wife, begs Prometheus to foretell her future. She is tormented by a cluster of stinging wasps, and two grotesque horns have sprouted from her head. She walks off, satisfied to learn that her future son will overthrow Zeus. A messenger of the gods ascends the rock as the faithful chorus maintains its vigil at the base of the rock. He offers Prometheus freedom if he will reveal the secret of prophecy. The chorus mounts the serpentine stair to implore Prometheus to agree, but he refuses. There is an angry rumbling representing the wrath of Zeus, and the chorus flees. The summit of the peak begins to crumble and smoke begins to rise from the fissures, and the whole top, along with the shackled Prometheus, crumbles into rubble.

There was little actual dancing in the spectacle, and Prometheus was completely a mime role, but the pageant had its effect especially in its appropriate outdoor setting. It was reminiscent of other outdoor performances that Shawn had staged as early as 1916 in the Greek Theater in Berkeley, California, and it showed once again the sympathy for ancient myth that he and the whole Denishawn influenced movement had. One of his pupils, Martha Graham, was to create a whole cycle of Greek-based dance dramas twenty years later.

KINETIC MOLPAI*

Choreography by Ted Shawn (with sections by Barton Mumaw, Dennis Landers, Foster Fitz-Simmons, Fred Hearn, and Wilbur McCormack). Music by Jess Meeker. First performed at the Clark School, Goshen, N.Y., October 5, 1935, by Ted Shawn and Burton Mumaw, Frank Overlees, Wilbur McCormack, Dennis Landers, Fred Hearn, Foster Fitz-Simmons, William Howell, and Ned Coupland. Also performed at Jacobs Pillow, Lee, Mass., July 3, 1962, and at the New York City Center, New York, N.Y., November 16, 1972, by the Alvin Ailey City Center Dance Theater.

When he established his own company of male dancers, Shawn was determined to create a repertory of works that would show off male prowess in dancing. One of the finest of the dances surviving from this time is *Kinetic Molpai,* which was revived as recently as 1972 by the Alvin Ailey Dance Theater. The piece is divided into twelve parts and features the company of eight men, who form a chorus, and a solitary man, the leader, who joins them sporadically.

The leader strides out and steps proudly around to each of the four corners of the stage, where he beckons his followers. These appear in pairs at each summons, and they bow to him. As he turns, they form a circle and then split into groups of four. One of the men separates himself and is tossed back and forth between the two opposing groups and then is carried forward on their shoulders and set down. The men leave. Their movement has been full of strong, angry accents, but when the leader reappears he restores tranquillity.

His solo is marked with extended pleading motions of the arms, and as he moves about the space four men whirl on and stop with arms thrust downward and their feet straddled. A second group of four appears as the leader exits and the two quartets march in blocs around one another with great dynamic energy. Suddenly individuals begin to spin rapidly and exit, leaving a trio of men. Their dance features high leaps and rotating gestures of the arms in jerky circles like a violent minute hand on a powerful clock. With a series of jumps from one side to the other and circling leaps they rush off.

* Later Section 3, "Future," of *O, Libertad!*

The quartets return and en masse take large steps first to one side and then to its opposite, after which they all step carefully in large arcs. Each grouping keeps to its own pace and is independent of the other. They cross and recross the area until they suddenly stand erect, extend one leg to the side, and leave. The leader walks on, only to sink to the ground and then to rise again. This is repeated several times and he almost seems to draw strength from the ground as he rises. In the final ascent he stretches his arms high over his head and abruptly his wrists appear to be lashed together. He wrenches them apart and the open arm gestures become a beseeching cry. He drops to the ground and makes an obeisance, and though he tries to rise again he is pressed to the ground by an unseen but powerful force.

The first of the returning men sees him and covers his eyes and then shakes his fist at the sky. Four men carry the leader off and the others create a tableau of stylized grieving with arms held angularly over their eyes. All sweep around in arcs, turning periodically and giving the impression of disorder and distress like men "running in circles." Their bodies rock with sobs and they fall to the ground in a wreath of sorrow.

The leader returns full of the vibrancy that he had had previously, and hauls one man up by the arm as he passes. That man draws up the next in a similar fashion, and the whole circular group is brought to its feet in a beautifully simple way. They dance the finale displaying all of the vigor and energy that they can project. At the end of their celebration all kneel to the leader, who stands at the center of their file.

The dance has some of the piston energy that is associated with massive machinery, but its design is based on the descent and resurrection theme that Shawn observed in the dances of many cultures. He created the movement for bare-chested men in belted trousers so that it would have a contemporary look to the audiences of the 1930s for whom it was created, but it was a continuation of the thematic currents that he examined throughout his long career. The piece was very popular and the gesture of arced parallel arms over the head became a personal trademark for Shawn, and drawings of him in this pose turned up regularly on his programs.

CHOREOCHRONICLE
OF TED SHAWN

1911

A French Love Waltz

1912

Diana and Endymion

1914

Cymbal Dance
Dagger Dance
Grecian Suite
Modern Dances
National Suite
Oriental Suite
Ourieda
Pierrot and the Butterfly
Rondo Capriccio
Vintage Dance
Earth Cycle
Pipes of Pan

1915

Hawaiian Ballet
Josephine and Hippolyte
Nature Rhythms
St. Denis Mazurka
South Sea Ballet
Joseph's Legend

1916

Arabic Suite
Savage Dance
Sculpture Plastique

1917

Bach's Fugues
Bach's Inventions
Botticelli

1919

Flamenco
Gnossienne, No. 1
Japanese Spear Dance
Julnar of the Sea
Miriam, Sister of Moses
Three Part Invention, No. 12
Two Part Invention, No. 4

1920

Frohsinn
Gavotte
Javanese Shadow Play
Les Mystères Dionysiaques
Two Chopin Mazurkas

1921

The Abduction of Sita
Contrapuntal Dance
Le Contrabandier
Invocation to the Thunderbird
Malagueña
Pierrot Forlorn
Revolutionary Étude
Schérzo Waltz
Spanish Suite I
Street Nautch
The Twenty-third Psalm
Xochitl

1922

Cowboy
Danza Espagnol
Egyptian Ballet
Moszkowski Waltz
Siamese Ballet
Spanish Suite II

1923

Cuadro Flamenco
Flamenco Dances
Legends from the Vienna Woods
Pasquinade
Polonaise

1924

Around the Hall
Boston Fancy—1854
The Crapshooter
*Death of Adonis
Eagle Dance
The Feather of the Dawn
Gringo Tango
Voices of Spring

1925

Choeur Dansé
Pas de Quatre
Spanish Suite III
Straussiana
Tango and Alegrías
Valse Denishawn

1926

Allegresse
Cosmic Dance of Siva
Danse Cambodienne
Danse Profane
General Wu's Farewell to His
    Wife
Momijii-Gari

Sinhalese Devil Dance
Spanish Suite IV

1927

Glazounow Waltz

1928

Grief and Joy
Mazurka de Salon
Orpheus

1929

Bazaar Scene
Chopin Ballet
Death of a God
Death of the Bullgod
Fingal's Cave Overture
Idyll
Jurgen
*Mevlevi Dervish
Pacific 231
*Prometheus Bound
Ramadan
La Rumba
Shawl Dance
Temple Dancing Girl

1930

Baba Jaga
Brahms Opus 79, No. 2
Caunpore Nautch Girl
Divine Idiot
Hispanic Suite
Group Dance for Male Ensemble
Mental Fantasy
Osage-Pawnee Dance of Greeting
Scarf Plastique
Orpheus Dionysus (with
    Margarete Wallmann)
Souvenir of Bavaria

1931

The Camel Boys
Dance of Greeting
Dance of the Redeemed
Job, A Masque for Dancing
O Brother Sun and Sister Moon
Pièces Froides
Rhapsody
Stick Nautch
Waltzes from Der Rosenkavalier
Workers' Songs of Middle Europe
Zuni Indian Ghost Dance

1933

Charlie's Dance
Cutting the Sugar Cane
Doxology
Los Embozados
Fetish
The French Sailor
John Brown Sees the Glory
Kankakee at Cannes
Negro Spirituals I
Negro Spirituals II
Sixth Prelude from the Well-
    Tempered Clavichord

1934

Choric Dance from an Antique
    Greek Comedy
A Church Service in Dance
Dance of the Thrashing Floor
Dayak Spear Dance
Dynamo
Ferruca Triana
Hopi Indian Eagle Dance
Hound of Heaven
Labor Symphony
Maori War Haka
Mule Team Driver's Dance
Pierrot in the Dead City
Pioneer's Dance

Pleasantly Satiric Comment
Ponca Indian Dance
Primitive Rhythms
Turkey in the Straw
Variations on a Theme of Diabelli
Walk Together, Children

1935

Danza Afro-Cubana
A Dreier Lithograph
Gothic
*Kinetic Molpai
Movement Naif
Mule Skinner's Dance

1936

Finale from a New World
New World Symphony
Pirate's Island

1937

Mozart's Fortieth Symphony
O, Libertad!

1938

Dance of the Ages

1939

The Persians

1940

The Dome
Excursions into Visible Song
Four Dances Based on American
    Folk Music
Free Fantasia for Capes
God of Lightning
I Call Upon Thee, My Lord
Jacobs Pillow Concerto
Jesu, Joy of Man's Desiring
Toccata and Fugue in D Minor

1941

Mongolian Archer
Polka Militaire
Valse Brillante

1944

Mountain Whippoorwill

1946

Barcarolle
Gypsy Rondo-Bout Town

1948

Minuet for Drums

1949

Dreams of Jacob

1951

Song of Songs

1964

Siddhas of the Upper Air

The Founders

As the pioneer generation of modern dance had revolted against the unserious attitude of previous dancers, so too did the founding generation revolt against the first generation. The favorite word for designating former efforts at serious theatrical dance outside of the ballet tradition was "expressionist." It connoted the "dancing gods and goddesses" period of modern dance and served as a warning of what to avoid in dance. The new generation felt that too much in the way of compromise had taken place among the forerunners in their attempts to come to terms with public taste. The younger dancers felt that their predecessors had not held onto the original vision that had driven them to create dance companies and to tour as concert artists and not as incidental accompaniment to musical plays. The younger generation wished to establish further the freedom and the independence of modern dance, and it was willing to dispense with popular audience favor altogether if need be. The most famous choreographer of her generation, Martha Graham, admitted years later that, as a young dancer/choreographer, she "went on stage with a whip in my hand."

That whip was a form of movement requiring body configuration that had none of the pleasing lyrical quality of the Denishawn dances she had previously performed. Instead she made the body assume attitudes of stressed tension. Where once there were curves of movement interconnected, now the public was shown sharp percussive beats that finished without the gentle transition into another movement. It was a march compared to a ballade. Martha Graham might have been the most extreme in her attitude, but it was a feeling shared by the others such as Hanya Holm, Lester Horton, Doris Humphrey, Tamiris (Helen Becker), and Charles Weidman. Dance had to assert its independence, and one of the first changes that were made besides the style of movement was in the nature of the costuming. Harem pants were replaced by floor-length severely cut dresses among the women and the men abandoned dervish cloaks for less exotic garb such as shirts and trousers worn by workmen. In making such changes the dancers were responding to the current of the times in much the same way that the previous generation had been sensitive to its time. It was no longer appropriate for dancers to draw on the *art nouveau* sinuosities of line and luxuriant imagery. That had been the expression of a time which in the United States was known as the Gay Nineties, in England as the Edwardian age, and in France *la belle époque;* it was a time of peace, the longest that Europe has ever enjoyed, and commercial prosperity. It was destroyed in the trenches of World War I. The industrial revolution confirmed its technical expertise by producing machines of war that were more lethal than anything the world had ever seen, and while the longing for the refinements of the prewar period lingered on entire societies were torn loose from articles of social faith and sent looking for new ones.

In Italy the futurist painters were intoxicated with the energy and brute power of the machine, which they continually strove to replicate on still canvas. They even conceived of a new dance form which would utilize the sounds of machines instead of conventional music, and in one dance an aviator's flying suit replaced the usual type of costuming. In Germany, Oskar Schlemmer was working with the idea of dance as an expression of machine energy and precision, and in the United States, Martha Graham declared that her dances, though they did not imitate the motions of machines, did reflect the rhythm of an industrial society. The work of the emerging choreographers was designated "modern dance" to distinguish it from the previous expressionist dance and ballet. Prior to this time serious dancing outside of the ballet tradition had a place in the theater and the public eye but did not have a name because individual dancers like Isadora Duncan, Loie Fuller, Ruth St. Denis, Ted Shawn, and Maud Allan did not think of themselves as belonging to a movement but simply as individual artists.

The newly coined "modern dance" group did think of itself as a movement, and at times as a crusade. It was against decorative prettiness, against previous subject matter, against beguiling styles of movement, against ornate settings and costumes and was wary of the commercial theater. It was strongly committed to explore individual styles of movement in search of the language of dancing honesty. At times this resulted in extreme movement deformation that was characterized by some viewers as ugliness. To the members of the group it was identified as an expression of artistic integrity. Each of the choreographers of the modern dance family strove to find the logical basis for developing a vocabulary of dance movement that was based on some natural body rhythm. Martha Graham examined the basic breathing of the body and the changes wrought in it by the inhalation and exhalation of breath. From this she developed her ideas of contraction and release of energy and founded her technique on the discovery. Doris Humphrey conceived of all human motion as a transitional state between disequilibrium and equilibrium. The imbalance which is involved in taking a simple step forward would be the commonest example. A stable stance is exchanged for progress forward, but stability has to be re-established before further progress can be made by taking another step. She called the process fall and recovery and thereby instituted another broad line of dance development.

But no matter what special technique each of the founding generation developed for personal reasons, all agreed that the fundamental process of dance movement had to be examined in order to find a logical and honest base so that each choreographer could create meaningful dance works. It would have compromised their integrity to take a fully fashioned style of movement and use it to create their works. It would have been the language of another, and a gestural language which had been formed in response to another's creative needs. It would have been ultimately inhibiting. So each set out to create the style that most perfectly suited individual creative needs.

One of the strongest beliefs of the generation was in logic, whether it was the logic of the conscious mind or the associative logic of the unconscious mind. It rejected fairy tale as being too closely interwoven with the conventions of the ballet. The emphasis was on the individual through the mind and through the emotions. Eventually the whole world of psychological motivation as it had been developed by Freud, Jung, and others in the field became a rich source of dance subject matter for the founding generation.

The act of courage for these dancer/choreographers was to abandon commercial success in pursuit of artistic expression. The previous generation was brave in asserting that dance was a serious mode of expression or could be, when the prevailing theater world did not believe it to be so. The forerunners strove to demonstrate their belief to the existent audience; the new generation looked for a new audience and a home outside of the commercial dance field. Eventually that home was found in the academic world beginning in the early thirties, when dance departments were established at a few schools in the country. The development was helped immensely by the creation of the Bennington Summer School of the Dance in 1934. Each year the school offered students and teachers from around the country the opportunity to study and work with the most famous names in the modern dance field. They could learn technique and they could observe finished work, and they returned to their own schools with an enhanced zeal for modern dance.

The rise and development of modern dance was coincident with the development of dance criticism as a form, independent of theater or music criticism, in newspapers and magazines where previously no specialist dance critics were employed. The number was at first small but grew with time, and dance became accorded a respect in critical treatment that it had not enjoyed when the forerunners were first beginning their struggle for recognition. Most if not all of the criticism they received came from theater or music critics, some of whom had a sympathy for movement and its possibilities but did not possess any expertise in the broad field of dance.

Mostly in New York but scattered around the country in some other cities such as Los Angeles, the movement which began in the twenties as the interest of a dedicated few developed enormously by the forties. At that time modern dance choreographers virtually replaced standard show choreographers in the popular musical theater and had their own concert touring companies besides. The choreographers who had revolted from the commercial theater and its conventions had convinced their detractors of their worth and had created a new dance audience of serious theatergoers as well. There were dance departments in numerous colleges and modern dance companies were beginning to tour in other countries. It was an enormous leap forward.

ANGNA ENTERS

Born Anita Enters, she changed her name at the request of her manager, who believed in the mystical significance of certain combinations of letters. She was educated privately and took only social dancing as a young lady. She was only encouraged to go on the stage when concert soloist Michio Ito asked her to be his partner in the early twenties. She made her creative debut in 1924 on a joint program with three musicians; the combined dance and song recital being a common occurrence at the time. The first solo program consisting only of her dance works followed two years later in October 1924. She spent the following years up to the outbreak of World War II touring in the United States and abroad.

She created a style of dance-mime that was unique. To some she appeared to be a "wordless monologist," which is probably the closest one can come to describing her art, which almost defies strict categorization. She specialized in character vignettes, and one of her most famous was *Moyen Age*.

After she curtailed active performing, Enters settled in Southern California, where she wrote movie scripts for Metro-Goldwyn-Mayer. During her active performing days she always costumed her own programs and even had exhibitions of her paintings. She opted for semiretirement after having written two volumes of her autobiography, a novel, and a treatise on the art of mime. Even in an age of spectacular talents she stands out for her broad range of expertise.

MOYEN AGE

Choreography by Angna Enters. Music by Girolamo Frescobaldi. First performed at the Little Theatre, New York, N.Y., October 17, 1926, by Angna Enters.

When Enters first began to explore the idea of a medieval dance, she thought of the great stone statues to be found on the entranceways and in the interiors of European cathedrals. Accordingly she designed her first costume in gray so as to give the impression of a living statue flowing from one pose to another. When she tried the costume she was dissatisfied with its appearance and switched to the red- and black-trimmed dress that became the final costume design.

A small crown sits on her head with a small gold knob at the top, and small leaves peel outward from the rim at the four major directional points.

The collar is high and the skirt is full. Her sleeves are decorated at the cuffs with the same roll of gold and turquoise fabric that encircles the neck. When she begins to move, her feet are invisible beneath the long folds of the dress. She is enacting the story of a woman's reaction to the story of the Crucifixion, adoration, and Annunciation. She seems to have stepped out of a Fra Angelico painting as she melts seamlessly from one attitude of apprehension to another of attentive listening or devout adoration.

No attempt is made to duplicate the exact gestures that one might find in a medieval painting but just to capture the pious spirit of the time through the composition of the figure as she assumes succeeding poses.

Obviously the dance pleased Enters, since she kept it in her active repertory almost from the beginning of her concert career. It prompted one critic to remark at its first performance that it "suggested medieval richness stiffness and atmosphere not only by costume but by pantomime that might have sprung from some wistful old tapestry. She evoked the spirit of another day."

CHOREOCHRONICLE
OF ANGNA ENTERS

1922

Devotion

1924

Dance of Death

1926

Second Empire
Sapphic
Promenade
Polonaise
Piano Music
Moyen Age
Habanera
Geschichten aus dem Wiener
Wald
Feline
Cardinal
Bourée

1927

Odalisque
Le Petit berger

1928

Cakewalk—1897

1930

Shaking of the Sheets; a Dance of Death

1932

Vienna Provincial—1910
Plumb-line and Ornament
Pique-nique—1860
Life Is a Dream
Boy Cardinal

1933

Pagan Greece
Pavana
Santa España de la Cruz

1934

Back to Childhood
Danse macabre
Vodvil
Let's Go to Town
Holy Virgin Pursued by Satan

1935

Saturnalia

1952

Fleur du mal
Tango Dancer
Paris 1900

1955

Les Sons et les parfums tournant
   dans l'air du soir

n.d.

Aphrodisiac—Green Hour
Barbary Coast—1849
Contre Danse
Renaissance

MARTHA GRAHAM

Martha Graham was born in Allegheny, Pennsylvania, in 1894 and in 1908 moved to Santa Barbara, California, where she grew up. She attended the Cumnock School in Los Angeles after graduating from high school and there had her first dance instruction. She attended the summer session of the Denishawn school in 1916. She taught at the Denishawn school subsequently and from 1919 till 1923 was a member of the Denishawn company and school. She danced for two seasons in John Murray Anderson's Greenwich Village Follies and in 1925 was an instructor of dance at the Eastman School for Dance and Dramatic Action in Rochester. She formed her first independent company, consisting of herself and three other dancers, in 1926 to present her own work in New York, and a year later opened her own studio.

By 1929 she had enlarged her company to sixteen dancers and was having an annual New York season. She presented *Heretic*, an example of her changing dance style, and two years later her first unanimously acclaimed masterpiece, *Primitive Mysteries*. She was on the staff of the Bennington School of the Dance from its first year, 1934, until it closed in 1942, although she continued as artist-in-residence each summer until 1944. Her first male dancer was Erick Hawkins, who joined the company in 1938 and remained with it until 1950. Their marriage in 1948 was terminated by divorce in 1954.

She was asked to take her company on a foreign tour under the sponsorship of the State Department during 1954–55, when she performed in major cities in Japan, Indonesia, India, Pakistan, Iran, and Israel among others. By the end of the 1940s she had completed a series of dances on American themes, among which are *Frontier, Letter to the World,* and *Appalachian Spring.* During the 1950s and subsequently she created dances such as *Clytemnestra* and *Errand into the Maze* with subjects drawn from Greek mythology. Examples of her interest in theological subject matter are dances like *Seraphic Dialogue,* based on the legend of St. Joan of Arc, and her interest in Hebrew saga is shown by her *Judith.*

For the bulk of her career she chose to work with music specially commissioned for dance under the guidance of her long-time musical collaborator Louis Horst. Her technique of dance movement based on the principle of contraction and release of the torso is the most widely taught system of instruction in colleges and universities. She retired as a performer in 1969 in a dancing career that spans over fifty years, but she continues as an active company director, choreographer, and teacher. She has created over 150 dances.

HERETIC

Choreography by Martha Graham. Anonymous music (Bréton Têtus). *Costumes and lighting by Martha Graham. First performed at the Booth Theatre, New York, N.Y., April 14, 1929, by Martha Graham and Kitty Reese, Louise Creston, Irene Emery, Ethel Rudy, Lillian Ray, Hortense Bunsick, Sylvia Wasserstrom, Mary Rivoire, Ruth White, Lillian Shapero, Virginia Briton, Sylvia Rosenstein, Evelyn Sabin, Betty Macdonald, and Rosina Savelli.*

In 1929, almost three years to the day after she gave her first public independent concert, Graham introduced her new concert group to the public. The dancers were sturdy, well schooled in the percussive movement that was the basis of the Graham technique as it was emerging, and almost carbon copies of one another in general appearance. They were stern faced, used white make-up, and were clothed identically in the company dances. Graham presented four new works for herself and her new group and the outstanding one was *Heretic.*

The dance has three sections, and in each the company of twelve women pits itself against a solitary figure in white. They are dressed in dark dresses that almost reach the floor; their hair is clamped severely down beneath dark caps. The solitary figure stands away from them with her hair flowing freely down her back, in the shaft of bright white light which serves further to distinguish her from them. She moves alone; they are bound together and move as one.

As the dance begins, the group stands shoulder to shoulder, resolute against any incursion from the outside. The figure in white slowly begins to circle around the group looking for a way through their opposing tightness. A lilting Breton folk tune accompanies her movement. It is repeated over and over as she approaches the group, which has formed itself into a wall to repel the intruder. As she nears the group, it sways backward as if recoiling from a poisonous infection. She extends an arm but she is regarded suspiciously. They stamp their heels with an ominous thump to deny her entrance. Twice she manages to break through but they continue to resist her. She kneels before them and they face her in two ranks with clenched fists raised above their heads. Her third attempt to break through their resisting line fails and the dance concludes with her noiseless fall to the ground.

The dance was stark but prophetic of the type of simple, powerful works that would continue to come from Graham for the next ten years. She strongly felt herself to be like a heretic, challenging old conceptions about dancing, and the piece indicated that she held no illusions about the power of her opposition.

PRIMITIVE MYSTERIES

Choreography by Martha Graham. Music by Louis Horst. Costumes and lighting by Martha Graham. First performed at the Craig Theatre, New York, N.Y., February 2, 1931, by Martha Graham and Lillian Shapero, Grace Cornell, Mary Rivoire, Joane Woodruff, Ruth White, Gertrude Shurr, Louise Creston, Anna Sokolow, Lillian Ray, Ethel Rudy, Hortense Burkin, Virginia Briton, Martha Todd, Pauline Nelson, Bessie Schönberg, Ailes Gilmour, Dorothy Bird, and Georgia Graham.

This work was the most important single piece of choreography during the first five years of Graham's independent career. She had demonstrated first her quick and powerful dancing skill and then her ability to assemble dances that were different and could stand on their own merits. With the creation of *Primitive Mysteries* she exposed a profundity of conception that had previously only been hinted at. She was no longer one of many promising choreographers; she moved to the center of modern dance development.

The dance has three sections: "Hymn to the Virgin," "Crucifixus," and "Hosannah." The first section begins in silence with twelve women, all dressed in long dark blue dresses walking unhurriedly onto the stage in three lines. They step forward on one leg, draw the other leg up to it, then pause before stepping off on the first leg again. The walk thus achieved is deliberate and has a processional pace. Until this point there has been no music. The file farthest from the audience extends horizontally, and the two others stretch vertically down toward the audience. When the dancers are in place they form a three-sided "box." The Virgin is in white, an expression of her innocence and suggesting an initiation dress, a color which clearly distinguishes her from the rest of the group. As the group marches on she steps into their midst. Then a melody for flute begins and she moves first to one of the side groups and then to the other. She stops at each, and they form a halo of arms around and behind her head.

Sharp chords on the piano indicate the force and thrust of the group movements. The Virgin is the only person who moves alone; all others move in clusters. She is the subject of their attention and at one point she leads the horizontal group around the stage in a file that passes between two lines of women who face one another. As the Virgin passes each of the pairs of facing women, they greet her. One crooks an arm and holds it up, while the other crooks hers in a similar fashion but rests the forearm on the floor and extends her body out to the side. Thus, one of the women salutes the sky and the other the ground, and together they form the parameters within which the Virgin moves. To conclude the section, the dancers form a circle around her, stepping first to the right and then to the left. In silence they resume the opening formation and pass slowly off the stage.

Trios predominate in "Crucifixus" with the Virgin in the center of the trio farthest away from the audience. The two women flanking the Virgin arch their arms over her head and again the opening is done in silence. At the first note of the music she bursts forward and holds her arms straight out. The group compacts into a tight square off to one side. In the first row, one now raises her leg higher and higher and then suddenly turns the motion into a giant step by shifting her weight forward. The others follow, forming a large circle around the Virgin. They clasp their hands behind their backs and bend forward, giving an animalistic configuration to the body. They are all impelled forward by some force that is beyond their questioning. As they circle, the music increases in tempo and the steps take on a quality of driven frenzy. It is the climax of their ceremonial. It concludes with a stately walk off.

For the third and final time the group returns in silence. The Virgin now has an attendant. Two lines of five dancers each stretch out horizontally across the stage. One group dashes toward the audience while the other moves away. The groups fraction into clusters of twos and threes. The Virgin sinks to the ground and is assisted by her attendant, who places her hands behind the Virgin's head in a blessing. The entire group sits with her and then rolls over onto its knees, the head of each dancer bent to the floor. It is a concluding obeisance. All walk off with the Virgin and her attendant in the center.

When Graham first worked on the piece with her company, she explained it to them in terms of the Virgin in Christian ritual and over thirty years later explained it to another company that was going to dance it as a dance having reference to the Sabbath queen of Hebrew myth. Undoubtedly in coaching other dancers she might adduce similar figures from other religious traditions to make the import of the dance clear. The Virgin energizes the group by her pure presence; the group honors and cherishes her. She is the manifestation of religious creative power. The audience at the first performance cheered without restraint, little knowing that Graham had spent the previous night in an agony of doubt as to the dance's worth.

FRONTIER (PERSPECTIVE NO. 1)

Choreography by Martha Graham. Music by Louis Horst. Costumes and lighting by Martha Graham. Scenery by Isamu Noguchi. First performed at the Guild Theatre, New York, N.Y., April 28, 1935, by Martha Graham.

By the time she created this dance in 1935, Graham was totally committed to the use of new music for her works. She was influenced in this decision by Louis Horst, who was her musical director and who had composed several works for her including the first commissioned score, *Three Poems of the East* and the profound *Primitive Mysteries*. Throughout her career he proved specially sensitive to her needs and in *Frontier* gave her the simple but eloquent score that accompanied this beautiful solo. She also used décor for the first time, commissioning a set from Isamu Noguchi. It consisted of a short length of fence with a length of rope in the shape of a "V" which spread outward and upward from the fence to disappear in the "flies."

The dancer is seated on the fence wearing a long dress such as a plainswoman might choose and staring away so that she is seen in profile. With her first movements, a series of tiny steps, she delineates a large square area in front of the fence. The steps almost form a visible perforation marking the space she regards as her own in this broad, undivided expanse of territory. She returns to the fence, then bounds forward in a straight line, conquering the space in another way. Later she moves forward again on the same direct line, but now she jumps up and extends her leg at a right angle to the side, like the tolling of a pendulum measuring off the time in a confident and secure manner. The wildness of her first assault on the area has been replaced with a calm exploration of her zone of mastery. At the end of the dance she again rests on the fence and gazes off in profile, but now makes a folding gesture of the arms that suggests the closing of a gate.

Graham's domination of space and its organization was never so clearly demonstrated as in this solo. She was able to conjure up the vision of a limitless land in which she had settled herself and had tamed one portion of it for her own use. There was also the characterization of the frontier woman resolute, unafraid, but with spontaneous joy bursting forth from meeting the challenge she faced. An important by-product of this work was her delight with the spare set created by Noguchi. It inaugurated a collaboration that produced three dozen dance décors that remain among the great achievements of the American stage.

LETTER TO THE WORLD

Choreography by Martha Graham. Music by Hunter Johnson. Costumes by Edythe Gilfond. Scenery and lighting by Arch Lauterer. First performed at Bennington College Theatre, Bennington, Vt., August 11, 1940, with the following cast: characters in the real world: Margaret Meredith as the One in White, Nina Fonaroff and Marjorie Mazia as Two Children; characters in the world of imagination: Martha Graham as the One in Red, Erick Hawkins as the Lover, Jane Dudley as the Ancestress, Merce Cunningham as March, Nelle Fisher as the Happy Child, George Hall as the Boy with the Birds, and Sophie Maslow, Ethel Butler, Jean Erdman, Frieda Flier, Elizabeth Halpern, David Campbell, and David Zellmer.

When the ballet was first presented at Bennington College, Vermont, during the summer of 1940, it was suggested by an eminent critic that the dance had best "be interred in the hills of Vermont." Fortunately the advice was disregarded, and when the piece was presented the following fall in a New York concert it was hailed as a masterwork. It is a pivotal piece in the Graham *œuvre,* incorporating as it does spoken poetry in the very fabric of the dance.

Emily Dickinson's poetry and life were the inspirations for the piece, and her part in the dance is performed by two women, One Who Dances and One Who Speaks. The first section is "Because I see New England," and the Speaker and Dancer encounter one another and express a kinship in the lines of a poem that concludes "I'm nobody too." They retire to a bench together as a man enters to dance a solo variation. Four couples enter to perform a social dance that suggests school youngsters as they pass one another and sweep around in a large circle. The Postponeless Creature introduces the figure of the Ancestress, who is dressed in stark Puritan black and white and follows the Dancer. The latter shudders at her approach and tries to flee, but the Ancestress follows and helps her up after she falls to the floor. They go together to kneel by a bench, and the couples return in a somber procession. The men lift the Dancer and lower her to the floor, where her lover, who did the opening male solo, goes to her and lifts her. Two of the other girls are raised aloft as if dead and the Ancestress passes under the arches formed by their bodies. She leans heavily on her lover and seems powerless to stand on her own after the intimidating visit of the Ancestress. The Dancer receives encouragement from the Lover, though, and makes a defiant gesture to the Ancestress as the Speaker says the poeticized blessing "In the name of the bee, the butterfly, and the breeze. Amen."

"The Little Tippler" portion of the dance shows a slightly giddy Dancer, who is enlivened by alcohol into doing a happy solo that suggests faintly a sailor's hornpipe as she shields her eyes with one hand and leans forward to peer from time to time. She hunches up her shoulders frequently as little spasms of silliness sweep through her. Her solo is immediately followed by the jolly entrance of a man in a green coat who bounds around as the creature conjured up by the poem "Dear March, come in." Together the Dancer and he overturn the stern bench, lift it high in the air, and move it to another place from its appointed one. It is a duet of innocent mischief which is dispelled as the Ancestress reappears and forces the Dancer to return the bench to its rightful place and glares at her as she leaves.

The light, joyful atmosphere of the section concludes with a little Maypole dance around a figure called the Fairy Queen, and then the warm group dance of young love in which March reappears.

The fourth movement finds the Speaker and the Dancer walking slowly with veils held over their heads. The Dancer pushes her arms forward as if calling to someone and leans back over the bench. Her lover and the Ancestress reappear and she stands between them, turning first to one and then the other. She and the Lover dance together, and he lifts her and she appears ecstatically happy, but the Ancestress returns and separates them with large chopping sweeps of her arm.

The concluding movement, "This Is My Letter to the World," contains one of the finest solos that Graham ever created, in which the Dancer sweeps around, bows down under the weight of her grief, rebuffs the Ancestress, and sits on the bench with her hands clasped securely together.

One of the most immediate results of Graham's use of spoken text in this and others of her dances is that it influenced a broad range of choreographers to try the same device. The affirmation of her life as an artist is profoundly moving and her confident stillness at the end of the dance the conception of dance genius. As a voracious reader, Graham demonstrated her extreme sensitivity to the lonely talent of Emily Dickinson's poetry, selecting texts of varying mood to portray the inner landscape of the poet's soul. It remains the most successful linkage of verse and complementary movement to be brought to the stage.

DEATHS AND ENTRANCES

Choreography by Martha Graham. Music by Hunter Johnson. Costumes by Edythe Gilfond. Scenery by Arch Lauterer. Lighting by Jean Rosenthal. First performed at Bennington College, Bennington, Vt., July 18, 1943. First performed in New York City at the Forty-sixth Street Theatre, December 26, 1943, by Martha Graham, Sophie Maslow, and Jane Dudley as the Three Sisters; *Ethel Butler, Nina Fonaroff, and Pearl Lang as the* Three Remembered Children, *Erick Hawkins as the* Dark Beloved, *Merce Cunningham as the* Poetic Beloved, *John Butler and Robert Horan as the* Cavaliers.

Deaths and Entrances takes place in an interior that could be one room or could represent an entire house. It contains three pieces of furniture: a stepped platform on the right-hand side close to the audience, directly across the stage on the left a vanity table with what might be a mirror or the reredos of an altar, and at the back of the stage on the same side a rectangular box about the size of a chest of drawers. Dominating the entire setting is a huge curtained window with the curtains permanently drawn. The atmosphere is close, and the bearing of the three women, who are seated on the platform as the dance begins, suggests tenseness and a suppressed antagonism.

Each in turn dances a short solo; one is a bit flirtatious, another has a stately, erotic quality, and the protagonist, the woman in the black dress, projects repressed fury. The dance as it develops is as much about the past as it is about the present. Episodes from the past are danced by the women with men from the past, and periodically dancers dressed as small children pass through to observe, at times to deposit or take up some symbolic object, a dark goblet, a shell, or a vase. These in turn set off chains of memories.

The main character is the woman in black, who in her past has two men, the Dark Beloved and the Poetic Beloved. They are dressed almost identically in velvet jackets, ruffled shirts, and dark trousers and are destined to clash despite the mitigating presence of the woman between them. Again from the past are drawn two other men called the Cavaliers, who at one point become polite tea dance partners for the sisters except that what one sees as their supposedly graceful holding of their partners hands is in fact a clenched encounter between hands struggling against one another. And then the struggle is over and partners are exchanged and the antagonism begins again, for another moment of confrontation, which again vanishes almost immediately.

On the lower step of the platform a board with two chess pieces stands throughout the dance. One piece is white the other red. The contending men move them angrily at one time, and the sisters are seated around the board at the beginning, engaged in some type of play. The woman in black is torn by conflicting emotions and in a great solo appears to be on the edge of breaking down but manages to retain her psychic hold as she runs and turns around, going from one to another of the curious pieces of furniture.

At the end of the piece all of the characters from the past have vanished and only the three sisters remain. They seat themselves around the game board as they were in the beginning, and the woman in black takes the goblet she has been holding and places it firmly and dramatically between the two chess pieces to conclude the mysterious game.

When it was first given in the attic theater at Bennington College in Vermont, it was interrupted by a violent summer lightning storm. Flickers could be seen through the skylight, and halfway through the performance the power failed, and the theater was darkened. It was a suitably dramatic setting for this work, which is concerned with the storms of the inner landscape.

Its intensity, its allusiveness, and its utter conviction make it one of Graham's most outstanding dances. It began as a conscious examination of the three Brontë sisters but developed into a much more personal statement about life and family conflicts, and one is reminded that Graham herself was one of three sisters. Its use of flashback techniques to compress time is one of the most brilliant achievements of the work. This was the second score that Hunter Johnson did for Graham. The first was *Letter to the World*, and both dances are among her most accomplished creations.

APPALACHIAN SPRING

Choreography by Martha Graham. Music by Aaron Copland. Costumes by Edythe Gilfond. Scenery by Isamu Noguchi. Lighting by Jean Rosenthal. First performed at the Library of Congress, Washington, D.C., October 30, 1944, by May O'Donnell as the Pioneering Woman, *Merce Cunningham as the* Revivalist, *Nina Fonaroff, Pearl Lang, Marjorie Mazia, and Yuriko as the* Followers, *Erick Hawkins as the* Husbandman, *and Martha Graham as the* Bride.

Everything and everyone connected with this extraordinary dance seemed to be blessed with a special aura. Graham was at the height of her creative powers, Aaron Copland produced one of his most beloved scores, Noguchi sketched in the farm setting with elegant spareness, and Jean Rosenthal bathed it with one of her most brilliant light designs.

The scene is a farmyard in which a section of fence rail indicates the territory possessed by the young couple. The house is nothing more than a peaked entrance and a clapboard wall with a bench. An inclined stump which later functions as a pulpit thrusts out of the ground. A rocking chair of bladelike slimness furnishes the house. On the surface it is the story of a husbandman and his bride taking possession of their new house and starting a new life together. The two young people are observed, examined, and ultimately approved of by the older generation, represented by the Pioneer Woman and a fire and brimstone Revivalist. The action occurs in the early settlement days.

The Husbandman's first entrance brings him to the side of the cabin where he and his bride will dwell, and he runs his hand reflectively over the surface of its overlapping boards. There is a sense of both possession and questioning. As the work progresses, the Husbandman and his bride dance a warmly joyous duet that reveals their shared hopes for the future. The Revivalist with his broad-brimmed hat is a formidable figure, more concerned with rectitude than with love and warmth. He represents one aspect of the experience the young are entering. His sternness is softened by the Pioneer Woman, who has already experienced the emotional joys and pains that will become the lot of the young woman.

The simple tale of the man and his bride examining their farm gives no inkling of the ramifications of gesture with which Graham composed the dances for her principals. The Bride's joy is not expressed by simple hopping up and down but is a surge of happiness that seems too good to be admitted, so that she draws back from the full expression of her happiness for fear of driving it away. The slow expansive gestures of the Pioneer Woman indicate her sharing of the younger woman's joy, though tempering it with wisdom. The Bride has steps that are buoyed up with hope for the future, while the Pioneer Woman, like a ship breasting waves, sweeps along with calm resolution. The Husbandman settles his feet into the ground like one who is drawing sustenance from it in the way that any living thing might. He is as solid as the fence posts that hold up his railings, but he appears to be someone who could grow. He is open and firm. The Revivalist, filled with fervor, is equally firm. In effect he carries around with him a congregation-audience which listens to and applauds his words. In a beautiful fusion of two different types of gesture, the congregation of four women cup their hands as if in prayer and then clap them together as if applauding. Surrounding it all, Copland's singing score wraps itself like a benign thread, while Noguchi's setting, more like a spatial drawing than a sculptural block, gives indications of place without obtruding.

Audiences recognized a story that was simultaneously personal to a couple and their kin and an expression of a country's growth. The musical quotes from a traditional hymn that Copland incorporated into his score emphasized the warm, religious, and joyful values expressive of the sinew and heart of a young country that, though still struggling, was confident of a happy outcome. The piece became a signature work for Graham, and years later audiences had only to hear the score to be reminded of her special achievement.

DARK MEADOW

Choreography by Martha Graham. Music by Carlos Chávez (Hija de Colquide, *1944*). *Costumes by Edythe Gilfond. Scenery by Isamu Noguchi. Lighting by Jean Rosenthal. First performed at the Plymouth Theatre, New York, N.Y., January 23, 1946, by May O'Donnell as* She of the Ground, *Erick Hawkins as* He Who Summons, *Pearl Lang, Natanya Neumann, Marjorie Mazia, David Zellmer, Yuriko, Mark Ryder, Ethel Winter, and Douglass Watson as* They Who Dance Together, *and Martha Graham as* One Who Seeks.

In her published notebooks Graham devotes a great deal of space to her jottings about this work. In them she refers to her readings in Jungian psychological theory in which great stress is laid upon universal ideas implanted in the race's collective unconscious. She speaks of Roman, Greek, and Indian myth as well as her own experience of standing atop a ruined pyramid in Mexico. All of her experiences went into the construction of this mythic dance that draws its inspiration from diverse sources and refuses to be locked into any one mythic tradition.

Noguchi's setting suggests a primitive prenational locale. Three dark mounds are at the right. Another mound with a sheer white face not yet visible stands at the left and functions as an inclined platform at first. One Who Seeks stands on the platform with arms upraised. Then she begins her wandering course through the dark stones, including the one she was standing on. Five women who inhabit the space like a curious herd reflect her broad gestures with similar motions but more compressed in their reach. Her questing has a brute intensity emphasized by the rough simplicity of her movement.

She of the Ground passes through and the other women leave. One Who Seeks continues her wandering as She of the Ground walks through the space again with great calmness and serenity. He Who Summons steps out from behind the large mound at the rear of the stage and prances back and forth, bringing She of the Ground into the clearing again. This time she does not remove herself and remains immobile but close to the center of the action. One Who Seeks goes off to return with the whole of the group called They Who Dance Together, which consists of five women and three men. They bring a black cloth with them.

One Who Seeks takes the shroud-like cloth and begins a strong meditative solo, returning again and again as if to exorcise something from the past, and appears almost to be a penitent wrapping herself in the cloth. He Who Summons stands behind a mound on whose summit is fixed a small white cross. She of the Ground takes the cross, turns up the white face of the stone at the left, and leaves. One Who Seeks braces herself on the stone until He

Who Summons draws her away for a duet, but at its conclusion turns her resolutely back toward the stone and conceals himself behind the mound at the rear. Three couples dance through the still scene and depart. The men return with shafts in their hands, thrusting them into holes in the white stone. During this whole section they weave in and around the principals, who gravely go through their ritual.

In the final portion She of the Ground returns in a green cloak, suggesting the fecundity of the earth, and turns one of the mounds so that its yellow side shows. She places a small pronged tree in it and dances a worshipful solo before it. He Who Summons and She Who Seeks return as the solo finishes. Together all gather at the mound where the tree sprouts green leaves, and One Who Seeks whirls gently and happily.

The dance celebrates the cycle of birth, growth, death, and rebirth in abstract symbolical terms. The personages of the dance have an epic character and carry out the terms of ritual that was ordained before words, before thought but not before feeling. They occupy that crossroad where the animalistic and the protocivilized beings touch. In the piece Graham created some of her most striking ensemble work for They Who Dance Together, who wove throughout the piece in a unifying flow.

ERRAND INTO THE MAZE

Choreography by Martha Graham. Music by Gian Carlo Menotti. Costumes by Martha Graham. Scenery by Isamu Noguchi. Lighting by Jean Rosenthal. First performed at the Ziegfeld Theatre, New York, N.Y., February 28, 1947, by Martha Graham and Mark Ryder.

In the years 1946–47, Graham was beginning a new cycle of works based on ancient myths of the Greek and Hebrew traditions as she turned from her preoccupation with Americana. One of the strangest and most powerful of these dances, *Errand into the Maze* takes the classical legend of Ariadne and turns it into an exploration of personal psychology. In the original, Ariadne, who is the daughter of the King of Minos, gives her beloved Theseus a golden thread by which to guide himself out of the maze after killing the monstrous Minotaur. In this version the conflict is between Ariadne and the Creature of Fear.

The stage has a large "V" shape at the left, which suggests a huge bone of some description. Leading from it to a small block toward the rear of the stage is a white tape. A rope extends upward from the block and disappears in the flies. Another rope attached to it stretches diagonally into the wings. A crescent and a circular shape are attached to it, lightly suggesting a skyscape.

At the base of the block a woman stands in an obvious state of anxiety, turning first one way and then the other. She moves to the side, staying well to the rear of the stage, and her torment increases. Suddenly an odd figure jumps into view; it is a man with a bone like a yoke over his shoulders and his hands are draped helplessly over it. He wears tiny bull's horns and after jumping agitatedly, rolls off.

The woman now picks up the white tape and draws it through her hands as she follows it to the "V" at the front of the stage. Her frenzy continues as she bounds with the tape in her hands, as if she were being drawn to something that could harm her. The creature returns and she approaches him tentatively and then begins a passionately awkward duet with him.

Again he leaves and her movements become more lyrical and not as spasmodically driven as they were, but then the anxiety reasserts itself and the creature returns. She sweeps up the tape and dashes behind the "V" and stretches it back and forth across the entrance as a barrier to him. It is effective, though she still gives a convulsive shudder at his presence. He finally slides to the floor and she undoes the crisscrossed tape to complete her liberation.

The location of the conflict is in the mind of the heroine, who has to conquer her own fear, represented by the yoked creature. He is a curious menace, in that his bull-like energy is seriously hampered by the hindrance placed across his shoulders. He can rush about but he cannot strike or stifle the woman. He is essentially a powerless menace but must be resolutely faced down. The woman is forced to encounter him directly so that she can see how groundless her fears were and only with that self-knowledge vanquish this shadowy villain. It is a brilliantly simple duet but resonant of common human problems that exist on the psychological plane of reality.

DIVERSION OF ANGELS

Choreography by Martha Graham. Music by Norman Dello Joio. Costumes by Martha Graham. Scenery by Isamu Noguchi (but not used after the first performance). Lighting by Jean Rosenthal. First performed at Palmer Auditorium, Connecticut College, New London, Conn., August 13, 1948, by Pearl Lang, Helen McGehee, Natanya Neumann, Dorothea Douglas, Joan Skinner, Dorothy Berea, Dale Schnert, Mark Ryder, Robert Cohan, and Stuart Hodes.

This is one of the best known of Graham's works and is the one that has been most widely performed. It has been included in the repertories of several companies other than Graham's own and has won audiences for itself all over the world. It was created for the first season of the American Dance Festival at Connecticut College, which succeeded the Bennington College Summer Dance Festival, which had been formally discontinued in 1942.

It is a lyric dance for four couples and three solo women who are archetypes of the young girl, the passionate woman, and somewhat exalted lady. These are dressed in yellow, red, and white. As the dance begins the woman in white is at the center of a circle of men who turn and fall away from her like the opening of big powerful flower petals. At times, as they circle around her, they resort to a simple and childlike expression of happiness by turning cart wheels.

The others of the cast, dressed in shades of brown, dash on, and the work develops in a series of rapid entrances and exits full of the enthusiasm and athletic vigor of youth. There is no character development as such, but the energy of the piece in pure dance terms has a compelling zest of amorous play; as much play as amorousness. At one point the woman in red suddenly zooms on the stage in a rapid dash that takes her across it diagonally like a streak of crimson passion. It startles and also makes one smile at the audacity. The lady in white concludes the dance, resting immobile at the rear of the stage while one of the men puts his hands, with fingers splayed, behind her head in a halo of benediction.

The dance is one of the most accessible in the Graham repertory because of its immediate emotional appeal. It does not have the literary structure that many of her pieces do, nor does it explore the dark side of human nature, which has proved so attractive to Graham's mystical nature. It is a celebration and expresses itself as such in the first bars of the music and the muscular good spirits of the dancers.

SERAPHIC DIALOGUE

Choreography by Martha Graham. Music by Norman Dello Joio. Costumes by Martha Graham. Scenery by Isamu Noguchi. Lighting by Jean Rosenthal. First performed at the ANTA Theatre, New York, N.Y., May 8, 1955, by Linda Margolies as Joan, *Patricia Birch as the* Maid, *Mary Hinkson as the* Warrior, *Matt Turney as the* Martyr, *Bertram Ross as* St. Michael, *Lillian Biersteker as* St. Catherine, *and Ellen van der Hoeven as* St. Margaret.

There is no dance in Graham's repertory that has benefited more from reworking than *Seraphic Dialogue,* which began creative life as a solo called *The Triumph of St. Joan.* Accustomed as she was to redoing parts of dances after they had received their first performances, Graham usually was spurred by dissatisfaction with specific elements of the choreography. In this case she rethought the structure of the dance because of the extraordinary beauty of the décor offered to her by Noguchi, who succeeded Frederick Kiesler, the original designer.

The polished brass set shines like finely drawn gold. On the right are three seats upon which the dancers who portray aspects of Joan's life sit stiffly upright while one or the other of them dance. Opposite them on the other side of the stage is a stand on which hang a cross and a sword, done in the same openwork brass. To the rear rises a structure of circles, triangles, and rectangles resembling the tracery of a stained-glass window. It contains no glass, however, just the outlining metal, glistening. Within it is seated Joan's patron saint, St. Michael, attended by Sts. Catherine and Margaret. His hands with fingers outstretched flutter beatifically. Joan herself is seated before the structure.

She rises and the three dancers who portray aspects of her character march in, draped with long cloaks that brush the floor. Solemnly they take their seated places, and the essay into memory and reflection begins. Joan in effect dances dialogues with aspects of her being and then retires to allow the individual to dance out that portion of her life which each represents. The first is the maid, who joyously jumps and affirms her enthusiasm for life. She whips her scarf around like a banner but then yields it up and returns to her place as Joan then reflects on this segment of her life. She retires once more as the warrior steps out of her cloak and approaches the stand on which her future sword hangs. She approaches it as if in a church, moving forward on her kness. St. Michael emerges from his sanctuary and takes the sword from its place to pass it over the body of the young warrior. She clasps it to herself with a passionate fervor. Joan returns to express her feelings of mixed pride and sorrow for the fate of the idealistic young zealot.

The warrior resumes her cloak, and the martyr steps forward. There is the affirmation of the cross, which she carries proudly, but events conspire to force her martyrdom. She cannot deny the voices which have guided her, and in a solemn processional attended by St. Catherine and St. Margaret, who hold the hem of her cloak high, she marches off with the cross held steadily before her.

The cycle is complete; youth and innocence have been succeeded by war, contention, and finally sacrifice for an ideal. Joan returns in a resplendent gold dress for her beatification. She is beyond time now, and St. Michael opens the doors of his sanctuary to allow the saints to run, thrusting their hands up in celebration, to proclaim the entrance of Joan into blessedness. He leads her to her niche behind the tracery guarding the sanctuary, and they extend their arms out to the sides with their accepting and satisfied palms turned upward.

Joan is the story of heroic virtue and was one of a series of dances that used the device of memory to allow a play between the past and present. For Graham the past was a very real part of the present, affecting the course of events and exerting an influence that had to be dealt with consciously so that one did not become a helpless plaything of its unseen pressures. In its choreography, design, lighting, and music *Seraphic Dialogue* represented a superb fusion of theatrical elements.

CLYTEMNESTRA

Choreography by Martha Graham. Music by Halim El-Dabh. Costumes by Martha Graham and Helen McGehee. Scenery by Isamu Noguchi. Lighting by Jean Rosenthal. First performed at the Adelphi Theater, New York, N.Y., April 1, 1958, by Martha Graham as Clytemnestra, *Paul Taylor as* Aegisthus, *Yuriko as* Iphigenia, *Helen McGehee as* Electra, *Matt Turney as* Cassandra, *Ethel Winter as* Helen of Troy; *Bertram Ross as* Agamemnon *and* Orestes; *Gene McDonald successively as* Hades, Paris, *the* Watchman, *and the* Ghost of Agamemnon; *David Wood as the* Messenger of Death, *and Ellen Siegel, Richard Kuch, Akiko Kanda, Carol Payne, Ellen Graff, Bette Shaller, Lois Schlossberg, Dan Wagoner, and George Nabors.*

This was Graham's first evening-long work and was a considerable departure from her own and modern dance practice in general. The ordinary length of even a large-scale work was ordinarily not more than an hour, but Graham was thinking on a monumental scale and needed the creative time granted by a full-evening work to recount the tangled tale of the wronged Clytemnestra and her own misdeeds.

The dance consists of a prologue, two acts, and an epilogue. In the prologue Clytemnestra sits and ponders the events of her life from her unquiet stay in the land of the dead. She is dishonored before the king of the dead for her actions while on earth and has been denied rest because of it. One hears rumbling and muted sounds of alarm from the orchestra. Two singers in formal contemporary dress stand, one at either side of the stage. The male intones a low moaning ah-h-h-h-h-h that rises into a piercing e-e-e-e-e-e-e sound. The woman begins "I, Clytemnestra . . ." and throughout the evening both will accompany the action on stage with commentary like that of a chorus in a classical Greek play.

The messenger of death, with bald head, bare chest, and red sheath draped around his lower body, walks across the front of the stage thumping his staff. Three sculptural pieces, isolated from one another, are on the stage. To the left an elaborate chair on which a man conceals his face with branches, at the rear a circle of strips hanging from above within which is Clytemnestra, and on the right a wooden platform having two levels, one supporting a man and the other two women. Clytemnestra moves forward to begin her meditation as the circle of streamers is lifted. She drops to her knees, curves her arms in toward herself questioningly, rises, kicks her outstretched palm with her foot, and sinks to her knees again.

The man with the branches before his face is the King of Hades, and he descends from his throne to approach her. She retreats from before him, attempting to shield her face from his gaze. He crosses to the opposite platform to stand and she goes to his throne. He stands with Helen of Troy,

Apollo, and the goddess Athena. The sight of Helen brings back the memory of the siege and sack of Troy and four couples dash on to detail the terrible events that took place. They wear black costumes and their dance is a grotesque lament. All those watching except Hades go off, and Clytemnestra is left pressing her anguished palm to her forehead. She crosses to him. He stands straddling her body as she sinks to the floor arching backward. He then circles her. The memories begin to flow again.

A young girl is dragged in to lie athwart huge crossed war lances. The men stamp around her in a circle, raise her up on one of the crossed lances like a sacrifice, and two of them carry her off. It is Iphigenia, Clytemnestra's daughter, who was sacrificed by her war-bound husband Agamemnon, to secure favorable winds from the gods. The memory of the loss stings Clytemnestra afresh. Hades approaches her and she stands on his empty throne but dismounts to look painfully at the great angular dagger lying beside it.

Another episode in her past swims to the fore. It is her murdered husband, Agamemnon, whom she slew in revenge for Iphigenia. She goes to conceal herself in the circle of streamers as the messenger who opened the prologue walks across the back of the stage. Once again the eerie wordless plaint ah-h-h-h-h-h-e-e-e-e-e-e is heard. During the passionate duet the story of their life together is sung, and now a flood of memory causes all of the characters in the entwined tale to emerge. As each appears, the chorus of two gives a brief summation of the part that each plays in the legend, including her unlawful consort Aegisthus, and the vengeance sworn against her by her two other children, Electra and Orestes, who enters with the Furies. All whirl and leave. Clytemnestra grasps the fatal dagger and exits while holding it aloft.

The first act begins with a long solo by the watchman in Mycenae, Agamemnon's and Clytemnestra's home, and it announces the news of Troy's fall. The action of the dance has been shifted from the underworld to the kingdom of the living, and many of the dancers now assume two or more roles in succeeding sections. The watchman in the world of the living is the same as the one who danced the king or overseer of the kingdom of the dead. Clytemnestra enters, robed in violet, escorted by six Furies who clutch at their stomachs and then sweep their elbows in, while they circle her, in a dance of grim jubilation.

Suddenly the mighty war lances are brought on again and form a fence at the rear while in front the young Clytemnestra dances with Aegisthus and Paris entreats Helen of Troy in a passionate dance. They drink from a cup and do an intoxicated duet in which he spins off with her. Young Clytemnestra and Aegisthus now return to embrace tenderly but intensely while the older Clytemnestra watches this part of her past intently from behind the fence of spears. Iphigenia enters and is borne away, sacrificed. The stage is emptied except for Clytemnestra, who does her dance to seduce Aegisthus. She is not the innocent betrayed but rather the active participant in the shameful union. While they dance he brings her attention to the dagger, and she suffers from the consequences of its use, but her ardor for him replaces good sense.

Agamemnon returns in triumph standing erect on top of the crossed spears, which have been transformed into his victorious litter. Clytemnestra greets him wearing an enormous red train borne by two servants. He leaps arrogantly down to put a robe about Clytemnestra, who tosses it off. He then insultingly places it at the feet of his new love, Cassandra. Clytemnestra is caught in a spasm of hurt and pain as he mounts the litter again. Her great cloak is spread across the entire front of the stage. She falls at his feet and raises her hand, but he rudely pushes it aside and tosses her away. She gathers herself and draws the cloak about her body and by so doing suggests a blood resolve. Cassandra, who is blessed with the gift of prophecy, is also cursed in that no one believes what she says, and her frantic warnings go unheeded.

Clytemnestra begins a seductive dance to attract Agamemnon, who is swollen with pride and enters into their home. The servants make an entranceway out of the cloak and Clytemnestra enters with the fatal dagger. She raises it and thrusts it into his body and Hades extends the branches of death behind Agamemnon's head. Cassandra, who was the daughter of Priam, Troy's king, is Agamemnon's prize of war, and her fate is sealed when he dies. She leaps wildly about in terror and scuttles along on her knees beseechingly for anyone who will save her from Clytemnestra's revenge. There is no savior and she perishes by the same blade that drew Agamemnon's blood.

The Furies enter to decry the scene of revenge and murder, and Aegisthus and Clytemnestra do a brief dance of exultation. He storms around brandishing a spear while she indulges and feeds his pride. The messenger returns to view the carnage and opens his mouth in a silent scream.

The second act opens in the bedroom Clytemnestra shares with Aegisthus. The ghost of Agamemnon staggers past in the gloom. Clytemnestra rises from her troubled sleep wearing a deep red gown and returns to Aegisthus' side, but her sleep is still disturbed. Her son, Orestes, dances out his hostility against his mother and her lover but also shows his indecision. His sister, Electra, comes to him to remind him of his duty to avenge their father. All is still as Clytemnestra rises again to expel her anxieties and fearful anticipations. She collapses by the throne. Her children observe her from a little distance; it is obviously a moment for decision. Clytemnestra offers them a curse as they shuffle toward her on their knees, and then rolls in front of them. Orestes takes the dagger and stabs her and then hurls it into the body of Aegisthus, who wakes and attempts to flee. Orestes collapses.

The epilogue finds Clytemnestra back in the underworld. The messenger crosses in front of the black curtain as a procession of women, Hades, and Clytemnestra passes behind it. The chorus inquires "Why dishonored among the dead?" and then proceeds to relate the story. Clytemnestra sits and watches the Furies and rises to take the branches of death from Hades to run forward and back with them. She acknowledges her guilt and strides before the curtain as all others stand immobile.

The achievement of the work marked a high point in Graham's career. She had woven the strands of the Greek myth into a towering dance that was rich and dense with invention. She took the themes of passion and duty that she had worked with throughout her career and resolved the tension that resulted from their clash. It was inevitable that the dictates of the heart should run afoul of the commands of duty, but it was only through an admission of guilt that the sentence of condemnation could be removed. Clytemnestra had paid with her life for the murder of her husband and her liaison with Aegisthus, but it was only when she acknowledged her passionate infatuation with Aegisthus that the curse of an unquiet death was removed from her.

Once again, Graham called upon Noguchi to design her sets, and he responded with the imagination that always characterized their collaborations. He gave her individual units with which to work. Each of the sculptural pieces was independent of the other and could be isolated with a shift in lighting. It greatly facilitated the changes in time from the present to the past, and in designing the crossed spears he in effect provided a triumphal carriage, a fence, a sacrificial altar, and a funeral bier, all with the greatest economy.

When the dance was created in 1958, Graham was in her sixties and past her dancing prime, but she still possessed tremendous theatrical presence. During a performance it was impossible to take one's eyes from her and she dominated the action throughout. When the story demanded that she dance a duet with her beloved, she simply retired to the background and observed herself as a young person through memory. It was a device that she was to use frequently during the latter part of her career with great success. While it was a physical necessity, she turned it to her own advantage.

PART REAL–PART DREAM

Choreography by Martha Graham. Music by Mordecai Seter. Costumes by Martha Graham. Scenery by Dani Karavan. Lighting by Jean Rosenthal. First performed at the Fifty-fourth Street Theatre, New York, N.Y., November 3, 1965, by Mary Hinkson, Matt Turney, Robert Cohan, and Bertram Ross, with Takako Asakawa, Juliet Fisher, Carol Fried, Phyllis Gutelius, Noemi Lapzeson, Gene McDonald, Clive Thompson, Peter Randazzo, Gus Solomons, Jr., and William Louther.

Two men and two women inhabit a sensuous twilight world of myriad colors that suggests a Persian miniature. Motivations are obscure but follow a rational course of shadowy logic. The whole feeling of the piece is that of a frolic in an exotic garden.

Accompanied only by the sound of a fish-scale chime which she agitates, a woman crosses the stage. Three strange objects decorate the space: a stand with a cylinder atop it, a metal disc with beads on wire spurting from its center, and a narrow screen of metal mesh. After she crosses and disappears, the woman crouching at the disc walks back and forth in front of the screen. A man reaches out to pluck bits of clothing from her and dances with her veil. Suddenly a chorus of four women enter and a second man swivels around to reveal himself nestled inside the cylinder. He wears a green sash. He runs to draw the fountain of wire and beads out of the disc, and the woman standing in a long robe near it runs after him as he dashes off.

In front, the man with the red sash emerges from behind the screen and scoops up the long robe and fashions the shape of a cloaked woman out of it. He does a clever solo dance while maintaining the illusion that the tucked and draped robe is actually a woman. It is a fetishistic impulse lifted to the realm of art and totally appropriate in the hothouse passion of the dance. The man in the green sash returns to dance a brief duet with the woman who agitated the fish scales.

Four supporting couples enter as golden curved shapes are lowered into view. These are like protoalphabet characters. The lead men watch from their respective perches and then all join in a sensuous quartet. The woman who left the robe returns in a voluminous dress which the two men entwine around themselves and her. They are joined by the first woman, who also links herself to the long skirt, and they all look upward as the golden squiggles are replaced mysteriously by streamers of white bubbles. The other men return the fountain of beads and wire to the disc.

The supporting women bring out rich, glittering robes for the principals. After a brief restrained dance the men return to their places at the beginning of the dance and one girl to the disc at the rear. After a moment the first woman enters, again in silence, accompanied only by the gentle clatter of the fish-scale wind chimes, and crosses the stage diagonally as she did to open the dance.

The dance occupies no definable country, although it suggests a Middle Eastern dream of heavenly sensual opulence. The partners pass easily from one to another, and there is a luscious sumptuousness to their costuming and dancing that lifts the work to an appealing level. There is no telling what are the ties that bind the protagonists to one another, but they follow rules that guide them to satisfaction and pleasure.

CHOREOCHRONICLE
OF MARTHA GRAHAM

1925

Pompeiian Afternoon (with
    Esther Gustafson)
A Serenade in Porcelain (with
    Esther Gustafson)
Spanish Dance (adaptation of
    Ted Shawn's *Serenata morisca*)

1926

Chorale
Novelette
Tänze
Intermezzo
Maid with the Flaxen Hair
Arabesque No. 1
Clair de lune
Danse languide
Désir
Deux valses sentimentales
Masques
Trois gnossiennes
From a XII-Century Tapestry
A Study in Lacquer
The Three Gopi Maidens
Danse rococo
The Marionette Show
Portrait—After Beltram—Masses
Suite from "Alceste"
Scène javanaise
Danse degli angeli
Bas Relief
Ribands
Scherzo
Baal Shem
La Soirée dans Grenade

Alt-Wien
Three Poems of the East
Arabesque
Pictures in Melody
May Time in Kew (*Valtse*)
Flute of Krishna
Then and Now (*Gavotte*)
A Corner in Spain
A Dream in a Wax Museum
    (*Dance of French Dolls*)
A Forest Episode

1927

Peasant Sketches
Tunisia: Sunlight in a Courtyard
Lucrezia
La Canción
Arabesque No. 1 (revised)
Valse caprice
Spires
Adagio
Fragilité
Lugubre
Poème ailé
Tanzstück
Revolt (originally *Danse*)
Esquisse antique
Ronde
Scherza

1928

Chinese Poem
Trouvères
Immigrant
Poems of 1917

Fragments
Resonances

1929

Dance ("Strong Free Joyous
    Action": Nietzsche)
Three Florentine Vases
Four Insincerities
Cants mágics
Two Variations: Country Lane,
    City Street
Figure of a Saint
Resurrection
Adolescence
Danza
Vision of the Apocalypse
Moment Rustica
Sketches from the People
*Heretic

1930

Prelude to a Dance
Two Chants
Lamentation
Project in Movement for a Divine
    Comedy
Harlequinade

1931

Two Primitive Canticles
*Primitive Mysteries
Rhapsodics
Bacchanale
Dolorosa
Dithyrambic
Serenade
Incantation
Electra (p)

1932

Ceremonials
Offering
Ecstatic Dance

Bacchanale (No. 2)
Prelude
Dance Songs
Chorus of Youth—Companions

1933

Tragic Patterns
Elegiac
Ekstasis
Dance Prelude
Frenetic Rhythms
Lucrece (p)
Six Miracle Plays (p)
Romeo and Juliet (p)

1934

Transitions
Phantasy
Celebration
Four Casual Movements
Intégrales
Dance in Four Parts
American Provincials
Valley Forge (p—minuet)

1935

Praeludium (No. 1)
Course
*Frontier (Perspective No. 1)
Marching Song (Perspective No.
    2)
Panorama
Formal Dance
Imperial Gesture
Panic (Choral Movement)

1936

Horizons
Salutation
Chronicle

1937

Opening Dance
Immediate Tragedy
Deep Song
American Lyric
A Doll's House (p—tarantella)

1938

American Document
Preview Pageant, New York
    World's Fair

1939

Columbiad
Every Soul Is a Circus

1940

El Penitente
*Letter to the World

1941

Punch and the Judy

1942

Land Be Bright

1943

Salem Shore
*Deaths and Entrances

1944

Imagined Wing
Hérodiade
*Appalachian Spring

1946

*Dark Meadow
Cave of the Heart

1947

*Errand into the Maze
Night Journey

1948

*Diversion of Angels

1950

Judith
Eye of Anguish
Gospel of Eve

1951

The Triumph of St. Joan

1952

Canticle for Innocent Comedians

1953

Voyage

1954

Ardent Song

1955

*Seraphic Dialogue

1958

*Clytemnestra
Embattled Garden
A Guide to the Life Expectancy
    of a Rose (Dance Movement)

1959

Episodes: Part 1

1960

Acrobats of God
Alcestis

1961

Visionary Recital
One More Gaudy Night

1962

Phaedra
A Look at Lightning
Secular Games
Legend of Judith

1963

Circe

1965

The Witch of Endor
*Part Real – Part Dream

1967

Cortege of Eagles
Dancing-Ground

1968

A Time of Snow
The Plain of Prayer
The Lady of the House of Sleep

1969

The Archaic Hours

1973

Mendicants of Evening
Myth of a Voyage

1974

Chronique
Holy Jungle
The Dream

1975

Lucifer
Adorations
Point of Crossing
Scarlet Letter

HANYA HOLM

Widely respected as a teacher, Hanya Holm has also made her impact upon concert dance, theater, film, and television as a choreographer. She was born in Germany and studied in Dalcroze schools in Frankfurt and Hellerau and also at the Mary Wigman school in Dresden. Wigman made the most lasting impact upon her, and she joined the Wigman company in 1919 and toured with it for a dozen years. During this time she also appeared in one of the early productions of Max Reinhardt's theatrical spectacle *The Miracle,* which had an international success.

When the Wigman company toured the United States under the sponsorship of Sol Hurok, he encouraged Miss Wigman to found a school in the country. She asked Holm to head the staff, and the Wigman School opened in New York in 1931. For the next five years Holm devoted most of her energy to teaching and explaining the Wigman method to students and audiences. By 1936 she decided to form her own concert dance company and changed the name of the school to the Hanya Holm Studio.

During the summer of 1937 she was in charge of the workshop group at the Bennington College Summer School of the Dance and created her most famous work, *Trend,* with which she introduced her company to New York in the fall. She continued to create dances for her company and in 1941 established a summer dance program at Colorado College in Colorado Springs which continues to attract students.

Her interest in various forms of theatrical dance for other media resulted in an early (1939) television broadcast *Tragic Exodus.* She also wrote an instructional article for dance teachers, "Dance, a Basic Educational Technique," included in the World Book Encyclopedia. Following her early interest in the theater she created the dances for many musicals starting in the late 1940s. Among her outstanding productions have been *Kiss Me, Kate, Out of This World,* and *My Fair Lady.* She has also worked on operas and film.

The special quality of her teaching has been its success in creatively stimulating her students. Holm has eschewed doctrinaire formulas in favor of a creative approach stressing principles and not particulars of style. Among her better known students have been Alwin Nikolais and Valerie Bettis, both of whom have evolved individual styles of movement.

TREND

Choreography by Hanya Holm. Music by Wallingford Riegger and Edgard Varèse (Ionization and Octandre). Costumes by Betty Joiner. Lighting by Gerard Gentire. First performed at the Bennington Festival, Bennington, Vt., August 13, 1937, by Hanya Holm with Louise Kloepper, Lucretia Wilson, Carolyn Durand, Elizabeth Waters, Bernice Van Gelder, Henrietta Greenhood, Keith Coppage, Marva Jaffay, Miriam Kagan, Ruth Ledoux, Lydia Tarnower (members of the Concert Group), and Mary Standring Adair, Helen Alkire, Mary Alice Andrews, Carol Beals, Caryl Cuddeback, Elizabeth Ann Davis, Hermine Dudley, Helen Ellis, Marianne Elser, Mary Gillette, Margaret Jewell, Helen Knight, Hildegarde Lewis, Caroline Locke, Victoria Payne, Josephine Reddin, Harriet Roeder, Jeanette Saurborn, Dorothy Smith, Edith Vail, Florence Warwick, and Martha Wilcox (members of the Workshop Group). First performed in New York City (with scenery and lighting by Arch Lauterer) at the Mecca Auditorium, December 28, 1937.

Holm first presented the dance at the Bennington College Summer School of the Dance as part of the workshop program in 1937. It incorporated students for the summer as well as members of her own company. In the winter, when the piece was first shown in New York, Holm increased the scope of her own solo in the "he, the Great" section and added the final portion, "Assurance." However, even in its incomplete state at Bennington, it was recognized as a great dance. For its realization Holm had created a set roughly U-shaped with the mouth of the letter toward the audience. A ramp on either of the legs of the letter led up to an elevated platform, as did a flight of stairs in the center. Free-standing square columns stood at either end of the elevated platform. The dresses of the cast extended soberly to the floor. Holm had the orchestra blocked off for seating and required that viewers watch from the balcony so as to see the pattern of the work.

The group tramps heavily and sharply delineating the dehumanized and severely regimented working conditions of the industrial laborer to open "Our Daily Bread," the first of the dances criticizing society. It stresses the mass and has a strongly architectural look, as do the other group dances, in which angular repetitive machine movements characterize the regimented working classes. Contrasting to the workers are the world-weary and bored idlers who lounge about in "Satiety."

A series of individual solos skewer other social injustices as in "The Effete," where the soloist moves before a surfeited group that is incapable of sustained movement but sways and stirs fitfully. The pursuit of money is caricatured in "lucre lunacy" and salesmanship religion in "From Heaven Ltd.," where the group joins in a mass revival meeting as it is being exhorted to pursue higher values. The war maimed are recalled in "Lest We Remember" as the dancer tries varieties of ways to suppress the memory of the injured, dashing from one narcotic escape to another. Dictatorship is shown to be empty hero worship in "he, the Great" as a soloist interacts with the group.

In "Cataclysm" all of the elements of the first half of the dance are brought together in a struggling, seething collection of bodies moving in groups across the stage up and down the ramps with a solo figure enduring and then beginning a new mood in "The Gates Are Empty." The whole of the first section has been a detailing of the woes of the society and now begins a slow but optimistic rebuilding. In "Resurgence" there is a quiet certitude and confidence as the group leans and stretches its arms hopefully overhead, and the mood is continued through the final movement, "Assurance."

Holm created a panorama of solo and group dances that showed a society being destroyed by its own false values which could only be reborn when these were banished in a cataclysm of some sort, reflecting the inner conflicts and divisions of the society. The trajectory of the dance was thus plotted as a long descent, then a brief transition and slightly longer reaffirmation. Among the interesting elements associated with the work was the sustained use of recorded music, at a time when this was very unusual for modern dance, and the inclusion of two uncompromisingly advanced selections by Edgard Varèse in the final two sections, "Ionization" and "Octandre."

METROPOLITAN DAILY

Choreography by Hanya Holm. Music by Gregory Tucker. First performed at the Bennington Festival, Bennington, Vt., August 1938, by Elizabeth Waters, Henrietta Greenhood, Louise Kloepper, Valerie Bettis, Caroline Locke, Miriam Kagan, Barbara Hatch, Harriet Roeder, Hanya Holm, Marva Spelman, and Charlotte Sturges.

The plainly humorous rather than satiric side of Holm was shown in this dance, which depicted projected scenes from various departments of a daily newspaper.

Fashionably tailored costumes in stark black and white dress the women who dance the financial pages as they depict highs and lows on the stock charts. Two women in plaid gossip earnestly in the center of the stage, and two others stretch their heads eagerly to pick up a scrap of information or misinformation from the sides of the stage in the scandal column. The haughty and slightly burlesqued airs of the women in the society section do not prevent them from posturing to catch the attention of the daily press.

Two women in shawls soberly portray the feelings of those scanning the want ads while bright color and exaggerated dynamics identify the characters of the comic pages. The women of the sports section proudly walk on with identifying numbers to mime the actions of a variety of sports contests such as bowling, archery, fencing, football, golf, tennis, and the like before forming a pyramid at the center to conclude their display.

Holm drew on her experience of cafe comedy in the European tradition to create the dance and allowed her humor full sway. The piece was very popular when first presented and Holm kept it in her repertory for many years, though making small adjustments to it. When it was first presented, the work only had women portraying its parts, but later Holm added men for balance.

CHOREOCHRONICLE
OF HANYA HOLM

1928

Euripides' Bacchae
Dramatization of Plato's Farewell
  to His Friends

1929

L'Histoire du soldat

1930

Das Totenmal (with Mary
  Wigman)

1936

Salutation
Drive
Dance in Two Parts
Sarabande
In Quiet Space
City Nocturne
Four Chromatic Eccentricities
Primitive Rhythm
Festive Rhythm

1937

*Trend

1938

Études
Dance of Introduction
Dance Sonata
Dance of Work and Play
*Metropolitan Daily

1939

Tragic Exodus
These Two Are Exiles

1941

The Golden Fleece
From This Earth

1942

What So Proudly We Hail
Namesake

1943

Parable
Suite of Four Dances
Orestes and the Furies

1944

What Dreams May Come

1945

Walt Whitman Suite
The Gardens of Eden

1946

Dance for Four
Windows

1947

And So Ad Infinitum (The
  Insect Comedy)

1948

Xochipili
The Eccentricities of Davey Crockett
The Insect Comedy (p)
$E=MC^2$ (p)
Kiss Me, Kate (mc)

1949

History of a Soldier
Ionization
Blood Wedding (p)

1950

Five Old French Dances
The Liar (mc)
Out of This World (mc)

1951

Prelude
Quiet City

1952

Kindertotenlieder
Concertino da camera
My Darlin' Aida (mc)

1953

Ritual
Temperament and Behavior

1954

Preludes I and II
Presages
L'Histoire du soldat
The Golden Apple (mc)

1955

Desert Drone
Pavane (from Gian Carlo Menotti's *Sebastian*)

Sousa March
Reuben, Reuben (mc)

1956

Preludio and Loure (Bach's Partita No. 3)
My Fair Lady (mc)
The Vagabond King (mp)
The Ballad of Baby Doe (opera)

1957

Ozark Suite
Chanson triste
You Can't Go Home Again
Where's Charley? (mc)
The Dance and Drama (tv)
Pinocchio (tv)

1959

Orpheus and Euridice (opera)

1960

Christine (mc)
Camelot (mc)

1961

Music for an Imaginary Ballet

1963

Figure of Predestination
Toward the Unknown Region
Dinner with the President (tv)

1964

Theatrics

1965

Anya (mc)

1967

Spooks

LESTER HORTON

The intense but sometimes indiscriminate zest for dance expression drove Horton to create works that ranged from the slimmest revue sketches to powerfully moving concert pieces. He designed outdoor pageants, choreographed night-club acts, worked on movie musicals, and shaped searing domestic drama like *The Beloved*. Horton was born in Indiana and developed a passion for American Indian culture and artifacts. While in Chicago he was engaged by the producer of the pageant *The Song of Hiawatha* and he traveled to California, where he supervised its presentation.

The move to California became permanent. After a few years wandering through the state collecting Indian artifacts and giving occasional solo performances of his dances he settled in Los Angeles. In 1932 he formed his own company and continued to present pageants based on Indian lore and ritual. These were greeted with some enthusiasm for their occasionally brilliant touches of dance, but more often for their décor and costuming.

Two years later he presented his first dance based on the story of Salome, which was unquestionably a success. His own physical skills as a dancer were limited, and his best roles were solidly based on character portrayal rather than on sustained lyric dancing. The technique which emerged from the performing and teaching of his group tended to feature a solid "composed" torso and asymmetrical arrangements of the arms and legs springing from this secure center.

In 1944 he suffered a severe neck injury which dictated his retirement from the stage as a performer, but he continued his work as a choreographer for the rest of his career. His school was staffed by himself and members of his company, who were drawn primarily from the Los Angeles area. His enthusiasm for the school and new productions saw him offering large numbers of scholarships, keeping the school on the edge of insolvency and continually in debt while paying for the staging of new works. His somewhat helter-skelter collecting eventually produced one of the finest collections of percussion instruments in the country, and his interests in design led him to dress and set most of his works in addition to creating the dances for them.

He continued to rework some of his dances right up until his death in 1953, as shown by his *Salome,* which was presented in that year in its fifth revision and retitled *The Face of Violence.* He pursued an individual course, scarcely bothering with the rest of the dance world outside of California, and his company ventured to dance centers in the East only twice. He established in Los Angeles the first theater in the United States devoted entirely to dance and called it Dance Theater. His company performed there for three to nine months out of every year on the weekends.

His company was also the first racially integrated company in the country, including black, Mexican-American, Japanese, and white dancers before any other company had so open a policy. His influence has been exercised mainly through his talented company members and pupils, among whom are Alvin Ailey, Janet Collins, Carmen de Lavallade, Bella Lewitzky, Joyce Trisler, and James Truitte.

SALOME (THE FACE OF VIOLENCE)

Choreography by Lester Horton. Music by Lester Horton. Costumes by William Bowne. First performed at the Dance Theater, Los Angeles, Calif., April 11, 1950, by Carmen de Lavallade, Luisa Kreck, Sondra Orans, George Allen, Kenneth Bartmess, and Jack Dobbs.

Salome was a character who fascinated Horton, so much so that he made six separate versions of his dance about her. The last and presumably his final word on the subject was created around the extraordinarily talented and beautiful dancer Carmen de Lavallade. Horton renamed the piece *The Face of Violence* when it was presented in 1950, and for this version reintroduced the character of the Eunuch, who functioned as a commentator as well as a participant in the action.

The multilevel stage has ramps, platforms of various elevations, and a well representing the cell of John the Baptist (Jokanaan). The face of Salome is seen first and then her whole body as the spotlight's circle widens, and she parts a curtain and advances down a ramp. She carries a fan which she flutters coquettishly as she descends. She is spoiled, willful, and petulant. Her eyes turn to a guard watching over the cell of John and she seductively crawls across the set toward him. The guard averts his gaze and she plays her fan up and down the length of his back but fails to arouse his interest. Standing with knees apart and bent, she begins a sensual undulation that attracts him to dance with her. They stay close to the cell as he lifts her repeatedly and her swaying, loosened hair signals the abandonment of her nature. She demands to see John.

The prophet emerges with his long cloak hanging in folds from his arm. It carries the early Christian symbol of the fish. Salome watches him intently and stalks around the throne, where he is standing. She embraces his feet then throws herself at him. He moves away from her and she pounces on the throne he has vacated to bend backward suggestively, each time coming closer to the ground. The prophet returns to his cell, rejecting her, and she in her fury rejects the guard, who kills himself. Salome's pelvis churns in frustration as she straddles the cell.

Herod, Herodias, and the Eunuch enter. Herodias is angry and Herod tipsily frolics with the Eunuch. Salome turns her back on them, but the Eunuch touches her and she goes to sit on the throne, glancing angrily at them, as they continue their decadent play. Suddenly she rises to commence her seduction of Herod. As the turning, twisting dance proceeds, the drunken Herod becomes more and more entranced with her sinuous body. After she slips out of her long veil and slides to the floor Herod draws her up to his throne.

Then the successful Salome demands her reward by extending her arm slowly and chillingly toward the cell of the imprisoned prophet. Herod is appalled, but the evil imprecations of Herodias and the Eunuch prevail and Herod, with face painfully and shamefully bent away, extends his commanding arm behind him toward the cell. The lights are darkened and a red glow appears from the cell. Salome crawls to it. The cloak of the prophet is thrust upward, soiled with bloody hand prints.

She grasps the garment in her teeth like an animal that has taken its prey, and then begins an orgiastic dance with it. She draws it across her body again and again as the others watch in fascinated disbelief. Finally Herod can no longer endure the flaunting of his crime and strangles Salome, whose hands flutter weakly as life leaves her body. Her head hangs back limply and the Eunuch walks away, his face drained of expression.

The work was one of the most successful that Horton ever created. It was a work that was totally his in concept, staging, costuming, and even the score, which he composed using percussion and human voice with some wind instruments. It delineates the willfulness of an evil, inbred court in which whim can destroy human life and only pleasure is the governing principle, though even here there are some excesses which cannot be tolerated.

THE BELOVED

Choreography by Lester Horton. Music by Judith Hamilton. First performed at the Dance Theater, Los Angeles, Calif., May 22, 1948, by Bella Lewitzky and Herman Boden.

In a program note to the dance, Horton wrote that it "attempts to state in pure dance terms the bigotry and sexual chauvinism that held women subservient in fin-de-siecle New England, a kinetic projection of the social savagery of the double standard."

The "savagery" imbues every moment of the dance, from its repressed opening to its brutal ending. A tapestry hangs behind a table that has a cloth that reaches to the floor. On either side is placed a high ladder-back chair, suggesting probity of the most unyielding sort. The woman wears a dress with a high-necked collar and a skirt that extends primly to the tops of her feet. The man wears a red house jacket buttoned carefully and his trousers tailored impeccably.

As she stands near the audience with her hand clasped to one cheek in burning shame and the other curled over the front of her thigh, he sits with one forearm resting sternly on the table and the other hand cupped on his knee. He is the picture of rectitude, sternly listening from his ramrod posture.

He stands and stomps toward her, his anger barely repressed. She has transgressed and must be punished. In a brutal, systematic way he sends her reeling again and again, and his own rage seems to grow as the social barriers recede. He maintains his stiff posture as she bends under his fury but finally in a fit of uncontrollable rage he bends over her, but not in compassion. He strangles her.

The double standard of sexual conduct, allowing men freedom not accorded to women, was not a product of the Victorian age alone, but did receive a considerable boost in that moralistic time. For all its righteousness the age concealed a brutality and harshness that were lurking in the best drawing rooms though not expressed overtly. Horton created one of his most moving and physically violent pieces to expose what he considered its hypocrisy.

CHOREOCHRONICLE
OF LESTER HORTON

1928

The Song of Hiawatha

1929

Siva-Siva

1931

Kootenai War Dance

1932

Voodoo Ceremonial
Takwish the Star Maker

1933

Oriental Motifs

1934

Allegro Barbaro
May Night
Hand Dance
Lament
Salome
Incantation from Aboriginal
    Suite
Dances of the Night
Two Arabesques
Danse Congo
Salome (revision)
Aztec Ballet
Second Gnossienne
Concerto Grosso, Second
    Movement
Painted Desert Ballet

Chinese Fantasy
Bolero
Ave
Maidens
Salutation
Gnossienne No. 3
Vale

1935

Mound Builders
Passacaglia
Pentecost
Dictator
Rain Quest
Conflict
Ritual at Midnight
Tendresse
Sun Ritual
Rhythmic Dance
Salutation to the Depths
The Mine
The Art Patrons

1936

Growth of Action
Two Dances for a Leader
Flight from Reality
Lysistrata
Ceremony

1937

Prelude to Militancy
Chronicle
Salome (revision)
Prologue to an Earth Celebration
Exhibition Dance No. I
Le Sacre du printemps
Salome (revision)

1938

Pasaremos
Haven
Conquest

1939

Departure from the Land
Five Women
Something to Please Everybody
Tierra y Libertad!

1940

Sixteen to Twenty-four
A Noble Comedy

1941

Pavanne

1942

Moonlight in Havana (mp)

1943

Rhythm of the Islands (mp)
White Savage (mp)
Phantom of the Opera (mp)

1944

Climax (mp)

1945

Salome Where She Danced (mp)
That Night with You (mp)
Frisco Sal (mp)
Shady Lady (mp)

1946

Tangier (mp)

1947

Barrel House

1948

Totem Incantation
*The Beloved
Salome (revision)
Siren of Atlantis (mp)

1949

Warsaw Ghetto
The Park
The Bench of the Lamb
*A Touch of Klee and Delightful
    Two*
Tongue in Cheek (mc)
Bagdad (mp)

1950

Estilo de Tú
Bouquet for Molly
El Rebozo
*Salome (The Face of Violence)
    (revision)
Brown County, Indiana
Rhythm Section

1951

Tropic Trio
On the Upbeat
Another Touch of Klee
Medea
Girl Gershwin (mc)
Annie Get Your Gun (mc)

1952

Seven Scenes with Ballabilli
Liberian Suite
Prado de Pena

1953

Dedications in Our Time
South Sea Woman (mp)
3-D Follies (mp)

DORIS HUMPHREY

Combining an intellectual sense of craft with an emotional commitment to humane values made Humphrey design dances that were heroic in the best sense. At times her interest in the sheer mechanics of making a dance consumed her attention, but the works of her mature genius show a sympathy for human suffering or sacrifice and an artistic attempt at consolation and betterment of that condition.

She began dancing in childhood and early displayed a talent for it. She was encouraged to continue by several teachers and benefited from instruction in a variety of styles including ballet. Almost alone among the founding generation of modern dancers, she received a good foundation in ballet technique. She opened her own school in Oak Park, Illinois, but left it to study at the Denishawn school in Los Angeles since she desired to have a performing career.

Ruth St. Denis was attracted to her and later when St. Denis took her own company on tour included Humphrey in it. At this time Humphrey was very much under St. Denis's influence and co-choreographed several dances with her, which were presented by the St. Denis company. She toured with St. Denis and Shawn in the Denishawn company until the late 1920s, when she and Charles Weidman left to form their own company and found a school.

The first years of her independent career were spent forming her distinctive approach to dance movement, based on the fall from and recovery of balance. During this time she created simple but intensely intelligent pieces such as *Water Study,* and *Life of the Bee.* Later as she developed her vocabulary of movement, the works of her maturity began to emerge, such as *New Dance* and *Passacaglia and Fugue in C Minor.* With Weidman she gave regular concerts in their New York studio and taught each summer at the Bennington College Summer School of the Dance until it was dissolved in 1942.

She was forced to withdraw from the stage as a performer in 1945 because of an arthritic hip, and arthritic seizures plagued her till her death. Deprived of an outlet as a performer, Humphrey continued to choreograph and teach and became the artistic director of the José Limón company, which was the direct successor to hers and Weidman's old company. As a dedicated teacher of creative composition courses, she eventually codified her technique in her book *The Art of Making Dances.* It is marked by practical good sense and a reliance on the imaginative exercise of the intellect.

She was instrumental in establishing a dance department at the Juilliard School and regularly taught there. At the time of her death she left her autobiography in uncompleted manuscript. Her name is most frequently linked with that of Martha Graham as being one of the two main influences in modern dance development. Graduates of the Humphrey-Weidman and José Limón companies include Sybil Shearer, Eleanor King, Katherine Litz, William Bales, Ruth Currier, Louis Falco, and Jennifer Muller, all of whom have gone on to found their own companies, using the Humphrey-Weidman technique in their own individual ways.

SOARING

Choreography by Doris Humphrey with Ruth St. Denis. Music by Robert Schumann (Fantasiestücke, Op. 12, "Aufschwung"). First performed at the Spreckels Theatre, San Diego, Calif., September 20, 1920, by Doris Humphrey with Dorothea Bowen, Ruth Austin, and Katherine Laidlaw (Ruth St. Denis Concert Dancers).

As the dance begins four women hold down the corners of a large scarf beneath which another woman is lying. The four suddenly hoist the corners and the scarf balloons into a vault over the head of the fifth dancer, who performs a series of little skipping steps. The scarf is curved over in front of her like a wave and is then gathered up by two of the dancers, who hold it like a low wall, and three leap in front of it. The scarf is curled over them, and the original woman returns to the center, where the scarf is once again arched over her head. When it is placed down, she delicately steps on it while drawing one corner up over her head to touch it down at its diagonally opposite corner, and then she opens it up to its full size again. All stand for a moment and then exit with the scarf in tow.

This work, like another dance, called *Scarf Dance,* uses a large amount of material but unlike the way that Loie Fuller of a previous generation used it. In Fuller's case she concealed the person inside the cloth property, while Humphrey used the material as a way of showing the dancing body and not hiding it. Again these early works showed the influence of Denishawn styling in their romanticism but also indicated a changing emphasis. In revivals the work clearly shows its historical era but significantly also holds up as a dance creation and not just as a period piece.

HOOP DANCE
(SCHERZO WALTZ)

Choreography by Doris Humphrey. Music by Ilgenfritz. First performed at the Academy of Music, Newburgh, N.Y., October 6, 1924, by Doris Humphrey.

As its title indicates, *Hoop Dance* was designed to use a large hoop as the protagonist in this solo that Humphrey designed for herself. At the beginning she rolls the large hoop out and steps inside it to balance on one leg with the other flexed to the side while holding onto the upper part of the hoop in a pose that is reminiscent of the Hindu god Shiva. She pushes the hoop away from her and runs to catch it, bowing her head inside its circumference. The movements are playful and she rocks it from one side to another before lifting it aloft so that her arms arc around it and its bottom edge curves across her chest. The mood of the dance suggests a hymn to happiness, and at one point Humphrey lays the loop flat and does a small variation within its circle that reminds one of a woodland nymph. Picking it up again, she spiritedly pushes it away and catches it several times and concludes with the opening pose of the dance.

When she created this dance it was at the beginning of her career, and Humphrey had not yet created the distinct style of movement that is to be observed today in her mature pieces. It was frankly influenced by the lyrical style of Denishawn but shows an intelligent use of the dance conventions of the time with an indication of her individuality.

WATER STUDY

Choreography by Doris Humphrey. In silence, originally with gong accompaniment. Costumes by Pauline Lawrence. First performed at the Civic Repertory Theatre, New York, N.Y., October 28, 1928, by Georgia Graham, Virginia Landreth, Celia Rauch, Gertrude Shurr, Dorothy Lathrop, Sylvia Manning, Jean Nathan, Cleo Atheneos, Evelyn Fields, Jane Sherman, Rose Yasgour, Justine Douglas, Margaret Gardner, Eleanor King, and Katherine Manning.

The dance is designed for fifteen women crouched onstage, heads facing to the left. They are arranged in two intersecting zigzag lines and begin the slow movement of arching their backs, beginning with the women on the right traveling across to those on the left. The first time the movement is a small swell and the second time a surge. The third time a more vigorous rise is combined with a twist of the torso, which all of the group does except for the leading two, who prostrate themselves forward. It is like the sight of a wave hitting a beach and then subsiding as the women on the left arch hands over heads while straightening up to show the curl of the wave.

In the second portion of the dance the group divides and faces across the width of the stage. Individuals rush out to a collision in the center space, where they jump upward and then lie on their sides. After these spurting jumps caused by the collisions the group collects to bend forward and lean back. The group rushes to the left, and those in front roll over as those in the back kneel and arch hands, and again the group divides. Those left stand in a row and in a rapid sequence each jumps in the air and then holds a single pose so that when the movement is over the first girl is standing, the second leaning, the third on one knee, the fourth leaning toward the floor, and the fifth crumpled on the floor at the end of a small cascade.

The other group turns, bends knees, and tucks elbows in toward the waist and then extends arms until all join in and everyone is swaying. All drop to one knee to re-create the opening formation and then start the small wave motion. Each slides forward on one knee and lies prone until all have completed the final ripple.

The dance is a delightful re-creation of the movement of water to be observed both at the seaside and at a stream and now is accompanied only by the breathing of the dancers (though in the first performance they were cued by taps on a gong). What sets it off from other evocations of nature, such as the flame and moth studies of Loie Fuller, is that the whole dance is carried through movement exclusively without the assistance of any stage properties or special costuming.

THE SHAKERS
(DANCE OF THE CHOSEN)

Choreography by Doris Humphrey. Traditional music. Costumes by Pauline Lawrence. First performed at Hunter College, New York, N.Y., November 12, 1930. First professional performance at the Craig Theatre, New York, N.Y., February 1, 1931, by Doris Humphrey, Sylvia Manning, Evelyn Fields, Rose Yasgour, Cleo Atheneos, Ruth Allred, Celia Rauch, Dorothy Lathrop, Katherine Manning, Rose Crystol, Eleanor King, Ada Korvin, Letitia Ide, Ernestine Henoch, Virginia Landreth, Helen Strumlauf, Charles Lasky, José Limón, and Charles Weidman.

A curious offshoot of the Quakers, the Shakers lived communal lives of prayerful simplicity and chastity. Because marriage was forbidden by the tenets of the faith, the Shakers diminished in numbers and found it difficult to recruit new members to their sect. Only a few believers still exist at this time and are of an advanced age. They dressed soberly and danced out the fervor of their prayer meetings in mass formations. The first performance had many more women than men, but the description is of a contemporary, more sexually balanced production.

A half-dozen men and like number of women kneel with hands clasped and fingers interlaced, facing a woman who sits on a simple bench toward the rear of the stage. The groups are separate and do not cross a line that parts them. The four men on the side rock back on their heels and the four women facing them do the same. The two men and two women with their backs to the audience sway from side to side. The pace accelerates, men jump up to throw hands high, and women do likewise, conveying the feeling of intensely felt emotion bursting forth. But yet each group keeps to its respective isolated side.

There is a sense of frustrated sexual passion about the vigor with which they express religious emotion. The groups file around to face one another at the center, and the solitary woman strides between the two columns, at which they form into two large wheeling "X's," the spokes of which mesh but do not touch. This dissolves into group jogging which is repetitive and insistent as the two formations move to and away from the center division.

The female leader mounts the bench and claps for order and all sink to their knees. She exhorts them and jumps down to bounce up and down. All follow her lead and the pace increases. She turns in the center but stops suddenly to thrust her arms heavenward, at which they sink to their knees and clasp hands reverently.

The dance was modeled on illustrations depicting the Shaker ceremonial and captures its special feeling astutely. The society was dominated by women, and its hypnotic jogging transported the believer into a passionate affirmation of religious fervor, all of which Humphrey captured in this brief dance. Like *Water Study,* it was included as part of a musical, *Americana,* which Humphrey did in 1932. At two points in the dance Humphrey included brief spoken recitations, which represented her first attempts at combining motion and words meaningfully. Subsequently she would use words to a much greater extent.

NEW DANCE

Choreography by Doris Humphrey with Charles Weidman. Music by Wallingford Riegger. Costumes by Pauline Lawrence. First performed in a six-part version at Bennington College, Bennington, Vt., August 3, 1935. First performed in a seven-part version at the Guild Theatre, New York, N.Y., October 27, 1935, by Doris Humphrey, Charles Weidman, Beatrice Seckler, Sybil Shearer, Katherine Litz, Edith Orcutt, George Bockman, Katherine Manning, Ada Korvin, Joan Levy, Miriam Kradovsky, William Matons, Kenneth Bostock, Morris Bakst, Noel Charise, Jerry Davidson, Maurice Gilbert, Lee Sherman, Harris Poble, William Bales, and Ezra Friedman.

Oddly enough this part of the trilogy was completed before *Theatre Piece,* which should logically precede it. In the latter Humphrey unmasked those underlying drives of competitive acquisitiveness which were distorting the society, and in *New Dance* she gave her idea of what life should be like. In her program note she states that it "represents the growth of the individual in relation to his fellows in an ideal state."

A couple stands in the center, behind them at the right are four women and on the right two other women. The couple breaks into movement: she carves great arcs in the air, and he darts and lunges. The women behind raise their arms above their heads in salutation. The couple circles, touches palms, and the man exits. In the "First Theme" she raises her arms while balancing on one leg, bending the other slightly behind her. She kicks a little to the right and then the left, increasing in amplitude as she advances to the audience. The group is drawn into the leaping dance that she has begun and forms a circle around her. She repeats her opening dance this time more rapidly, and pairs of women do a short variation on it and all go off.

In the "Second Theme" two seated women extend one leg upward and stretch back, to be followed by the others. All seated again, they sway softly and stand to turn and cluster together. Turning halfway to the right and then to the left, they traverse the stage, accelerating to full turns before going off.

The four men who dance the "Third Theme" stand at the four corners of the stage. They dash diagonally at each other in pairs, leaping as they meet in the center and continuing on to the opposite corner. After several crossings one pair meets at center, bracing palms against the other's. The second pair also does the same, and one of the men backs off as the other chases. Three surround the fourth, who waves his arm in comradely fashion and invites them all to join him in a series of attitudes and turns. They continue with vigorous strides and balances, turning toward the center several times as they walk off.

In the "Processional" the woman from the lead couple advances to the center and walks to a group of three women and a man who follow her, pausing to extend one foot slightly every few steps. At the opposite side of the stage the rest of the company joins and steps around the lead couple at the center, in a manner that suggests good breeding.

The "Celebration" finds all circling vigorously. They halt and form three groups facing the audience with the men in the center. Short "quotes" from all of the preceding sections are woven together, and the section concludes with the lead woman in the center, while all extend an arm toward her like spokes of a wheel.

After a short pause in which the curtain is lowered the "Variations and Conclusion" of the dance is given. This shorter portion of the dance draws upon a joyful mood of fulfillment and flows forward with a gracious and happy sweep that concludes with all of the dancers facing the audience turning to the right, reversing quickly, and turning to the left continuously as the curtain is lowered on a stage that seems the mass of energetic and harmonious citizens that Humphrey imagined in her "ideal state."

New Dance is both the name of the trilogy and one of its parts and has some of Humphrey's most joyful invention. There is a sunny quality to it which is in quite a distinct contrast to the two other sections of the over-all work. Together these pieces are a powerful expression of Humphrey's talent for developing arresting and fresh movement within her strong philosophical convictions. Charles Weidman was equally inspired in creating the "Prelude" and "Third Theme" at Humphrey's request.

THEATRE PIECE

Choreography by Doris Humphrey with Charles Weidman. Music by Wallingford Riegger. Costumes by Pauline Lawrence. First performed at the Guild Theatre, New York, N.Y., January 19, 1936, by Doris Humphrey, Charles Weidman, José Limón, Edith Orcutt, George Bockman, Katherine Manning, Katherine Litz, Letitia Ide, Ada Korvin, Beatrice Seckler, Joan Levy, Sybil Shearer, Miriam Kradovsky, Lily Verne, Louise Allen, Kenneth Bostock, William Bales, Joseph Belsky, and Jerry Davidson.

Humphrey's satiric intent begins with her title, which reduces the actions of the society described in the piece to the level of actors in a stage space. With only one notable exception, her own solo "Interlude," the work is a series of bitter vignettes portraying the often venal motivations of the society.

In the "Prologue" the roles are given to the dancers as they would be to actors on stage preparing for a play, roles reflecting business, sports, and male-female relations. "Behind Walls" begins the nightmarish competition of the business world. Startling dislocations occur. Through a gap in the long wooden platforms two pairs of legs are seen walking back and forth while a single head moves along with them. Suddenly the head (belonging to a dancer concealed in the horizontal box above the opening) takes off in the opposite direction. The action of money changing and all of the other activity are controlled by a dominant figure who directs it as would a dictator. Only one girl rebels against this demon-driven system and remains dancing in opposition to it. The women exit from their offices and stores donning (in mime) hats and continue their predatory searching, "In the Open." The pursuit now is not money and power but a man. When one is seen they preen and contend among themselves for his attention.

The woman who has set herself in opposition to the others now does a solo that breathes quietude and everything that is remote from the destructive contentiousness that preceded it. It is, however, only a brief interlude in the satiric drive of the dance, which moves ahead to expose the false basis of much of contemporary society.

Immediately after, the desire to gain prominence in sports is detailed, "In the Stadium," where team sport such as football is shown to have the same motivating influence as the individual game of golf. The crowd cheers on the football hero to ever-greater exertions and is a most amusing section in the dance.

The crowd once again is courted, "In the Theatre," where actors vie with one another for the attention of the onlookers, who are easily distracted, and even the frantic actions of the performers do not hold their attention. Forced by the system to maintain their efforts, the performers hop up and down in pleasure at the least hint of applause, appearing like marionettes dancing on strings. "In the Race" brings the business world, personal relations, sports, performing together in a race which is the basic reality behind each of the separate façades. In the "Epilogue" the solo woman continues to move in counterpoint, posing her own deeply felt gestures against the facile motions of the large group. Her lyricism is a rebuke to their distorted energy, but she fails to change them, though she remains a rebuke to their lives.

The piece is logically seen with *New Dance,* in which the lyricism of the individual is transferred to the group. The theme of the individual and the place of the individual in society occupied Humphrey throughout her career, but the great trilogy of *New Dance* was her first definitive attempt to handle so large a theme. She was always interested in moral values, and the difficult transitional years of the 1930s were to spur her to eloquent statement on the difficulties of the just man in an unjust system. The witty and mostly pantomimic "In the Theatre" was created by Charles Weidman, who used the stock triangle situation, the chorus girl, and the silliness of the star system to good effect.

WITH MY RED FIRES

Choreography by Doris Humphrey. Music by Wallingford Riegger. Costumes by Pauline Lawrence. First performed at Bennington College, Bennington, Vt., August 13, 1936, by Charles Weidman as the Young Man, *Katherine Litz as the* Young Woman, *Doris Humphrey as the* Matriarch, *Lillian Burgess and Maxine Cushing as* Choric Figures, *with William Matons, William Bales, Ada Korvin, Beatrice Seckler, Joan Levy, Sybil Shearer, Edith Orcutt, Miriam Kradovsky, Lily Verne, Louise Allen, José Limón, Paul Leon, Philip Gordon, William Canton, and members of the Bennington Workshop Group.*

This was the last of the three dances which comprised the heroic trilogy *New Dance,* and it is a more personal piece than the other two. Like the others it was designed with a setting of long, low risers and columns from which the dancers would depart and to which they would return. The most striking costume was that of the Matriarch, which featured a skirt of enormous breadth that required great dexterity to manage. It was heroically effective in giving the character a larger-than-life-sized quality compared to that of the other dancers. Alone among her generation, Humphrey had an analytical intelligence regarding dance and wrote tellingly about the craft. Below is an extract from a letter written to her husband in the summer of 1936 describing *With My Red Fires.*

First a hymn to Aphrodite, or Priapus or Venus, anyway to the excitement, the greatness the rapture, the pain of frustration that is love. A voice will speak of that from a temple and the ever willing victims will respond with utterings, stabbings, listenings, impatience, fire in the blood. . . . Next the process will begin. Put the force to work, seek out the mate rush from one to the other, buffet the rest out of the way. Yes, there are two lovers at last, the end is all but achieved, the heat and thirst quenches. But what and who is that beckoning in the window? It's a woman, old, she's beckoning to the girl's lover, she's the mother, she says it's late and no time for young girls to be lugging around with unknown young men and goodness knows who he might be or what sort of a family he comes from. Come in this moment, your virtue's at stake, the world will say you're a bad girl. You won't? You will do as I say. Sew the seam, mop the floor, walk like me, talk like me, come away from the window. How can I mop the floor and sew the seam with my lover outside? I have danced in the Hymn to Priapus and I belong to my love. The old one is quiet now in the house; steal away through the window to the waiting lover. In the shadows find him, wrap him round. The old one has missed you, she's screaming now from the top of the house, the alarm is spreading, people are running, shouting, they're on the morbid scent, they gleam with virtuous hate. She's run off with a nobody? Which way? To the town? To the Inn? No, here by the wall. Tear them apart, the dirty things. What shall we do, old one, marry them with a gun and giggles or run them out? See that they're well battered, punish, pinch, tear, beat and I shall shut the door. So, let's take them over the rocks, up, down through the rocks, leave them at the Priapic stone. Moralists point the finger, sentimental ones weep over young love's impetuosity. Scandal mongers laugh.

As in the other parts of *New Dance,* Humphrey was concerned with the individual and his or her relationship to the surrounding society. In this case two younger members heeded an emotional call that made them disregard the wishes of the Matriarch. She wins a momentary vindication from the others, but one wonders, which will crumble first, society's strictures or love's urgings?

PASSACAGLIA AND FUGUE IN C MINOR

Choreography by Doris Humphrey. Music by Johann Sebastian Bach (arr. for piano by I. Philipp). Costumes by Pauline Lawrence. Scenery by Arch Lauterer. First performed at Bennington College, Bennington, Vt., August 5, 1938, by Doris Humphrey and Charles Weidman, with Billy Archibald, William Bales, Mirthe Bellanca, George Bockman, Harriette Anne Gray, Frances Kinsky, Katherine Litz, Katherine Manning, Edith Orcutt, Beatrice Seckler, Sybil Shearer, Lee Sherman (members of the Concert Group), and Barbara Page Beiswanger, Sara Jean Cosner, Gloria Garcia, Maria Maginnis, Ethel Mann, Claudia Moore, Pegge Oppenheimer, Ruth Parmet, Barbara Spaulding, Patricia Urner, and Mildred Zook (members of the Workshop Group).

A cluster of dancers is arranged at the center of the stage on a multilevel platform facing left. There are two lower platforms, one at either side of the central grouping. A woman from the right one rises and walks toward the audience and is joined by a second woman from the same side. They begin a stately procession before the others, taking a step and then extending one leg behind themselves and one arm in front. In this manner they complete a circuit in front of the other dancers, who now turn to face toward and slip out of their robes. The two women on the platform at the left stand and bow to the first two women, who return to their opposite platform, balancing off the larger group.

The dance now unfolds its fugue section with first one man stepping forward, breasting the air with his arms, followed by two other dancers and then four until the whole company has been set in motion. The man who started the company action is joined by one of the women who did a stately promenade initially, and they dance a duet as the group form an arc behind them. The man passes through them to mount the tiered platform while the woman remains in front, and they continue their duet at a distance, walking and extending their legs. When the group reascends the structure, the man and woman place themselves on opposite sides of the stage near the audience, to do a series of turns with one arm extended in the air and then retire, while three men do split leaps in the air and four women walk in straight lines to form a square.

The couple returns and the whole group stands clasping their hands in the air above their heads and swaying from side to side. All step forward and then turn to walk away from the audience and mount the platform again, where they lean to one side, presenting a profile view of themselves.

The dance continues as one girl rises, followed by a man, and then a second girl stretches her arm forward and leans back for support. The group kneels and rocks slowly. The first couple is joined by a second couple in a diagonal line before the group. The movement is stately in keeping with the character of the whole piece. The lead male does his variation, and more and more of the group are drawn into the dance. Four women stand at the corners of an imaginary square. Within its boundaries eight dancers move as a body to the left, and a three-dancer cluster moves to the right and then reverses the directions, and all lie on their sides as a trio steps among them. The lead male descends again from the platform to dance a variation, and all watch him from a seated position. He is then joined by his female partner. All drift back to the structure and whirl and then all stop dramatically. Then one by one they start to move again and lean back with arms opened in an accepting gesture. The lead couple faces the group and bows. The members of the group bow respectfully back.

The work, which was not widely appreciated when it was first performed, has come to hold a high position of respect in the body of Humphrey's dances. It shows her analytical and formal skill at arranging a group dance which offers a movement structure that draws from the strength of Bach's score but is not subservient to it. It is a piece showing great formal invention and is the best of the "abstract" works that Humphrey created.

LAMENT FOR IGNACIO SÁNCHEZ MEJÍAS

Choreography by Doris Humphrey. Music by Norman Lloyd. Costumes by Pauline Lawrence. Scenery by Michael Czaja. First performed at Bennington College, Bennington, Vt., July 11, 1946, by José Limón as Mejías, Ellen Love as the Figure of a Woman, and Letitia Ide as the Figure of Destiny. First performed in New York City at the Belasco Theatre, January 5, 1947, with Meg Mundy as the Figure of a Woman.

The barest sculptural indications of a doorway into a house and a portion of a room are the setting for this melancholy dance. A man and two women stand in subdued light on a platform on the right. He extends his hand downward and steps off the structure but is restrained by a cloth held momentarily by the two women. He moves through it and they extend their hands toward him with an anxious stretching. He walks off proudly and erectly, carrying himself with the arrogance and confidence of a matador. They move after him but retreat as he goes off; one buries her face in her hands, and the other starts after him again.

He returns wrapped in a cape and falls to the floor, rolls over, and then lies motionless. He stands and allows his cape to drop. While the women watch him, he mimes the action of a bullfight, his arms are curved like horns, then he displays the imaginary wave of a cape followed by a dramatic drop to one knee. His restless movement all over the area indicates the continuous action of a bullfight.

One woman holding a cord opposes him, and they dance a combative duet. He makes repeated scissors motions of his hands and then his arms across the front of his body. She lashes him with the cord; he trembles and loses strength. She goes to the platform room and stands dominatingly as he ascends the small flight of stairs to recline on the table, later to be his coffin. She cradles him in her lap, after which he slides beneath the table and vanishes.

She spreads her arms widely and laments. The other woman moves to the center of the stage and does the same. They walk about declaiming, and suddenly he steps in and does a brief solo, mounts a small box, and turns slowly. The women's clamor ceases.

The dance shows Humphrey examining a dramatic conflict with great intensity and compassion for all those involved in the conflict of a man driven to danger. There is the general observer, who represents the overview of fate, and the other woman, who grieves passionately for him. At the beginning of the dance they are all united by a thin red scarf which entangles their lives. The dance progresses with interludes of recitation and music. For the poetry Humphrey selected suitable passages from various translations of Lorca's poem but did not attempt to create a dance which was merely programmatic. She wished to have the words and the motion interact but not be subservient to one another.

DAY ON EARTH

Choreography by Doris Humphrey. Music by Aaron Copland (Piano Sonata). Costumes by Pauline Lawrence. First performed at the Beaver Country Day School, Brookline, Mass., May 10, 1947, by José Limón, Letitia Ide, Melisa Nicolaides, and Miriam Pandor (the José Limón company).

Three figures are seen at the rear of the stage: a woman seated on a low platform, a young girl by her side, and a small child in front of her. A man strides in and the young girl leaves the group to run to him. He kneels and she leans back on him. They run from side to side and he embraces her and then releases her. She tumbles and he lifts her tenderly and she flees. He arches himself backward in an agony of loss and then goes off.

The woman who has been seated rises and casts off her cloak. She reaches after him, draws him back, and they walk hand in hand to the rear of the stage, where the little girl stands, and they play with her. The man embraces the little child tenderly while the woman goes off. When she returns they all dance together. The child leaves and the man and woman dance a long duet that explores the emotions of hope and fear that a couple might experience. Alternating moods of struggle and support are created.

The young girl re-enters, the man goes to the woman and lifts her up, and the child enters. The woman seats herself on the platform, and the three others lie feet to feet and spread the cloak over themselves like a shroud, completing the generational cycle.

The dance is cast in an intimate style of one family grouping that includes several age groupings, but in her treatment of the group Humphrey makes a comment about all humanity by extension. The movement is vigorous and heroic in force and is strongly compelling.

CHOREOCHRONICLE
OF DORIS HUMPHREY

1920

Valse caprice (Scarf Dance)
Bourée
*Soaring (with Ruth St. Denis)
Sonata Pathétique (with Ruth
St. Denis)

1923

Sonata tragica

1924

*Hoop Dance (Scherzo Waltz)

1926

A Burmese Yein Pwe (with Ruth
St. Denis)
At the Spring
Whims

1928

Air for the G String
Gigue
Concerto in A Minor, Allegro
Moderato (Grieg)
Waltz

Papillon
Color Harmony
Pavane for a Sleeping Beauty
The Fairy Garden
Bagatelle
Pathetic Study
The Banshee
Rigaudon
Sarabande
*Water Study

1929

Air on a Ground Bass
Gigue
Concerto in A Minor, Allegro
Marcato (Grieg)
Speed
Life of the Bee
The Call
Quasi-Waltz
Courante (from Antique Suite)
Mazurka to Imaginary Music

1930

A Salutation to the Depths (with
   Charles Weidman)
Breath of Fire
Drama of Motion
La Valse (Choreographic Waltz)
Descent into a Dangerous Place
   (Gargoyle)
March (Parade; Passing Parade)
Salutation
Étude No. 1
Die Glückliche Hand (opera)
Lysistrata (p)
Les Romanesques

1931

*The Shakers (Dance of the
   Chosen)
Dances of Women
Burlesca
Lake at Evening
Night Winds
Tambourin
Three Mazurkas
Variations on a Theme of Handel
Two Ecstatic Themes
   Circular Descent
   Pointed Ascent
String Quartet (Bloch)

1932

The Pleasures of Counterpoint
Dionysiaques
Carmen (opera with Charles
   Weidman)
Aida (opera with Charles
   Weidman)
Americana (mc)

1933

Suite in E (with Prelude by
   Charles Weidman)

Run Little Chillun'! (p)
The School for Husbands (p)

1934

Rudepoema
Pleasures of Counterpoint No. 2
Pleasures of Counterpoint No. 3
Exhibition
Theme and Variations
Credo
Christmas Oratorio
Orestes

1935

Duo Drama
*New Dance
Variations and Conclusions from
   New Dance
Iphigenia in Aulis (opera)

1936

*Theatre Piece
*With My Red Fires

1937

To the Dance

1938

American Holiday
Race of Life
*Passacaglia and Fugue in C
   Minor

1939

Square Dances

1940

Variations (with performing
   dancers)
Song of the West

1941

Dance "ings"
Decade

1942

"Rivers" from Song of the West
Four Chorale Preludes
Partita in G Major

1943

Él Salón México

1944

Inquest
Canonade
Swing Out, Sweet Land (mc with
  Charles Weidman)

1946

Story of Mankind
*Lament for Ignacio Sánchez
  Mejías

1947

*Day on Earth

1948

Corybantic

1949

Invention

1951

Night Spell

1952

Fantasy, Fugue in C Major,
  Fugue in C Minor

1953

Ritmo Jondo (Deep Rhythm)
Ruins and Visions
Poor Eddy (p)

1954

Felipe el Loco

1955

The Rock and the Spring
Airs and Graces

1956

Theatre Piece No. 2
Dawn in New York

1957

Descent into the Dream
Dance Overture
The Child and the Apparitions
  (opera)

1959

Brandenburg Concerto No. 4
  (with Ruth Currier)

EDWIN STRAWBRIDGE

While attending Lafayette College in Pennsylvania, Strawbridge came into contact with the school's dramatic society, which left him with a longing for the stage. However, he was studying law and it was intended that he become his father's successor. When his father died, leaving him with a small inheritance, he decided to pursue his career on the stage instead of at the bar.

His introduction to dance came after he had appeared first as an actor, and the development of his career was as a dance mime rather than as a dancer pure and simple. In his own words, "It was my endeavor to act which led me back to dancing. In learning how the body released emotion I discovered the true essence of the dance."

As a child, Strawbridge had studied social dancing, but his first professional appearance was as a camel boy in Adolph Bolm's production of *Prince Igor* in the early twenties. It was a simple walk-on part but quickly led to further involvement with dance. In 1923 he staged dances in *Fantastic Fricassé* at the Greenwich Village Theater and three years later gave his own first solo recital, and then joined the Ruth Page company at the Ravinia Opera. He toured with the company on a Far Eastern trip that included Japan, China, and Russia before returning to the United States.

The League of Composers commissioned him to stage the movement for Prokofiev's *Le Pas d'acier* in 1931 at its debut performance in New York. He continued with solo concerts and then in the middle thirties established his Junior Programs Ballet Company, which specialized in children's productions. These included *Pinocchio, The Princess and the Swineherd,* and *Daniel Boone.* Strawbridge withdrew more and more from the concert dance stage to appear in and to direct these youth programs and finally ended his active stage career in the middle fifties.

THE EAGLE

Choreography by Edwin Strawbridge. Music by Edward MacDowell. First performed at the Guild Theater, New York, N.Y., November 3, 1929, by Edwin Strawbridge.

Strawbridge was a striking-looking man, and he made the most of his physical force and grace. In his solo numbers he chose to portray either abstract mood, such as the restlessness and power of the sea in the work of that name, or the solitary reverie of some creature either human or animal, such as that portrait he created in *The Eagle*.

Alone and proud, he stands surveying the land below from his high perch. He is a traveler of the roads in the sky and soars close to the sun in his isolated wanderings. He is remote and free, with the sky spread out behind him and the land and sea beneath his feet.

One has the feeling that great strength is ready to be loosed at any moment and that the repeated swoops and dips of the beast are not without a keen-eyed purpose. His natural home is high among mountain crags from which he descends quickly. In the words of the Tennyson poem that inspired the dance, "And like a thunderbolt he falls."

The piece was one of the most effective in Strawbridge's repertory, and he continued to perform it up until he discontinued his solo concerts. It was a blend of traditional mime and newer movement elements which placed him at the crossroads of the artistic currents then flowing through the dance world. It had some of the romantic feeling of the Denishawn era but also some of the tough-minded exploration of movement that characterized the founding generation. Strawbridge did not establish a school to perpetuate his own artistic concerns but rather went his individual way throughout his career.

CHOREOCHRONICLE
OF EDWIN STRAWBRIDGE

1923

   Fantastic Fricassé

1929

   Allegro Barbara
   White Peacock
   Prelude to Revolt
   Dance for Victory
   *The Eagle

1930

   The Sea

1930–31

   March
   Vagabond
   Driver of Storm Winds
   Poème satanique
   Charity
   Youth
   Delusion
   New Visions
   Pas d'acier
   Prometheus
   Golliwog Cakewalk
   I Danced with a Mosquito
   David and Goliath Impressions
   Heroic Hymn

1932

   Harlequin Dance
   Bartered Bride Polka
   Les Petits riens

1933

   Orestes

1936

   Pinocchio
   The Cat and the Mouse
   The Little White Donkey
   In Theatre Street

1938

   The Princess and the Swineherd

1941

   Daniel Boone

1942

   Christopher Columbus

1948

   Simple Simon

1953

   Pecos Bill

HELEN TAMIRIS

Helen Becker decided that she needed an exotic stage name when she took up the serious study of dance, and she selected Tamiris. She was first attracted to ballet and unlike most others of the founding generation achieved a fair degree of competence in it. In the early twenties she studied at the Metropolitan Opera Ballet school and appeared for three seasons with the opera ballet doing the interludes of dance that were called for in the various operas in repertory. Since the opera management had little regard for ballet, there were no opportunities for independent evenings devoted to ballet, as was the custom in the European opera houses upon which the Metropolitan was patterned. Tiring of second-rate status, she left the Metropolitan for touring with the Bracale Opera Ballet in South America and then returned to try her hand at show dancing in New York in the Music Box Revue.

    Deciding to create her own dances, she gave her first solo recital in New York and began to develop a repertory of concert works. She chose 1927 for her debut, the year after Martha Graham made her first appearance as a concert artist and a year prior to the appearance of the Humphrey-Weidman troupe. She did not, however, share their experience with the popular

(LEFT) Maud Allan in *Vision of Salomé*. (RIGHT) Loie Fuller. (BELOW) Isadora Duncan.

Ted Shawn and Ruth St. Denis.

Helen Tamiris in *Negro Spirituals*.   PHOTO BY MARCUS BLECHMAN.

Charles Weidman and Doris Humphrey in *New Dance*.

Martha Graham in *Deaths and Entrances*.   PHOTO BY CRIS ALEXANDER.

Denishawn aesthetic and so developed in a somewhat less self-consciously doctrinaire way. She was not fighting clear of a show business career which hampered her but was expanding her own personal horizons in whatever manner she saw fit.

She found it congenial to work in the musical theater as well as in the concert dance field. She had a tour of major festivals in Western Europe decades before any of her co-dancers did, and she also started work on dances exploring Americana before any of the others. She joined with them in 1930 as part of the first Dance Repertory Theater season, in which each company presented individual programs but shared publicity and rental expenses for the theater. She established her School of American Dance, which she maintained until 1945. During the Depression she participated in the Dance Project N.Y., sponsored by the Works Project Administration, and also coached actors in techniques of dramatic body movement.

She choreographed a number of Broadway musicals including *Up in Central Park, Show Boat, Annie Get Your Gun,* and *Touch and Go,* for which she won a Tony award. During this time she was not active as a concert dancer and had in effect retired from the performing stage although she reformed her company after her marriage to Daniel Nagrin, calling it the Tamiris-Nagrin Dance Company. Among her most enduring works are *Negro Spirituals* and *Walt Whitman Suite.* She had a great love for the spirituals and was the first choreographer, white or black, to select them for concert dance production.

NEGRO SPIRITUALS

Choreography by Helen Tamiris. Traditional music arranged by Genevieve Pitot. Costumes by Helen Tamiris. Nobody Knows the Trouble I See; Joshua Fit de Battle ob Jericho *was first performed at the Little Theatre, New York, N.Y., January 29, 1928;* Swing Low, Sweet Chariot *at the Martin Beck Theatre, New York, N.Y., April 7, 1929;* Crucifixion *at the Craig Theatre, New York, N.Y., February 7, 1931;* Git on Board, Lil' Chillun; Go Down, Moses *at the New School for Social Research, New York, N.Y., December 18, 1932;* When the Saints Go Marchin' In *at the Tamiris Studio, New York, N.Y., February 2, 1941; and* Little David, Play Your Harp; No Hidin' Place *at the Rainbow Room, New York, N.Y., April 1, 1942. All were danced by Helen Tamiris.*

This version of the dance, revised for eight men and women, utilizes eight spirituals, one of which is sung for each section. "Nobody Knows the Trouble I See" opens the work, and all of the dancers walk slowly across the stage in a line. They stand and let shoulders droop and then kneel, each lost in some private sorrow. They rise and slowly walk past one another to leave the stage. "Go Down, Moses" is a male solo in which an arm stretches up and the legs are spread powerfully. He lurches forward, slowly bending forward, and swings his arms right and left as if tearing off fetters, and concludes with his arm raised in a noble tragic pose.

In "Swing Low, Sweet Chariot" a lone woman sways from side to side and reaches over her head to sway her arms. She stamps her feet as she runs backward and then leans body back and steps forward while flapping her arms open and closed. She repeats the sequence for the second verse and kneels with one arm outstretched. "Git on Board, Lil' Chillun" features a man trippingly dancing toward the audience on a diagonal. He reaches out and opens and closes hands in the happy frenzy. He suddenly pauses to dig his heel in the ground and rotates the foot from side to side, indicating that the happy dance is over and he has to go home.

The man who dances "They Crucified My Lord" extends his arms to the side at shoulder height and steps rapidly away from the audience. Near the back of the stage he turns and holds his palms forward. He brings his hands into his sides with the palms held forward and slides them up and down his body from mid-chest to thigh as if they were running in a groove. He approaches the audience and then returns to the back of the stage to repeat his variation and finally faces front, stretches arms to the side, the lowers his head. This is followed by the martial "Joshua Fit de Battle ob Jericho." A man is in the center of the stage striding vigorously in place and swinging his arms. He stamps his heels as he walks around and thrusts his arms aggressively forward. Finally he bends his body forward pugnaciously.

In "Little David, Play Your Harp" two women accompany a man onstage, all doing little doll-like steps. The women hold their arms as if they were harps, and circle around him as he mimes and dances feats of daring. In a final parade they walk off in single file and just before disappearing lean back and snap heads around to take a quick look at the audience. The entire company of eight joins in the concluding "When the Saints Go Marchin' In." Each enters singly and all arrange themselves in a circle. Individuals leap up as if possessed by a holy ecstasy. They stamp their feet then extend one leg and swing their arms around happily. All form a large circle again, to skip then turn to approach the audience, touching one hand then the other hand to their chests and throwing it out to the side again. The dance ends with all thrusting one arm to the side.

The dance is one of the most popular that Tamiris ever created and showed her talent for combining a social consciousness with charming dance movement. It was one of the first pieces to incorporate black music with concert level dance and remains a beautiful suite of dance episodes.

WALT WHITMAN SUITE

Choreography by Helen Tamiris. Music by Genevieve Pitot. First performed at the Booth Theatre, New York, N.Y., January 14, 1934, by Helen Tamiris, Sydne Becker, Hilda Sheldon, Dvo Seron, Ida Soyer, Ida Tavrin, and Molly Bornn.

The opening of the dance finds its nine men and women standing around or on two large wooden structures. The one at the right side of the stage is three steps in profile, and a right-angle platform is at the opposite side. The dancers are motionless until the man at the top level of the "staircase" raises his arm and moves it around in a scanning motion to include everyone on-stage. As they begin stamping he goes quietly off. The dancers repeatedly rise to the balls of the feet and bring the heels down and bounce up again. The movement is lively and they begin to swing their arms upward and downward like scoops. A second man leaps from the "staircase" while the company in groups of three swing their arms up over their heads and then reverse the direction downward. The motion is passed from trio to trio until all join and face the audience. This is followed by all pumping up and down in place and raising their arms in large arcs which stop short of meeting over the head. They return to the platforms, where some extend their arms to the side like a bird's wings and others sit and bow their arms in front. As the original man who made the scanning motion with his arm returns, all stop.

The second movement begins as he brings his arm up, looks at his hands, and places one hand over his heart. This section is a dance for the women, who make large, open gestures in a tempo slower than previously. They form themselves into a "Y"-shaped chain and move across the stage and sway as if in sea waves. Their formation dissolves into a "J" shape and then into two parallel lines, and then they form a tight watch-spring spiral which unfolds. They bow individually and finally face the audience while extending one arm up and then freeze in position.

The men enter to do the third movement and the women scatter. The pace is energetic and characterized by much leaping. The men dash from one side to another, then begin a section of mime showing men at work, hauling, and tugging with one another, after which they return to leaping and swinging their arms overhead in a way that suggests lariat twirling.

The women rejoin the group and all repeat the pumping up and down in place that was seen in the opening section; some are mounted on the plat-forms and others are at stage level. To conclude, all form themselves into two lines across the stage one behind the other and extend their arms to the side and slightly above shoulder level in a gesture that is exuberant and suggests triumph. At the end the front line kneels while the back line remains standing.

The mood of the dance is energetic and positive in its approach. It reflects the enthusiastic celebratory sense that one receives from Whitman's own poetry. He embraced experience with an all-inclusive grasp, and the spritely dancing of the men and women in the piece has a similar openness to it; a relentlessness that has great drive and warmth.

CHOREOCHRONICLE
OF HELEN TAMIRIS

1927

Florentine
Melancholia
Portrait of a Lady
Circus Sketches
The Queen Walks in the Garden
Three Kisses
Two Poems
Impressions of the Bull Ring
Tropic
Amazon
Subconscious
1927

1928

Gayety
Perpetual Movement
Country Holiday
Hypocrisy
Harmony in Athletics
*Negro Spirituals
   Nobody Knows the Trouble
      I See
   Joshua Fit de Battle ob Jericho
Twentieth Century Bacchante
Prize Fight Studies
Peasant Rhythms

1929

American Serenade I
American Serenade II
Popular Rhythms
Dance of the City
*Negro Spirituals
   Swing Low, Sweet Chariot
Revolutionary March
Fiesta (p)

1930

Sentimental Dance
Play Dance
Romantic
Dirge
Triangle Dance

1931

Woodblock Dance
Olympus Americanus—A 20th
   Century Ballet
Mirage
South American Dance
Dance of Exuberance
Transition
Mourning Ceremonial

Eroica
Maenad
Dance for a Holiday
*Negro Spirituals
    Crucifixion

1932

Composition for Group
*Negro Spirituals
    Git on Board, Lil' Chillun
    Go Down, Moses
    Gris-Gris Ceremonial

1933

Cymbal Dance

1934

*Walt Whitman Suite
Toward the Light
Group Dance
Gold Eagle Guy (p)

1935

Cycle of Unrest
Mass Study
Dance of Escape
Flight
Harvest 1935

1936

Momentum

1937

How Long, Brethren?

1938

Trojan Incident (p)

1939

Adelante

1940

These Yearnings, Why Are They?
Floor Show

1941

*Negro Spirituals
    When the Saints Go Marchin'
        In
    As in a Dream
    Song of Today
    Liberty Song

1942

Bayou Ballads
*Negro Spirituals
    Little David, Play Your Harp
    No Hidin' Place

1943

Porterhouse Lucy

1944

Marianne (mc)
Stovepipe Hat (mc)

1945

Up in Central Park (mc)

1946

Show Boat (mc)
Annie Get Your Gun (mc)
Park Avenue (mc)

1947

The Great Campaign (mc)
The Promised Valley (mc)

1948

Up in Central Park (mp)
Inside U.S.A. (mc)

1949

Touch and Go (mc)

1950

Great to Be Alive (mc)
Bless You All (mc)

1951

Flahooley (mc)

1953

Carnival in Flanders (mc)

1954

Fanny (mc)
By the Beautiful Sea (mc)

1955

Plain and Fancy (mc)

1957

Memoir

1958

Dance for Walt Whitman
The Vine or the Tree

1960

Women's Song

1961

Once upon a Time . . .

1963

Arrows of Desire
Rituals
. . . Versus . . .

CHARLES WEIDMAN

During the severely serious 1930s Charles Weidman possessed a warm, spontaneous humor that allowed him consistently to see the lighter side of experience as well as the darker. He created many dances drawing on both aspects of life, but his comic sense dominated his creative energies, and he is best known for those dances celebrating the incongruities of human encounters. As a performer, he demonstrated a subtle sense of mime that was unique. He could in a moment transform himself from a blustering man into a demure young girl with the deft manipulation of a scarf and a quick alteration in bodily posture.

Weidman was born in Lincoln, Nebraska, and showed no great desire to follow his father's career of civil engineering. He did later commemorate his father's membership in a volunteer fire department in *And Daddy Was a*

Fireman, but not until he had left home and received his dance training. He went to the Denishawn school in Los Angeles and was immediately accepted as a pupil by Ted Shawn, who sent him out to tour in his production of *Xochitl* with Martha Graham only a few months after his arrival. It was the sink-or-swim school of dance instruction, and Weidman demonstrated a knack for dance that rapidly developed into demonstrable skill.

He remained with the various Denishawn companies until the autumn of 1927, when he and Doris Humphrey left to give a concert of their own works and to establish their own company. Both contributed to the formation of the technique of movement that is now known as the Humphrey-Weidman technique, with its emphasis on the idea of dance as the result of restoring the balance after an imbalance induced by any form of movement. In popular terms it has been characterized as "fall and recovery."

The Humphrey-Weidman studio and company dissolved in 1945, when Humphrey was forced to retire because of an arthritic hip. Weidman went on to form his own company and subsequently his own school. After extensive touring in the 1940s and early 1950s he devoted most of his energy to teaching both on the West Coast and in New York. When he returned to that city, he created a studio and performing space out of a loft on Twenty-ninth Street with Mikhail Santaro, where weekly concerts were given, including revivals of past works and creation of new dances. These latter, such as the *St. Matthew Passion,* were distinguished mostly for Weidman's own skill at mimetic action rather than any imaginative dance design. He continued his teaching assignments both at his own school and in a variety of colleges until the time of his death. To the last he involved himself in a variety of projects including restagings of his own and Doris Humphrey's works.

OPUS 51

Choreography by Charles Weidman. Music by Vivian Fine (Op. 51). Costumes by Pauline Lawrence. First performed at Bennington College, Bennington, Vt., August 6, 1938, by Charles Weidman, Harriette Anne Gray, Beatrice Seckler, Billy Archibald, Mirthe Bellanca, George Bockman, Katherine Litz, Lee Sherman, Pauline Chellis, Maxine Cushing, Eleanor Frampton, Molly Hecht, Maxine Hunt, Dorothy Ross, and Anne D. Stern.

The solemnity of the summer of 1938 at the Bennington College Summer School of the Dance had an opposite effect on Charles Weidman. He resolved to do a dance that was not concerned with social betterment or any elevated feeling other than the sheer joy of dance movement. While casting about for a name to give the dance he mentioned the difficulty to his long-time associate Doris Humphrey. She asked him how many dances he had created up to that time and he replied that it came to "about fifty." "Then call it Opus Fifty-one," she replied pragmatically, and he did.

The first movement begins conventionally enough as two women walk forward and do an attitude turn followed by extensions of the leg to the side. They are joined by two other women and then a third and all turn together. Legs are extended backward and all bend forward, and the five join in a circle after stepping grandly around for a moment. In the circle they step backward, pause for a moment, and file around slowly, swinging crooked arms right and left. All stand in a vertical line. First three jump to the side and return, and then the two others follow, and the impression is of a bell tolling. One begins a turn which is then picked up by all. They bow to the center, swing their arms, extend their legs and then walk off. It is the last that the audience sees of conventional dance, but in its own quiet way it introduces the playfulness that will characterize the rest of the dance.

Four men immediately follow them with a march. It begins with one man standing on a low box weaving a flickering pattern of hand gestures in front of his face and over his body with fluttering fingers and then slowly extending his arm and snapping his fingers. Immediately the three other men rush in and join him is a slightly cockeyed version of a march. Then the whole company of men and women enter to perform "Commedia," a madly dense collection of individual mime segments whose relationship existed purely in terms of the motions and not the characters. In one instance a woman telling her beads like a pious nun would push each bead firmly downward as she finished the individual prayer, and nearby a man would tug upward rhythmically on an imaginary fishing pole to balance the gesture. There were gestures drawn from acrobatics, daily tasks of sweeping and gardening, all linked together in a blizzard of movement that did not attempt to tell a story but just to present kinetically related gestures no matter how incongruous their juxtaposition.

The group leaves and a single man does a mazurka that displays his skill in achieving chains of turning leaps. Two women leap on diagonally to follow his odd mazurka with an even odder waltz, which leads into the culminating finale called "Spectacle." It is designed with circus flair and even the simplist gestures and steps are underlined with flourishes in the music that make them seem quite spectacular. To open, a man swings his legs from side to side, leading one to anticipate a large concluding gesture which in reality in only a modest ascent of a low box, from which he jumps down with a fanfare. In a similar fashion another man on the box begins a slow rolling forward; suddenly two women enter and throw their legs out to the side in a firm straddle over him and flourish their hands upward to emphasize their quite modest feat. It all concludes with gracious bows.

Weidman's development of "kinetic pantomime" as opposed to representational pantomime was one of the major contributions of his career. He simply followed the trajectory of a gesture as it metamorphosed into a whole skein of movement that suggested bits and fragments of characterization as it progressed but did not tarry or linger over any. It was and is inspired foolishness that transcended the linear mode in which most dances of the time were composed. Weidman had first shown *Kinetic Pantomime* in a work of that name in 1934 but fulfilled its promise in this piece. Like many overtly foolish things it concealed a quite revolutionary approach to composition beneath the surface laughter.

FLICKERS

Choreography by Charles Weidman. Music by Lionel Nowak. Book by Alan Porter and Charles Weidman. First performed at the Humphrey-Weidman Studio, New York, N.Y., December 27, 1941, by Charles Weidman and Doris Humphrey, with Katherine Litz, Lee Sherman, Maria Maginnis, Charles Hamilton, Gloria Garcia, Beatrice Seckler, Nona Schurman, Molly Davenport, and company.

In the early 1940s the generation that had grown up with the conventions of the silent movies felt a little nostalgic for them. They were all conceived according to a formula which featured several shorts, some humorous, and then a longer, more serious film with a famous star. The musical accompaniment was either supplied by a single piano player selecting "mood" music or a pit orchestra doing much the same. To underscore the humorous tone of this dance about the early movies, Weidman asked his composer to include period songs like "Dardanella" and "Hearts and Flowers" in the body of the score which he was preparing, and Weidman designed the movement so that it reflected the slightly jerky movement that was a mark of early films. The dance is divided into four "reels."

"Hearts Aflame" tells the classic story of the young man from the city who falls in love with the farmer's daughter. As a backdrop to all of the sections, there is a large white screen at the rear. In his first production of the work Weidman had background slides projected on it from the rear to set the scene, but he later abandoned the device, since it was too clumsy technically to travel with, and in subsequent revivals the "reels" are all played in front of a large empty white screen. The hero arrives from the city, with his hat perched squarely and somewhat foolishly on his head, and is looking for a job. The farmer hires him and gives him a broom. The stage properties are all large cutouts adding to the sense of old-fashioned moviegoing. The hero waves shyly to the daughter as he begins sweeping, and it is obvious that he is in love with her. The two villains enter, and one runs his hands roguishly up and down the farmer's daughter's arm, which she withdraws. He presents the farmer with a mortgage and asks him to choose between his home and his daughter's hand in marriage. The hero intercedes and begins to rout them in a pie-throwing contest but is suddenly struck down and tumbles over an old stump. He emerges holding up a bag of gold triumphantly and the villains are dispatched and everyone lives happily ever after.

"Wages of Sin" is a spoof on the vamp concept of female sensuality, and we first see her escaping from a leper colony in the dead of night to make her way to the big city. She wears an ankle-length skirt and slinks along with her body tilted backward staring out from heavily darkened eyes. At times she draws her palms upward along her thighs. She locates her prey in a party and invites him to visit her, alone! She is reclining fetchingly on a low couch as he parts the curtains to her hideaway. They embrace passionately and she slinks away, leaving him in a tormented spasm of scratching. She has located her betrayer and paid him back.

"Flowers of the Desert" shows the plight of an innocent young couple when a sinister sheik decides to pay attention to the young woman. His appearance is greeted by a frightened rattling of cups and saucers on the part of the party guests, and the high point is a tango in which he bends and sweeps the young woman around in an abandoned manner, including a brief walk up the side of the proscenium as his mighty arm circles her waist.

The final "reel" is "Hearts Courageous" and shows a stalwart pioneer family fighting off the incursions of the Indians as they defend their log cabin home in the wild West. Just as the stalking Indians seem to be about to strike, a sign is dropped, "TO BE CONTINUED," as it was in many old-time movie serials to keep up interest for the next week's segment.

Weidman's talent for pantomime dance was never better than in this small and perfect replica of early movie days. The jerky movements and the cardboard cutouts all added to the feeling of days gone by. Weidman himself was the oafish hero in the first section and the devilish sheik, and he presented his co-artistic director, Doris Humphrey, delightfully as the vamp in a role that was not associated with her normally serious professional appearances.

AND DADDY WAS A FIREMAN

Choreography by Charles Weidman. Music by Herbert Haufrecht. First performed at the Humphrey-Weidman Studio, New York, N.Y., March 7, 1943, by Charles Weidman as Daddy, Doris Humphrey as Vesta, Nona Schurman as Grandmother Hoffman, Peter Hamilton as Young Fire and Older Fire, and Maria Maginnis as Victim of Fire, with Molly Davenport, Helen Douglas, Doris Goodwin, Ethel Mann, Helen Waggoner, Patricia Balz, Madge Friedman, Marion Scott, Joseph Gifford, and Frank Westbrook.

In actual fact Charles Weidman's father was a fireman in his home town of Lincoln, Nebraska, and this dance is biographical. Previously he had examined his maternal relatives in *On My Mother's Side,* and this is a fitting companion piece to it.

Items are read from the daily newspaper periodically to show us the stages in the fireman's advancement against his rival, Chief Malone, and the arch villain, fire itself, in appropriately colored tights. Both of these characters are danced by one person.

The time is the turn of the century. All of the props including the fire engine are cardboard cutouts that remind one of miniature toy theaters. The eager, restless young "Daddy" is taken with Vesta, who visits the town. He demonstrates the various parts of the fire engine and how they work. She follows the demonstration with tenderly feigned interest.

He has first demonstrated his prowess at extinguishing a small fire in a booth at the State Fair and continues his tussle with the stealthy "fire" as he presses his somewhat timid suit with Vesta. He finally manages to see her at home, and her mother leaves them alone long enough for him to get out a proposal, which is accepted.

The climactic fire is one at the Lindell Hotel, where he rescues a frightened woman. The papers announce his election to the leadership of the fire department in the Panama Canal Zone for his good work. He leaves wearing his straw skimmer and suitcase, preceded by the pesky "fire."

Like others of his pantomime pieces, this one finds Weidman in good humor, dealing with his subject in friendly fashion. Striving for success as a fireman was a serious business in his father's day, but Weidman saw the witty aspect of the struggle, and his combination of the rival chief and the demon "fire" was a masterly touch. His chorus of women who read from the newspapers also formed a pleasing transition from one section to another.

A HOUSE DIVIDED

Choreography by Charles Weidman. Music by Lionel Nowak. First performed at the Humphrey-Weidman Studio Theatre, New York, N.Y., June 24, 1945, by Charles Weidman, Peter Harris, Albert Manny, Paul Wilson, Ann Dunbar, Betty Osgood, Pat Shafer, Barbara Thomas, Jane Thompson, Nadine Gae, Saida Gerrard, and Peter Hamilton.

In addition to his comic talent, Weidman at times displayed a more somber side of his nature, and in this dance examined the Civil War conflict and the character of President Abraham Lincoln.

A small group of women and a man stare at a cross draped with a black cloth. A speaker carrying a wreath announces Lincoln's death and passes the wreath to one woman, who places it at the foot of the cross. Another woman stretches her leg to the side and laments. Others in blue costume enter with their hands clasped and stretched out in front. The cross is removed as the three do a split and bow. The lean, sober figure of Lincoln enters and he slowly stretches his hand from side to side. Women in gray enter and face those in blue. A man in blue leads his group and a man in gray leads his.

Lincoln faces the two antagonistic groups and mimes the conciliatory words of a speaker, but the groups dash at one another with angry hand gestures. Lincoln endures in silence. The speaker asserts that the nation is in danger of committing suicide, but the only response from the opposing camps is a rocking of their bodies in derisive laughter before they retire. Lincoln parades sadly around the areas they have vacated with his arms over his head and the fingers of his hands interlaced like the contending forces.

He faces heavenward and begins to mime a sermon about the fruits of labor as four girls in brown suggestive of slave labor crawl and work while two men menace them with clenched fists. In contrast to this degrading and unprofitable labor another woman, well dressed and seated, does decorative sewing. One of the women defies the overseers as the others crawl off, and she is killed for her audacity. Lincoln and the speaker carry her off and he rages with anguish as pounding drums are heard. The speaker declaims "A house divided against itself cannot stand."

The blues and the grays all enter to shake fists at one another. Lincoln turns first to one side and then the other, but they each slash at him as they shake with evil and foolish laughter. There is no stopping the conflict which has been so long in building, and the parties engage. Ultimately the forces in gray lose. Lincoln mimes the generous mercy shown in his speech after the cessation of hostilities. All, now brought to their senses, stand and incline toward him.

The mime of the piece is by far and away the most important aspect of the work, which does not have any great choreographic inventiveness apart from it. But with a strong central figure the historical pageant does take on a sincere and tragic aspect. In this case Weidman chose to use representational pantomime rather than the fluid "kinetic" pantomime that he made his own special trademark.

FABLES FOR OUR TIME

Choreography by Charles Weidman. Music by Freda Miller. Book by James Thurber. Costumes by Charles Weidman. Lighting by Jack Ferris. First performed at Jacobs Pillow Dance Festival, Lee, Mass., July 11, 1947, by Charles Weidman, Felisa Conde, Betty Osgood, Carl Morris, Betts Lee, Emily Frankel, and Sharry Traver.

The disarmingly soft but pointed humor of James Thurber was bound to have attracted the interest of Weidman sooner or later, and it did in the year 1947. He created a pantomime work that included four of the stories for the Jacobs Pillow Dance Festival in the summer. By the time that he brought the work to New York in the fall, he had eliminated "The Little Girl and the Wolf" and substituted "The Shrike and the Chipmunks." The work remained in this state of completion until recent years, when Weidman created another sketch, "The Clothes Moth and the Luna Moth," but for the sake of nostalgic history the work is described as it appeared in that first New York season.

With an utter stroke of genius Weidman introduces a narrator, who is dressed in street clothes and wanders through the various sections reciting the tale as it is expressed in mime. He remains somewhat distant from the proceedings though intimately involved in them. He begins with the story of "The Unicorn in the Garden," as the hero rises happy and jolly from his bed to greet the day. It is not a day like any other, since through an open window he sees a unicorn wandering in his garden. He does not return to his breakfast but moves about gracefully and then returns to his bedroom to tell his wife what he has seen. He extends one pointed forefinger from the middle of his forehead and flutters his hand like a swishing tail at the base of his spine. She rises in curlers and in wrath. "The unicorn is a mythical beast," the narrator states. The man goes to the garden, picks a flower and gives it to the munching beast and rushes back to tell his wife again. "You are a booby and I will put you in a booby-hatch," he is informed. Her fingers dial an imaginary telephone and she summons a doctor and a policeman. To them she mimes the actions of a unicorn. The husband remains passively observant. The officials seize and draw her away, and he denies her story. When she is gone he reclines contentedly.

In "The Shrike and the Chipmunks" a man and a woman tuck their elbows into their sides and dangle their hands in front of their chests like paws. Wrinkled noses and munching teeth complete the transformation. The narrator manipulates the menacing large shrike around on the end of a long pole. The female is a busy scold tidying and warning her lazy husband about the menace of the strike. He is more interested in a basket of acorns, tucking them between his toes and using them like castanets as he dances happily around. He is obviously a ne'er-do-well, but the shrike scoops up his industrious, sharp-tongued wife before making off with him.

"The Owl Who Was God" finds the hero settled on his perch rolling his shoulders like a bird settling his feathers. His back is to the audience. Two moles are impressed with his grave dignity and confer with other forest creatures. His sober mien suggests special wisdom, perhaps even divine wisdom. The owl turns blinking and fluttering to face the secretary bird, who questions him on his knowledge. He is puzzled and his muttered "to whit's" and "to whoo's" punctuate the serious questions so perfectly that he is acknowledged to be divine. Resigned to being their leader, he ambles down and leads them in a procession over the edge of a cliff to their destruction.

"The Courtship of Arthur and Al" again underlines the silliness of conventional wisdom and is told exclusively by the narrator. It is the tale of two beavers in love with the same girl beaver. She marries the older and more industrious one, who works himself to death for her. And the moral of the tale, at least for Al, is "Better to have loafed and lost than never to have loafed at all."

Weidman subsequently went back to Thurber for his subject matter in *The War Between Men and Women,* but he caught all of the ironic twists of the stories the first time around in *Fables.* It was a marriage of sensibilities that were made for one another.

BRAHMS WALTZES, OPUS 39

Choreography by Charles Weidman. Music by Johannes Brahms (waltzes for piano, four hands, Op. 39). First performed at the Village Theater, New York, N.Y., June 12, 1967, by Carol Geneve, Joan Matthew, Joan Weigers, Maya Doray, Carlos Sille, and Frederick Courtney.

These waltzes for piano four hands, published early in Brahms' career, have been attractively choreographed by Weidman as a homage for his late dance partner, Doris Humphrey. At the premier of the piece he included the program note "Dedicated to Doris Humphrey because it is the kind of movement she loved and could do so beautifully."

The dance opens with five women taking high steps diagonally across the stage then moving rapidly in a closed circle, touching each other's fingertips. Two men join and three of the women go off. The two others face the men, who lift one bent leg and sweep it to the side while opening a hand, palm up, as a greeting. The women extend the same gesture to the men and they slide to a split.

One man does a solo turning and then rushing to one side, where he pauses to make a serpentine wriggle in the air with one hand. He repeats this several times and leaves as two girls tear on like whirlwinds. Pausing, they slide one leg forward and then draw themselves up composedly. A man joins them and all do a coy little heel-and-toe step sideways toward one another. The women start away from him momentarily but he attracts them back.

In another burst of energy two women sit and whirl on the ground, halting at times to thrust one leg high and then resume the turning, only to roll over and kneel. A trio of women quickly sweeps along, leaning to one side and extending the trailing leg. A man enters and exhorts them to leaps, then dances before them exuding puckish charm. The entire company joins momentarily and then exits.

Three women re-enter to turn in place. One woman leads the trio of men and the fifth woman joins the group. All dance in unison, sweeping around the stage and pausing dramatically to do a deep bend with legs spread widely. The formation fragments as all walk slowly in individual paths, and they seem to be in casual conversation with one another. Abruptly the pace picks up, they throw themselves down, first on one side and then on the other, then twirl and sit. One of the men begins a solo and draws one of the seated girls up as a partner. Others follow and soon the company is dancing the final waltz, which concludes with polite bows to one another and then to the audience.

While Weidman is most famous for his skill at constructing pantomime dances, he had a facility for pure dance movement which he also exercised from time to time, and this work is a beautiful example of his talent at constructing a plotless work that sails along on the emotional breeze of these lovely waltzes. When the work was first presented it was designed for two men and four women, but later Weidman enlarged it for five women and four men.

CHOREOCHRONICLE
OF CHARLES WEIDMAN

1928

> *Minstrels*
> *Ringside*
> *Japanese Actor*

1929

> *Compassion*
> *Marionette Show*
> *Passion*
> *Two Preludes*

1930

> *Lysistrata* (p, with Doris
>   Humphrey)

1931

> *La Puerto del Vino*
> *Danse Profane*
> *The Happy Hypocrite*
> *Music of the Troubadours*
> *Two Gymnopedias*

1932

> *Dance of Sports*

> *Dance of Work*
> *Carmen* (opera, with Doris
>   Humphrey)
> *Aida* (opera, with Doris
>   Humphrey)
> *Prologue to Saga*
> *Studies in Conflict*

1933

> *Candide*
> *As Thousands Cheer* (mc)

1934

> *Alcina Suite*
> *Exhibition Piece*
> *Kinetic Pantomime*
> *Life Begins at 8:40* (mc)
> *Iphigenia in Aulis* (opera, with
>   Doris Humphrey)
> *Memorials to the Trivial, the
>   Connubial, and the Colossal*

1935

> *Traditions*

1936

    American Saga
    Atavisms
    Quest
    I'd Rather be Right (mc)

1938

  Opus 51
    This Passion

1940

    On My Mother's Side

1941

  Flickers
    The Happy Farmers

1943

  And Daddy Was a Fireman
    La Comparsa
    The Dancing Master

1944

    The Heart Remembers
    Sing Out, Sweet Land (mc, with
      Doris Humphrey)

1945

    David and Goliath
    Dialogue
  A House Divided

1947

  Fables for Our Time
    Lynchtown

1949

    Rose of Sharon

1951

    A Song for You
    Classroom, Modern Style

1954

    *The War Between Men and
      Women*

1956

    Medea

1960

    *Is Sex Necessary? or, Why You
      Feel the Way You Do*

1961

    Christmas Oratorio

1963

    Dialogue Situation Two
    King David
    Saints, Sinner, Scriabin

1967

    Easter Oratorio
  Brahms Waltzes, Opus 39

1972

    Letter to Mrs. Bixby

1973

    Bach's St. Matthew Passion
    In the Beginning

1974

    *Visualization, or From a Farm
      in New Jersey*

In and Out of the Steps
of the Founders

The conclusion of World War II found modern dance in a state of triumphal vindication. The difficulties of poverty and public indifference had both been overcome to a major degree if not entirely conquered. The period of the 1930s were marked by doctrinaire stridency, struggle, and great accomplishment. The forties and fifties found younger choreographers alternating between the desire to consolidate the artistic victories won by the previous generation, all of whom were still working, and the urge to strike out in creative directions that were particularly their own. They respected and drew sustenance from the previous generation's accomplishments, but from time to time each would create a work that did not fit exactly into the mold cast by the founding generation. The work of these newer artists was marked by both deferential respect to previous wisdom and a restless search for more personalized ways of embodying their own artistic concerns.

There was a great optimistic turbulence created by World War II, when much of the rigidity of the previous decade was broken. The newer dancers and choreographers were not aware of the struggle that had been needed to establish modern dance as an independent art worthy of serious respect. They simply accepted its existence and went on from there. Of course they were in contact with the great figures of the time and joined their companies and studied in their schools, but there was a change in the sensibilities of the younger artists. They had to work hard for artistic respect, but they did not have to struggle for the very existence of their art form. The dancers of this generation were not imbued with the hostility that the historic generation felt toward ballet. These dancers recognized that ballet training was useful to them and helpful in making them more accomplished dancers, so they started to attend ballet class as well as to take class with the special school of modern dance that most attracted them. Even among the various modern dance schools there was a sense of rivalry which the younger dancers did not feel as keenly as their predecessors. Each naturally felt that he or she was working with the finest of the modern dance companies in the field but did not carry the feeling to the extremes of partisanship that existed in the thirties, when supporters of one company felt obliged to denigrate the accomplishments of any other company. Most of the younger dancers took varieties of dance classes before they settled on the particular style of movement which suited them most perfectly. Once committed to a company they discontinued class with other modern dance schools, but many often concealed the fact of continuing ballet study from the choreographer with whom they were dancing.

One of the accomplishments of modern dance had been the easy integration of black dancers into its fold. These dancers were found in all of the modern dance companies, and many were beginning to try out their own choreographic skills. Previously there had been black dancers and choreographers, such as Pearl Primus and Katherine Dunham, who had their own companies. These groups toured extensively and drew heavily on African and Caribbean dance styles to use in their repertories. They were popular and well received by the theatergoing public, but eventually were disbanded and the black students went to other modern dance companies for professional opportunities.

When they decided to strike out later on their own as leaders of their companies they created a style of dance movement which borrowed from the approaches of the various choreographers they worked with, but they also added the fluid energy that had been so abundantly seen in the Primus and Dunham companies. A style of dance loosely called jazz dance emerged, which relied on a strong rhythmic impulse and an alert, bouncy carriage to the body. The style is still to be seen in companies with black choreographers and almost everywhere in a modified form in popular theater or television variety entertainment.

Some of the chief legacies of the historic generation were the idea of linear development, i.e., that dances had a beginning, developed a clear, frequently psychological theme and came to a conclusion in an unambiguous sequential way and that the body should stress the emotional and dramatic in movement. To a great extent these ideas were accepted, but then periodically one of the choreographers of this generation would create a dance which did not adhere so strictly to the dictates and practices of the historic generation. To a great extent, when these dances appeared they were treated critically as if they were odd exceptions to the rules and not to be taken seriously as essays for a new direction in creative development.

The choreographers of this group did not feel themselves to be in a conscious state of revolt from the rules and thus did not conceive of themselves as a movement, much less a crusade, as the historic generation did. They were accustomed to working within the system as it had been established and which they found for the most part congenial. They did not want to discard totally the styles of movement which they had inherited; they thought highly of them and wished to extend their expressive possibilities a little bit further than they were when they first began to work. But there was a certain buoyancy of attitude that had not been part of the climate of the thirties. Many more things seemed creatively possible, and the impact of ballet training did have its effect.

The newer choreographers who experienced ballet training simply did not move in the way that the previous generation did. A lightness and a quickness were developed which were in marked contrast to the solid strength of the older dancers. The newer dancers were sleeker and attacked movement in a more lyrical manner than did their predecessors. This ability, which was not needed for the older dances in the repertory, was used in the newer pieces that were being choreographed and that extended the expressive range of the various established styles.

Many of the dancers found work in the commercial theater, designing the dances for musicals, and others found dancing jobs in Broadway productions. Modern dance had come a long way from its outcast days, when reviewers would regularly dismiss the efforts of modern choreographers as being ugly and not at all appealing. It was a time of transition for the field; there were dances created in the familiar traditional manner but there were also strange glimmers of change to be discerned.

ALVIN AILEY

Ailey spent the first eleven years of his life in Texas, where he was born, but his dance career received its first boost in 1942, when his family moved to Los Angeles, and he eventually had the opportunity to study with Lester Horton. After Horton's death, Ailey guided the company through its first appearance at Jacobs Pillow in the summer of 1953 and its fall appearance in New York. The company disbanded subsequently and Ailey formed his own troupe, American Dance Theater, including members of the defunct Horton company such as Carmen De Lavallade, Joyce Trisler, and James Truitte. The company was sponsored on a tour of the Far East, and Ailey also appeared in Europe.

He had by this time created a substantial number of works, including his most famous *Revelations* and also *Blues Suite*. In addition to his concert work Ailey has appeared in several Broadway productions, including *House of Flowers*, and has choreographed several others. He has created dances for other companies in addition to his own, including the City Center Joffrey Ballet and American Ballet Theater. As a strong organizer, he has attempted to maintain his company intact in a variety of locales. For several years it was the resident modern dance company of the Brooklyn Academy of Music, leaving only when offered the opportunity to become the first resident modern dance company in the history of the City Center in Manhattan. His company performs regular spring and fall seasons there at the Fifty-fifth Street theater and has performed in the Center's other house, the State Theater at Lincoln Center.

Though he no longer appears as a performer, Ailey is active as a teacher in his school, which offers substantial scholarship aid to minority group students. Though Ailey now rarely shows the influence of Lester Horton movement technique in his work, he gives considerable acknowledgment to Horton's eclectic activity in the scope of his own concerns.

In recent years he has become interested in finding a middle choreographic ground between modern dance and ballet and has created a number of works both for his own company and American Ballet Theater, exploring these possibilities. He is keenly aware of the lack of a modern dance repertory company which would perform modern dance classics by a variety of choreographers. To help remedy the deficiency, he has instituted a program of revivals that seek to show the roots of modern dance development. Among the choreographers whose work he has revived have been Ted Shawn, May O'Donnell, Katherine Dunham, and Pearl Primus. He regularly includes works of other choreographers, such as Lucas Hoving, Paul Sanasardo, Donald McKayle, Talley Beatty, and Joyce Trisler in the repertory of his own company.

His dancers are among the most exciting appearing anywhere, and the company has created audiences for dance attractions wherever it has appeared. It scored a notable success in a tour of the Soviet Union when it was the first modern dance company ever to make a national tour there. In a footnote to his other activities Ailey has the distinction of having created ballets for the musical productions which opened the new Metropolitan Opera House, Samuel Barber's *Antony and Cleopatra,* and, in the opera house in Kennedy Center, Leonard Bernstein's *Mass.*

BLUES SUITE

Choreography by Alvin Ailey. Music by Pasquita Anderson and José Ricci. Scenery and costumes by Geoffrey Holder. First performed at the Ninety-second Street YM-YWHA, New York, N.Y., March 30, 1958, by Clarence Cooper, Nancy Reddy, Julius Fields, Lavinia Hamilton, Tommy Johnson, Audrey Mason, Charles Moore, Charles Neal, Dorene Richardson, Liz Williams, and Claude Thompson.

As the title indicates, the dance is permeated with the sound and the feelings of the "blues," that special musical plaint that has become part of meditative popular culture. It is a cry from the anonymous tormented masses that took shape in "sporting" districts up and down the Mississippi.

The setting is in one of those "sporting" houses and details the lives of the women who work there and the men who visit. As it opens the men and women are scattered across the stage lounging on stools and chairs. A tall ladder stands at the right. Three large windows are projected on the back cloth, and the stage is suffused with cool green light. It is the time of "Good Morning Blues" as the men and women begin to stir and wake up. All move slowly and clear away from the center. One of the men dances alone in a solo that bespeaks lonely desire. Four other men join him in "Mean Ol' Frisco"; they are all wary and very alert. Their movements suggest a world of missed connections and things that might have been.

The four women immediately succeed them with a dance of their own, suggesting the disappointment felt in the "House of the Rising Sun." A large, softly luminous orange circle glows on the back cloth as they turn and stretch their arms in pleading movements to the heavens above. A couple begins a combative duet. She flounces around in a long feather boa and he is attracted to her. The dance turns into a scuffle and she rejects him emphatically, to the point of pushing him so that he falls. She then sashays off to pose on the ladder and look at him. He dusts himself off, goes to pull the boa angrily from her shoulders, and surprisingly she indicates her interest in him by hanging onto the end. She drops into his arms and he carries her off.

"In the Evening" the festivities of the house begin again, and the four fancy ladies high-step on, awaited and admired by four men who welcome their appearance enthusiastically. One of the women, as much as she tries, cannot be the sexy little strumpet and is comically awkward. The mood of the piece for the next three songs is gay and carefree. Two more women appear to join the festivities, and a young man who wants to be like his elders but who is pushed out whenever he is detected. It doesn't happen, though, before he has had a chance to dance with several of the girls and even be mistakenly embraced by one of the other men, who pushes him away with distaste and goes off to seek his girl.

The riotous good times, however, are brought to an end with the return of "Good Morning Blues"; all the men and women are reminded that another day is near and the cycle will begin again. They cluster and stretch their hands toward the sky hopefully. The sound of a church bell and the passing hoot of a train whistle are heard.

Ailey quite frequently puts this dance on the same program with *Revelations,* and the combination is like the revels of Saturday night and the repentance of Sunday morning. Both absolutely throb with vitality and have the artistic cohesion of accurately presented sentiments.

REVELATIONS

Choreography by Alvin Ailey. Set to traditional music. Costumes by Lawrence Maldonado. Lighting by Nicola Cernovitch. First performed at the Ninety-second Street YM-YWHA New York, N.Y., January 31, 1960, by Joan Derby, Minnie Marshall, Merle Derby, Dorene Richardson, Jay Fletcher, Nathaniel Horne, and Herman Howell. The soloists were Nancy Redi and Gene Hobgood, assisted by the Music Masters Guild Chorus of the Harlem Branch YMCA under the direction of Frank Thomas. The piece as originally performed consisted of danced portions and musical interludes grouped under three broad headings "Pilgrim of Sorrow," "That Love My Jesus Gives Me," and "Move Members Move." The work was revised extensively a month after its first performance and was again given at the Ninety-second Street YM-YWHA. Since then it has seen other revisions as well as an augmentation of the cast, along with new costuming by Ves Harper.

Every company has what is known as a "signature piece," that is, a work which expresses something about the artistic direction and the spirit of the company in the clearest manner. For the Alvin Ailey American Dance Theater that piece is undoubtedly *Revelations*. It has been seen in every country that the company has toured and has been universally acclaimed. It was originally done for the small company that Ailey started with and, though it has been expanded in numbers of performers, it has lost nothing of its creative vibrancy.

The six women and three men are densely packed in a wedge at the center of the stage, and as they flex their knees the stress lines in the women's dresses are beautifully picked out by the hot golden light that pours down over all of them from above as they extend their arms like wings. They separate but cluster again at the end of "I Been Buked," with arms stretched quiveringly overhead and fingers splayed. Then the arms stutter down in stiff, jerky motions to rest at the dancers' sides.

A trio of two women and one man follows to the plea for deliverance for "Daniel" trapped in the lions' den. The final dance of the first section, "Pilgrim of Sorrow," is "Fix Me Jesus," an exceptionally beautiful adagio for a man and woman. It has lovely sculptural poses that underlines its pleading for help, and concludes with the striking image of the woman with her feet braced on her partner's thigh, reaching upward. He holds her other arm and leans backward.

The bright energy of the piece picks up with the three parts of "Take Me to the Water," which begins with "Processional." The shadowy dramatic lighting of the first section is replaced by bright white light as the line of dancers is led in by a man carrying a long pole with small, fluttering bits of cloth. All are dressed in white trousers or dresses and in one floridly magnificent case a woman holds aloft a giant white umbrella that even has its own white chiffon covering over the silk. The woman pumps it up and down with splendid brio. The dancers turn and circle sparklingly. Two long, broad cloth streamers are suspended just above the surface of the stage. One is white and the other blue, and they undulate slightly as a couple dances "Wading in the Water" under the watchful eye of the woman with the umbrella. They tumble and frolic in the waves and receive the cleansing benefit of the water. A man enters to do a solo of remorse to "I Want to Be Ready." He reclines on the stage but lifts himself to hold out pleading arms similar to the action of the woman in "Fix Me Jesus" and at the end sinks down once again.

The last major section of the work, "Move, Members, Move," begins with a dynamically driven trio of men running, running, running, trying to escape retribution. They spin and tumble as the song "Sinner Man" tells of their condition. "The Day Is Past and Gone" finds women with stools and fans gathering at sunset to relax and chat with one another. They are both formal and funny as they greet one another elaborately and settle comfortably onto the stools. The men of the company in bright shirts and neat vests join them in "You May Run Home" and the exciting finale, "Rocka My Soul in the Bosom of Abraham," as they dash ardently, pump their elbows in and out in delight, and create a feeling of warm scintillating humanity.

The piece is a brief recapitulation of the black response to adversity and an expression of life's joy. The spirituals carry their message of religious comfort and the choreography expresses it clearly in movement that carries an edge of excitement throughout. Quite often audiences simply refuse to leave the auditorium until they are given a reprise of the last section. It is a request that is frequently honored by the company.

QUINTET

Choreography by Alvin Ailey. Music by Laura Nyro. Costumes by Matthew Cameron and George Faison. First performed at the Church Hall Theatre, Edinburgh Festival, Scotland, August 28, 1968. First performed in New York City at the Billy Rose Theatre, January 27, 1969, by Sylvia Waters, Linda Kent, Michele Murray, Consuelo Atlas, and Alma Robinson.

This work unites five glossily dressed women in eye-popping dresses that cling to them. They are smartly costumed and each woman wears a large, puffy blond wig. They are entertainers such as one might see in a supper club or performing at a large rock music concert.

The popular music has a regular and insistent beat, and the five are lined up side by side. They sway and undulate and from time to time one will tear away from the group to do a solitary variation that is a private expression of distress. After each "soliloquy" the woman rejoins the group. Two of them break away to dance lonely solos as the song "Stoned Soul Picnic" is played.

To the strains of "Luckie" one woman tosses herself around violently and rolls on the floor as the professional veneer of the dance begins to wear a little thin and the women become more forthright in showing their private selves in the context of a public performance. Together again as "Poverty Train" begins, the five wiggle and strut, when suddenly one of them slips out of the skin-tight glamorous dress, throws her wig to the ground, and begins a driven, tortured solo. All of them mouth the ironic words of the song.

One woman in a white dress begins to dance alone in an unhurried manner, seemingly reflective and looking toward the future. Three others in contrast move with a fast, edgy eagerness that expresses more of a sexy here-and-now attitude, and they leave her stretching and reaching upward. She too leaves moments later. Another one of the group steps in without her wig but in her brassy dress, which she slips out of, and begins to dance in her slip. It suggests regret and a simple longing for good times. She suggests what might have been, but then picks up her clothes and leaves.

The glittering look of the opening dance is repeated as all return in their "pop" entertainer gowns, but angrily they begin singing against the sound of the song that accompanies the dance. They are fighting against the music that is stifling them personally. They walk in small defiant circles, but the sheer weight of the music draws them back into the stylized performers that they were at the opening of the piece, and they conclude with a glamorous ensemble dance.

Ailey, who used spirituals, jazz, and varieties of classical music, took a long, hard look at the popular music scene when he created *Quintet*. It is a devastating comment on the private lives of performers and by extention anyone else who presents one face to the world when they are living another life behind what can be seen in public. Here he allows that private life to peep out a little at first and then lets it stand revealed before encasing it once again in the popular glamorous look that first concealed it. The dance has been very successfully performed by the Ballet Hispanico in addition to Ailey's own company.

MASEKELA LANGUAGE

Choreography by Alvin Ailey. Music by Hugh Masekela. Costumes by Christina Giannini. Lighting by Gilbert Hemsley. First performed at the Palmer Auditorium, Connecticut College, New London, Conn., August 16, 1969. First performed in New York City at the Brooklyn Academy of Music, November 21, 1969, by Kelvin Rotardier, Judith Jamison, George Faison, Renee Rose, John Medeiros, Sylvia Waters, Michele Murray.

The music of South African trumpeter Hugh Masekela is used throughout the dance, which details the grim plight of being black in South Africa. The setting is a bar in an obviously hot climate. Comfortable lounging chairs are scattered about, a fan turns slowly overhead, and a neon sign brightly projects the name of a popular beer.

The men and women stand, sit, and stare outward aimlessly. They have the air of being trapped in the large room. It has become their world and outside forces have ordained that this is where they have been forced to remain. They begin to remove jackets, hats, and other outer clothing as the music drives them into a group dance that features wriggles and pelvic thrusts that gradually subside, and the group drifts apart.

A woman with a vibrating walk storms around the area pursued by three men who follow her in the background. She is a sensual dynamo and they are unable to keep up with her. A man who wears a rakishly tilted fedora laconically steps forward. He has an air of mystery and sexual allure. His long solo is almost like that of a modern day hypnotist weaving a spell. He directs the rest of the men and women almost the way that an orator can play on the feelings of a crowd. One of the men breaks loose of the spell and momentarily tussles with him, but their fight is inconclusive and the crowd disperses.

Another woman now takes the center boldly. She turns repeatedly and almost seems possessed of a motor twitch that she cannot control. The surroundings by now seem particularly seedy and shabby. A third woman attracts a trio of men who make up to her, even the narcotics addict is attracted to her, though he lives in his own world of pleasant unreality for the most part. During the desultory mating game a man stumbles into the room wounded. He has been shot and is dying. His movements and those of the addict have a great similarity. The crowd flees from the man, and then all rush to look out the door from which he tumbled. He is a victim of the outside world and a grim reminder of its hostility. With the dying man still lying on the floor, the others begin to slip into their outer clothes again and push their chairs and stools forward to the edge of the stage. They sit or stand and stare angrily.

The run-down bar is obviously one of the few refuges that the people in the dance have. There they can relax with one another, enjoy themselves, and forget about the outside world. But that world won't let them alone, and the wounded man is a reminder of its enmity. At the beginning the people were able to put aside some cares along with their street clothes, but now they assume cares again as they put on those same street clothes.

CHOREOCHRONICLE
OF ALVIN AILEY

1954

   La Création du monde

1958

   Cinco Latinos
   *Blues Suite

1959

   Knoxville: Summer of 1915

1960

   Three for Now
   *Revelations

1961

   Hermit Songs
   Roots of the Blues

1962

   Feast of Ashes

1965

   Ariadne

1966

   Macumba

1968

   Reflections in D
   *Quintet

1969

   *Masekela Language

1970

   Gymnopedies
   The River
   Streams

1971

   Archipelago
   Choral Dances
   Cry
   Flowers
   Mary Lou's Mass
   Mingus Dances
   Myth

1972

   The Lark Ascending
   Love Songs
   Sea-Change
   Shaken Angels
   A Song for You

1973

   Hidden Rites

1975

   The Mooche
   Night Creatures

MANUEL ALUM

A native of Puerto Rico, Alum did not begin his dance training until he came to the United States in 1959. At that time he studied with Neville Black in Chicago and two years later took up residence in New York. He took ballet class with Margaret Black and Mia Slavenska and also studied at the Martha Graham school. His most important influence both as a teacher and a creative influence, however, was Paul Sanasardo, with whom he also studied.

In a short time he was invited to join the Sanasardo company and quickly established himself as one of its leading dancers and ultimately its assistant artistic director. During this time he began his own choreographic career and prepared eight works for the company. For several summers he functioned as assistant director of the School of Modern Dance at Saratoga.

He has toured extensively with his company and has been in demand as a guest choreographer. He is currently living and teaching in New York.

CELLAR

Choreography by Manuel Alum. Music by Kilar. First performed at the Festival of Two Worlds, Spoleto, Italy, June 1967, by Manuel Alum.

As a study in quiet obsession, the work has few equals. It is a solo for a man suitably garbed in gray who wears a tight-fitting gray headpiece that covers his hair and the back of his neck. It gives an alien look to the dancer as if he inhabited a different world. Though the piece has been performed with a variety of settings, the essential elements are a triangular wooden shape that suggests a corner and a low-standing light bulb.

The ticking of a clock, the large, old-fashioned noise made by a metal bedside alarm clock, is heard. The dancer stands and peers out from behind a large slatted construction. He emerges from behind it in a crouch and takes tiny "duck walk" steps over to the bulb, which is shaped like a candle flame. He sits beside it with his knees pressed closely together and passes one foot over the other, almost in the way that a man would anxiously rub one hand over the back of another.

Mechanical rustling sounds are heard and he tilts over on his back, and the light casts shadows of his feet and hands as he pedals them in the air like an insect upended. He tosses himself around but stays close to the ground. He spins on his knees; he seems weighed down by some force that keeps him in its power. Then he returns to sitting as the ticking of the clock reasserts itself over the mechanical sound. Again in a squatting position he traverses the area. He encounters nothing until he comes to the slatted construction. He stops, stands, and goes behind it to stare out for a moment.

Alum is a most accomplished dancer, and this solo shows his skill at its subtle and impressive best. The pauses between movements are filled with intense passion. Literally nothing dramatic happens except for the solitary searching of the man in the odd gray costume and cap, but Alum creates a world of lonely seeking and waiting that everyone has experienced at one time or another.

CHOREOCHRONICLE
OF MANUEL ALUM

1963

Familial Trio
Wings I Lack

1966

Nightbloom
Storm
Offering

1967

Dream After Dream and After
Fantasia
*Cellar

1968

Dream and Trial
Palomas

1969

Overleaf

1970

Roly-Poly
Era

1971

Terminal

1972

Sextetrahedron
Woman of Mystic Body . . .
  Pray for Us

1973

Juana
Deadlines
Steps
East—to Nijinsky
MOONsCAPES

1974

Yemaya
Escaras
Ilanot

MARY ANTHONY

Because of sympathetic teachers in grade school and high school Mary Anthony was encouraged to express herself artistically from an early age. A viewing of Martha Graham giving a solo concert at Ohio Wesleyan determined her dance career. She came to New York and received a three-year scholarship at the Hanya Holm Studio in 1940 and three years later appeared with the Holm company.

During the rest of the decade she appeared with various companies and taught at the New Dance Group as well as at the Holm Studio. In 1948 she presented the first of her own dances and began to appear in Broadway musicals. She then appeared in *Touch and Go* in London, was invited to choreograph an Italian musical, *Votate per venere*, and taught in Paris for a year. She returned to New York to work with a variety of companies and to create her own works.

Throughout the fifties and early sixties she shuttled back and forth from engagements in England, Italy, and Mexico. She has maintained her company and a studio between her outside assignments and regularly presents yearly concerts. Her work is meticulously crafted with strong dramatic accent.

IN THE BEGINNING
(ADAM AND EVE)

Choreography by Mary Anthony. Music by Peter Sunthorpe (Sun Music I and II). *Costumes by Leon C. Warner. Part I (Adam) was first performed in 1969. Part II (Eve) was first performed at the Fashion Institute of Technology, New York, N.Y., December 20, 1970, by Ross Parkes and Yuriko Kimura.*

The subject of the first man and woman encountering one another in remote loneliness is one that has exercised considerable fascination for a variety of choreographers. It is the story of the most facinating adventure that any individual can have, the discovery of someone like himself and yet provocatively different.

A silvered disc inclined upward hugs the earth to the left and rear of the stage. Adam first performs a solo of self-discovery in which he finally manages to rise and leave the disc asserting his newly found confidence and awareness. In the second part he lies face down and she rests on top of him. As he arches his back he raises her up. She continues upward and stands over him. She curves her arms and ripples her hands down the front of her body, makes a brief cradling motion, and then steps off the disc. He stands to watch her, then they clasp one arm and lean the weight of their bodies back. With the free arm they stretch toward one another; linked in one way, they are still strangers reaching to one another. They cautiously but passionately approach. Suddenly he cocks his head as if he hears an alien and dangerous sound. Quickly he carries her to the security of the disc.

They step down to do a lyrical dance, and he draws her firmly away from the tree which stands opposite the disc, and together they recline. He sleeps and she steals to the tree, which unleashes a powerful erotic drive in her. She returns to the disc and they circle one another, fall to their knees, and bend forward in shame over the expression of their passion. They leap and separate, he returns to the disc and she to the tree. It is obvious that their innocent encounter is a thing of the past, but they need one another and so return to their tempestuous union.

In a short space of time the dance encompasses self discovery, aroused physical passion, remorse, and acceptance of mutual dependence. It is like a miniature saga of the human race being played out by two individuals. For maximum effect the dance requires performers of great emotional intensity to bring out the full pungency of the work.

CHOREOCHRONICLE
OF MARY ANTHONY

1949

Chaconne (with Joseph Gifford)
Genesis (*XIX*)
Giga

1956

Songs
Threnody

1957

The Purification

1958

Blood Wedding

1967

Gloria

1968

Antiphon

1969–70

*In the Beginning
   (Adam and Eve)

1971

A Ceremony of Carols

n.d.
The Dialogue
Plaisanteries d'amour
The Wind
Apéritif

TALLEY BEATTY

Like jazz, Talley Beatty was born in New Orleans and moved up the Mississippi to Chicago. As a young man, he was taken into the Katherine Dunham company and danced with her for seven years. When he left the company, he formed his own small group, which he later expanded and toured Europe in 1949 and the United States for the next several years. His company was inactive for periods of time but re-formed as needed for concert commitments as recently as 1969.

Among his credits are an outstanding film with Maya Deren, *Study In Choreography for Camera,* made in 1945 and extensive work with Broadway and Off-Broadway theater. He created the movement for Jean Genet's acclaimed *The Blacks* as well as dances for a variety of other Off-Broadway productions among his various commitments. Several of his works are to be found in the repertories of other companies, including the Alvin Ailey American Dance Theater and the Boston Ballet. For the latter he also created *A Wilderness of Mirrors.* Beatty works in a dance style that is loosely termed jazz, and includes elements of main-stream modern dance, Caribbean movement, touches of ballet, and the rhythmic edginess that is associated with jazz music. He has taught extensively abroad and in the United States.

ROAD OF THE PHOEBE SNOW

Choreography by Talley Beatty. Music by Duke Ellington and Billy Strayhorn. Costumes by Lew Smith. First performed at the Ninety-second Street YM-YWHA, New York, N.Y., November 28, 1959, by Joan Peters, Mini Marshall, Herman Howell, Mabel Robinson, Talley Beatty, Altovise Gore, Tommy Johnson, Georgia Collins, and Jerome Jeffrey.

There really was a railroad train with the name *Phoebe Snow,* which was only retired from active service in 1967. It ran along the Erie-Lackawanna rail system, and Beatty grew up in a home that was near the train tracks. The name was created as an advertising ploy to characterize the cleanliness of the train as being white as snow inside, at a time when the grime from coal-powered locomotives was the rule rather than the exception.

The world of young men and women beside the railroad tracks is a world illuminated by red and green signal lights which flash alternate stop and go signals rapidly. The men and women enter and look with hard eyes. There is a feeling of suspicion in the way they creep on, stare around, and then dash off. The tempo picks up and the men set themselves off with a cocky stroll and they slide on their knees. Couples and individuals dance, and for a climax to the group activity, the six women vault on the men exultantly.

A milder range of emotion replaces the first group dance as a solitary man reaches out in lonely fashion. Three women follow him and then two men and a woman. A couple dances a love duet isolated from the roil of other activity that preceded them. It is, however, an exploitive exercise for the man, who summarily and cruelly leaves the woman after their sexual coupling. A second couple is not even so lucky as to be left to one another. As their duet is interrupted by a stranger who presents a danger to them. They are separated and the whole group engulfs them, the man is beaten senseless trying to protect his girl, and she is assaulted. It is life in the dangerous raw, and we again see the signal lights, concluding with their stop and go flashing.

Life near the railroad tracks is a mixture of fear, fun, romantic yearning, and violent assault. These little vignettes are all pulled together by Beatty to present a picture of that tumultuous life. The work has been presented by several companies but most successfully by companies with an integrated or all black cast.

CONGO TANGO PALACE*

Choreography by Talley Beatty. Music by Duke Ellington, Miles Davis, and Gil Evans. Costumes by Georgia Collins. First performed at the Ninety-second Street YM-YWHA, New York, N.Y., October 29, 1960, by Georgia Collins, Mini Marshall, Altovise Gore, Joan Peters, Mabel Robinson, Herman Howell, Jerome Jeffrey, Tommy Johnson, Ronald Platt, Dudley Williams, and Albert Popwell.

Originally the last movement of *Come and Get the Beauty of It Hot,* this portion has achieved an independent concert life all of its own. It is totally self-contained and has the aggressive vitality that the best jazz works manage to capture. The music is an impression of Spain, but the choreography is an impression of a Spanish ghetto in the United States.

The company moves around restlessly; the men and the women eye one another warily. The men are elegantly thin and draw themselves upright frequently with reining-in motions of the arms. The location is a night club where the men and women have come to meet one another.

Men grasp women around the waist, but it is not the tender embrace of young lovers; it is sensual brutality raised to an approximation of the social encounter but teetering on the edge of savagery. Couples are formed but abandoned for group dashes and sweeps. Everything is transient, individuals halt and engage one another for a while, but the suspicious loneliness of their emotions prevents anything resembling gentle encounters. They are poised for flight at the least unusual move. The lights dim on their still-driven prowling.

Beatty's evocation of life in a ghetto area, hardened to disappointment and mistrustful of easy happiness, is masterly. One has the continual sense of time being the enemy. One has to take what one can now and not wait for tomorrow, and taking involves a certain roughness. There is no time for polite exchange. The emotions are raw and the dancing gives them full vent.

* Originally Part 6 of *Come and Get the Beauty of It Hot.*

CHOREOCHRONICLE
OF TALLEY BEATTY

1949

Southern Landscape, 1865

1954

Parranda (mc)

1959

*Road of the Phoebe Snow

1960

*Come and Get the Beauty of It
   Hot
*Congo Tango Palace
Bring My Servant Home

1961

The Blacks

1962

Look at All Those Lovely Red
   Roses

1963

Danse au Nouveau Cirque, Paris

1964

The Migration
Toccata

1967

Montgomery Variations

1968

The Black Belt
House of Flowers (revival, mc)

1969

Antigone
L'Histoire d'un petit voyage
But Never Jam Today (mc)

1970

Don't Bother Me I Can't Cope
   (original production, mc)
Billy Noname (mc)

1971

Croesus and the Witch (mc)
Ari (mc)
Bury the Dead (mc)

1974

Caravanserai

1975

Tres Cantos

VALERIE BETTIS

She started dance study in her native Houston with Rowena Smith and Tina Flade, and when she attended Bennington she was attracted to study with Hanya Holm. She continued study with Holm when settled in New York and made her first professional appearance in Holm's epic *Trend*. For the following two years she toured with the Holm company.

She began creating her own work and appearing in solo concerts in 1941. Her piece *The Desperate Heart* won critical praise two years later. She formed a company and created one of her best known works, *As I Lay Dying,* based on the Faulkner novel from which passages were read connecting the individual sections.

Her interest in spoken dramatic texts and dance movement has continued to the present, and her work group performs using both voice and body motion to shape pieces. She continues to work and teach at her studio in New York.

Through the years she has been active in television, on Broadway and Off-Broadway, and in movies. One of her most notable productions was the 1958 Off-Broadway staging of *Ulysses in Nighttown*. She has also created ballets for the now disbanded National Ballet of Washington and the Slavenska-Franklin company.

THE DESPERATE HEART

Choreography by Valerie Bettis. Music by Bernard Segall. Based on a poem by John Malcolm Brinin. First performed at the Humphrey-Weidman Studio Theatre, New York, N.Y., March 24, 1943, by Valerie Bettis.

When the dance was first given, it struck commentators as being of an exceptional quality. John Martin, the dance critic of the New York *Times,* had the custom of drawing up a roll of honor at the end of each season and mentioning those works which he felt were outstanding. *The Desperate Heart* was named in August 1943 to this list. An even greater praise came from Louis Horst, who was Martha Graham's musical director and a father figure to the whole world of modern dance. He called it "the finest solo work in the entire modern dance repertory of this decade and it takes its rightful place alongside the solo masterpiece of a previous decade, Martha Graham's *'Frontier.'*"

As the solo figure dances, she is accompanied alternately by music and by a poem by John Malcolm Brinin. She is costumed in a long dress, and the cloth facing on the torso outlines a huge heart. She is tormented and caught in an emotional vise. Her body turns and twists; she is thwarted by restraints that set her quivering. She runs and suddenly bursts into a leap. She hesitates and seems to find some solace but is driven again. Her search is endless, though she pauses in a crouch, inevitably she rises to circle and search. It is a dilemma that is without final resolution, as she passes out of sight still reaching and searching.

Remarking on the drama in Bettis's work, Edwin Denby noted, "One has not the sense of watching a dancer's dance inventions, she looks like a beautiful young woman who is agitated, like a character in a situation." Bettis continued to impress the theater world with her skill as a performer and choreographer, but in this piece she achieved a level that could scarcely be improved upon.

CHOREOCHRONICLE
OF VALERIE BETTIS

1942

> And the Earth Shall Bear Again

1943

> Daisy Lee
> *The Desperate Heart

1946

> Yerma

1947

> Virginia Sampler
> Status Quo

1948

> As I Lay Dying

1949

> Domino Furioso
> It Is Always Farewell

1952

> A Streetcar Named Desire

1955

> The Golden Round

1956

> Circa '56

1958

> The Past Perfect Hero

1959   1964

 Closed Door   *He Who Runs*
                                        Inventions of Darkness
1960   *Songs and Processions*

 Early Voyagers

JOHN BUTLER

Born in Tennessee, Butler came to New York to study with Martha Graham and subsequently appeared in her company dancing such roles as the Poetic Beloved in *Deaths and Entrances*. He left the Graham company to create his own works and began to design dances for opera, including *The Consul*, as well as Broadway and Off-Broadway shows. He formed his own touring company in 1955 but after a few years abandoned the idea of a permanent group in favor of work with a variety of companies.

Prior to disbanding the group he appeared in the festival at Nervi and also at the Festival of Two Worlds in Spoleto, where he was the dance director in 1958. Among his most notable pieces is *Portrait of Billie*, a dance detailing the life of blues singer Billie Holiday.

Among the opera companies for which he has worked are the Metropolitan Opera and the New York City Opera. He has created dances for American Ballet Theater, Harkness Ballet, Pennsylvania Ballet and has staged works for New York City Ballet and Netherlands Dance Theater. Besides serious concert work he has also staged ice shows and industrial shows for various companies.

CARMINA BURANA

Choreography by John Butler. Music by Carl Orff. Scenery by Paul Sylbert. Costumes by Ruth Morley. First performed at New York City Center, New York, N.Y., September 24, 1959, by Carmen De Lavallade, Veronika Mlakar, Scott Douglas, and Glen Tetley, with singers of the New York City Opera.

Tracking down all of the various productions of *Carmina* would provide enough material for a book all by itself. Butler initially staged it for the New York City Opera Company in the late-1950s. When he was invited to work for the Netherlands Dance Theater in the sixties, he staged it for that company as well. A film was made of the work in a ruined castle in Holland, and Butler mounted it for the Pennsylvania Ballet and for the Alvin Ailey American Dance Theater, when he returned to the United States. It offers many choice roles for both dancers and singers, and scarcely a season passes without its being presented by one or another major company.

The people of the dance are monks and nuns who have ceased to obey the religious discipline of their orders and are following a naturalistic round of life related to the joys and sorrows of a more secular calling. The composer discovered a collection of poems at a Benedictine monastery in Bavaria, written in the thirteenth century by monks and minstrels in a mixture of Latin and German. His musical setting for the poems selected features strongly rhythmical melodies that sweep the action forward irresistibly.

The dance is divided into three broad sections: "Springtime," "In the Tavern," and "Court of Love." It begins with the robed chorus singing "O Fortuna," a poem that reflects on the changing seasons of life and the wheel of fate. One first rides its rising trajectory and then when the crest has past finds the sorrow of the descending arc. The company enters in somber robes and moves with the precision and gravity of a religious ceremony. There are eight couples, and the lead dancers perform a courtly *pas de quatre*, slipping out of their outer clothing to reveal their flesh-colored costumes.

The involvement of the principals with one another surfaces periodically throughout the course of the dance as a subplot to the general sweep of the rest of the company. The dance is full of passion tugging against the strict and demanding rules of the religious life. After the first blush of spring passion the dance develops life further in the raucous life of the tavern, where there is even a song lamenting the fate of a bird being roasted for a meal. The twistings and turnings of a woman, supported by two men, suggest powerfully the rotations of a spit upon which such a bird would be cooked over an open fire.

"The Court of Love" continues the saga of life now touched by some of the bitterness of loss experienced by those subject to the ever-moving wheel of fate as it passes into its descending phase. A particularly telling projection shows a large wheel with a figure tumbling off. At the conclusion the company returns once again clothed in the dark monks' robes that signal the conclusion of the cycle, and the chorus repeats the lament "O Fortuna," which opened the piece.

The sheer energy of the dance reflects the score marvelously. It combines elements of folk dance along with beautifully sustained adagio passages for couples. Always there is a sense of force driving everything and everyone before it as the wind would drive a sailing ship. The couples play out their roles like actors in a vast drama over which they exercise little control. The discipline of the religious habit is thrown away for a while but then reasserts itself with a certain inevitability. The songs linger in the memory as tantalizing reminders of the exuberant fullness of life.

PORTRAIT OF BILLIE

Choreography by John Butler, set to Billie Holiday's songs with a libretto based on Billie Holiday's life. First performed at Jacobs Pillow, Lee, Mass., August 16, 1960, and in New York City at the Ninety-second Street YM-YWHA, May 8, 1961, by Carmen De Lavallade and John Butler.

Selecting documented episodes from the life of blues singer Billie Holiday, John Butler created this intensely moving portrait of the decline and fall of a talented performer. He divided the work into three broad sections: "Young Billie," "Billie's Blues," and finally "The Stuff." The last refers to the grip that drugs had on the singer, which ultimately caused her death. But even in the first appearance of Billie, she has a nervous twitchy movement that is characteristic of drug dependence. Interwoven throughout the dance are the recorded songs of Miss Holiday.

As the slightly kittenish and raspy voice of Miss Holiday is heard singing "Who do you think is coming to town, lovable Henry Brown," the woman steps smartly about. She paces impatiently and is dressed in street clothes reminiscent of the styles popular in the 1940s. She wears a large white flower in her hair. The man approaches her and together they begin to dance, at first with tenderness but then increasing combativeness. The man has the sleeve on one arm rolled up, indicating his own drug dependence. He is obviously intent on taking advantage of her, and the background music provides an ironic comment on her innocence. "What makes me treat you like I do, Gee baby I'm good to you." At the conclusion of their duet he takes the flower from her hair and arrogantly crushes it and throws it to the ground.

Stunned at his betrayal, she rushes to recover it and clutches it tightly to her chest; the singing voice warns, "You ain't gonna bother me no more, no how, love goes just so far." Isolated and lonely, she weaves her way around obviously hurt and in need of some support. She finds it in the use of drugs, which dull the pain of her isolation. As a performer, though, she continues to present herself and her songs to a public which does not have any inkling of her private tragedy, "Oh!, Oh!, Oh!, what a little moonlight can do" the voice insinuates, and then at the conclusion of the song applause is heard and she looks startled by the spotlight that illuminates her, but she recovers her professional poise and continues to act her public role. The private sorrow eats away at her and the drugs take their toll and she finds herself sinking slowly to the stage, and the performer's voice is heard murmuring, "Thank you, thank you very much, ladies and gentlemen," as the life drains from her.

Butler's choreography matches the subject with great sensitivity, and in the work he created a genuine sense of black jazz dance, which few white dancers have been able to do. The selection of songs is also commendable as they present Billie Holiday's own portrait of Billie through her voice and vocal art. It is a vehicle for a great dancer making demands both on sheer energy and also dramatic talent.

CHOREOCHRONICLE
OF JOHN BUTLER

1953

Malocchio
Masque of the Wildman

1954

The Brass World

1955

Davy Crockett
Frontier Ballad
Three Promenades with the Lord

1956

*The Unicorn, the Gorgon, and
    the Manticore*

1957

Seven Faces of Love

1958

Unquiet Graves
Triad
The Letter and the Thee
The Glory Folk

1959

Album Leaves
In the Beginning
The Sybil
*Carmina Burana

1960

Turning Point
Saul and the Witch of Endor
David and Bathsheba
*Portrait of Billie

1961

Ballet Ballads (with Glen Tetley
    and Mavis Ray)
Ballet of the Nativity
Esther
Hypnos
Letter to a Beloved

1962

Alone
Brief Dynasty

1963

The Mark of Cain
Sebastian

1964

Ceremony of Innocence
Ceremonial
Catulli Carmina

1965

Chansons de Bilitis

1966

After Eden
Jephthah's Daughter
Villon

1967

Aphrodite
The Captive Lark
Landscape for Lovers
Touch of Loss
A Season in Hell

1968

Ceremony
The Initiate
Labyrinth

1970

Itinéraire

1971

Hi-Kyo

1972

According to Eve
Moon Full

1973

Amériques
Black Angel
Intégrales
Kill What I Love
Trip

1974

Puppets of Death
Cult of the Night

1975

Medea

n.d.

Encounters
The Minotaur
Nativity and Adoration
The Parliament of Heaven
Herod and the Kings

JACK COLE

As an adolescent, J. Ewing Richter (Cole) of Brunswick, New Jersey, became entranced with the idea of a dancing career. It was the result of seeing a performance by Ted Shawn and Ruth St. Denis. He enrolled at the Denishawn school and toured with the company for several years. When Shawn established his all male company, Cole joined it and subsequently left to perform with Denishawn alumna and alumnus Doris Humphrey and Charles Weidman. His dance interests were wide and he began to work on his own choreography using oriental movement and jazz improvisation in addition to ballet and modern dance. He appeared in supper clubs and danced on Broadway, attracting substantial attention to himself in the *Ziegfeld Follies of 1943*. He was invited to Hollywood by Columbia Pictures and during the mid-1940s created the dance movement for a series of musical films including *Moon over Miami*. His style of dance became the recognized standard for musical films and theater productions for the next twenty years. While at Columbia Pictures he formed a dance company which rehearsed on the studio lot and gave performances in addition to the work that the individual members did in the movies. Cole never stopped working in the live theater and returned to Broadway frequently, choreographing such shows as *A Funny Thing Happened on the Way to the Forum,* and *Man of La Mancha*. His movie credits include *Gentlemen Prefer Blondes* and *Some Like It Hot*.

HINDU SERENADE

Choreography by Jack Cole to songs arranged by Baldwin Bergerson and sung by Ilona Massey and Jaye Martin. Costumes by Jack Cole. First performed at the Ziegfeld Follies of 1942, February 1943, by Jack Cole and three women dancers.

The dance was created, as were so many of Cole's, to the fairly set pattern of time allowed Broadway choreographers in musical shows of the early 1940s. It was an amusing interlude in a panoply of separate sketches, but within the limitations of the form he made a deftly amusing and entertaining dance vignette in his special style of ancient Hindu gesture and contemporary jazz.

The resplendently costumed man is seated at the center of the stage with one leg tucked under him and the other extended and bent at the knee. One hand rests confidently on his thigh and the other droops casually over the knee of the bent leg. Gold necklaces are placed across his chest, a large gold ring decorates one forefinger, and a daub of red paint in the center of his brow designates his caste. Three women in native costume stand behind him with one hand bent back and the other held up to the side of the head shielding the face. The air is heavy with pseudo-contemplation and repose.

Suddenly the man rises and begins an exhausting, sinuous, and frantic dervish dance that has him alternately lost in ritual postures and whipping his supple body like a possessed jazz dancer. The three women are a decorative frieze for his energetic and engaging dancing. At one point they sink to the stage tilting their bodies to one side and extending their legs outward. He pauses in his frenzy to give one of them a kick, dispelling the meditative calm of their formation. The piece ends with a decorative frenzy combining high voltage energy and the ritual hand gestures of traditional Hindu dance.

Cole made his discovery of combining Hindu dance gesture with thirties jazz and swing music when teaching at Adelphi University. He had finished a traditional class in oriental dance and put on a recording of swing to relax for a moment. He started doing the hand gestures to the novel music and subsequently built a career with the discovery. He created concert dances as well but the Hindu modern idiom remains his special distinction.

CHOREOCHRONICLE
OF JACK COLE

1934

Dance for a Pack of Hungry
    Cannibals
Appassionetta (with Alice
    Dudley)
Blue Prelude
Minnie the Moocher

1938

Oriental Impressions

1941

Polynesian Fawn

East Indian Classic to Jazz
    Tempo
Ethnic Dance Theme and
    Variations
Latin American Dances

1942

Something for the Boys (mc)
Moon over Miami (mp)
Keep 'Em Laughing (mc)

1943

Ziegfeld Follies of 1942 (revue)
*Hindu Serenade

1946

Cover Girl (mp)
Down to Earth (mp)
Gilda (mp)

1947

East Indian Dance
"Jitterbug Ritual"

1948

Magdalena (mc)

1950

Alive and Kicking (mc)
The Odyssey of Harlequin

1953

Carnival in Flanders (mc)

1954

Gentlemen Marry Brunettes
(mp)

1955

Kismet (mp)
Three for the Show (mc)

1957

Les Girls (mp)

1958

Some Like It Hot (mp)

1961

Donnybrook (mc)
Let's Make Love (mp)

1963

A Funny Thing Happened on the
Way to the Forum (mc)

1965

Man of La Mancha (mc)

1968

Bomarzo (opera)

RUTH CURRIER

The most important creative influence in Currier's career was that exercised by the late Doris Humphrey. Currier was her assistant starting in 1952 and for eight years until Humphrey's death in 1958, after which she completed *Brandenburg Concerto Number 4,* a work that Humphrey had begun but left unfinished.

Currier had previously been a member of the José Limón company, dancing many featured roles. She began her own choreographic career in

1955. She has added steadily to her body of works, in which *The Antagonists* reveals her creative exploration of a small dramatic incident. She has taught at the Juilliard School, Bennington College, and Sarah Lawrence and currently is the artistic director of the José Limón company, a post she assumed after Limón's death.

THE ANTAGONISTS

Choreography by Ruth Currier. Music by Igor Stravinsky. Costumes by Lavina Nielsen. First performed at the Palmer Auditorium, Connecticut College, New London, Conn., August 20, 1955, by Ruth Currier and Betty Jones.

One of the favorite confrontations in dance is between two people who find themselves in close proximity but are of differing temperaments in their approach to the encounter. In this work two women find themselves on opposite sides of a fence.

Three lengths of fence and fence post define a triangular enclosure within which a woman sits in a long dress. The other woman runs on, agitatedly darting her arms stiffly across the front of her body. The woman in the enclosure sits disinterestedly and stares ahead while the woman outside continues her leaps and outstretching arm gestures. She finally ceases and lies down. The seated woman shows a little activity, flopping her tightly pressed knees side to side then standing to curl an arm around her head.

She steps from one rail to another then straddles the fence to swing one leg in idle arcs. She stands on one of the posts but always keeps carefully inside the enclosure. The woman on the outside watches everything intently and now jogs from side to side in an inviting gesture that has a touch of impatient frenzy to it. She makes imploring gestures but the other woman remains cautiously inside.

The woman outside prowls its perimeter and with a quick dart destroys the refuge by opening the fence into a straight line. The woman inside is startled but continues to cling to the protective fence even though it no longer encircles her. When she does try her "freedom," she is still timid and then antagonistic to the outside woman. Their duet is harshly combative. Each tries to mount the other and weight her down. They push away from one another, try to reconcile differences, but the timid woman returns to the protective fence.

In its short duration the piece develops the mutually mistrustful feelings of the two women and throws them sharply to the fore. What looks like a liberating gesture to the one outside seems dangerously hostile to the one inside. It is a mismatch that will never be resolved and one feels their frustration.

CHOREOCHRONICLE
OF RUTH CURRIER

1955

*The Antagonists
Idyl

1956

Becoming
Resurgence
Triplicity

1958

To Lean, to Spring, to Reach,
   to Fly
Dangerous World

1959

Brandenburg Concerto No. 4
   (with Doris Humphrey)

1960

Transfigured Season
Toccanta

1961

Places
Quartet
Resonances
A Tender Portrait

1963

Diva Divested

1965

To wish . . . together . . .
   fearsomely

1966

Triangle of Strangers
Night Before Tomorrow

1967

Fantasies and Façades
Arena

1975

Phantasmagoria

DUDLEY—MASLOW—BALES DANCE TRIO

The members of this highly trained and highly acclaimed company came together quite by accident. Jane Dudley, Sophie Maslow, and William Bales each independently created a piece for a program sponsored by *Dance Observer* in 1942. They decided to join forces and danced together for the next dozen years until Dudley was forced to retire from active performing due to an arthritic hip. Besides creating an excellent small company the three represented as many diverse strains of the modern dance world and expressed the freer and more tolerant attitude that began to develop after the 1930s.

Bales had been a featured member of the Humphrey-Weidman company, Maslow had trained with Martha Graham, and Dudley had studied with Hanya Holm and subsequently became a member of the Graham company. Ignoring the unwritten law against the study of ballet, all of the members of the trio took ballet class for the advantages that it gave them. In their creative work they expressed a lively appreciation of theatrical values and toured very successfully for many years.

The three were not afraid to include humorous pieces in repertory and rejected the somewhat somber face that modern dance presented to the world in the 1930s. One of their curtain-raiser dances was *As Poor Richard Says*, which illustrated wittily a selection of Benjamin Franklin's aphorisms. As a group, they were sympathetic to Americana, and Maslow created one of her finest pieces, *Folksay*, mining this vein. Dudley took some drawings from the pen of the ironic cartoonist William Steig and made *The Lonely Ones*. In quite another mood Bales created the study of a sailor and his on-shore relations with various women in *Es Mujer*. The trio had variety, life, and three excellent performers.

All of them had had summer residencies at Bennington when they were members of other companies and all had taught successfully there and elsewhere, including a substantial commitment to the New Dance Group, which was formed in 1932. Maslow continues her teaching with this school to the present day. Jane Dudley has lived in England for the past several years and is a member of the staff of The Place, the first modern dance school established in England. Bales organized the dance division of the performing arts college established at Purchase, New York, as part of the state university system. Though the trio has passed into performing history, the members continue to exert an influence on a new generation.

THE LONELY ONES

Choreography by Jane Dudley. Music by Zoe Williams (sound effects). Costumes by Charlotte Trowbridge. Based on cartoons by William Steig. First performed at Cornell University, Ithaca, N.Y., June 1, 1946, by Jane Dudley, Sophie Maslow, and William Bales.

The collection of noise and music that accompanies this dance was one of the little innovative touches that the choreographers of the dance trio brought to popular attention. The costuming was as broad as the cartoon characterizations themselves and presented the characters in larger-than-life-sized terms.

The dance develops as three independent but related solos. The Woman's solo is "Revenge Is Sweet," the Man's is "I Have Recreated Myself," and the Other Woman's is "Convention Be Damned." Each of the characters is drawn from the conventional amorous triangle.

In a proper green bustle the Woman is full of prim and grim resolution to have her revenge on her muscle-bound husband. He has transformed himself into a caricature of muscular development, narcissistically wrapped in his own posturing. He is slightly dull mentally and is left exhausted by the simple task of slipping out of his own jacket. The Woman clings to him with the tenacity of a barnacle to the side of a ship.

The Other Woman is a dynamo of unfocused energy. She is liberated in spirit and wears a wide grin as she launches herself into the other lives. She casually shines a shoe with the hem of the Woman's dress. She kicks the Man's chair and for good measure wraps her knees around his neck. She has a giant rose pinned to her thigh and is in general quite outrageous. The three play out their foreordained roles hilariously and sadly locked within an orbit that none can escape.

The characters are truely lonely and in achieving their heart's desire have only come to realize that it too is a prison. The "liberated" Other Woman is nothing more than a petulant child who has eluded adult maturation. The Man has made himself into a grotesque through his body-building and the Woman, who has her man, finds that she hasn't achieved the stability that she thought she would by the accomplishment. The humor is relentless and sugar-coats a basically sad situation.

CHOREOCHRONICLE
OF JANE DUDLEY

1934

In the Life of a Worker
Time Is Money
The Dream Ends
Death of Tradition (with Sophie
    Maslow and Anna Sokolow)

1935

Middle Class Portraits

1936

Songs of Protest

1937

Under the Swastika
Fantasy
Satiric Suite (with Sophie
    Maslow, William Matons, and
    Anna Sokolow)
My Body, My Carcass

1938

Jazz Lyric
Women of Spain
Nursery Rhymes for Grownups

1939

Ballad of Molly Pitcher
The Betrayed

1940

Harmonica Breakdown

Adolescence
Short Story

1941

Pavane
Skatter-brain
Dissonance
Gymnopédie (with Sophie
    Maslow)
The Kiss of Judas

1942

Bach Suite (with Sophie Maslow
    and William Bales)
Caprichos (from *Women of
    Spain,* with Sophie Maslow)

1943

"As Poor Richard Says . . ."
    (with Sophie Maslow and
    William Bales)

1944

Spanish Suite (with Sophie
    Maslow)
Swing Your Lady

1945

New World A Comin'
Furlough: A Boardwalk Episode
    (with William Bales)

1946

*The Lonely Ones
  Ballads for Dancers

1949

  Vagary
  Out of the Cradle Endlessly
    Rocking

1950

Passional

1953

Family Portrait

FOLKSAY

Choreography by Sophie Maslow. Set to American ballads sung and spoken by Woody Guthrie. Text by Carl Sandburg (The People, Yes), spoken by Earl Robinson. First performed at the Humphrey-Weidman Studio, New York, N.Y., March 10, 1942, by Sophie Maslow, Hilda Hoppe, Anne Marcus, Minna Morrison, Sylvia Shand, Anne Wiener, Lou Rosen, Pearl Lang, Marjorie Mazia, David Campbell, Mark Ryder, and David Zellmer.

Among the most popular dances that the trio (augmented for this piece) ever performed was this combination of mime, music, and movement. It was created as a series of eight incidents, and the musicians were onstage with the performers talking and singing and playing their guitars. The words that they spoke were those of humorous, casual banter, but those that were recited were all taken from Carl Sandburg's *The People, Yes,* and they were sung and spoken by Woody Guthrie and Earl Robinson, two of the country's leading balladeers.

The dances are designed to reflect the folk rhythms of rural America and the concerns expressed in each of the songs, beginning with the curious inquiry "Where Are You from, Stranger?" At times the chief movement is mime and at others rollicking leaps and runs. It has a zestful humor and also a reflective side as expressed by the duet detailing the unhappiness caused by "courtin' too slow" from "On Top of Old Smokey."

"Sweet Betsy from Pike" shows the other side of courting, the energetic, bursting-with-life side. Maternal concern is tenderly depicted in the duet designed around "Hey, You, Sun Moon and Stars," in which Maslow counseled her "daughter" on the ways of the world. Her "daughter" being danced by Majorie Mazia, who was Guthrie's wife. The dance ends with an affirmative finale in silence as each of the dancers crosses over the stage and disappears to be followed by the balladeers.

The piece was a perfect expression of the pride, energy, and spunkiness that followed the ending of the Depression of the 1930s. The people had survived; the country had survived most difficult times and wanted to celebrate the fact. There were dozens of such dances created at around the same time, but none had the advantages of the talented collaborators who made this one. It had a strongly constructed core onto which was grafted barn dance movement, and it was able to rouse audiences to stamping, clapping, and cheering over three decades after it was first presented.

CHOREOCHRONICLE
OF SOPHIE MASLOW

1934

> *Themes from a Slavic People*
> *Two Songs About Lenin*
> *Death of Tradition* (with Jane Dudley and Anna Sokolow)

1936

> *May Day March*

1937

> *Satiric Suite* (with Jane Dudley, William Matons, Anna Sokolow)

1938

> *Runaway Rag*
> *Women of Spain* (with Jane Dudley)

1939

> *Silicosis Blues*

1941

> *Sarabande*
> *Gigue*
> *Bourée*
> *Exhortation*

> *Melancholia*
> *Americana*
> *Gymnopédie* (with Jane Dudley)
> *Dust Bowl Ballads*

1942

> *Bach Suite* (with Jane Dudley and William Bales)
> **Folksay*
> *Caprichos* (from *Women of Spain* with Jane Dudley)

1943

> *"As Poor Richard Says . . ."* (with Jane Dudley, William Bales)

1944

> *Llanto*
> *Spanish Suite* (with Jane Dudley)

1948

> *Champion*

1950

> *The Village I Knew*

1951

Four Sonnets

1952

Snow Queen

1953

Suite: Manhattan Transfer
Israel in Dance and Song

1954

Celebration

1955

The Gentleman from Cracow

1956

Anniversary

1958

Raincheck

1963

Poem

1964

The Dybbuk
From the Book of Ruth

1965

In the Beginning
Dance of the Sabras

1966

Collage '66
Invocation of David

1969

Ladino Suite

1971

Country Music

1973

Touch the Earth

n.d.

Three Sonnets
Neither Rest nor Harbor
Prologue
Diamond Rocks

ES MUJER

Choreography by William Bales to traditional music. First performed at the Humphrey-Weidman Studio, New York, N.Y., March 10, 1942, by William Bales as the Man and Teru Osato as the Child, with Muriel Brenner, Carol Kobin, Reba Koren, Joan Lesser, Hortense Lieberthal, Rosabel Robbins, and Patricia Schaeffer. A preliminary version of the piece was first given in the summer of 1940 at the Bennington College Summer School of the Dance.

In the relatively small body of work which he turned out, Bales's meditation of the life of a sailor and his relations with the women he encounters and the women he left behind ranks near the top. As a performer, he had great force and mimetic talent, both of which elements are used in this work.

The sailor stands alone removed from the various women in his life, who are at first just as insubstantial as memories. They stand and stare away and only come to life with his appearance. He returns to his mother and two sisters in "Three Who Love Him," and there is no hint of his rough calling and way of life. He is obedient and deferential to his mother as he had always been, and to the younger sisters he is protective as an older brother should be.

The tone changes as he encounters a couple of other girls in "Two Who Have Known Him." He peels off his jacket and has a tough swagger as he approaches them for a lustful tussle. It is a far cry from his benign feelings for his family. When he leaves them he dances a duet with the girl whom he loves in "One Who Is in Love with Him." The feeling of romantic tenderness replaces the erotic tumbling of the dance with the prostitutes. And then he leaves them all to return to his calling, the sea. They again group themselves to stare off at empty horizons until he returns.

The dance centers around one man and the various faces that he presents to the women in his life. Each of them sees only one part of him, and so even when he is with them a good part of him remains hidden, almost as much as when he is completely removed at sea. Everyone plays various roles with others and in this dance we see three of them clearly delineated, although there could be many more, as the sailor passes from port to port. He is like everyone in their daily encounters, but his profession dramatizes the process.

CHOREOCHRONICLE
OF WILLIAM BALES

1941

Il Combattimento (with Nona Schurman)

1942

Bach Suite (with Jane Dudley and Sophe Maslow)
*Es Mujer
Peon Portraits: Adios

1943

To a Green Mountain Boy
"As Poor Richard Says . . ." (with Jane Dudley and Sophie Maslow)
Peon Portraits: Field Hand

1945

Sea Bourne
Furlough: A Boardwalk Episode
   (with Jane Dudley)
Three Dances in Romantic Style
A Winter's Tale (p)

1947

Soliloquy

1949

Judith
Rip Van Winkle (p)

1950

Impromptu

1951

The Haunted Ones

JEFF DUNCAN

Originally Duncan studied to be a pianist, but soon his interests turned to other aspects of the theater and he studied both drama and dance. He took class with Hanya Holm in her summer school of the dance and when he came to New York he studied with her former pupil Alwin Nikolais. He performed with Nikolais's company as well as the New Dance Group, in addition to devising his own creative works.

After a period in which he shared concerts with other choreographers and had danced in several of Anna Sokolow's works, he decided that he needed a permanent home and studio in which he could appear regularly and also teach. He gathered together several like-minded fellow dancers and choreographers and founded Dance Theater Workshop, which continues to function as a studio school and performing space. It has enabled many choreographers to have a number of performances of their works because of the repeat-performance policy which governs its series presentations. This is a great improvement over the single appearance that is usually the fate of the young or even established choreographer who does not want to have the burden of his or her own company.

WINESBURG PORTRAITS

Choreography by Jeff Duncan to traditional American music. Libretto by Sherwood Anderson. First performed at the Fashion Institute of Technology, New York, N.Y., January 12, 1963, by Don Redlich as Reverend Curtis Hartman, *Carol Wallace as* Mrs. Willard, *Jeff Duncan as* George Willard, *Kate Friedlich as* Alice Hindman, *and Jon Lightfoot as* Elmer Cowley.

Sherwood Anderson's memories of the small town in Ohio where he grew up were the basis for his book *Winesburg, Ohio,* and the dance is based on episodes from it.

The element that relates all of the specific characters is the storyteller himself, whom we encounter in the first section, "Anticipation." He is crouched and has his chin resting on his hand. He is thinking and then stretches. The sound of Bluegrass fiddling finds him dashing around, kicking his heels, full of energetic good spirits. He pauses, crouches again, and then sweeps around the stage before leaving, and his place is taken by the various characters in the dance.

"Mother" is danced by a woman who is first seen rocking in a chair and the music of an old song is heard. She stops and reaches over the back of the chair as if plunging her arm back into time. She becomes young again in memory and circles around as if she were at a ball where she greets friends. The sound of a waltz sends her into a happy twirl, and she touches the chair warmly and embraces the small footstool that stands with it. The weight of years asserts itself and she drags the chair around. Cradling the stool like a baby, she rocks slowly once more in the present.

The storyteller approaches a girl in a nightdress and presses her hands to his face. It is an emotional pledge but she flees from him. Together, however, they begin their duet with a formal walk in which they go arm in arm. As the dance progresses it becomes sensuously warmer and more passionate until they embrace without hesitation.

"Queer," in the sense of being mentally slow, describes the awkward young man with square-set shoulders and a mop of hair, whose features have a heavy look to them. He turns right and left with stiff jerks of his torso as a voice sings a mournful song. The man's body twitches increasingly until he shoots his arm up and lurches forward. He resumes the rigid torso turns and tries for a graceful pose but ends in an inept approximation of an arabesque. He kneels and shuffles and then stands to shield his face. He turns slowly and again lurches forward, twisting his slab-like torso to the right and left. He is a prisoner of a limited understanding and he strikes out, shadow-boxing against the cloud that makes him different from the others. He collapses, then rises to lumber off clumsily as the song ends.

A lonely woman lies in her half of a double bed and a song about husbands going to a tavern to talk to strange girls begins. She touches the empty spot in the bed, rises to sit on the edge, and rocks slightly. She folds and unfolds her hands in a worried fashion. The sound of Bluegrass music turns her into a flirtatious young girl again as she begins a square dance, but when the music stops she is deposited into the lonely and older present. She rolls the bedclothes to simulate her missing mate, wanders about, and then sits and broods.

A man of the gospel now dances his sermon for the parishioners. He walks with his arms held behind his back thoughtfully. Clasping a lectern, he rests his head on it momentarily and then mimes a sermon wiggling his fingers and striking his palm with his fist. The mood catches him and he drops to his knees. He rolls over and arches his body up, then launches into a large circle of ecstatic jumps. Finally the religious din brings him back to the stern and proper present of a church meeting. The lectern is laid on its side and he stretches out beside it, caressing it as if it were his beloved. He exits carrying it on his back like a cross.

In the final section the storyteller sits by the woman in the rocking chair and the restless Bluegrass music alternates with the old song. He wants to go and she falls as he stands up. After they embrace he pushes her away. She returns as if dazed and then lies on her side. He piles the stool and the chair near her and then walks in a measured manner away from her. It is the closing of one chapter in his life and the sound of the Bluegrass music opens up another one. He starts to kick his heels and tap his feet and leaps off.

The structure of *Winesburg Portraits* follows the episodic structure of the original book in that it presents vignettes of life in a small town. It is a life which has a settled order but which produces a chafing in a restless spirit. That restlessness is symbolized by the Bluegrass music that beckons to the hero. The town represents the past and it is what he must escape from. The story is familiar but beautifully told in motion and in music.

CHOREOCHRONICLE
OF JEFF DUNCAN

1954

Image

1957

Antique Epigrams
Three Fictitious Games

1958

Frames

1959

Terrestrial Figure

1960

Opus I, No. I
Outdoors Suite

1961

Il Combattimento

1962

Rite of Source
Quartet

1963

Duet
Trio
*Winesburg Portraits

1964

Revelation
Six Bagatelles
Diversions for Five

1965

Glimpse
Summer Trio

1966

Canticles
Statement
Studies for an Ominous Age
Preludes
Diminishing Landscape

1967

Three Studies
View – Part I

1969

Royal Hunt of the Sun (p)
Body Parts
Vinculum
Les Sirènes
Resonances

1970

The Glade

1971

> *Douprelude*
> *Lenten Suite*
> *Space Test*

1973

> *Canticles No. 2 for Three*
> *View* (entire piece)
> *Cantique de Cantique*

1972

> *Shore Song*

1974

> *Pieces in May*
> *Phases of the Oracle*

KATHERINE DUNHAM

In addition to her work in the theater Dunham found time to acquire a doctorate in anthropology. She was born in Chicago and attended the University of Chicago. During part of the thirties she was associated with the Chicago dance program of the Federal Theater program set up by the Works Project Administration, and came to popular attention with her work on Broadway and in the movies.

She appeared in and choreographed a series of musicals, the most famous being *Cabin in the Sky*. As a performer, she was vividly flamboyant with great reserves of energy ready to burst out at any moment. She organized her own concert group and toured in the United States and abroad. She was the subject of a book by Richard Buckle, the English critic, and Roger Wood, the photographer, and has written an autobiography of the early part of her life.

Between appearances onstage she studied dance forms in several of the Caribbean islands and lived in Haiti for several years. She has regularly published articles about her researches and has collected honors and recognition for her anthropological work from the Scientific Fraternity of the University of Chicago and the Royal Society of Anthropologists in London. She has worked for the past several years in St. Louis directing a center for the development of black studies and culture.

RITES DE PASSAGE

Choreography by Katherine Dunham. Music by Paquita Anderson (percussion by Gaucho). Costumes by John Pratt. Lighting by Dale Wasserman. First performed at the Biltmore Theatre, Los Angeles, Calif., October 30, 1941, by Lavinia Williams as the Maiden in the Community, *Laverne French as the* Man in the Community, *Talley Beatty as the* Boy Initiate, *Roger Ohardieno as the* Warrior, *and Katherine Dunham as the* Matriarch.

Dunham was asked to deliver a lecture at Yale University and decided that it would be most effective if it had some practical illustration. She prepared the lecture, which was titled "An Anthropological Approach to Theater," and the dance which demonstrated it was later incorporated, without the lecture, into her regular repertory.

A young man sits in the center of the stage with his feet spread and knees drawn halfway up. His arms are extended to the side as he arches his body yearningly upward. He relaxes again into a sitting position and bows his head forward.

He lies back and a man enters wearing a mask. He is the chief warrior of the community and an envied figure to the young man on the brink of adulthood. The warrior looks at the reclining youth, who rises and goes to meet him. They clasp one another's arms and balance their weight against one another as they sink slowly toward the ground. Three other men with short masks enter and see the pair. They leap, dramatically thrusting their arms outward to welcome the young man into the tribe of men. They stomp around him and hoist him aloft and bear him off. His fists are powerfully clenched.

In the second scene we are in the midst of a village and its life, women make pounding motions as if grinding grain, men are seen engaged in games. A marriageable young woman stands at the back of the stage where she is seen by an interested young man. He approaches her. She drops to her knees, arcing her arms above her head. She rises and he places his arms around her as if to place her in a frame, but he does not touch her.

They grow more ardent and clasp each other's shoulders and begin their love duet. At its conclusion they turn away but return to one another. Their dance, which has been observed by the men and women of the village, has reached its logical conclusion, and the villagers join to celebrate their union. The finale throbs with energetic life with the women leaping and stretching one leg to the side and the men sliding to the floor at one point to thrust one leg high in the air. The union of the couple is confirmed.

The piece does not confine itself strictly to the characteristic steps of traditional African dance but blends them with Western movement as well. As

Dunham announced in the title of her talk, it was an anthropological "approach" to theater and not a strict reconstruction. Given the effectiveness of the piece on stage, it would be pedantic to pick at the decision to reject step-for-step authenticity. It artfully draws on African forms and shapes them for performance, and presents us with significant episodes in the development of a man and a woman at crisis points in their lives.

CHOROS*

Choreography by Katherine Dunham. Music by Vadico Gagliano. Costumes by John Pratt. Lighting by Dale Wasserman. First traceable performance Portland, Ore., 1943, by Katherine Dunham, Syvilla Fort, Claude Marchant, and Tommy Gomez.

As a direct development of her interest in the Caribbean area, this small-scaled but vivacious dance for two couples and solo woman based on original folk materials was created by Dunham. She ascribes the origins of the dance to a trip she took to northern Brazil, in which the music of Vadico Gagliano and the nineteenth-century architecture impelled her to think of the quadrille as the basis for her dance. The revised version is described below.

The music has a Latin lilt and bounce. A man and a woman enter and step slowly and in a restrained manner toward one another and then make an accelerated run together. They whirl and skip in a small circle as another couple dips and moves to one another. They join in a line with hands around each other's waist and then separate. The men move behind the women, who hop on one foot, while the men turn with one arm stretched over their heads. The women clap as the men come to the front, and they in turn clap as the women whirl. The couples join embracing as in a ballroom dance, and then the women return to the center to do tiny kicks, and the men circle their arms around the women's waists to conclude the section.

The pace is slower as the second section begins, and the men support the women's turns then do small scissor crossing of their legs. The whole has a softly emphasized allure as the men wiggle their hips. The girls reflect the erotic jiggle later and then they all halt. The solo woman enters and the two men each support her in a turn by taking one of her hands. They return to their partners, who leap from side to side, and then the men go to the solo woman again. Together the three prance from one side to the other. The pacing of the piece is absolutely relentless, and the men perform a small circle of leaps around the solo woman.

The final movement has the group clapping hands over their heads as

* Choro: A nineteenth-century Brazilian quadrille.

they leap straddling their feet to the side. All form a circle, and then with the solo woman in the center the others make a square around her. They move in tiny circles as she energetically wiggles her shoulders and hips. All suddenly stop and shout, *"Choros."*

The slow entrance of the first pair of dancers does not prepare one for the nonstop drive of the dance to follow. It is a cleverly designed set of variations of the quadrille that quivers with infectious movement. There is no message other than the sheer joy of living and being able to move so securely and joyfully. None is needed!

CHOREOCHRONICLE
OF KATHERINE DUNHAM

1940

Tropics
Le Jazz Hot
Pins and Needles (revue)
Bre'er Rabbit an' de Tah Baby
Plantation Dances

1941

Star Spangled Rhythm (mp)
Stormy Weather (mp)
Carnival of Rhythm (mp)
*Rites de passage

1942

Rara Tonga

1943

Tropical Revue
Bahiana
*Choros
Island Songs
Mexican Rumba
Peruvienne
Rumba, Santiago de Chile
Tableaux of Spanish Earth

Ti' cocomacaque
Woman with a Cigar
Florida Swamp Shimmy
Callata
Plantation Dances

1944

L'Ag'Ya
Flaming Youth 1927
Havana Promenade

1945

Carib Song (mp)
Shango

1947

La Comparsa
Bal Nègre

1948

The Octoroon Ball
Casbah (mp)

1950

Brazilian Suite

JEAN ERDMAN

Erdman found a rich dance source in James Joyce's *Finnegans Wake,* creating a dramatic movement work, *The Coach with the Six Insides,* which was given critical acclaim and several awards. Her company toured extensively with the work, and it was also adapted for several television presentations.

Erdman was born in Hawaii and attended Sarah Lawrence College near New York. She studied with Martha Graham at the Bennington College Summer School of the Dance and also studied at the School of American Ballet. She was taken into the Graham company and danced many notable roles, including One Who Speaks from *Letter to the World,* in which she also recited the verse of Emily Dickinson. The part originally taken by an actress has been performed by Erdman since shortly after its premiere in 1941 and as recently as 1970.

Early in her career she was co-choreographer of several pieces with Merce Cunningham, who was also a member of the Graham company at the time. Erdman has created dance movement for several plays on Broadway and Off-Broadway and served as the head of the dance program of New York University's School of the Arts. She is currently the director of The Open Eye, a multimedia group that brings dance, drama, and music together as equal partners in theater pieces.

THE COACH WITH THE SIX INSIDES

Choreography by Jean Erdman. Music by Teiji Ito. Libretto by Jean Erdman, adapted from James Joyce's Finnegans Wake. *Scenery and costumes by Robert DeMora. First performed at the Village South Theater, New York, N.Y., November 26, 1962, by Jean Erdman, Anita Dangler, Sheila Roy, Leonard Frye, and Van Dexter.*

Erdman had the only speaking role in Martha Graham's great dance about the poet Emily Dickinson, *Letter to the World.* She was the One Who Speaks and recited lines of verse that accompanied the choreographed episodes of the work. The experience had a profound effect on her and she has throughout the remainder of her career explored the theater of words and dance. In this piece she won popular acclaim for her achievement in evoking the dream world of James Joyce's *Finnegans Wake.*

There are five persons and the central one is Anna Livia Plurabelle, who is the dancer. The four others are actors who assume two roles each and speak all of the lines, and the episodes reflect aspects of the book though none is drawn directly from it. As the crone, the dancer eloquently sums up the whole of the first section. At another moment she is the keening Irishwoman bemoaning the sorrows of her life and her race's difficulties. At another moment she is Belinda the hen, who scratches and reveals a letter that no one can read and she transforms herself into a dancing rain. The actors move in stylized fashion reciting words and making sounds, all of which have been drawn from the book itself. It is a world full of puns and reality dimly perceived and barely grasped and concludes with a long, rambling monologue reflecting a peasant acceptance of existence and experience.

Erdman made one basic change in Joyce's book by establishing the multifaceted woman Anna Livia Plurabelle as the central character. For Joyce it was the man HCE, Humphrey Chimpden Earwicker, whose unconscious night thoughts were the subject of the novel, which ranged back and forth through history with scant regard for any logic other than the associative one of the unconscious. It is the story of one woman and all women in myriads of roles.

CHOREOCHRONICLE
OF JEAN ERDMAN

1941

Departure
Rigaudon
Baby Ben Says Dada

1942

The Transformation of Medusa
Forever and Sunsmell
Credo in Us (with Merce
    Cunningham)
Ad Lib (with Merce
    Cunningham)
Seeds of Brightness (with Merce
    Cunningham)

1945

Dawn Song
Creature on a Journey
Daughters of the Lonesome Isle
Ophelia

1946

Passage
People and Ghosts
Changing Moment

1947

Les Mouches (p)

1948

Four-Four Time
The Perilous Chapel
Sea Deep: A Dreamy Dream
Jazz Maze
Hamadryad
The Enchanted (p)
Dawn Song

1949

Festival

1951

The Fair Eccentric

1952

Changingwoman
Sailor in the Louvre

1953

Song of the Turning World
Broken City
The Burning Thirst

1954

Upon Enchanted Ground
Otherman—Or the Beginning of
a New Nation
Salutare
The Weather of the Heart
Strange Hunt
Pierrot, The Moon

1956

Duet for Flute and Dancer

1957

Harlequinade
Fearful Symmetry

1958

Four Portraits from Duke
Ellington's Shakespeare Album

1959

Bagatelle
Elegy
The Road of No Return
Salutatio
Io and Prometheus
Now and Zen—Remembering
Solos and Chorale
The Gates of Arallu

1960

Twenty Poems by e. e. cummings

1961

The Solstice
Dance in 5/8 Time

1962

*The Coach with the Six Insides

1964

Yerma (p)
Hamlet (p)

1965

The Partridge in the Junglegym

1967

The Marriage on the Eiffel
Tower (p)

1968

The Municipal Water System Is
Not Trustworthy

1969

Ensembles
Voracious (with Luciano Berio)
Safari
Vulnerable as an Island Is
    Paradise

1970

The Castle (with Jimmy Giuffre)
Twilight Wind

1971

Two Gentlemen of Verona (mc)

1972

Moon Mysteries (three plays by
    Yeats)
Marathon

1974

The Silken Tent
Rapid Transits

GEORGE FAISON

The first theatrical recognition that Faison received was an award in high school for his work with school productions. He grew up in Washington, D.C., and when he graduated from high school began to study dentistry. He also spent a great deal of time with the work of the theater department, and this led him to serious dance studies. He went to New York, where he was a scholarship student at the Harkness School, and he also studied with Elizabeth Hodes. His modern dance classes were taught by Thelma Hill, James Truitte, Louis Johnson, and Dudley Williams.

He joined the Alvin Ailey American Dance Theater and danced with the company for three years. Recognizing his interest in costume design, Ailey had him redesign *Blues Suite*. After leaving the Ailey company he founded his own group, the George Faison Universal Dance Experience, for which he also designs all the costumes as well as choreographing the dances. He has appeared on television and Broadway and has drawn on all of his dance experiences to create his pieces. In addition to creating smaller-scaled works he has also prepared several full evening dances. His company made its debut in the spring of 1971, dancing *Poppy*, his stern kinetic lecture against the perils of drugs. He choreographed the award winning musical *The Wiz*.

POPPY

Choreography by George Faison. Music by Miles Davis, Sister Stone, Béla Bartók, Dionne Warwick, Lee Michaels, Isaac Hayes, Giuseppi Verdi, Gyorgy Ligeti, Melba Moore, Black Sabbath, and Brute Force. Costumes by George Faison. Lighting by Johnny Dodd. First performed at the Riverside Church, New York, N.Y., April 4, 1971, by George Faison, Loretta Abbott, Harvey Cohen, Eugene Little, Jason Taylor, Al Perryman, Lettie Battle, Peter Colly, Renee Rose, and Sandy McPherson.

This dance collage is a collection of vignettes all designed to discourage people from using drugs through dramatic incidents drawn from life. Through the whole piece there wanders a figure called Poppy, who represents the drug menace and interacts with the other dancers.

Poppy's costume is black and has a spider web traced on it. He stands in the center of a group of boys and girls whom he pushes away. He does a solo that portrays his grasping evil nature. The kids stand with hands at their sides and palms turned forward, they smoke and become dreamy and removed and wave good-by to the audience. They don't even seem much involved with one another.

Now they cluster afresh but with a twitchy, itchy way of moving. Poppy returns, content to see that they are "hooked" on his brand of poison. The young men do a finger-snapping jazz dance by themselves but then are joined by the young women, and all just stumble around in a large crowd. They fall, laugh, and get up again. Poppy is content.

A young girl dances and is jeered at by her friends, who strike at her. She is not like the others and does a balletically based solo. Poppy stalks her and finally sinks his teeth into her arm like a vampire. She becomes his victim as well. Suddenly a figure in a long robe with white beard and hair enters to sing Verdi's *"Pace, pace, mio Dio!"* He is the just, pious figure and Poppy flees but returns in a moment with some of the trapped kids and wins his fight against this religious man by showing how irresistible he is.

In a surrealistic scene the company portrays insemination beneath large plastic sheet costumes. One couple bursts out of the plastic sheeting and the others go off to return in carnival-bright clothes for an orgy. One woman becomes the leader of the revels and grinds her pelvis provocatively. All tumble into a restless pile and then roll off.

Poppy exults once more over the victims. The lighting presents him in silhouette very effectively. The men and women now strip out of their gaudy clothes to stand with their plain leotards. "The thrill is gone" accurately reflects their mood in music. Poppy now crawls menacingly and invitingly forward to entice the audience into trying his wares. He smiles and continues to plead and invite participation.

The group at the rear of the stage trembles, then pleads, and is swept by a whirlwind of pain and anguish. Poppy laughs. The men and women are in the throes of withdrawal from drugs. Shots are heard. He points at them and laughs.

The piece is frankly melodramatic but in performance is effective in its portrayal of the evils of narcotics addiction. Faison is not hesitant about putting any element into a dance, such as the singing religious figure, if it will advance the story that he wishes to tell. The effect may be untidy but these interpolations contribute to the spinning of the yarn. There is a certain naïveté involved, but the directness of the expression is winning.

CHOREOCHRONICLE
OF GEORGE FAISON

1971

The Gazelle
Slaves
*Poppy

1972

Don't Bother Me, I Can't Cope
  (mc)
The Coloureds
Black Angels
Ti-Jean and His Brothers (p)
We Regret to Inform You

1974

In the Sweet Now and Now
Suite Otis
Reflections of a Lady
Yesterday, Today, and Tomorrow
  (Eartha Kitt revue)
Boedromion

1975

The Wiz (mc)

LOUIS FALCO

Remarkably skilled as a performer, Falco made an immediate impression when a member of the José Limón company. He started studying dance at fifteen, and when he graduated from New York's School of Performing Arts, he joined the Limón company. A tour of Central and South America introduced his talent to the public in 1960. Prior to establishing his own company he danced regularly with the Limón company and was featured with several other modern dance companies.

He has studied with a wide range of teachers and schools, including the Henry Street Playhouse, the American Ballet Center and the Martha Graham School of Contemporary Dance. He began to create his own dances in 1967 and established the performing ensemble Louis Falco and Featured Dancers in that same year. The following summer he created *Huescape*, a beautiful trio for himself, Juan Antonio, and Jennifer Muller, and gave its premier performance at Jacobs Pillow. The following year the company appeared at the Spoleto Festival of Two Worlds. In addition to concert work Falco has staged opera productions and worked on Broadway. Displaying a keen sense for design, he has commissioned costumes and décors for his dances from a distinguished group of artists including Robert Indiana, Stanley Landsman, Marisol, and William Katz.

HUESCAPE

Choreography by Louis Falco. Music by Pierre Henry, Pierre Schaeffer, Jacques Lasry, and Bernard Baschet. Scenery by William Katz. First performed at Jacobs Pillow Dance Festival, Lee, Mass., June 27, 1968, by Jennifer Muller, Louis Falco, and Juan Antonio.

The setting is literally a landscape of solid bands of colors running horizontally along the back and sides of the stage. Falco prepared the dance for his first appearence at Jacobs Pillow with his newly formed company. He selected a *musique concrète* score full of electronic blendings of voices, gunshots, and conventional orchestral playing to accompany this triangular relationship.

The dancers are dressed in solid-colored leotards and tights. One man in red, another in yellow, and the woman in blue. These same colors, with the addition of the intermediate orange and green, are the colors of the horizontal stripes. The three dancers occupy the stage together but seem linked by only the most casual of relationships. At first the two men disport by themselves and the woman is content to display her beautifully strong and elegant self, extending a leg dramatically and dashing in small circles. Then she approaches the two men and balances, first resting on one of them and then on the other.

The man in red is attracted to her and shifts his interest gradually to her at the expense of the man in yellow, who continues to move on the periphery of their duet. He then begins to assert himself, moving more closely to the man in red, but the woman keeps inserting herself between them, preventing them from returning to the world they inhabited before she exerted herself. Discouraged, the man in yellow departs, the man in red leans back, and the woman bends backward for support and leans on him.

While the simplicity of the involvement and its resolution of the trio into a duo is conventional, its execution by three talented dancers is very engrossing. Falco's choreographic interest always seems to develop from personal relations no matter how unusual the settings of his dances. In this as in other pieces he tends to use music as a form of aural décor rather than a metrical or rhythmic guide to the dance, further drawing one's attention to the persons of the dancers themselves as people and not as musical athletes.

CHOREOCHRONICLE
OF LOUIS FALCO

1967

Argot
The Gods Descend
Translucens

1968

*Huescape

1969

Timewright

1970

Caviar

1971

Ibid
Journal

The Sleepers
The Gamete Garden

1972

Soap Opera

1973

Avenue
Tutti-frutti
Twopenny Portrait

1974

Storeroom
Eclipse

1975

Caterpillar
Pulp

NINA FONAROFF

Though born a native New Yorker, Fonaroff traveled to the West Coast to study dance at the Cornish School in Seattle, and because of her intense interest in painting also studied with George Grosz while he was a resident of New York. She went to Zurich to study stage and costume design, and currently she is on the staff of the London School of Contemporary Dance.

The start of her performing career was spent as a member of the Martha Graham company, and for several years after she left the company she was an assistant to Louis Horst, who had been its musical director. She created the largest part of her own dance repertory after leaving the company, although she had shown some of her own work previously. In addition to her own modern dance training she also studied at the School of American Ballet and has made a substantial reputation as a teacher both in her own studio and on the staff of Bennington College, Teachers College, the Martha Graham School, and the Neighborhood Playhouse.

MR. PUPPET

Choreography by Nina Fonaroff. First performed at the Ninety-second Street YM-YWHA, New York, N.Y., November 16, 1947, by Ray Malon as Mr. Puppet *and Nina Fonaroff*

During the mid-1940s there was a great deal of interest shown by choreographers in the possibilities of combining the spoken word with dance movement. Many of these experiments came to naught, but one of the pieces which displayed a special liveliness and accomplishment was this one, and perhaps it arose from the fact that Fonaroff not only designed the dance movement but also wrote the monologue. It was a dance play that came from one hand. It so impressed Dame Alicia Markova and Anton Dolin that the international ballet stars toured through Europe with it on one of their tours.

The male puppet, who has freed himself from his bonds, stands and moves from place to place as he recites the words which carry his aspirations and dreams. He is dressed as Harlequin and the woman who rarely moves is Columbine. Her remarkable strength consists of maintaining different fixed poses which vary periodically to reflect the changing tone of his discourse.

The mood progresses from loneliness to utter frustration and finally a fine madness as he appeals to her for some sort of reaction so that he may break out of his isolation and share his feeling with another person. He is awkwardly ardent and intense, and she is galvanized into a flash of life only when he has despaired of his.

The piece makes almost inordinate demands on the female, who must remain the passive object of the male puppet's attention throughout his tortured meanderings. She is without life and he loses his way seeking the confirmation of his own through an exchange of feelings with another.

CHOREOCHRONICLE
OF NINA FONAROFF

1942

Theodolina, Queen of the
   Amazons
Yankee Doodle, American
   Prodigy
Hoofer on a Fiver
Cafe Chantant, Five A.M.

1946

Of Tragic Gesture
The Feast
Born to Weep
Of Sondry Wimmen

1947

Recitative and Aria
*Mr. Puppet

1948

The Purification

1949

Masque

1953

Requiem

MIDI GARTH

One thing that most agree upon is that Garth is a dance individualist who has constantly striven to find her own creative way. As a performer, she possesses a precision of gesture which enriches her own solos in a way that others have not been able to achieve when dancing in her works. She emerged as a creative force in the mid-1950s, showing her spare and elusive pieces at a time when no one else had taken such an unusual approach.

She is a native New Yorker who studied at the New Dance Group, and at the Martha Graham School while also studying composition with Louis Horst. She settled in Chicago for several years, attending Roosevelt University. At the time she studied ballet with John Petri and Berenice Holmes as well as taking modern instruction with Sybil Shearer.

When she returned to New York, she began giving regular solo concerts and formed a small company shortly afterward. She teaches and continues to present concerts of her work, although these have tended to diminish in frequency in the 1970s.

ANONYMOUS

Choreography by Midi Garth. First performed at the Henry Street Playhouse, New York, N.Y., March 8, 1959, by Midi Garth.

Probably the best known of Garth's dances, it is a perfect example of her fascinating creative approach. When Garth began work on this piece, the modern dance world was dominated by the creative approach of the generation of the 1930s. It placed great stress on linear development of dance themes, insisting that dances have a clear beginning, middle, and conclusion. The movement vocabularies developed for such dances tended to have a powerful thrust, and gestures were overtly colored with emotional significance.

Garth rejected the idea of direct statement in favor of the indirect indication of emotion. By so doing she had to modify her own movements so that they did not "shout" but instead "whispered" their significance. It was a bold decision but one which required tremendous performing concentration to make its performance fully effective.

The stage area is bare except for a lone figure. She is garbed in black with her head covered. The only sound which accompanies the dance is a metronome which ticks away the precious seconds of existence. The figure is driven into quick gestures that are angular and convey a sense of malaise. These sharp twitches are punctuated by slow languorous periods of desultory swaying. But the figure is pricked anew by the ticking into sharp but isolated movements of the arms and legs. It is almost as if she does not have control of her destiny and she concludes as alone as at the beginning.

The dance does not have the smooth curve of rising dynamic energy which then diminishes. It begins at one level and continues it throughout the dance without emotional peaks and valleys. The figure is truly anonymous and the victim of an indifferent time which passes without hurry but inexorably.

CHOREOCHRONICLE
OF MIDI GARTH

1949

No Refuge
Predatory Figure

1951

Dreams

1958

Double Image

1959

*Anonymous
Ricordanza
Prelude to Flight
Sea Change
Juke Box Pieces
Retrospect

1961

Voyages
This Day's Madness

1963

Imaginary City
Versus

1969

Day and Night
Impressions of Our Time

n.d.

Night
Other Voices
Suite of Dances
Summer
Time and Memory
Voices

RODNEY GRIFFIN

A native of Philadelphia, Griffin started to take tap dance lessons at the age of eight and soon after began ballet and modern dance classes. After receiving a scholarship for the Martha Graham School he settled in New York. One of the teachers in the school, Donald McKayle, was impressed with him and cast him in a Broadway show and invited him to join his own touring company. Having a good memory, Griffin became indispensable to McKayle for staging his works. Among other companies for which Griffin has mounted McKayle's works are the Alvin Ailey American Dance Theater and Eliot Feld's American Ballet Company.

While pursuing his own career on Broadway, Griffin also did film and television work and started to create his own pieces in 1972. One of the first companies he worked with was the Interboro Ballet, which has developed into the Theater Dance Collection, a company for which Griffin has choreographed most of his pieces, including the hilarious *Misalliance*.

MISALLIANCE

Choreography by Rodney Griffin. Music by Jacques Ibert. Costumes by Tyrone Browne. First performed at the Ninety-second Street YM-YWHA, New York, N.Y., May 1972, by Carole Flemming as the Bride, *Clay Taliaferro as the* Groom, *Natasha Grishin as the* Bridesmaid, *Lynne Taylor as an* Attendant to the Groom, *Richard Anderson as a* Priest, *and Loretta Abbott, Miriam Welch, Roger Briant, and Byron Wheeler as the* Children. *A revised version with costumes by Holmes Easley and lighting by Edward M. Greenberg was performed at the Clark Center for the Performing Arts, New York, N.Y., February 1974, by the Theatre Dance Collection.*

In the early days of modern dance development there was a feeling of hostility toward the technique and theatricality of ballet dancing. Modern dancers would from time to time make satiric works commenting unfavorably about one or another of the balletic conventions, but recently this has diminished considerably. It has diminished to a point where choreographer Rodney Griffin can make a dance that spoofs the conventions of modern dance and ballet with an elfin and friendly glee.

Initially three women on point and dressed in fluffy tutus flutter frivolously about the stage and then dither off casting roguish glances at the audience. They are obviously there to entertain. They are succeeded by a woman in bare feet who stomps on and holds a dustpan like a religious ikon at arms length in front of her. She has a no-nonsense air to her. A man in a floor length white cloak follows her. He enfolds her and suddenly she ends up with the cloak and her dustpan is taken by him. He stands revealed bare chested in brief trunks.

The three balletic women tiptoe in and one takes the sacred dustpan and uses it as a fan. The five form a group and the man drapes the cloak on himself like a Roman toga. The balletic women continue to flutter as the barefoot lady emotes with dramatic arm gestures. The man continues to follow her as she does her variation. The women go off and he does a solo that throbs with sexual suppression, contorting his body in a parody of the Martha Graham technique. A ballerina enters daintily, the contrast is like

Beauty and the Beast. Her tutu has an elastic band and he hoists it up in a lightning move so that it is about her throat like a collar. She attempts to continue her light gauzy movements but he simply drags her offstage. She returns pregnant!

An elaborate deployment is made of a sheet behind which she gives birth to a most remarkable offspring. It is a perfect cross between the two dance worlds. One foot is unshod and the other has a toe shoe; it is a male *en travesti*. It has one breast and is torn by contradictory dance impulses. The resultant solo shows the creature attempting a most balletic leap to be doubled up by a modern dance contraction at just the wrong moment. The whole cast seems to have been transformed. The serious woman enters to do a buck-and-wing. One ballet woman wears tap shoes and another sneakers. The ballerina's movements are totally concealed beneath the modern dance man's white cloak, and the piece ends in an utter emotional tangle.

The accuracy with which Griffin pointed out the performing conventions of each mode of dance is the nub of the dance joke, but even audiences not familiar with the particular schools of dance would laugh at the obvious mismatch between the personages of the work. As a final fillip when the cast takes its bows, a man presents the ballerina with flowers. She graciously turns to the man and offers him a single bloom in what has become accepted balletic curtain call behavior. He disdains the offer, snatches the whole bouquet, and runs off!

CHOREOCHRONICLE
OF RODNEY GRIFFIN

1972

Cave Paintings
Guaranteed Pure
Misalliance (first version)
The Lady Doth Protest
Race
Not in Your Hands
Virginals
Spanish Steps
Canon
Dawning
Duetino
Chamber Music
Twelve Days of Christmas
Winter Lady
The Ugly Duckling
The Sleigh Ride
The Nest

1973

Tintype
Tombmates
Puppets
For the Birds
The Lovers
Ends
Ancestral Voices
The Tail of the Bumblebee
Courtly Dances
Mandragor

1974

The Miraculous Mandarin
*Misalliance (revised)

1975

Summer Lightning
The Fool's Almanac

STUART HODES

While interested in the theater from an early age, Hodes had never taken any serious dance training until he enrolled at a beginner's course at the Martha Graham School. He was just out of the Army Air Force, where he had spent three years as a bomber pilot, and was, like everyone of his generation, impatient for results. He resolved to discontinue training at the school unless he was promoted to a more advanced class within six months. He eventually wound up as Graham's partner and a mainstay of the company.

In addition to his concert work he was a leading dancer on Broadway and assisted Donald Saddler in staging several shows. He began creating his own works for concert appearances in the 1950s and has continued to choreograph for his own dancers and for other companies in the United States and abroad. As a teacher, he has been on the staffs of the Harkness Ballet, Juilliard School of Music, and of course the Martha Graham School. At present he is the head of the dance department of New York University's School of the Arts.

BEGGAR'S DANCE

Choreography by Stuart Hodes. Music by Johann Sebastian Bach. Words by Henry Wadsworth Longfellow. First performed at Wollman Hall, New York, N.Y., May 17, 1973, by Stuart Hodes and Susan McGuire.

The bitterest moment in any dancer's life is the moment when the physical demands of the profession are more than can be met. The moment comes sooner for some than others, but it inevitably arrives. Hodes retired to a career of choreographing and teaching and in an inspired moment, devised a way to get himself back onstage as a performer in this dance. He has subsequently created other works, and it appears as if it might develop into a full-blown series, but this was the first.

A man stands in a white linen suit with a straw Panama hat on; he is of mature years. A young woman with an Indian headband circling her forehead wears a leotard and flared long pants. The sound accompaniment alternates between a singsong reading of the *Song of Hiawatha* and passages of baroque music. She moves sinuously and sensuously across the front of the stage, and he moves behind her sketching in his movements. She launches into all of her dancing with the full intensity of a young performer. In a sense she is like the young Hiawatha, who has a full life stretching out in front of him, and her partner has the majestic fullness of the Bach music.

At one point she begins a series of arabesques and he approaches, almost but not quite touching her supportively. During the whole of the duet he maintains a watchful and careful distance between them. He is attentive and frames her with a vocabulary of gesture that has great emotional weight even though it is presented in the shorthand that dancer's call marking a role. At the end he lies on his side with head bared giving her homage.

The male character did not have a name when the dance was presented for the first time, but subsequently in another work identically dressed he was identified as Philo. The Greek word *philos* is the word for "loving" and in English is used in combination with other words to denote a liking, a loving, or a predilection for, all of which Hodes has for dancing and dancers. In this piece he graciously presents a young dancer within the frame of a duet combining youthful energy with mature gesture.

CHOREOCHRONICLE
OF STUART HODES

1950

Lyric Percussive
Surrounding Unknown
Drive
Flak

1952

I Am Nothing
No Heaven in Earth
Musette for Four
Murmur of Wings

1953

Reap the Whirlwind

1955

La Lupa

1958

Suite for Young Dancers

1959

Offering and Dedication
*Folk Dances of Three Mythical
    Lands*
The Waters of Meribah
First Impressions (mc, with
    Jonathan Lucas)

1960

A Good Catch
Offering and Dedication
Simon Says
Balaam

1961

Milk and Honey (mc, with
    Donald Saddler)

1962

We Take the Town (mc, with
    Donald Saddler)

1963

After the Teacups
Sophie (mc, with Donald
    Saddler)
Persian set

1964

To Broadway with Love (revue,
    with Donald Saddler)

1965

The Abyss

1966

Gymkhana

1967

Akimbo
A Music of Sighs
Persian Gymnasts
Breugalesque

1968

Prima Sera
Zig Zag

1969

Hocus Pocus
Responsive Readings
Bird of Yearning

1970

We
Hear Us O Lord, From Heaven
   Thy Dwelling Place
Conversation Piece
Vocalise
Audio Visual
Dance for Film/Whale Trip

1971

The Honor of Your Presence Is
   Requested
Trace
A Dancing Machine

1972

Voice Over
I Think I Can Express

1973

*Beggar's Dance
A Game of Silence
Transit Gloria

1974

After the Teacups (revised)
Boedromion
Domaine

1975

Bolder and Bolder

LUCAS HOVING

Hoving is almost equally well known in terms of roles that he has created for himself, such as Daedalus in his *Icarus* or the friend in José Limón's *Moor's Pavane*. A particularly expressive dancer in terms of dramatic gesture, he also showed a great comic skill in several dances he created for his own company.

Hoving began to study dance in his native Holland with Florrie Rodrigo and the expressionist dancer Yvonne Georgi. He traveled to England to study at Dartington Hall, where Kurt Jooss established his school and company after he had left Germany, and was invited to join the Jooss Ballet.

He came to the United States in the middle 1940s and later became an American citizen. He danced with several companies including those of Martha Graham and Valerie Bettis before joining the José Limón Company, with which he had a long association. He has taught extensively both in the United States at the Juilliard School and the summer dance program at Connecticut College. Since his retirement from active performing he has devoted himself to teaching, dividing his time between the United States and Holland. *Icarus,* one of his most popular works, has been staged for several companies, including the Alvin Ailey American Dance Theater.

ICARUS

Choreography by Lucas Hoving. Music by Chin-Ichi Matushita. First performed at the Ninety-second Street YM-YWHA, New York, N.Y., April 5, 1964, by Lucas Hoving as Daedalus, *Patricia Christopher as the* Sun, *and Chase Robinson as* Icarus.

The classical Greek legend of man's attempt to escape from a maze provided the basis for this dance. In the story a young man Icarus and his father Daedalus make themselves wings of birds' feathers held together with wax. His father cautions him not to fly too close to the sun lest the wax melt, dissolving his wings, and cause him to crash fatally to earth.

As the dance opens Icarus lies on the ground in a simple white leotard while Daedalus in a gray overshirt and trousers stands behind him almost like a cautionary figure. The young man stirs. He leaps and dives toward the ground, breaking his fall with his outstretched arms and slowly lowering himself. He is like a bird swooping.

The older Daedalus catches him about the legs and holds him as Icarus stretches out his arms overhead. He then makes a series of leaps using the older man's braced legs as a taking-off point, but eventually he falls. Daedalus slides his hands up and down worriedly along his body and then taps Icarus, who rises to walk around in an exploring fashion. Daedalus remains in the background looking on solicitously as the emboldened Icarus begins to dash to and fro. Daedalus stretches his arms to the side, and he and Icarus both fall to the ground as a woman dressed in a resplendent robe slowly moves across the back of the stage.

Her movements are majestic and confident in a totally self-contained manner. She pauses on her path to undulate her arms from time to time, making one think of some vast solar flare. The two men sit and watch her but the younger is drawn to move closer and closer to her while the older man sits and quietly observes her progress. He bows his head in resignation as Icarus approaches nearer to her. She turns slowly in place, twisting the long train of her gown about her ankles like some shimmering vortex that is drawing Icarus to his destruction.

Icarus falls and rises again but he has voyaged too close to danger and collapses. Daedalus rises with arms held before him as if in pleading while he walks around the tumbling Icarus. The woman unwinds her train slowly and passes off, leaving the older man to walk slowly and painfully to the prostrate Icarus. He gathers his legs and clasps them to his chest and the dead Icarus hangs with his head and arms limply touching the ground.

The story has been used many times, but Hoving's economy in telling it with a trio of dancers is masterful. As a tale, it is straightforward and, as an allegory for the conflict between young men's yearning and older men's wisdom, it carries considerable weight.

CHOREOCHRONICLE
OF LUCAS HOVING

1950

The Battle

1953

Electra (with Lavina Nielsen)
Perilous Flight (with Lavina Nielsen)
Satyros (with Lavina Nielsen)

1955

The Love of Three Oranges

1960

Wall of Silence

1962

Divertimento
Has the Last Train Left?
Parades and Other Fancies
Strange to Wish Wishes No Longer
Suite for a Summer Day

1963

Aubade

1964

*Icarus
Incidental Passage*

1965

*Satiana
The Tenants*

1967

Rough-In

1970

*Aubade II
Opus '69
Reflections*

1971

Zip Code

n.d.

Newsreel

MYRA KINCH

While attending the University of California in Los Angeles, Kinch also studied dance with a variety of teachers and then moved to the East Coast for further study. She had experience with modern dance, ballet, and ethnic forms and made her own debut in Europe as a solo dancer. During the 1930s she was active in the West Coast chapter of the Federal Theater Project and toured throughout the country giving solo recitals or company concerts with her small group.

In 1948 she began a long association with the Jacobs Pillow University of the Dance where she headed the modern dance section. She is best known for her satirical dances, among which *Giselle's Revenge* is one of the finest. In addition she has created serious works and has imparted her knowledge to a generation of students.

GISELLE'S REVENGE

Choreography by Myra Kinch. Music by Adolphe Adam (Giselle), *arranged by Manuel Galea. Scenery by Liz Matus. Costumes by George Horn. First performed at the Henry Street Settlement Playhouse, New York, N.Y., November 22, 1953, by Myra Kinch as* Giselle, *Rhoda Johannson as a* Wili, *and William Milié as* Albrecht.

The world of dance is full of stories in which an unlucky maiden is betrayed by an unfaithful suitor. Her usual recourse is to die of a broken heart, but the traditional resolution of the story seemed far too one sided to be allowed to stand unchallenged, so Kinch decided to tell it another way.

A cloth-shrouded mound stands to the left with a cross surmounting the pile. A mysterious woman in a black dress enters and waves a wand. The cloth is drawn off to reveal a coffin. As she departs a sorrowing man enters with a cloak draped around him and timidly approaches the coffin. He stares apprehensively then lies on his side to pump his leg out and back as an expression of woe. He rises, twirls smartly, and approaches the coffin. He is a repentant romantic lover expressing his feelings in conventional romantic terms that are only slightly exaggerated. His solo of remorse continues as he tosses off his cape, covers his eyes, and sinks before the coffin, where he lies motionless.

Silently the lid hinges open, though he remains totally unaware of the motion. Two hands grasp the sides of the coffin and Giselle hauls herself upright and peers inquiringly at the inert form. She sits daintily on the edge of the coffin and swings her legs over the side. She steps away and makes malevolent gestures to the grieving Albrecht. She is dressed like a cartoon vampire. Dashing to the recumbent form, she touches his shoulder and flees before he sees her. He does see the open and empty coffin, however, and reels backward. As he peers inside a Wili in a black tutu rapidly dances past, but he does not see her either.

When Giselle returns he is drawn to her and once again pumps his leg in and out as he reaches over to touch her. She easily ducks beneath his arm and rushes through a door at the right. He follows and she returns almost instantly through a door standing immediately next to the first. It's like the entrance and exit doors leading to a restaurant's kitchen. Their chase includes several more disappearances and reappearances, and then they dance a duet which includes steps from the original choreography at the conclusion of which she tosses him a flower and vanishes. The menacing Wili in the black gauze tutu crosses in front of him.

Distraught, he presses the back of his hand to his forehead and then slides into a classically correct arabesque. At its conclusion, Giselle sneaks up behind him coyly and pops him on the head with another flower, kisses his hand, and tosses herself into his arms. Their duet is an artfully awkward rendering of the original as she sweeps closer and closer to the open coffin. She lies in it and twiddles her feet at him. He follows. Suddenly her hands appear over the edge of the lid as she closes it on him. She frolics about joyously. She is now free. To make sure, she accepts hammer and nails from the helpful Wili and is last seen securing the lid with precise blows.

The dance is obviously funnier to those who are already familiar with the plot of the romantic ballet but even amusing to those who do not know the conventions of the work. Kinch has a keen eye for the absurd and for the posturing that occurs in even the most serious works. She tastefully exaggerates the original for her own humorous ends, and has poked at the pomposities of both ballet and modern dance.

CHOREOCHRONICLE
OF MYRA KINCH

1948

American Suite
Entrances and Exits
Song of Sabra

1949

The Six Mrs. Tudors
Of Dreadful Magic

1950

Fatima from Sarasota

1951

Along Appointed Sands

1952

The Bird Watcher
Tomb for Two

1953

*Giselle's Revenge
Sarabande for the Erudite

1955

Variation on a Variation
Sundered Majesty
Salade
Nymphscarf

1956

The Bajour

1958

Beautiful Dreamer
The Sound of Darkness

1960

Sad Self Hereafter
A Waltz Is a Waltz Is a Waltz

1971

Sappho Synkopto
Devil's Tattoo

n.d.

Slavic Suite
Greek—1915
Ecossaise

ELEANOR KING

King established herself as a performer with the original Humphrey-Weidman company, which she joined in 1927, and remained as a featured performer for the better part of a decade. During this time she formed the core of her own style and it drew heavily on the Humphrey-Weidman technique. She established her own company after she left the Humphrey-Weidman group and toured for several years with it.

She has often found inspiration for her work in the writings of classical writers and has created pieces which combined dance and recitation as well as pure dance works. Her work has a meditative, literary base to it and deals with sober subject material ordinarily.

ROADS TO HELL

Choreography by Eleanor King. Music by Genevieve Pitot. First performed at the Humphrey-Weidman Studio, New York, N.Y., May 28, 1941, by Eleanor King.

This suite of four satirical dances was created for solo dancer. It is a particularly difficult type of dance to sustain interest, since it does not have the support of dramatic conflict, augmented ensemble passages, or even glamorous costuming.

In "Pride," the first section, a woman in a shapeless voluminous garment bends over, crouches, and then bounces up. She steps grandly and bursts her arms widely. When she hops forward she sweeps her arms haughtily downward and then bounds up. It is only a semblance of humility that she can bring herself to. At another moment she almost drives her arm into a stiffly held fascist salute. Altering her stance, she rolls her hands over and over one another, dripping condescension, then stands bolt upright, hands on hips, and jumps up and down petulantly. She concludes with a number of turns which she launches with one pounding foot. She reaches up arrogantly and sinks to a crouch. She exits, bounding up and down, circling one arm.

"Sloth" finds her seated, yawning and stretching. She brushes feet over one another and slumps down. She crawls off supporting her weight on knees and elbows, then begins to rock her body to achieve leverage enough to rise. She doesn't manage to. Finally she stands still, yawning and tottering slightly. For a moment she pursues some purposeful movement, but it is really only dithering back and forth. She never really organizes any large pattern of movement, and finally the dithering becomes less and less frenzied and she sinks down stifling a yawn.

The large, shapeless garment is now cinched at the waist for "Envy." It is a dance of some affectation. She sashays and mimes, sitting daintily. Her shoulders wag back and forth excessively as she walks. The whole carriage of her body has an artificial tilt as she carves out an area of her own domain. Once done, however, it is unsatisfactory, since she sees something or someone else who appears to have more appeal. Her jaws snap repeatedly and with a hostile acquisitiveness. She experiences frustration in her coveting mood and is reduced to running in place futilely and reclines unsatisfied.

The suppressed fury of "Wrath" is first seen as she begins a slow gyration of her whole body while maintaining a tight grip on one wrist. Suddenly the arms fly apart and she makes grasping motions in the air. Fighting for control, she clasps her hands behind her, but the force of her anger drives her into a series of pounding leaps. She tosses her head and then her freed arms as she leaps. She turns furiously and steps forward, crossing one leg in front of the other awkwardly while making a refusing wag of her head. Inner spasms thrust her limbs out and she sinks quivering into a crouch and then lies down.

The piece is a study of four methods of self-destruction. The feelings generated from within the person all turn back upon the individual and cause personal harm. It's a grim study of the debilitating effects of base feelings upon the person who has them and not upon the others to whom they are directed.

CHOREOCHRONICLE
OF ELEANOR KING

1931

Study
Mazurka (with José Limón)
B Minor Suite (with José Limón)

1934

Song of Earth

1936

American Folk Suite

1937

Icaro

1941

*Roads to Hell
Characters of the Annunciation

1944

Moon Dances
To the West

1950

The Libation Bearers (after Doris
    Humphrey)

1951

Dance in the Afternoon
Transformations
Soliloquy in the Morning

1952

Four Visions

1954

Song for Heaven

1959

Miracles

1960

Gilgamesh

1963

Salutation

1967

Synthesis (Well Tempered
    Dancer)

1970–71

Toward New Noh

1975

A Fantasy on Tai Chi

n.d.

Ode to Freedom
Bach Partita No. 6 in E Minor

PAULINE KONER

Despite her long association with the José Limón Company, Koner has always maintained her own choreographic approach to dance. She has both created major roles within that company and designed her own dances with her concert group. She was born in New York and while attending regular academic school she studied ballet with Michel Fokine, making her first appearance in the children's corps of his company. She continued her study with Michio Ito and toured with his company for two years. She presented her own work in her first solo concert in 1929. She traveled to the Soviet Union and danced there for a year, then she returned to the United States and further touring.

Her teaching credits include schools abroad in Italy, Holland, Chile, Brazil, and Japan as well the United States. In addition to her appearances in

New York she has appeared at the two major summer dance festivals at Jacobs Pillow in Massachusetts and the American Dance Festival in New London, Connecticut. *The Farewell,* which she created as a tribute to Doris Humphrey, artistic director of the Limón Company, is one of her most dramatic works. Her most recent teaching has been at the North Carolina School of the Arts.

THE FAREWELL

Choreography by Pauline Koner. Music by Gustav Mahler (Das Lied von der Erde). *First performed at the Ninety-second Street YM-YWHA, New York, N.Y., April 30, 1962, by Pauline Koner.*

The dance was created as a memorial to the late Doris Humphrey by Koner four years after Humphrey's death. It represents the most beautiful tribute that one artist can give to another, a living creative work. The romantic Mahler score, with its tragic undercurrents, was a perfect choice for the dance.

A transparent gauze curtain shields the stage and softens the outline of the solitary woman who emerges. It is as if she had appeared in the mist. She has a limp cloth tape lying across her upturned palms. The ends of the tape are not visible, since it extends diagonally across the stage, starting beyond where we can observe it and passing off on the other side again beyond our vision. This is the farewell-to-the-earth section, and she wears a deep red floor-length dress as she moves meditatively along the length of the tape. A long arc of rope stretches along the left side of the stage crosses the tape and comes to an end to the rear of the stage in the middle. As the dancer leaves bursts and bouquets of colored lights are projected.

She returns in a pink dress and dances with a joyful sense of freedom as she prepares to bid farewell to the happiness of youth. The arc of her life as symbolized by the rope is prudently and partially folded up. The progression of her life brings her to her farewell to love. She gradually enjoys and then relinquishes the joys that are the cycle of life. She bends quickly and folds up the rope further to the point where it crosses the cloth tape. She again evokes the happiness of love but is drawn fatalistically to gather up the remaining portion of the rope and carry it off.

When she returns in the final section, which is her final farewell, she is dressed in black. She now turns her total attention to the tape as she picks it up and examines it carefully, searchingly. She measures it out with sliding motions of her hands along its length. She anguishes over it and wraps herself in it. She travels along its length attempting to "read" it as one might a message on a perforated strip. She embraces it but is inevitably drawn slowly away from it until finally she must release her grip on it. As she disappears, the tape stretches out taut and shimmering in the air.

The dance is a touching personal memorial and Koner performs it with such loving intensity that it is almost impossible to imagine anyone else doing it. Even in its expression of youthful joys it has an autumnal undercurrent that finally dominates as the dancer takes the final farewell.

CHOREOCHRONICLE
OF PAULINE KONER

1929

Mazurka
Joy
Hungarian
Habanera

1930

Nilamani
Beginning (from *Cosmic Poems*)
Extase russe
Minstrelesque
La Cani
Fantasia (*Japanese Scarecrow*, with Nimura)
Desespoir
Allegretto gracioso
Blue Flame
Mora Gitana
Altar Piece
Rustique
Visions
Upheaval
Triana

1931

At the Fair
Three Interpretations of a Theme
Spanish Impressions
Barbaresque
A Love Poem
Exotique

Two Laments
Dance in a Religious Mood
Without Rhyme or Reason

1932

Moorish Ritual
Impressions of a Bullfight
Waltz Languide
Ya-lel (*O Night, O Beautiful Night*)
Chassidic Song and Dance
Farruca
Tableau d'Autel
Gitanaza
Cycle of Masses

1933

Danse Macabre
Rondo
Waltz Momentum
Dance of Longing
Three Small Funeral Marches
Palestinian Pictures
  Yemenite Prayer
  Ya-lel
  Debka
La Maja maldita

1937

Free Day
Lullaby to a Future Hero
Hindu Dance of Radha
Bird of Prey
Alegrías
La Corrida

1938

Summer Time
Song of the Slums
Harvest Festival
Sailor's Holiday

1939

It Ain't Necessarily So
Among the Ruins
Study of a Nude
Tragic Fiesta
Portrait of a Child
Pas de deux

1941

Ravel Valse
Judgment Day
Flamenco Song
Ballerina: Her Greatest Triumph

1944

In Memoriam
Out of This Sorrow
City Song
Passing Love
Song of the Prairie

1945

Mothers of Men
    Lullaby to a Future Hero
    Out of This Sorrow
    Song of the Prairie
Sarabande and Capriccio

1945–46

Choreotones (Fifteen-minute
    ballets for TV)
    Star Dust Blues
    Park Bench
    Summertime
    Dance Sketches
    It's a Date
    Mississippi
    Grandma's Sofa
    Nightspots

1946

Jitterbug Sketches

1948

Voice in the Wilderness

1949

The Visit

1951

Amorous Adventure

1953

Cassandra

1955

Concertino in A Major

1956

The Shining Dark

1960

Barren Sceptre (with José Limón)

1962

*The Farewell

1963   n.d.

  Dance Symphony   *Tides*
  Solitary Song   *Upheaval*

1969

  Poème

PEARL LANG

In addition to being the first dancer that Martha Graham ever permitted to take one of her own roles, Lang has pursued a career on Broadway and has also maintained her own company. As a performer, she has an exceptional lyricism and as a choreographer has drawn on this same quality most notably in *Shirah*, a work she created after a mystical Hasidic tale.

The pronounced dance influence in her life was study with Martha Graham during a decade spent dancing with the Graham company. She only formed her own company in 1952 after leaving the Graham company, and it was then that she began her own independent creative career. She has taught at Jacobs Pillow, the Juilliard School, and the Yale University School of Drama. Abroad she taught in Germany, Switzerland, and Sweden and was granted a fellowship from the Guggenheim Foundation. She continues her teaching and makes regular appearances with her company.

SHIRAH

Choreography by Pearl Lang. Music by Alan Hovhaness. Costumes by Pearl Lang. Scenery by Tom Watson. Lighting by Tom Skelton. First performed at the Palmer Auditorium, Connecticut College, New London, Conn., August 19, 1960, by Pearl Lang, Dale Sehnert, Bruce Marks, Patricia Christopher, Paul Berensohn, Bettie De Jong, Victor Melnick, Koert Stuyf, Rina Schenfeld, Tryntje Ostrandon, and Jennifer Muller.

The hebrew word *shirah* means song, and the dance celebrates a legend drawn from the Hasidic mystical literature about the loving contemplation which exists between a spring and "the heart of the world." Essentially these two face one another in rapture, and their adoring relationship is the life-affirming force that maintains existence.

A dozen men and women stand and in unison perform a pious rite that includes lowering the body into a squatting position and tipping the forehead so that it brushes the ground in a prayerful exercise. They stand and bend backward, and the women circle their arms over their heads in a mild delirium, and the men, who have been lying on their backs, raise their legs and torsos upward to form shallow "V's." One of the men crosses in front of the group, walking with tiny steps in a squatting position. Moments later he returns, thrusting his leg to one side, leaping forward, and repeating the motion until he completes a diagonal across the stage. The company arranges itself in two parallel lines, and he walks along outside of them while another man walks between the columns of reclining dancers. The first man leaves once more and returns to bound around in a large circle. All then stand with arms over head and rotate them in a manner similar to that at the beginning of the section.

The woman who represents the spring walks on slowly, and the others bounce eagerly up and down; her arms curve upward in front of her. As the others leave, one man representing the "heart of the world" remains crouched at the opposite side of the stage facing her. She acknowledges him as she dances a spritely solo, frequently stretching her arms toward him. Their eyes create a bond between them. Three men cluster about his legs, holding them firmly in place as he swings his body in a wide circle beyond the point of his natural balance. The woman shivers in delight as the rest of the dancers return. She gathers in her hands elastic cords which she gives to the man, and these form a shimmering web across the stage. Members of the company each take a strand and pluck it. The "heart of the world" shakes them in shimmering waves, and she runs back and forth as they undulate. It is the visible sign of the song that is sent forth each day and touches the hearts of all living creatures. The first man gathers up all of the strands and presents them to the woman and then elevates her as she holds them in folds from her arms. The ritual is finished for another day and life has been reaffirmed.

There is a mysterious religious feeling throughout the piece from the faintly biblical costumes to the way in which the dancers almost seem lost in a contemplative transport as they rotate their arms above their heads periodically. The central role of the spring succeeds only in so far as the dancer is able to maintain a level of restrained joy as she moves back and forth from "the heart of the world." It is a considerable virtuoso feat but one which makes the dance keep the creative tension necessary.

CHOREOCHRONICLE
OF PEARL LANG

1949

Song of Deborah

1951

Legend

1952

Ironic Rite

1953

Rites

1955

And Joy Is My Witness

1956

Juvenescence
Parable for Lovers
Three at a Phantasy

1957

Persephone

1958

Nightflight

1960

Black Marigolds
*Shirah
Sky Chant

1962

Apasionada

1963

Broken Dialogues

1964

Shore Bourne

1965

Dismembered Fable

1966

Prayer to the Dark Bird

1969

Piece for Brass
Tongues of Fire

1971

Sharjuhm

1972

The Encounter
Two Passover Celebrations

1975

The Possessed

n.d.

Moonsung
Windsung
Moonways and Dark Tides

BELLA LEWITZKY

Because of her long and fruitful association with Lester Horton, Lewitzky's name is inextricably bound up with his, though she has successfully created a substantial body of work for her company on her own. Her early dance training was with Horton at his school in Los Angeles, and for many years she was the mainstay of his company, functioning as his most accomplished soloist and *régisseur* as well. She began teaching and together she and Horton formally founded Dance Theater, which housed both the school and the theater in which the company performed. When she decided to strike out as head of her own company in the early fifties, she established Dance Associates, which also based itself in Southern California. She has taught extensively throughout the United States and was made the dean of the School of Dance of the California Institute of the Arts when it was established. She began national touring with her company in the late 1960s, appearing several times in New York and at the American Dance Festival at Connecticut College among other locales.

ORRENDA (ONENESS)

Choreography by Bella Lewitzky. Music by Cara Bradbury Marcus. Costumes and lighting by Darleen Neel. First performed at Bowman Theater, Idyllwild, Calif., July 26, 1969, by Gary Bates, Fred Strickler, Melanie Alexander, Rebecca Bobele, Jan Day, Teresa Nielsen, Leslie Brown, Charles Edmondson, and Anna Zika.

Each member of the old Lester Horton company has been stamped with a certain style of movement favored by Horton, and each of them has developed or extended its scope in an individual manner. In this piece Lewitzky makes a contemporary statement about community, dramatically using that specially calm torso that Horton liked but adding her own dynamics.

A man leaps on stage, balances on one leg, and opens his arms in a greeting, then turns to the back, extends one arm up and one leg back for a moment, and repeats the movement facing to the side. He remains still while a second man bounds on to do the same, followed by a third who also repeats the sequence. Together they leap up, bend to the side, and roll on the floor before coming to rest again. As soon as they do, three women enter and perch on the men's backs momentarily and dismount. Each of the couples, face to face, leans back holding one another's wrists to make a "V" shape; the colors of their costumes are warm in contrast to those of the three

Alvin Ailey.   PHOTO BY ZACHARY FREYMAN.

José Limón and Betty Jones in *The Moor's Pavane*.   PHOTO BY WALTER STRATE.

Katherine Dunham.

Anna Sokolow.

Pearl Primus in *Prayer of Thanksgiving*.

women, who are in cool colors and who enter to course around the couples like slalom competitors. The couples separate, with the women moving in unison and the men running together. They join together again, and the three women in cool blue tilt backwards and squat down at the rear of the stage to watch them.

The three couples are toward the front of the stage, and one woman picks up her man and carries him off. The other two men lean back on the women, who support them as one would expect in a friendly community. One of the men carries a woman off, and the man in the center in turn supports the woman who had just been bracing him with her back. They walk off together and she half turns to him and then turns away, retaining her independence. The three women in blue stand and lean and then turn in unison. They are joined by the three women in the warmer colors and all do a variation but remain individually separate. As they pass into the wings, they shuttle in and out of one another, giving the feeling of community interchange.

One woman remains onstage as the men return to stand bending one foot up mechanically. They cluster and quiver, and then the five other women return to face the three men skittering their feet in place. The tempo accelerates. They join and all run together, with the former couples united. All cluster and loll heads, then individuals break away into small running patterns and exit.

The subtitle of the dance is "Oneness," and to a great extent the dance is conceived of as the action and interaction of bodies without any specific sexual differentiation. A woman is as likely to carry a man as he is to carry her. The same movement is given to all to do, and one does not have the feeling of sexual tension between the men and women. All are part of the dance; equal parts and equal partners, sharing in the community of movement.

ON THE BRINK OF TIME

Choreography by Bella Lewitzky. Music by Morton Subotnick. Décor and lighting by Darleen Neel. First performed at Bowman Theater, Idyllwild, Calif., July 26, 1969, by Bella Lewitzky.

When she prepared this dance, Lewitzky was already a mature dancer, but instead of making allowances for herself she choreographed it with passages of movement that would give a young dancer difficulty.

An arm flashes out from the wings on the right side of the stage and is withdrawn. The woman backs out a little distance, stands, extends one leg, and goes off. The arm appears again, then she comes a little farther out and ripples her body before exiting. With each succeeding entrance she moves further and further across the stage, and one can almost feel the tension that pulls her back repeatedly. She reaches the center of the stage and stays to do a brief variation. She is torn between two directions and teeters from side to side. She makes small curlicues with her hands, and her arms seem to float up as the torso descends. She scampers and her arms rotate like propellers, in union, and she dashes off, circling hands over one another in front of her.

She returns again to the center for another variation, which is almost touched with a sense of vertigo. She rises on the balls of her feet, flicks her hands, swirls her arms, drops to her knees, and then rises again. A flickering stroboscopic light catches her in a series of poses as she extends a leg to the right and then to the left and turns with one arm stretched upward, echoing the curve of the torso. She swirls around with her palm aimed directly upward. Then normal lighting is restored and she walks in measured steps and when exiting for the last time pauses to leave the spread fingers of her hand visible. The hand opens and closes several times and then is withdrawn.

The piece makes one think of Pascal's observation that man walks a narrow path between the infinitely large and the infinitely small; that he is surrounded by voids. In a similar sense one occupies only a small portion of the immensity of time and it is on the brink of time that Lewitzky chose to make her dance.

CHOREOCHRONICLE
OF BELLA LEWITZKY

1969

   Kinaesonata
   On the Brink of Time
   Orrenda (Oneness)

1971

   Pietas

1972

   Ceremony for Three

1973

   Game Plan
   Bella and Brindle

1974

   Five
   Spaces Between

1975

   V.C.O. (Voltage Controlled Oscillator)

n.d.

   Trio for Saki

JOSÉ LIMÓN

In addition to a career of serious concert dance, Limón has left a legacy in terms of his company. In ordinary circumstances the retirement or death of the major choreographer of a modern dance company has resulted in the dissolution of the company. His was the first to remain as a performing unit; in fact it had a brilliant success on a tour of the Soviet Union just after his death. His dancers have traditionally been some of the best trained and have been outstanding in interpretations of his dances as well as their own works.

Limón was born in Mexico to a family with a strong musical interest, and he himself played several instruments. When he was eight the family moved to the United States and settled in the Southwest. Limón pursued his academic studies at the University of California at Los Angeles and showed a desire to become a painter. He traveled to New York to continue his studies, saw his first dance concert, and resolved to pursue a career as a dancer. He studied at the Humphrey-Weidman studio and was invited to join their company. He danced with it for ten years until 1940, when he left to create his own works. During this time he also appeared in Broadway musicals. His career was interrupted for three years of service in the Army during World War II.

After his release from service he formed his own company with Doris Humphrey as artistic director and choreographer. This assrciation continued until her death. The Limón company was the first dance company sent abroad under the sponsorship of the State Department, and it toured South America in 1954. Several subsequent tours were undertaken under the same sponsorship, including the trip to the Soviet Union after Limón's death.

He was active on the faculty of several schools, most notably that of the dance department of the Juilliard School of Music and the summer dance festival held at Connecticut College each year since 1948. He was also artistic director of the American Dance Theater, which presented a selection of modern dance companies for the first time at Lincoln Center's State Theater. He is remembered for his total dedication to his chosen field.

THERE IS A TIME

Choreography by José Limón. Music by Norman Dello Joio (Meditations on Eccle-siastes). *Costumes by Pauline Lawrence. Lighting by Sharon Musser. First per-formed at the Juilliard Concert Hall, New York, April 20, 1956, by José Limón, Lucas Hoving, Richard Fitzgerald, Michael Hollander, Harlan McCallum, Pauline Koner, John Barker, Chester Wolenski, Lavina Nielsen, Betty Jones, and Ruth Cur-rier.*

The dance is based on Ecclesiastes, taking the titles of its sections from the verses in Chapter II of the book. It is a presentation of a dozen episodes in the life of a community, both as a unit in the beginning and end and through individual members in selected variations. The music is written as a theme and variations and the dance follows that structure. The composer was awarded the Pulitzer Prize for it in 1957.

The men and women of the dance are arrayed in a large circle holding each other's hands as they rotate slowly at first and then more animatedly. It is the circle of a rounded community. The group departs and a man alone creates a solo that combines movements that are air-borne and others that are earth-bound as he dances about first birth and then death.

Four men enter and lift him then are joined by four women, and all work at the placing of seed in the ground and gathering up that which has been planted in its season. In "A Time to Kill" a man is isolated and alone and is set upon by three others, who menace him and then stab him. He falls and is ministered to by a woman who goes to him when the others have left. Her care is beneficial and he revives as a demonstration of "A Time to Heal."

A solitary man struggles in "A Time to Break Down and a Time to Build Up." He moves sinuously and jabs at the air. He reaches as high as possible and then tumbles low. A couple dance to the sound of clapping hands com-ing from off stage in "A Time to Keep Silence, and a Time to Speak." She stands with her hands covering her face as he enters slapping his palms across his thighs. She does a sorrowful solo and he does a powerfully asser-tive one to the sound of wood pounding on the floor. After he has finished he leaves and she remains with her own thoughts.

Three women enter for "A Time to Mourn . . . a Time to Weep." Hope for the future has left them. They are realistic about the time, their heads bow in an acknowledgment that there are sorrowful times. In complete con-trast to their mood is "A Time to Laugh . . . a Time to Dance" when a woman dashes on to circle the stage with great energy and high spirits. She wears a ringlet of flowers in her hair and her costume is gaily colored. The look of the dance reminds one of a hoedown as three couples follow her and then exit happily clapping.

She returns in "A Time to Embrace and a Time to Refrain from Embracing" to dance a warm duet with her partner, but then they are separated by a group of men who take them off in different directions. A woman alone dances in front of a group of men in "A Time of Hate; a Time of War." She is obviously driven by powerful emotions and refuses to be comforted by the men. The opposite mood is portrayed by another woman in "A Time to Love . . . a Time of Peace." The dance is coming full cycle, and all of the dancers return to form a circle and then split apart to do individual variations which reflect the various moods that have comprised the dance. At the end all join hands again and sway in their huge circle as it was in the beginning.

The dance has a lovely balance to it, contrasting the joyous and the sad, repeating the motif of the circle in a variety of ways throughout, and is one of the most completely realized large-scaled works that Limón created. There are wonderful opportunities for both solo variations and group dances included in the piece which has been a staple of the Limón repertory since its creation.

THE EMPEROR JONES

Choreography by José Limón. Music by Heitor Villa-Lobos. Scenery by Kim Edgar Swados. Costumes by Pauline Lawrence. First performed at the Empire State Festival, Ellenville, N.Y., on July 12, 1956, by José Limón, Lucas Hoving, Martin Morginsky, Richard Fitzgerald, José Gutierrez, Michael Hollander, Harlan McCallum, and Chester Wolenski.

Dramatic conflict and the anguish of lonely heroes were always appealing subjects to Limón. His reading brought Eugene O'Neill's great play to his attention, and he decided to create a choreographic interpretation of it. When it opens, we find the tragic hero at a crossroads in his career: he has led a successful revolt by black slaves against their master but now in turn is facing such a revolt against himself.

A huge throne dominates the stage. Jones sits in it with his splendid hat, his large epaulets gleaming on his shoulders. His head is bowed forward. Bare-chested men leap forward and away like ugly figments of his imagination. They leave and he rises to dance a solo full of swaggering and posturing and also a little suspicious uncertainty. The White Man enters with mock humility and provocatively hangs his hat on the back of the throne. Jones flings it to the ground and stands angrily over the man. He threatens him with his gun, which he has withdrawn from a glittering holster slung near his crotch, a positioning which suggests the weapon is a surrogate for his masculinity. The White Man goes behind the throne and begins to rock it menacingly, a poignant reminder of the uncertainty with which it is held.

The second scene is in a clearing in the forest, and Jones is on the run. Three trunks of trees stand menacingly, an arm or a leg darts out from behind each one mysteriously. Jones continues his flight. He returns several more times, each time in a greater degree of dishevelment. Finally he is bare chested without his magnificent coat and hat. In the next scene he is brought back to the chain gang but not before he brandishes his revolver. It is of no use; he seems himself driven to be one of these tormenting phantoms. He remembers the whip of the White Man, the cruel auction where he was displayed like a fine carcass.

Alone again in the forest, he chances upon a man and kills him but is again tormented by fears and his superstitions. He sees a multiarmed and legged creature which becomes some avenging demon of retribution to the hunted man. The final scene shows the White Man seated on the throne and Jones's body being brought in by his fellow slaves. They toss it about and show no feeling for him but rather intense dislike. His body is tossed back ironically on the great throne and he is covered with his flamboyant hat and splendid coat.

When Limón created the work in the mid-1950s, he was working with a group of male dancers exclusively and successfully managed to keep the lack of female dancers away from one's consciousness. It is only on reflection that one becomes aware that it was a dance that did not have the dramatic, heightening presence of female dancers, and that it worked quite well in the confines of its own restrictions.

LA MALINCHE

Choreography by José Limón. Music by Norman Lloyd. Costumes by Pauline Lawrence. First performed at the Ziegfeld Theatre, New York, N.Y., March 31, 1949, by Pauline Koner as La Malinche, Lucas Hoving as El Conquistador, and José Limón as a Peon.

The work is for two men and a woman and is set in Mexico at the time of the Spanish invasion of the country. The woman is torn between her interest in her countryman and the invader. It is a morality tale but told with a lighthearted bounce.

The music is playful, with lapses into a more serious tone from time to time. Of the three the peasant, the man in white, alone carries nothing as the dance begins. The woman has a flower and the second man has a cross, which can also pass for a sword. The woman looks at it and the man gives it to her as a gesture of his interest. The man in white stares and shows his unhappiness. She passes the sword back to the donor and goes to the peasant and wraps her skirt about him, but he pushes her away. She had just a moment before done exactly the same with the sword.

The woman now slips out of the large skirt. The peasant is terribly angry with the man holding the sword, who ignores his fury. The woman returns to him to dance and re-establish their happy relationship. Her loyalty to him is the strength that he needs. The man holding the sword collapses, and the woman pledges her troth with a gift of the flower to the peasant. Now that the story has been told, the three gather together to dance a spritely trio as they had at the beginning of the work.

One of the few humorous works in the Limón repertory that succeed, *La Malinche* draws on both Mexican fable and the presentational methods of folk dancers. The characters first enter as performers and only then begin the actual relating of the story. When it is concluded they resume their roles as performers. It is a game as well as a morality tale.

THE MOOR'S PAVANE

Choreography by José Limón. Music by Henry Purcell, arranged by Simon Sadoff. Costumes by Pauline Lawrence. Based on Shakespeare's Othello. *First performed at the Palmer Auditorium, Connecticut College, New London, Conn., August 17, 1949, by José Limón as the* Moor, *Lucas Hoving as* His Friend, *Betty Jones as the* Moor's Wife, *and Pauline Koner as* His Friend's Wife.

Shakespeare's plays have provided the framework for many choreographers to design dances to, and one of the best known is this one. It is modestly scaled, being designed for two couples, but it has a large emotional impact. Limón himself was the original Moor, and no one has ever danced it as well as he, though the work has been given by a wide variety of companies other than his own. Its formal invention is rich within the strict requirements of the traditional pavane.

The four protagonists face one another in the center of the stage; they wear courtly dress. The Moor's back is to the audience and he looks directly across at his "friend." The friend's wife and the Moor's bride stare at each other. The dance begins as all bend backwards and separate. The women bow and the two men return to the center, where they touch palms and push lightly away from one another. The Moor gives a lace handkerchief to his bride as the other couple observes carefully.

The group separates again only to dash past one another making intersecting diagonals at the center. The two men together come forward and the two women retire to the rear of the stage and then are joined briefly by the men, who move forward again. The friend stands behind the Moor, who stares out intently. The friend's hands are on Moor's shoulders as he whispers in one ear. The Moor slowly tilts his head to listen with the other ear and abruptly snaps his head around to glance at the object of the vilification, his bride. She comes forward innocently as the friend backs off obsequi-

ously. The Moor suppresses his aroused anger and as the two dance the
friend inserts himself between them momentarily and then removes himself
to join his wife. They dance together as the Moor and his bride stand frozen
to one side.

The wife twists and turns and the friend supports her. She raises her arms
above her head in protest and he reaches his higher and dominates her. She
is agitated and glances fearfully at the Moor and his bride and then returns
to her husband and stretches her arms toward him. He supports her.

The Moor and his bride join them in the center for the formal dance and
the friend's wife plucks the lacy handkerchief from the bride's hand and
waves it gaily before returning it. While the couples go through the formal
dance, the handkerchief is dropped accidently and the friend's wife stealthily retrieves it. Together with the bride they retire while the friend pours
more poison into the ear of the Moor. The two move forward, hopping; the
Moor in front springs upward and the friend, behind him as ever, pushes
down on his shoulders to launch himself upward. The Moor turns angrily
and slashes at him with his arm.

The friend goes to his wife, who flaunts the lace handkerchief, and he
takes it from her. All join for the pavane before the friend draws the Moor
aside once again. This time the Moor angrily demands proof of his Bride's
infidelity, and the friend dramatically produces the handkerchief and flicks
it at him like a whip. The Moor backs away crushed. His fury is scarcely
suppressed as he tenderly cups his bride's face then roughly squeezes her
arms. She is bewildered and his fury has taken hold of him.

The other couple steps in front of them to conceal the murder, and one
sees only the furious flailing arms of the Moor. When the couple steps aside
the bride lies dead. The two reproach one another for the results of their
mischief, and the friend tries to throttle his wife, but the Moor tears them
apart and bids them look at the results of his own rampant temper. He then
lies mournfully beside his dead beloved.

The tragic tale is related in a series of "asides" wherein the action is
carried on. Between these, all of the participants join together for a polite
formal dance which conceals the jealousy that is tearing them apart. No one
ever leaves the stage during the asides. Those not participating in the dramatic action simply freeze as if suspended in time before resuming the
dance. It is a brilliant device that heightens the intensity of the work immensely.

CHOREOCHRONICLE
OF JOSÉ LIMÓN

1931

B Minor Suite (with Eleanor
   King)
Mazurka (with Eleanor King)
Two Preludes

1936

Hymn

1937

Danza de la Muerta

1939

Danzas Mexicanas

1942

Chaconne

1943

We Speak for Ourselves
Western Folk Suite

1945

Concerto Grosso
Eden Tree
Three Ballads

1947

Song of Songs

1949

*The Moor's Pavane
*La Malinche

1950

Concert
Exiles

1951

Antígona
Los Cuatro soles
Dialogues
El Grito
The Queen's Epicedium
Tonantzintla

1952

The Visitation

1953

Don Juan Fantasia

1954

Ode to the Dance
The Traitor

1955

Scherzo
Symphony for Strings

1956

*The Emperor Jones
King's Heart
*There Is a Time

1957

Blue Roses

1958

Dances
Missa Brevis
Serenata

1959

Tenebrae 1914
The Apostate

1960

Barren Sceptre (with Pauline
Koner)

1961

The Moirai
Performance
Sonata for Two Cellos

1962

I, Odysseus

1963

The Demon
Choreographic Offering

1964

Two Essays for Large Ensemble

1965

My Son, My Enemy
Variations on a Theme of
Paganini

1966

The Winged

1967

Mac Aber's Dance
Psalm

1968

Comedy
Legend

1969

La Piñata

1970

The Unsung

1971

Dances for Isadora
Revel

1972

Carlota
Orfeo

1975

The Waldstein Sonata (with
Daniel Lewis)

n.d.

Mexican Suite—Indian
Petite Suite
Zapata

KATHERINE LITZ

Offbeat humor has been Litz's trademark throughout her career. In addition to some remarkable solos such as *Fall of a Leaf* she has even prepared a dance version of Bram Stoker's Gothic tale *Dracula*. She is fond of paradox and will allow a tragic gesture to become humorous simply by following the trajectory of the gesture to its kinetically logical conclusion. She might bend back with a hand pressed over her eyes in anguish only to continue to bend and end up inelegantly in a pile on the floor. Beneath the humor there resides a keen appreciation of tragedy that gives her work its pungency.

She studied with Doris Humphrey and Charles Weidman and was a member of their company for seven years, starting in 1936. She was a member of Agnes De Mille's concert group in the early 1960s and also danced in several musicals, including *Carousel* and *Oklahoma!* While on tour with the latter she encountered Sybil Shearer and worked with her.

She returned to New York and began to give programs of her own work in 1948 and to teach. She established her studio in Brooklyn Heights and continues to choreograph and teach there regularly. She has appeared in dramatic productions of the Judson Poet's Theater and has also given concerts of her own work at Judson Church. She has appeared at the major American dance festivals at Jacobs Pillow and at Connecticut College in addition to regular teaching in colleges throughout the United States.

THE FALL OF A LEAF

Choreography by Katherine Litz. Music by Louis Moreau Gottschalk. First performed at Hunter College Playhouse, New York, N.Y., February 1, 1959, by Katherine Litz.

Litz has put together a simple costume property, a frilled band, and her own incredibly expressive arms and hands to create the character of a woman throughout a passage of time. The Gottschalk music brings to mind a bygone era of manners and convention.

The woman enters in a long dress of rich velvet. She wears a broad-brimmed hat that ripples softly. It is perched diagonally on her head. She makes a long, elegant parade through the space, sweeping her arms from front to back as she goes. It gives the impression of conversations on the move, little bits of chat exchanged in a formal social situation. Everything is fleeting and elaborately casual.

The "hat" is in reality a U-shaped frilled clip that she now slides down across her bosom like the border of a scoop-necked dress. She is in the full bloom of her womanliness as she steps energetically. She slides the band lower, to her hips, and the breadth of her stride diminishes somewhat. She still moves as in a social encounter, but some of the spring has left her step and she cannot make abrupt changes in direction as easily.

Again she moves the band a bit lower to the mid-thigh, where it further constricts her movement, but she continues on as best she can. When it is pressed down to encircle the knees, it becomes a quite formidable hobble to her movement. The area through which she can comfortably pass has been brought to its smallest. With courage but resignation she makes a tiny little chain of turns and then exits.

Litz's artistry makes of a very simple dance a very moving statement about age and decline. The device of the band effectively and symbolically restricts the freedom of the individual much as age with its grip does. Litz keeps her fading charm and spirits up, throughout the process, exiting with dignity and wistfulness. It's tragedy is like that of a wilting bouquet.

CHOREOCHRONICLE
OF KATHERINE LITZ

1949

The Argument
Daughter of Virtue
Fire in the Snow
Suite for Woman

1951

The Long Night
The Glyph

1953

Brief Song
Garden of Doubts
Madame Bender's Dancing School
The Story of Love From Fear to
    Flight

1954

Excursion
The Lure
Summer Cloud
Thoughts out of Season

1956

The Enchanted

1958

In Terms of Time (with Ray
    Harrison)

1959

Dracula
*The Fall of a Leaf

1963

Poetry in Motion (with Paul
  Taylor)

1967

Continuum

1968

Sermon

1972

Mabel's Dress

1974

*They All Came Home Save One
Because She Never Left*

n.d.

*Songs of Joy
To be Continued
Ballet Ballads
Territory
Blood of the Lamb*

LAR LUBOVITCH

Relentless energy is a characteristic of Lubovitch's choreography, and it also is a quality of his whole career since he began taking dance class in his childhood. He has been attracted to both modern dance teachers and to ballet instructors. He studied with Louis Horst, Anna Sokolow, and at the Martha Graham and José Limón schools. His ballet instruction came from Antony Tudor, Margaret Black, and at the American Ballet Theater School from Leon Danielian. He has danced with an equally mind-boggling assortment of companies, including the modern dance groups of Pearl Lang, Donald McKayle, John Butler, and Glen Tetley. His balletic credits include the Harkness Ballet and Manhattan Festival Ballet. In addition to creating works for his own company he has prepared pieces for the Bat-Dor Company of Israel, American Ballet Theater, the Gulbenkian Ballet of Lisbon, the Pennsylvania Ballet, and the Santa Fe Opera company. He has also appeared at major festivals.

THE TIME BEFORE THE TIME AFTER
(AFTER THE TIME BEFORE)

Choreography by Lar Lubovitch. Music by Igor Stravinsky (Concertino for String Quartet). *Costumes and lighting by Lar Lubovitch. First performed at the Brooklyn Academy of Music, New York, N.Y., October 31, 1972, by Jeanne Solan and Lar Lubovitch.*

The title of the piece has something of the confusing simplicity of a Gertrude Stein sentence, but it makes perfectly good sense as long as one takes a moment to parse its time sequence. Lubovitch has interested himself in varieties of subjects, from pure movement exercises to snarled emotional complications such as this one.

It is the here and now, and a man and a woman clasp one another and she slides toward the floor. He clenches his fists at her and both circle one another warily. He falls and she stands over him while his body spasms, and both are circling one another again. He reaches out to her and places a hand on her breast compulsively and reacts excitedly when she touches him. Then in a turnaround he approaches her tenderly and when she responds warmly he points and mocks her. She covers her face with her hands. He regrets his cruelty and tries to comfort her but mistrust has become a habitual response between them and they face off, tautly anxious. They launch into a perpetual motion round of circling, flexing, and crumpling. She leans backward on him and he pushes her forward. They fall and rise together, constantly driven to embrace, and they conclude as he roughly grabs her and they twist downward in a sensual embrace.

The man and woman suffer from the chronic affliction of not being able to live with one another and not being able to live without one another. Their attraction is physical in the extreme and is the tie that binds. They separate but somehow are always drawn back together in order to repeat past mistakes, suggesting that the past and the future are both united in the present.

CHOREOCHRONICLE
OF LAR LUBOVITCH

1968

Freddie's Bag

1969

Incident at Lee
Transcendent Passage
Unremembered Time—
Forgotten Place

1970

Ecstasy
In a Clearing
Variations and Fugue on the
Theme of a Dream

1971

Clear Lake
Social

Some of the Reactions of Some of
the People Some of the Time
upon Hearing Reports of the
Coming of the Messiah
Whirligogs

1972

Joy of Man's Desiring
Sans titre
*The Time Before the Time After
(After the Time Before)

1973

Scherzo for Massah Jack

1974

Three Essays
Zig-Zag

IRIS MABRY

There is one thing everyone agrees on and that is the intelligence that Mabry brought to her compositions. She was graduated with honors from Smith and majored in philosophy and went to the Neighborhood Playhouse to study dance and also the Bennington College Summer School of the Dance. She performed mainly as a solo artist, devising her own programs and costuming and frequently dancing to the music of her husband composer and accompanist Ralph Gilbert.

She was on the faculty of the Jacobs Pillow University of Dance and also the Perry Mansfield School of Theater, and directed the dance program in the Theater Department of Smith College. After dancing in the United States for several years she went to live and perform in Paris, giving several recitals there in 1949. She was one of the first modern dancers to appear in France and was the subject of much curiosity because of the novelty of her approach to movement.

DREAMS

Choreography by Iris Mabry. Music by Ralph Gilbert. First performed at Times Hall, New York, N.Y., May 7, 1946, by Iris Mabry.

At her first independent solo program Mabry impressed the New York critics, as indicated by John Martin's highly laudatory review. "Her slender body is completely alive and eloquent, controlled from tip to toe by inner compulsion, and what she thinks and feels and imagines with it is highly individual. Sometimes even though the movement is small in dimensions and placid in exterior there is behind it a burning intensity that gives it power." On the concert she offered a selection of solos which included this dance.

One of the characteristics of Gilbert's piano style was an insistent, driving rhythm against which Mabry floated along. In the crossovers she passes from one side of the stage to the other while an almost frantic jukebox selection of popular jazz style tunes pours from the piano. She appears totally, almost neurotically removed from the dance movement as she performs it. There is a sense of alienation heightening the dream aspect of the dance. Its basic style is the walk, but each of the walking series is a variant that satirizes both real and dream movements. The walk is developed into runs, punctuated by frozen poses, and one derives hints of frustration amid the psychological wandering.

Possessed of a long supple body and a formidable intelligence, Mabry made a case history dance for herself that was rich but allusive in psychological hints and touches. She dipped into the unconscious and came up with a character who was bombarded all day by the flux of popular culture and social inconsequentialities and in dreams, driven to play them out, to exorcise them by ironically imitating them.

CHOREOCHRONICLE
OF IRIS MABRY

1946

Litany
Witch
*Dreams
Sarabande
Scherzo
Bird Spell
Rally
Cycle
Blues

1947

Rhapsody
Allemande
Doomsday

1954

Apassionata
Entr'acte

n.d.

Lamb of God
Dilemma
Counterpoint

MERLE MARSICANO

Describing her own work, Marsicano has written, "Jumping and rolling on the floor do not particularly suit my mode of expression. I am less interested in hurling myself at the extremities of space than I am in moving, however fast or slow, within the infinite gradation of this vertical dimension. . . . The air around me seems to have the capacity to solidify or melt. It can be heavy, then rarefied or agitated and becalmed. Sometimes I have to force my way through it and at other times I am driven by it."

To arrive at her own creative direction, Marsicano broke with the traditional ballet and modern dance training that she had had. Born in Philadelphia, she first studied ballet with Ethel Phillips and joined the Philadelphia Opera Company as ballet mistress and lead dancer. Among her works were the dances for the first production of Deems Taylor's *Ramuntcho*.

She studied modern dance with Ruth St. Denis and Martha Graham and dance composition with Louis Horst. She moved to New York, where she presented her own solos and formed a company in the early 1950s. Notable among the works which she created was the solo *Figure of Memory*. She married painter Nicholas Marsicano and was deeply affected by advanced art and music. Among composers she commissioned for works were John Cage, Morton Feldman, and Stefan Wolpe. Though retired as a performer she continues to present concerts of her work and teach.

FIGURE OF MEMORY

Choreography by Merle Marsicano. Music by Morton Feldman. First performed at the Henry Street Playhouse, New York, N.Y., April 3, 1954, by Merle Marsicano.

Marsicano's pieces are all about an emotional mood but are developed with a style from which emotional gesture has been abstracted. There is no dramatic incident or stress laid upon the movement, and soaring jumps as well as earth-bound tumbles are rigorously avoided.

A single figure occupies the space developing languid gestures of the arms. She moves about the area with short, skittering little steps, darting this way and that, always seeking and never really finding the object of her search. The mood is like one that might be encountered in a dream where mists part and close again with mysterious purpose.

Her feet are in constant motion, carrying her to all corners in her search. Her hands flicker momentarily, and then she will suddenly stretch her arms straight out, but the object of her search remains beyond her grasp. The feeling evoked is that of perennial searching without violent anxiety. She glides from place to place and never pounces.

One does not detect the familiar beginning, middle, and end development of the dance. It always seems to have been there and, when it ceases, it does not finish with a sense of resolve. It just trails away. One is not so much concerned with the individual moments of the dance but more with the over-all web of movement that enmeshes the attention.

CHOREOCHRONICLE
OF MERLE MARSICANO

1951

   Idyl

1954

   *Figure of Memory
   Jet Pears
   Green Song

1956

   Fragment of Greek Tragedy

1958

   Il n'ya plus de raison

1960

   Queen of Hearts

1962

   Carnival of Imagined Faces
   Gone

1963

   Images in the Open

n.d.

   First Dance
   The Long Gallery
   Time out of Season
   Yellow Night

DONALD MCKAYLE

Born in New York City, McKayle studied with a variety of modern dance teachers and found time to pursue academic studies at City College of New York. He has danced in many of the leading modern dance companies, including those of Martha Graham, Merce Cunningham, Anna Sokolow, and Jean Erdman, while he also made appearances in Broadway musicals.

He formed his own performing group and created *Games* in 1951. His most successful pieces have drawn on some aspect of the black experience, whether it be the urban world shown in *Games* or the prison life depicted in

Rainbow 'Round My Shoulder. He has worked with the movement vocabulary created by Martha Graham, showing strong emotional configurations and stress, for the most part, but adding his own lyricism to it.

He has not attempted to maintain his own company intact, preferring to assemble dancers for specific seasons which he has mounted periodically since he first began to choreograph. Through his work as a dancer on Broadway in *House of Flowers* and *West Side Story,* to name only the best known, he has found himself in demand as a choreographer as well. He is represented by the successful *Raisin,* among others. He has taught at the New Dance Group school, Bennington College, and the Juilliard School and has appeared at the Festival of Two Worlds in Spoleto. For several years he was the artistic director of the Inner City Dance Company in Los Angeles.

DISTRICT STORYVILLE

Choreography by Donald McKayle. Music by Dorothea Freitag, Sidney Bechet, Duke Ellington, and Jelly Roll Morton. Scenery and costumes by Norman Maxon. Lighting by Nicola Cernovich. First performed at the Ninety-second Street YM-YWHA, New York, N.Y., April 22, 1962, by Pearl Reynolds, Gus Solomons, Jr., William Louther, Thelma Oliver, Mabel Robinson, and Alfred De Sio.

The red light area of New Orleans was known as District Storyville. It was like other "sporting" districts full of saloons, bordellos, and jazz. The last has survived and graduated to the mainstream of popular culture, and in this piece McKayle gives one a feeling for the ambiance out of which this music emerged.

The "Funeral Function" is just that, a social function that has its own governing rules. There is a sorrowful procession out to the graveyard which is observed by a young man full of eagerness for the sound of the music. The mourners and widow are in black. When the group returns from the burial, the mood has brightened. The lead horn player mimes playing the instrument, making musical shapes with his hands. The young man imitates his elders.

The second section is "The Sporting House Saga" and the proprietress is followed in by three of her girls and then by a slightly clumsy stumbling forth. There is a stand on which rests a horn. The madame instructs her girls in how to flaunt their wares. The young man awkwardly enters and goes to the stand to polish the horn. Then three men enter the house through a beaded doorway at the rear. The girls flounce on and begin to compete for the attention of the three.

During an "Entertainment" a wildly gyrating girl stands on top of a silver box doing a shimmy dance to the delight of the men. It is followed immediately by a passionate duet between one of the girls and the man who is

"King" of the horn players. She is a mass of feathers and fluff and he is full of the physical tension of being the most important man in the district.

While they are passionately engaged, the young man looks longingly at the horn on its stand. He goes over to it, touches it, and dances out his longing to be the master of such a splendid instrument. Emboldened, he takes the horn and the hat of the King but is caught by the madame. For a moment they play at his being the King and her being his girl, but she sends him away after a little while.

There is a music contest, but as previously the big man, the King, wins it again. The competitors go off, and the three girls move around mournfully until the sporting action begins again as it will repeatedly, but the parade of all the members at the end, led by the man with the horn, shows that the energy of the district is moving out to conquer others.

Sex and rhythmic expression of its high level energy were the loam out of which developed much of popular music. In uniting the bordello and the King of the instrumentalists, McKayle points out the connection precisely. A delightful subplot is that of the young man longing for mastery of the instrument and impatient to be King in his own right. There is no hiding the sadness of much of the life, but it is surpassed by the vibrant brilliance of the music.

REFLECTIONS IN THE PARK

Choreography by Donald McKayle. Music by Gary McFarland. Costumes by Norman Maxon. First performed at Hunter College Assembly Hall, New York, N.Y., March 6, 1964, by Robert Powell, Pearl Reynolds, Gus Solomons, Jr., Carmen de Lavallade, Jaime Rogers, Takako Asakawa, Mabel Robinson, Raymond Sawyer, and Sylvia Waters.

The Modern Jazz Society of Hunter College in New York decided to present a combined dance and music program in the mid-sixties, and asked composer Gary McFarland and McKayle to create a joint work. The resulting piece placed the musicians on stage lined up across the rear while the dancers performed in front of them. The two collaborators were in definite rapport and the piece looked stunning.

The principals are a man and a woman and the story is the story of how a man meets a woman and how love conquers all. It happens in a park, Central Park, to be exact. A host of characters are found there, including the unsavory. A young man with the restless edginess of one bred to and fed up with concrete comes to seek a little rest in the greenery. Like an overwound clock he is sprung with untapped drive power. A covey of pigeons and their feathery amours catches his idle eye. A woman casually strolls by and he is attracted. Some children play and an older lady comes along to shoo the pigeons.

Drawn one to the other, the couple steals off but is attacked by local predators. He is knocked down and she is assaulted. Each stumbles off to a separate section of the park after the incident. She recovers in the nightmare carnival of the merry-go-round and he in the noisy zoo. Some electioneering and a revival meeting transpire before they find one another, but they do.

The dozen episodes added up to an airy sponge of surpassing lightness, touching upon romance, religion, ribaldry, and rape. The last was coped with successfully and the locale provided McKayle with the opportunity to include a whole range of the activities of large city citizens, including some of the violence that is a part of city life. As in other pieces he mixes the good with the bad and emerges with a work that has a basic optimism. His invention for Carmen de Lavallade and Gus Solomons, Jr., was wonderfully effective, especially in their climactic duet "Does the Sun Really Shine on the Moon."

RAINBOW 'ROUND MY SHOULDER

Choreography by Donald McKayle. Music from the collection of John and Allen Lomax, arranged by Robert deCormier and Milton Okun and sung by Leon Bibb. Costumes by Domingo A. Rodriguez. First performed at the Ninety-second Street YM-YWHA, May 1959, by Mary Hinkson, Donald McKayle, Alfred De Sio, Harold Pierson, Charles Moore, Gus Trikonis, Jaime Rogers, and Jay Fletcher.

The chain gang working along rural roads in the South has become a thing of the past for most states, but at one time it was a common sight to see a group of men linked together at the ankles with a length of chain, going out from or returning to a prison farm. It is from the dreams and frustrations of these men that McKayle created this powerful dance.

A line of men stripped to the waist enters at the rear of the stage. They have their arms thrown over one another's shoulders and move as a unit, twisting their bodies from one side and then straightening up again and repeating the downward twist as if reacting to the touch of a lash. They separate and bend forward convulsively. They clasp their hands behind their backs and stretch backward as if being tugged by unseen bonds. The dull, unrewarding work of the gang is illustrated by a man slamming his arms downward as if he were hefting a heavy sledge hammer. The movements of the men are forceful but begin to reflect a weariness as the day progresses. They link hands and proceed to slump to the ground in a cluster. It is night and they toss from time to time in an exhausted sleep, starting up then sliding back again.

The first of the dreams is that of the sweetheart left behind. She enters to do a smooth, reflective solo with lovely turns and extensions in complete contrast to the twisted and powerful movements of the men's dance. She leaves to return a moment later as a saucy, bouncy girl who is joined by one of the men. They frolic and gambol while the accompanying song tells us that the man wants to get a "jug of brandy" and go to see his girl. She exits to finish that dream.

The young man now thinks back to the life that he had on his parents' farm before being put in jail. The woman returns with a kerchief over her head and takes the man and twists his shoulder this way and that way as if directing him in his many chores. He is pliant and to each of the questions posed in the song as to whether he has done this or that the reply is "Yes'm."

The man rejoins the group and they toss and turn as if continually tormented by dreams. Then they are up and dash back and forth restlessly. The lure of freedom exerts a continual pull upon them, and two men break away and run off. Shots are heard offstage and one man tumbles backward, to be gathered up in the arms of one of the other prisoners. The rest run back and forth making angry gestures, but it does not change the fact that "Another man done gone."

The second of the two has also been wounded, and we see him alone on the stage stumbling but driven by his vision to return home. His wife enters and he goes to her. She places his head on her lap. He has returned home but dies from his wounds.

The message of the chain gang is that there is no escape except through death and the living death of enduring imprisonment tormented by thoughts of the life left behind. The ensemble groupings for the men are powerful, and the role of all the women is taken by one dancer who must portray all of the feminine attributes. It is a tall order but rewarding when done by a first rate soloist.

CHOREOCHRONICLE
OF DONALD MCKAYLE

1951

  Games

1952

  Saturday's Child
  Her Name Was Harriet

1954

  The Street
  Prelude to Action
  Nocturne

1958

  Muse in the News
  Out of the Chrysalis

1959

  *Rainbow 'Round My Shoulder

1960

  Legendary Landscape

1962

  *District Storyville

1963

  Arena
  Blood of the Lamb

1964

  *Reflections in the Park
  Workout

1965

  Daughters of the Garden

1968

  Incantation

1969

  Burst of Fists

1972

  Barrio
  Songs of the Disinherited
  Migrations
  Sojourn

1974

  Raisin (mc)

n.d.

  Exodus
  Wilderness

JACK MOORE

Moore's connection with the founding generation of dancers has extended from his training to his choreography, but he has a stubborn streak of independence that inserts itself into his choreography in delightfully unusual ways. He sometimes shows a dadaesque gift for titling as in *Rocks,* which he created after another choreographer had created a ballet called *Jewels,* or in his props when his dancers scatter greens around in another dance or cavorted with an automobile tire in yet another.

He was born in Indiana and took jazz, tap, and baton twirling at a neighborhood school. After service in World War II he entered college and became an art major but also did some theater work, and he was offered a scholarship to the summer dance course run by Hanya Holm at the University of Colorado. The experience turned him definitely in the direction of a dance career and he came to New York in 1949. He was Louis Horst's assistant in his composition course and danced for a season with the Martha Graham company.

He was one of the founders of Dance Theater Workshop, which offered an alternative to single evening concerts in its series, and he continued his own creative work. He has taught at the Juilliard School of Music, and was the first of the Doris Humphrey fellows to have a summer residency at Connecticut College's American Dance Festival. He is currently on the faculty of Bennington College.

ROCKS

Choreography by Jack Moore. First performed at Bennington College, Bennington, Vt., November 1967. Revised version performed at the Dance Theater Workshop, New York, N.Y., April 10, 1970, by Leslie Berg, Nancy Green, Wendy Perron, Wendy Summit, Linda Tarnay, Linda Wilder, Aaron Osborne, Andé Peck, and Gene Stulgaitis.

Jack Moore's dances are created with spare good sense and are leavened with offbeat humor that is sometimes macabre. They have an air of calm and balance, somehow of mystical repose, even when the overt actions of the dancers are highly energetic. He sees the darker side of life with a wry smile.

A film of roof tiles is shown in "Pumice," the first section of the dance. The cast is costumed identically in brown shirts and white bell-bottomed trousers. Their bodies tremble as they stand with profile to the audience and look out over one shoulder. Individually each sinks to the stage to perform solo tasks. The wiping motion on the floor makes one think of generations of sailors who ground wooden decks clean with real pumice stones. Arms stretch out, then a hand is held over the mouth. Each rises separately and strides. All conclude walking in small circles with hands over mouths.

"Jade" begins with one man arching back. A woman jumps past him, then slides under him and clutches his arm. They repeat the small duet, and he drags her off. A quartet of women move back and forth across the rear of the stage in formation, after one woman has hand-walked around the stage with the others holding her by the legs like the handles of a wheel barrow. Two men and another woman spend most of the time seated making small positional changes in a tight cluster. Nothing is hurried or pushed out with a high dynamic level. A garbled version of a popular song is played. One man of the trio becomes superfluous when the woman shows a preference for the other.

A woman moving on a diagonal falls and rises to open the final movement, designated "Slag." Another dancer crosses on all fours using the palms of the hands as well as the soles of the feet. The entire cast of nine dancers enter linked together at the rear of the stage. They circle to the front, sing songs, clap hands, and break formation. Slides of rocks continue to be shown; all run and jump. They strike out in different directions doing a stiff-legged walk, moving their arms in a variety of positions derived from the ballet technique. The five dancers in the front jump and rise on the balls of the feet. The four at the rear move forward and all jump and turn on their own axes. They stop, clasp their hands behind their backs, bend at the knee, and hum "Rock of Ages." They walk again, crouch, and step from side to side, clap, kneel, and crawl toward the center of the stage. Two fine webs drop over them as they crawl.

The piece remains curiously aloof despite its somewhat mad elements. These are never allowed to get out of hand, and the balanced desperation that is an undercurrent in the dance is preserved intact. The men and women do varieties of dances and mimed tasks that strike one as being funny, and yet one has the feeling that all are trapped in a system that will eventually wear everyone down and send them to the slag heap despite a brief, semiprecious interlude.

CHOREOCHRONICLE
OF JACK MOORE

1951

Esprit de Corps
Clown '51

1957

Somewhere to Nowhere
The Act

1958

The Geek
Cry of the Phoenix

1959

Area Disabled
Figure '59

1960

Songs Remembered
Intaglios

1961

Target

1962

Opticon—A Vaudeville of the
   Mind
Excursions
Erasure

1963

Chambers and Corridors

1965

Vintage Riff
Assays (1963–5)

1966

Parsley All over the World
Four Elements in Five Movements
Figure '66

1967

Vintage Riff No. 2
Brew

1968

Five Scenes in the Shape of an
   Autopsy

1969

Puzzle
Tracks
Tracings
Residue—Variants 1, 2, 3, 4

1970

*Rocks (revival)

1971

Fantaisie pour deux
Ode

1972

Blueprint: Gardenstrip
3 Odes

1973

> *Ghost Horse Rocker*
> *Tracks and Side Tracks*

1974

> *Nightshade*
> *Garden of Delights*
> *Landscape for a Theater*

1975

> *Resume*
> *Love Songs for Jason Mayhen*
> *Six Easy Pieces for Anna* (tv)

DANIEL NAGRIN

There is belligerent and sinewy energy behind Nagrin's works that is beautifully seen in a work like *Strange Hero*, which pays a somewhat ironic tribute to a common gangster. Nagrin started with his own solo work while still a member of the Tamiris-Nagrin Company in the early 1940s. He was married to the late Helen Tamiris, and when he left the company he toured widely with his solo program.

He was born in New York City and studied with a variety of modern dance teachers including Tamiris, Hanya Holm, Martha Graham, and Anna Sokolow. From each teacher he selected movement approaches that suited his own choreographic ideas and blended them together in a jazz-oriented style that has a vibrant dynamic force.

Besides extensive work as a concert dancer he has also appeared on Broadway in *Annie Get Your Gun, Touch and Go,* and *Plain and Fancy* and he has choreographed the Off-Broadway productions of *Volpone* and *His Majesty O'Keefe*. He has taught at C. W. Post College and New York University as well as at his own studio, where he has currently formed a work group that explores improvisation within broad outlines set down before performance.

STRANGE HERO

Choreography by Daniel Nagrin. Music by Stan Kenton and Pete Rugolo. Costumes by Daniel Nagrin. First performed in a hotel ballroom, Eighth Avenue and Fifty-first Street, New York, N.Y., Spring 1948, by Daniel Nagrin.

The swaggering gangster has been the hero of innumerable films and plays, but Nagrin's translation of him remains one of the few convincing portraits that we have on the dance stage.

He walks on in a suit jacket that has grossly padded shoulders and is tightly fit to the torso. His trousers are full to the point of being baggy except at the ankle, where they are cuffed tightly to the leg. A cigarette dangles from his lips. He is wary as he steps forward. He halts and elaborately raises his hand to remove the cigarette from his mouth, and he replaces it a moment later.

His hand darts to his side and he slaps his thigh and points a forefinger as if training a gun at someone, but then he continues the gesture upward to withdraw the cigarette from his lips again. His body twitches like that of an animal that senses an enemy. He steps forward quickly and squats as if eying danger. Nothing challenges him and he strides away arrogantly then leaps and whirls around. He is constantly on the alert. He is startled now and runs to flatten himself against an imaginary wall where he looks around carefully.

He steps out with knees flexed, rolls over quickly on the ground, rises deftly, and points his forefingers at an enemy. His body recoils from the shocks of firing his two "pistols." He moves over to look at the fallen foe and kicks at the imaginary corpse, then leans forward to pound it furiously. As he stands to leave the conquered enemy, his body convulses with the impact of another enemy's bullets. He tumbles backward, is hit again and again. He touches his forehead as if to salute an unseen but victorious enemy.

The grim world of the predators portrayed makes one think of the jungle with its inexorable round of preyers and preyed-upon. Were it not for the ironic salute Nagrin's hero would be no different from the instinctive animals found there. Because of its recognition of superior stealth it is the trademark of a strange but recognizable warrior.

CHOREOCHRONICLE
OF DANIEL NAGRIN

1942

  Private Johnny Jukebox

1943

  *"Landscape with three figures,
    1859"*

1948

  Spanish Dance
  *Strange Hero
  Man of Action

1950

  Dance in the Sun
  The Ballad of John Henry
  Faces from Walt Whitman

1954

  Man Dancing
  Tom O'Bedlam

1957

  Progress
  Indeterminate Figure
  Volpone (p)

1958

  Three Happy Men
  Jazz, Three Ways
  *The Boss Man and the Snake
    Lady*
  With My Eye and with My Hand
  A Dancer Prepares
  For a Young Person

1959

  Dance in the Sun

1960–61

  An Entertainment
  An American Journey
  The Umbrella (p)
  The Firebugs (p)

1962

  Two Improvisations

1963

  The Man Who Did Not Care
  Emperor Jones (p)

1965

  In the Dusk
  Not Me, But Him
  Path
  A Gratitude
  In Defense of the City
  Why Not

1968

  The Peloponnesian War

1971

The Image
Duet
The Ritual
Polythemes
Wind I
Rondo
Mary Anne's Dance
Rituals of Power

1972

Signs of the Times
Fragment Rondo I and *II*
Ritual for Two
Ritual for Eight
Quiet Dance I and *II*
Wounded Knee
Sea Anemone Suite

1973

Hello-Farewell-Hello
Steps

1974

Untitled
Jazz Changes
Sweet Woman

1975

Nineteen Upbeats
The Edge Is Also a Center

MAY O'DONNELL

Like many of the dancers who performed with the Martha Graham company, O'Donnell left to create her own works, and while she showed some of the heritage she received in that company, she also displayed an intriguing originality.

She began to study dance in her native California with Estelle Reed in San Francisco. Her first professional appearances were made with Reed's company, and then she left to study in New York with Martha Graham. She joined the latter's company in 1932 and remained with it as a featured dancer for eight years.

With Gertrude Shurr, another graduate of the Graham company, and her husband, the composer Ray Green, she returned to California to found the San Francisco Dance Theater in 1939 and presented the first of her own works. She taught and then two years later joined the José Limón company and toured with it for three years.

She returned to the Graham company as a guest artist, creating memorable roles in *Appalachian Spring, Herodiade,* and *Cave of the Heart* as well as dancing major roles in the repertory. During this time she formed her own company and continued to create her own pieces, among them *Suspension.* After retiring from active performing she taught at a variety of schools including the School of Performing Arts. At present she continues to teach at the O'Donnell-Shurr studio in New York.

SUSPENSION

. . . at the still point of the turning world . . . there the dance is . . .

T. S. ELIOT

Choreography by May O'Donnell. Music by Ray Green. Scenery and costumes by Claire Falkenstein. First performed at the May O'Donnell Dance Studio, San Francisco, Calif., February 3, 1943, by Nancy Lang, Caryl Cuddeback, La Viva del Curo, Gregory Woodruff, Jessica Fleming, Lucy Herrick, and May O'Donnell.

Appearing as it did in the early forties, the dance puzzled most critics and delighted others. As one of the leading dancers of the Martha Graham company, O'Donnell was expected to reproduce works that bore the stamp of stressed drama, so familiar from Graham's work. Instead O'Donnell chose to design a serene piece that was calm and almost floating in its thrust. For an explanation she appended a quote from the poetry of T. S. Eliot ". . . at the still point of the turning world . . . there the dance is . . ."

A large mobile turns lazily at the left of the stage, and two boxes stand to the right. A woman bends back over the larger of the two as if she were offering herself on an altar, and then slowly turns lifting her arms like the cross members of the mobile. Her whole demeanor has a floating lightness as she moves on and about the two boxes.

Four women and two men walk slowly on and stretch their arms outward. They kneel, turn, and balance while she continues to work with the boxes. There is a studied lack of tension. The movement has the quality of people stirring at a great depth underwater. Individuals seat themselves and stretch their bodies upward; all behave as if they were isolated bits. People make momentary contact but they merely touch one another rather than establish a real bond. Their dealings with one another have a motor logic rather than an emotional tension, they exist to balance from one another more than to relate on a deeper level.

The pace of the movement is heightened in the third movement as the lighting becomes more intense and the dancers leap and march. The woman on the boxes, however, remains remote, still simulating the soft drifting of the mobile, and soon the others return to a less frantic state, walking and balancing as they had been at first. To conclude, all lie on their sides extending one leg as the solitary woman remains on her boxes and the others inhabit the remaining stage space.

The dance was really ahead of its audience when it first appeared, and only ten years later were audiences prepared to accept its unusual movement approach. It has been revived several times and most recently with dancers from the Alvin Ailey American Dance Theater company. O'Donnell created a poetical cloud of movement that refused to be hurried. She deliberately slowed down the timing of the piece and it ran contrary to the expectations of audiences, who were unable to appreciate its dreamlike quality because it was so contrary to its anticipations. The work didn't thunder, shout, or roar its message; it whispered but eventually achieved recognition.

CHOREOCHRONICLE
OF MAY O'DONNELL

1937

Of Pioneer Women
  a. Sarah Goes a Courtin'
  b. Markers on the Trail
  c. Jubilation for a Frontier

1939

Running Set

1940

So Proudly We Hail
  a. Cornerstone
  b. Hymn Tunes
  c. Of Pioneer Women
  d. Our Rivers Our Cradles
  e. Dance Set
  f. Epilogue from Cornerstone

1941

On American Themes (with
  José Limón)
  a. Curtain Raiser
  b. ". . . this story is legend . . ."
  *c. Three Inventories of Casey
    Jones*
Dance Theme and Variations

1943

*Suspension

1949

Celtic Ritual
Forsaken Garden
Horizon Song
Jig for a Concert

1952

Act of Renunciation
Dance Sonata No. 1
Magic Ceremony
The Queen's Obsession (*Macbeth
  1952–59*)
Ritual of Transition
Spell of Silence

1954

Dance Concerto
Legendary Forest

1955

Incredible Adventure

1956

Lilacs and Portals
Second Seven
  Part I—The Drift
  Part II—The Threshold
Dance Sonata No. 2

1958	1961
Dance Energies (1958–74)	*Sunday Sing Symphony*
Dance Sonatinas:	
Polka Sonatina	1962
Song Sonatina	*Dance Scherzos*
Cowboy Sonatina	

ELEO POMARE

The earliest part of Pomare's life was spent in Cartagena, Colombia, where he was born, and later in Panama, before he was brought to New York at the age of ten. He attended the School of Performing Arts and also studied with outside teachers like Louis Horst and Curtis James. Upon graduation in 1958 he founded a small company but four years later disbanded it and left for Europe on a John Hay Whitney Foundation fellowship. He studied at the Kurt Jooss school in Germany and organized another company abroad, where he toured in Northern Europe and the Scandinavian countries.

When he returned to the United States, he assembled another company, with which he toured extensively. He was the first director of the "Dance-mobile," which has brought professional dance companies to selected street locations to perform for the public at no charge. He has been the recipient of a Guggenheim fellowship and in 1971 founded the Vital Arts Dance School, which has as its aim the training of professional dancers "with knowledge of the history, the technique and performing capability of the dance."

BLUES FOR THE JUNGLE

Choreography by Eleo Pomare. Music by Harry Belafonte, Oscar Brown, Jr., Charles Mingus, and Michael Olatunji. First performed at the Ninety-second Street YM-YWHA, New York, N.Y., October 16, 1966, by Chuck Davis, Michael Ebbin, Strody Meekins, Al Perryman, Eleo Pomare, Ron Pratt, Bernard Spriggs, Shawneequa B. Scott, Lillian Coleman, Judi Dearing, Carole Johnson, Jeannet R. Rollins, Shirley Rushing, and Dolores Vanison.

The realistic depiction of current and historical events in this dance about black oppression inevitably calls to mind the tradition of the activist theater of the thirties. Pomare has a message that he wants to transmit, and his chosen medium is the performing stage.

A man stands on a platform while two women run past, and the strong sound of percussion fills the air. The voice of a slave auctioneer is then heard making a brutally frank evaluation of the women and their merits. Three men trapped in a prison and forced to work display their strong, athletic bodies as they bend to their tasks, but even their strength is worn down by the exertions continually demanded of them.

The focus of the dance moves forward rapidly, leaving overt slavery and chain-gang scenes behind to focus on the big cities. A saxophone is heard, but once again we see a man struggling against difficulties. He tries to advance but something keeps pushing him back and finally forces him to his knees.

Now in the longest portion of the dance a large cast of contemporary characters are presented in little vignettes that show a turbulent range of life in a black ghetto. A preacher enters and gospel music is heard, others watch as a woman acts out the gospel songs. Other women enter and men come to dance with them. The preacher arrives with a Bible and inspires a religious seizure among the dancers.

Events succeed one another rapidly. A man and a woman each drag a chair out to the center of the stage and make random dialing motions that produce a flow of everyday commercial messages from a radio. It all seems irrelevant and the man and woman become more and more disillusioned with one another until he finally strangles her after various conflicts, and a police siren sounds. A girl is confronted by a heroin addict who lives for injections of the drug. She stares at him as he writhes and twitches with desire for his narcotic.

Suddenly the slave auctioneer's voice is heard again as a night-club singer on a platform is seen in a tight dress.

Then a whole collection of people is seen filling the stage, there are blatant prostitutes, worn-out older people, swaggering young men, frisky kids, and an air of anger is felt from them. They all join hands to swirl around and are determined to escape from the trap that they are in. But they are restrained ironically enough by a black policeman who enters to restore "order."

There are varieties of dances that have been created on the miseries of the ghetto and the injustices endured by blacks, but no single choreographer is able to put the edge of resentment so integrally into the fabric of his work as is Pomare. His formal dance invention is not especially fresh, but his sense of selection and the placement of his theatrical elements are special. He has most successfully translated anger into choreographic expression.

NARCISSUS RISING

Choreography by Eleo Pomare. First performed at St. Mark's Playhouse, New York, N.Y., April 29, 1968, by Eleo Pomare.

This extraordinary dance is so much a vehicle for Pomare's own special talents that it might not survive transference to another dancer, but the vividness of its imagery and combination of erotic and social energy make it particularly relevant to Pomare's body of work. It is the rise and fall of a motorcyclist told with a minimum of movement but a world of theatrical intensity.

The first sound that is heard is the pounding acceleration and deceleration of a motorcycle engine. The dancer stands center stage facing the audience dressed in a minimum of clothes. His aviator's cap has a rakishly crushed crown and its visor juts forward. A leather gauntlet is worn on each hand, and heavy black boots come up over the ankles. A small leather dance belt completes the costuming, and large sunglasses mask his eyes. The total impression is a menacing one. With his hands spread as if gripping imaginary handlebars he rotates his wrists miming the gesture used to make a motorcycle accelerate and does a series of slow knee bends while facing the audience and then again in profile. His dark body glistens with a coating of oil.

Abandoning the act of driving a motorcycle, he thrusts his fists forward, punching and striking at unseen enemies. On the back of the stage his shadow is enormously magnified and adds to the hostility of his gestures. But ironically it is so large that it makes him seem puny in his rage. He is a man on the run and turns to the right and left. Suddenly his body is illuminated by a play of lights suggestive of police searchlights. He is on the run but has been tracked and cornered and, resigned to his entrapment, he slowly collapses.

One of the chief assets that Pomare has is his ability to take anger and use it effectively within a dance structure. Here the encircled motorcyclist could be read as having a relationship to any outlaw sensibility which is forced to lead an existence beyond the borders of what are considered the normal boundaries of behavior. And who must also pay the price for that rebellion.

CHOREOCHRONICLE
OF ELEO POMARE

1966

*Blues for the Jungle
Serendipity 1966

1967

Climb
Las Desenamoradas
High Times

1968

*Narcissus Rising

1969

Beginsville

1970

Movement for Two

1971

Black on Black
Burnt Ash
Movements

1974

Hushed Voices
Descent and Portals

1975

De la tierra
Radiance of the Dark

PEARL PRIMUS

A doctorate in anthropology is not the ordinary background for a successful concert dancer, but Primus has combined her interest in the study of black dance in Africa and the Caribbean, for which she earned her Ph.D., with a performing career. She has found the sources for a variety of dances in the rituals of the peoples she has studied, and has created a series of works based on them.

Her compact piston energy was first seen on the stage in 1943, and since then she has taught and toured regularly, both in the United States and abroad. She has devoted much of her time to study and performing in Africa, making her first visit there in 1948 and returning off and on for the next fifteen years. She created and shared a company with her husband, Percival Borde, but now confines herself to teaching and choreography. Most recently her works have been presented by the Alvin Ailey American Dance Theater as part of its continuing series of revivals designed to show the roots of modern dance.

THE WEDDING

Choreography by Pearl Primus. Set to traditional rhythms and chants of Africa (Oliwa, arranged by Solomon Ilorin). Costumes by Pearl Primus and Percival Borde. Scenery by Charles Rosen. Lighting by Marvin March. Commissioned by the African Research Foundation, Inc. First performed at the first annual African Carnival, 69th Regiment Armory, New York, N.Y., December 1961, by Chi Chi Ajuluchuku, Akwasiba Derby, Jocelyn Martinez, Delzora Pearson, Pearl Reynolds, Mary Waithe, Ruby Pryor, Edith Bascombe, Bangi Awallo, Matt Cameron, Tommy Johnson, Percy Nicholas, Oba-ya Okun, Marlo Timonz, Morton Winston, and Adetunji Joda.

The dance is a narrative based on an African model that tells of the evil that befell a young couple on their wedding day. The happiness that they feel is menaced by the appearance of a hostile magician who is clearly described as the Demon of Evil.

The wedding party enters led by the men, in long skirtlike costumes, who thrust and withdraw their hands in front of them and go off. They are followed by the women, who rock their pelvises rhythmically. They place one hand on the hip and push the other out repeatedly as they walk in a circle. All of this is by way of preliminary to the entrance of the bride, who now appears with her two attendants. She is much more restrained and takes tiny steps as she circles prior to sitting in the center on a low stool.

The men return to form a large circle that revolves clockwise around her, and the women make a smaller circle and move in the opposite direction in the middle of the stage. They all break away from this concentric formation and make two smaller circles, the men to one side of the bride and the women on the other. The bride sits very quietly in the center of this maelstrom of activity. The women also recline as the men leap energetically and form a line to stride forcefully forward and back. The women ripple and roll their shoulders while clapping to encourage the men to greater demonstrations of their prowess. The men respond, whirling animatedly and slashing at the air with the whisks they carry, and then leave. The women bound up and form a running circle which the bride joins excitedly, but she is made to sit on her stool.

Her attendant, who functions as a mistress of the ceremony, pounds and leaps as the other women clap. The women form a serpentine line, stretching out one arm and becoming a decorative background to the bride, who stands to leap and turn in a solitary dance. The scene is one of energetic and happy enthusiasm for the joy of the bride. Suddenly it is interrupted by the appearance of the demon, who frightens all into a cowering stance. He is accompanied by an evil assistant who abets his malevolence. The demon radiates a powerful influence which he uses to draw the women away from the group or to force them to collapse under the spell of his rapidly vibrating arms and hands. He drives all of the women away after he has demonstrated his power over them individually and now isolates the bride, who trembles and turns at his beckoning. The men return but are powerless and one by one are forced to the floor, where they thrash helplessly. When all appears completely lost, the "healer" appears to vanguish the demon and release the others from his power. The men and women celebrate with a communal dance as the demon and his assistant do a little stuttering step as they are banished.

The dance is a combination of original dance materials and choreographic shaping according to the conventions of the Western stage. It is gorgeously costumed and makes a striking impact visually. The demon has by far and away the choicest dance role in the entire piece, but as in all stories with a happy ending he has his power broken.

FANGA

Choreography by Pearl Primus. Set to traditional Gio Fanga orchestra music. Costumes by Pearl Primus. Scenery consisted of nature's palm branches and flowers. Lighting by Liberian Government technicians. First presented at a command performance for the Republic of Liberia, West Africa, at the Executive Mansion, Monrovia, Liberia, November 1949, by Pearl Primus and indigenous musicians who danced as they played in authentic fashion. Pearl Primus was decorated for this interpretation of Liberian culture with the Order of "Star of Africa" by the President of the Republic of Liberia, the late Dr. William V. S. Tubman.

This dance of greeting is one which ordinarily would be performed in West Africa by a large group of women. Primus has artfully extracted the essence of the original and shaped it as a solo for presentation in the proscenium theater. She danced it herself originally but has now passed on the role to others, and the work is currently in the repertory of the Alvin Ailey American Dance Theater.

The sound of drumming is heard before the curtain is raised. When it does rise we see a group of singers and percussion players seated at the front of the stage at the left. The solo dancer enters from the rear of the stage on that side and moves forward in a diagonal. She bends to the ground, pushing and retracting her hands from it. She stands and looks straight out, extending her hands, palms upward, and waggles her head gaily. She pushes her hands upward and does a series of little leaps. She walks alternately to the right and the left, shaking her head happily, then she goes to the rear of the stage and passes off once again, pushing her hands toward the earth and withdrawing them as she had done when she first entered.

Taking small steps, she re-enters with a cloth draped across her outstretched arms. She bows to the musicians, places the cloth down at the front of the stage, and with her hands on her hips pumps her elbows forward and back in a flapping motion as she walks off. She returns in a moment, again making the flapping gesture, and then begins to whirl kerchiefs in the air with each arm as she vibrates her legs. With her feet together she moves to the side, progressing by pivoting first on the ball of the foot and then on the heel. She enlarges the circles she makes with her arms and then stops to place her hands in front of her face. She waggles the fingers then spreads her arms widely, gives a few final ecstatic wags to her head, and runs off, kerchiefs trailing.

The dance is relatively short but contains a wealth of friendly hospitable gesture, and represents one of the more accomplished adaptations of folk dance materials for the contemporary stage.

CHOREOCHRONICLE
OF PEARL PRIMUS

1942

Hear the Lamb a' Crying

1943

African Ceremonial
Te Moana
Shouters of Sobo
Strange Fruit
Rock Daniel
Hard Times Blues
Jim Crow Train
The Negro Speaks of Rivers
Folk Dance
Afro-Haitian Play Dance
Yanvaloo
Café Society (mc)

1944

Study in Nothing
Our Spring Will Come
Slave Market
Caribbean Conga
Motherless Child
Good Night Irene
Take This Hammer
Mischievous Interlude
Wade in the Water
Gonna Tell God
Steal Away
Dark Rhythms (mc)

1945

Mean and Evil Blues

Twinsome Two Minds
Just Born
Scorpio
African Ceremonial (mc)

1946

Dance of Beauty
Myth
Dance of Strength
War Dance
Great Getting Up Morning
Folk Song
Chamber of Tears

1947

Emperor Jones (p)
Trio
Santos
The Witch Doctor
Legend
Shango
Calypso (mc)

1948

Caribbean Carnival

1949

*Fanga
Prayer of Thanksgiving
Go Down Death
Invocation
Chicken Hop
American Folk Dance

1950

Egbo Escapade
The Initiation
Everybody Loves Saturday Night
Fertility
Benis Woman's War Dance
Dance of the Fanti Fisherman

1951

Impinyuza

1953

Kalenda
Limbo

1954

La Jablesse

1955

Mr. Johnson

1957

Castilian
Calypso Suite
Calypso Revue (mc)

1958

Royal Ishadi
Temne
Yoruba Court Dance
Aztec Warrior
Ibo
Earth Magician
Engagement Dance
Unesta
Percival Borde and Company
  (mc)

1959

Ntimi

1960

Whispers
Story of a Chief
Naffi Tombo
Kwan
Zo Kengai
Konama (mc)

1961

  *The Wedding

1962

  The Man Who Would Not Laugh
  To the Ancestors

1963

  Mangbetu
  Zebola
  Life Crises

1965

  Anase (The Spider)
  Village Scene
  Hi Life

1969

  Masange

1970

  Dance of Lights

1975

  In Honor of a Queen Mother

DON REDLICH

The University of Wisconsin was the first institution of higher learning in the United States to have a full degree program in dance. Under its outstanding educator, Margaret H'doubler, it achieved a reputation which attracted students from all over the country, and Redlich took the bulk of his training there under H'doubler and Louise Kloepper. After graduation he moved to New York and began study with Hanya Holm, and he started to appear in Broadway musicals and to choreograph Off-Broadway and television productions. He presented the first concert performance of his own work in 1958 and subsequently formed his own company. He has done extensive touring and has participated for several years in the National Endowment Coordinated Residency Touring Program. His work is to be found in the repertory of the Bat-Dor Company in Israel, and his teaching assignments include Adelphi University and Sarah Lawrence College.

PASSIN' THROUGH

Choreography by Don Redlich. Set to traditional folk music. First performed at the Ninety-second Street YM-YWHA, New York, N.Y., May 27, 1959, by Don Redlich.

One of the stock characters in countless stories and jokes is the traveling salesman. In a previous age when communication between towns and cities was at a very low level, inhabitants would rely on travelers for information and news of the outside world. There was a certain glamour attached to these men who roamed from town to town and who saw things and went places that few others did. There was also a certain amount of suspicion directed at such travelers because of their restlessness. Redlich gives us a portrait of the type.

The stage is brightly illuminated and the lively music is plucked out on a banjo. A man dressed in a loud red and white striped shirt with sharply pressed trousers and a straw hat steps briskly on. He has just come to town and he circles the stage peering and looking around to see what he can see. One of the things that interest him is the sight of a pretty girl, and he halts his rambling to pay his respects to the imaginary lady.

He is encouraged by the favorable response and presses his suit. We are in effect the witnesses of half of the "conversation," but the piece is so expressively made that one does not have any difficulty in following the course of the dialogue. He is having some initial success in attracting the woman with his flirting, but then he loses her and is rejected. He wanders off dejected but then begins to revive his spirits with the thought of another town and another day and another girl and exits with the jaunty step that first brought him on.

The music very effectively sets the scene back in rural America of the nineteenth century, and the costuming completes the image of the irrepressible drummer, who takes each day as it comes and refuses to dwell on the lack of success today when there is always tomorrow to look forward to.

CHOREOCHRONICLE
OF DON REDLICH

1953

   Fall of the City

1955

   Thieves' Carnival

1956

   Measure of a Moment

1958

   Idyl
   Three Figures of Delusion
   Electra and Orestes
   The Zanies
   The Visited Planet
   Flight
   Mark of Cain

1959

   *Passin' Through
   Eventide

1960

   Age of Anxiety

1963

   Earthling
   Four Sonatas
   Tangents in Jazz

1964

   Cross-Currents
   Salutations

   Duet
   Concertino de printemps

1965

   Forgetmenot
   Eight + Three
   Oddities

1966

   Pococurante
   Set of Five Dances
   Comedians
   Trumpet Concerto
   Alice and Henry
   Couplet
   Air Antique

1967

   Comedians II
   Twosome
   Run-Through
   Reacher
   Struwwelper
   Cahoots
   Tyro

1968

   Tabloid
   Slouching Toward Bethlehem
   Untitled

1969

   Jibe
   Tristram and Isolt

1970

   Tristram, Isolt and Aida
   Woyzeck

1971

   Stigmata
   Tristan, Isolde, Aida, Hansel, and
      Gretel
   Implex
   Estrange

1972

   The Ride Across Lake Constance
   Harold

Opero
She Often Goes for a Walk Just
   After Sunset

1973

   Everybody's Doing It

1974

   Three Bagatelles
   Patina
   Ariadne auf Naxos (opera)

ROD RODGERS

Being born into a family of professional dancers is a sure way to be exposed to dance training at an early age. Rodgers, who grew up near Detroit, not only took all the jazz and tap lessons that he was given but also took them seriously enough to develop himself into a professional. He performed with a variety of companies and toured with the Erick Hawkins company before establishing his own performing group at the Clark Center for the Performing Arts.

He came to New York in the early 1960s and received a John Hay Whitney fellowship in 1965. He was one of the founders of the Association of Black Choreographers and has done television work in addition to his concert choreography. His own assessment of his company's creative direction was clearly expressed in his statement "The philosophy of the company reflects its director's feelings that black artists must maintain a tradition of being in the forefront of experimentation and innovation while, at the same time, celebrating positive black cultural images."

TANGENTS

Choreography by Rod Rodgers. Music by Henry Cowell and Lou Harrison. First performed at the Ninety-second Street YM-YWHA, New York, N.Y., February 10, 1968, by Ellen Robbins, Barbara Roan, and Ronald Pratt.

Rodgers' stated intention to combine innovative exploration and positive images of the black cultural experience was precisely fulfilled in this trio which has both elements.

The two women and the man wear identical brown leotards and tights, and each carries two yard-long white sticks, one in each hand. The accompanying music has a rhythmic ticktock sound, and as the dancers begin to move in unison they use the sticks as extensions of their arms. They tap the ground and then whip them around in arcs in the air. Then they hold them parallel and peer through the narrow space as if it were a slot or a gap in a venetian blind.

The music stops and in the silence the dancers tap the ground, and that sound, along with the swish they make slicing through the air, is the only sound that accompanies them as they move. The pace slackens somewhat and one stick at a time is dropped with a tiny clatter. The music begins again and, retrieving the sticks, one woman does a somewhat reflective solo. It is a distillation of the feelings that all of the brief encounters with the two other dancers have produced. They all course on their separate trajectories and never tarry long with one another. At the conclusion of her solo the two others enter and the music abruptly halts. The sticks slip from all three. They seem to have lost the necessary vitality to go on and they exit.

The movement itself is a development of the flowing style featured by Erick Hawkins in his works, and the sticks remind one of the many African dances in which such implements are used. Rodgers combined the two elements expertly in this dance that lays out insular isolation with geometric precision.

CHOREOCHRONICLE
OF ROD RODGERS

1965

Dance on a Line
Invention in Three Parts
Percussion Suite

1966

Discussion

1967

Inventions

1968

*Tangents
News . . . Recall
The Conjuring
Oscillating Figures
Primitive Suite

1969

Down in the Valley
Historical Tableau
Trajectories

1970

Dances in Projected Space
Harambee
Now! Nigga
Black Cowboys

1972

In Hi-Rise Shadows
Box
Shout

1973

Vuca (Awaken)!
Rhythm Ritual

n.d.

Eidolons
Assassination
To Say Goodbye
Quest

PAUL SANASARDO

There is a dark side to human experience where the painful and the mysterious combine to inflict psychic wounds. It is an area of particular fascination to Sanasardo, who has explored the dimensions of distress in a variety of imaginative pieces. He is a native of Chicago and was invited by Erika

Thimey to join her Dance Theater of Washington after graduation from art school. After two years he relocated to New York, where he has taught and performed for the following years.

Anna Sokolow selected him as one of the dancers for her epic of loneliness, *Rooms,* and later cast Sanasardo in her Broadway realization of Sean O'Casey's *Red Roses for Me.* He formed his first company with Donya Feuer and subsequently established his own performing group in the early 1960s. In addition to performing his own work he has also shown pieces by his talented pupils, including Manuel Alum. His works are in the repertories of several other companies, among which are the Alvin Ailey American Dance Theater and the Batsheva Dance Company of Israel.

METALLICS

Choreography by Paul Sanasardo. Music by Henry Cowell and Henk Badings. Scenery and costumes by Paul Sanasardo. Lighting by Gary Harris. First performed in New York City at the Ninety-second Street YM-YWHA, October 31, 1964, by Paul Sanasardo, Elina Mooney, and Willa Kahn.

As in many of Sanasardo's pieces, a large structure on stage assumes an important role in the dance. In this case it is a line of hanging metal tubes which looks like a large xylophone and also serves as a barrier between a woman in black behind it and a couple in white who are not bound by it.

The sound of a metronomically regular score highlights the feeling of passing time as the woman in black stands waving her arms behind the hanging rods. She does a mock military march back and forth and then a series of leaps in front of the bars. She tumbles to the floor and moves back toward the line of tubes, where she gathers a clattering armful of them and retires behind the line as the couple in white enters. The monotonous music stops.

The couple is obviously in a different time and emotional zone than the woman in black. The man lifts a bar that rests on two wooden supports, and the woman in white grasps the other end of it. They dance together, at times facing one another directly across the pole and then sliding away along its length and but always clinging to the pole that both unites and separates them. It is not, however, an impossible barrier to their association. At the end of their duet he walks off holding it firmly and dragging it along as the woman in white clings to it.

When they leave, the woman in black emerges again and the music that first accompanied her solo is heard. She is imprisoned more than ever and repeats her military march patrolling her lonely world. She conceals herself once more as the couple dances back and forth across the stage, but the engagement draws her compellingly. The man holds his partner close to him as she bends backward and the woman emerges to stare and stand closely to them while extending one leg longingly behind her.

In this precisely shaped trio Sanasardo captures in miniature a whole world of frustration and the feeling of being an outsider. The nature of the clanging barrier of metal tubes may represent her own manufactured difficulties or may in fact be a restraint imposed from outside. Either way it's marvelously effective.

CHOREOCHRONICLE
OF PAUL SANASARDO

1957

Doctor Faustus Lights the Lights

1961

Excursions for Miracles (with Donya Feuer)

1963

Of Human Kindness
Opulent Dream

1964

Laughter After All
*Metallics

1966

The Animal's Eye
Cut Flowers
Earthly Distance
Excursions
Fatal Birds

1967

Three Dances

1968

The Descent

1969

Pain

1970

Footnotes

1971

Sightseeing

1972

The Path

1973

Shadows

1974

A Sketch for Donna
Platform
The Amazing Graces

1975   **n.d.**

Pearl River   *Because of Love*
Sketches for Nostalgic Children *Poem*
A Consort for Dancers   *Two Movements for Strings*

MARION SCOTT

After study with Martha Graham, Charles Weidman, and Doris Humphrey, Scott then danced in their companies, being most closely associated with the Humphrey-Weidman group. She began presenting her own work in the late 1940s while continuing to work with other choreographers. She joined the Tamiris-Nagrin company in 1960 and remained with it until it was dissolved.

She was a teaching assistant to both Doris Humphrey and to Tamiris and also taught at the School of Performing Arts. Her own dance training included both ballet and modern, and she studied composition with Louis Horst. She danced at the summer festivals in Bennington, Jacobs Pillow, and Connecticut College and was made a Doris Humphrey fellow at Connecticut College in the summer of 1963. She was a co-founder of Contemporary Dance Productions, an organization designed to provide talented young choreographers the opportunity to present new works on jointly shared programs.

AFTERMATH

Choreography by Marion Scott. Music by Edgard Varese. First performed at Palmer Auditorium, Connecticut College, New London, Conn., 1963, by Marion Scott.

The late Doris Humphrey had an enormous impact on the shape and conduct of the American Dance Festival held each year at Connecticut College in New London. After her death annual fellowships for choreographers were established in her name, and during the summer of 1963, when she was a Doris Humphrey fellow, Scott created this solo for herself.

In the wings hidden red lights flash from one side of the darkened stage. As the performing area itself is illuminated, a woman backs in, crouching, and continues to move around with her arms grasping her knees. She is troubled about some event, and her whole body is collapsed inward defensively. She finally manages to loosen herself enough to stand, and she faces around a bit defiantly as if anticipating criticism. Her arms are tightly folded, but then she hesitantly unlocks them.

Her arms seem to have a life of their own, however, and seek each other behind her back. She frees them once again and they dangle limply at her side in a gesture of helplessness. She totters from one place to another, putting up a brave face as her hands seek one another protectively. They link once again but she forces them apart and then spreads them bravely far apart and leaves. Her initial protective crouch has been transformed into a more open and accepting stance.

The hands exist as individual elements, as if they were being directed by some primitive part of the brain intent on shutting the world out and protecting itself. When clasping in front does not work and they are forced apart, the hands stealthily join behind her back. The interplay between the open and the closed hands is the difference between perpetual defensiveness and a fresh start.

CHOREOCHRONICLE
OF MARION SCOTT

1940

Pastorale
Salute

1948

Museum Piece
As the Wind
Dangerous Crossing

1949

Tower of Babel

1953

The Afflicted Children

1955

Animal Courtship
Bacchanale

1956

The Tenderling

1957

Hymn

1958

Undercurrents

1960

From the Sea
From the Rocks
Night Quest

1961

Three Energies

1962

Dilemma
Rapt Moment

1963

*Aftermath

1964

Couplet
Going
Haiga

1965

Psalm
Matrix

1966

Jump! Jump!
Breakpoint

1967

Concerto for Three

1968

Life Begins on Childhood Wing

1971

Abyss

1972

Sevenfold

1974

A Celebration for Percussion and
     Dance
He That Has Time to Mourn
     Has Time to Mend

SYBIL SHEARER

For someone so relentlessly unconventional, Sybil Shearer had a very conventional background in dance, having studied both classic ballet and modern. She was a member of the Humphrey-Weidman company and later danced with Agnes De Mille and was her assistant during the production of *Three Virgins and a Devil*. She was extravagantly praised for her performing ability both as a member of the Humphrey-Weidman company and as a solo dancer. When she first began to present her own work in 1942, it was greeted with enthusiasm.

She abandoned the New York concert world soon after and relocated to Chicago and returned only sporadically for a few performances at widely scattered intervals. In the Midwest she first worked at the Winnetka Community Theater and then became the artistic director of a small company at the National College of Education in Evanston, Illinois, where she continues to work and teach.

As she developed artistically, Shearer became less and less bound by the conventions of the dance world she had grown up in. She rejected the use of stage make-up and at times insisted on presenting full evenings of dance without intermission. She used music as a background to her dances and not as a rhythmic guide for them. A typical dance program would consist of a loosely connected suite of solo dances with a wide variety of composers represented. She selected music that appealed to her and cheerfully mixed snippets of Brahms, Prokofiev, Debussy, and Scarlatti to create her provocative *Once Upon a Time*. Her artistic collaborator, Helen Morrison, has provided her with superior lighting designs, and her work has both elements of fey humor and a feeling for nature.

ONCE UPON A TIME

Choreography by Sybil Shearer. Music by Brahms, Prokofiev, Debussy, and Scarlatti. First performed at the Great Northern Threatre, Chicago, Ill., April 25, 1951, by Sybil Shearer.

The traditional first words of many a child's fairy tale were chosen by Shearer to characterize her own fanciful retelling of magical stories. The suite of eleven solos was first presented in a solid stream that lasted somewhat over an hour, including the inevitable costume changes, which tended to interrupt the flow of the piece somewhat.

The prologue begins in silence and is bathed in blue light. The dancer is dimly perceived as one might recall an elusive dream figure, as she wanders inquiringly through the stage area. And then with the start of the music she begins to create the dance pantomime characters whom she has fancifully named. There is a witch, Medmiga, who has long black ropes for hair and who dances slowly with an aura of mistrust and perhaps fear about her. As she moves into the shadows she extends one hand with fingers spread behind her and angrily clenches it before disappearing. Yanchi is oriental and sketches in her mood with delicate gestures of her slender wrists and hands. She is trippingly light on her feet, in contrast to the unfortunate Relluckus, who plays with a handkerchief. She is without lightness and grace and ends up losing the cloth and sinking in final despair at its loss.

Ceint's gaiety changes in tone, reflecting first the warm amber lighting of one part of the stage, where her movements are quick and wind-blown, to a dark green section where the slow motion of undersea gesture replaces them. Rundunse is stable, straightforward, honestly questioning, and a bit humorous as her feet keep skipping even after she is sitting. The aimless fluttering of Ziff's hands becomes a trembling fear as the movement becomes larger and larger. The veiled Oj moves in a film of cloth exploring, and Inigra dashes about confident and innocent. Lilloni invokes a world of spirit creatures moving easily through vast spaces with godlike swiftness and grace. The dance concludes with the epilogue, which closes the dream that the prologue opened.

While she created many dances for herself, Shearer brought her gift for fanciful titling, exceptional gestural eloquence and costuming to a peak in this work. It was atmospheric and episodic but added up to a world of fancy conjured up out of nothing and allowed to slip away as mysteriously as it came. The stories of the individual characters could be read as warning fables for the present time or simply as archetypal characters who exist throughout the mythical literature of all peoples.

CHOREOCHRONICLE
OF SYBIL SHEARER

1938

A Fable

1939

The Battle of Carnival and Lent

1941

In a Vacuum
In the Cool of the Garden

1944

Prologue
Vanity—or the Pulse of Death

1951

*Once Upon a Time

1953

Shades Before Mars

1959

Part I
Part II
Part III
Toccata for Percussion

1961

In the Shell Is the Sound of the Sea

1963

The Reflection in the Puddle Is Mine

1964

*Wherever the Web and the
   Tendril*

1971

*Afternoon, Evening, and the Next
   Day
Toujours le dimanche*

1972

*It's None of Those Blues
   Ticket to Where?*

ANNA SOKOLOW

No contemporary artist in the theater has hammered so relentlessly at the themes of isolation and resultant despair as Sokolow, except perhaps the playwright Samuel Beckett. And it is no surprise that Sokolow has designed movement for several of his plays without words. Sokolow was a student of Martha Graham and was a member of her company for the decade of the thirties.

She had her own concert group as well, and when she left the Graham company in 1939 she toured and taught in Mexico for nearly a year. During the forties she spent about half of each year teaching and working in Mexico, establishing the country's first modern dance company. Her intensity and skill as a teacher have brought her offers from other countries as well, including Israel and Japan. She has been associated for many years with the dance department of the Juilliard School of Music and has created many pieces for her accomplished student dancers, including *Session for Six*.

Her musical taste is wide ranging and she has worked with scores drawn from the classical repertory, such as Berg's *Lyric Suite,* to symphonic jazz band scores she used for *Rooms* (Kenyon Hopkins), and the aforementioned *Session for Six* (Teo Macero). She shows a particular sensitivity for the edgy urban rhythms of alienation. Stylistically her work has an energetic thrust that makes considerable technical demands upon her dancers. Her humor tends to be sardonic, and the tone of her pieces conveys concerned seriousness. She has worked for numerous companies in addition to her own groups and has staged or created works for Inbal, the Netherlands Dance Theater, and the City Center Joffrey Ballet among others.

LYRIC SUITE

Choreography by Anna Sokolow. Music by Alban Berg (Lyric Suite for String Quartet). *First performed at the Ninety-second Street YM-YWHA, New York, N.Y., March 30, 1954, by Donald McKayle, Mary Anthony, Beatrice Seckler, Eve Beck, Jeff Duncan, Leonore Landau, Sandra Pine, Laura Sheleen, and Ethel Winter.*

The six-part *Lyric Suite for String Quartet* provided Sokolow with a rich score to which she developed one of her most flowing and moving dances. It is a work which she has mounted for several companies.

It begins with a man's solo that features a series of sharp, controlled runs interspersed with deep *pliés*. The Andante amoroso introduces a solo woman who appears silently tormented as she clasps her hand and tosses her head. She takes a series of large steps backward and shields her eyes with her arm. She turns her head sharply, causing her hair to whip around, and steps forward, reaching her arm outward.

In the third movement another woman enters waggling her fingers as she bends forward and continues to flutter them in a backbend. She seems driven as she skitters about, arms clasped behind her and her face thrust forward. She stops her flight and sits in a pool of light then lies back. The dancers of the Largo desolato seem the healthy ideal boy and girl as they stand with their arms about one another's waists with their backs to the audience. They slide to the floor and lock arms in a circle, then rise to dance a restricted but recognizable ballroom sequence. They separate and she sits and he places his head in her lap. His body arches and he thrusts one leg upward with urgent energy and she receives him. He nuzzles her neck. They circle arms about one another's waists again and exit.

The man in Presto delirando is bound in emotional knots as he totters robotlike around the space. His anguish weighs on him until at the end of his solo he covers his face with his hands. The four women of the piece conclude with a display of individual variations and fast crossovers and then slide in the spaces between one another like fingers interlacing.

There is a craftsmanly suitability of the movement to the slightly astringent score, and the individual portraits of the performers alternate soundly between sadness and muted joy.

ROOMS

Choreography by Anna Sokolow. Music by Kenyon Hopkins. First performed at the Ninety-second Street YM-YWHA, New York, N.Y., February 24, 1955, by Jeff Duncan, Beatrice Seckler, Jack Moore, Donald McKayle, Eve Beck, Sandra Pine, Judith Coy, and Paul Sanasardo.

As the curtain rises four men and four women are seated immobile in eight separate chairs staring out directly in front of them. Individuals stand and sit, but all slump and then slide to lie sideways on the chairs. Each thumps a foot to the floor and then each slams palms to the floor and each sits straight up again, thrusting stiff legs before them and vibrating them up and down momentarily. Collectively their rigid torsos thrust forward and the first section ends with one man left alone.

He topples from the chair and rolls the length of the stage away from it, and make a scissors motion of his legs before sitting and drawing his legs up. His arm stretches upward and he rises to cartwheel happily for a moment but feels himself being drawn backward. He struggles but crawls on his stomach back toward the magnetic and malevolent pull of the chair. He tries an accelerating spin, takes a few steps in place, then seems to lose interest and runs stumblingly only to fall. Resigned, he straightens up and walks back to the chair to sit.

A girl sits on one of five chairs. She lolls her head as she stretches and clasps hands to her bosom. She scampers among the chairs and arches her back, slams her hips from side to side, and caresses the back of a chair. Then she steps from one to another as if they were real people, only to sit again and peer into her hands as if reading from a book. She tires of the "book" and like a social butterfly gets up to arrange the chairs and lies across two of them but sinks into a slump. Furious, she rises to knock the chairs down as she dashes from side to side, flailing her arms in the air. She stops abruptly, sinks into a depressed walk, and returns to stand motionlessly behind her chair.

A single chair stands alone when suddenly a man in a sports jacket dashes in and slides up to the chair. He snaps his fingers with a pulsating, eager rhythm and leans one hand on the seat. He sits and does a rapid little series of steps, then rises to leap and sashay around. He is bursting with energy trembling to be released. He opens and closes his fists and then leans forward as he runs in place. In a moment he is off again shadow-boxing and in the process knocks himself down. Even sitting, he vibrates but then allows his head to sink onto the seat of the chair.

Three couples are seated on chairs in a diagonal line, sliding the soles of their feet forward and back. They look up and stretch their arms out and then push their shoulders forward alternately. Convulsively they clasp their arms around their torsos and continue to slide the soles of the feet languidly forward and back. Sliding off the seats, they lie in a line, men and women alternately, when suddenly they spasm as if in pain, one after another. Together they rise to their knees but sink back to floor, where they intertwine one leg with that of the person next to them and caress the person's back. They return to sitting and sliding the soles of the feet back and forth, reaching out with their arms and slumping over. All stand on the chairs with heads forward and shoulders hunched up while rocking side to side slowly.

A bare-chested man stands. He steps forward and backward to lean on a chair. Three other men and one woman simply sit on theirs and stare forward, taking no notice of him as he dashes forward and back trying to attract their attention. Wearily he gives up and settles back on his chair. He tries staring in their faces and then a series of pounding jumps in place, but it is of no use, they do not notice him, and he returns to his chair to hide his face in his hands. The others leave without tossing him a glance. He bounds up to leap then falls and batters his head on the floor, and then he runs to clutch desperately at an empty chair.

Using the backs of three chairs like a dance practice barre, three women exercise, turning a formal arm movement into a farewell wave. They pump up and down, rising on the ball of the foot, and then step forward to lie down on one side and roll over. Rising to a kneeling position, they bounce gently and then lean their heads on the seats, only to return to the opening stance. They stop, stare questioningly off into space, circle the chairs mechanically, and sit.

Men and women walk past one another from one side of the stage to the other, as one girl places her chair in the center of the stage and sits. She then begins to extend her arms. Her fingers twitch and she tosses her head from side to side. She stretches one leg then the other while tossing her head. While seated she extends both her legs stiffly forward, vibrating them up and down. She rises to dash about distractedly. She slumps forward and her fingers tremble. She collapses and rises several times and begins a compulsive series of bows and bounces and finally stands on chair and flaps her arms slowly. All enter individually to place the chairs in their original formation. Each performs a brief sequence from the individual variations and returns to the prison of the chair.

The dance has a muted and at times overt air of desperation. All of the people shown attempt to escape from the isolation of their psychic "rooms" but none succeeds. The interest of the dance lies in the integrity and the imaginative failures that each is doomed to endure. The sophisticated and the simple are all condemned to endure the rigors of isolation, although each handles it in a different manner. The movement owes much to jazz in the accents and ritards of its execution, presenting the tragic in syncopation.

SESSION FOR SIX*

Choreography by Anna Sokolow. Music by Teo Macero (excerpts from What's New). *First performed at the Ninety-second Street YM-YWHA, New York, N.Y., February 19, 1958, as Session '58 by Eve Beck, Kate Friedlich, Dorothy Krooks, Jeff Duncan, David Gold, and Jack Moore.*

Restaged and renamed for student dancers in 1964, the dance has the energy and drive of a high-powered engine. The dancers in the cast (Martha Clarke, Ze'Eva Cohen, Paula Kelly, Dennis Nahat, John Parks, Michael Uthoff) were absolutely remarkable in their sensitivity to the choreography, and all of them have subsequently gone on to found their own companies or become integral parts of others.

The first part of the dance establishes the restless dynamism of the whole work, which develops as a series of encounters between the performers who rebound from one another with an elastic, antiseptic air of noninvolvement. A man and woman face the audience, dance momentarily, and go off, to be replaced by another couple who do the same. Two couples enter and the men leave. The two women hop around one another and they too leave.

Now the company begins to cross the stage in three separate lines, side-stepping quickly and facing the audience at all times. These rapid lines are replaced by diagonals as the dancers enter from the front corner of either side of the stage and whirl to the opposite corner at the rear, where they disappear. In a moment they return and now carve out arcs that start from the front right corner of the stage, reach their apogee at the center, and diminish at the rear on the same side.

In the second part of the dance two women begin to whirl with their arms at right angles to the torso and are joined by one of the men, who also is whirling. The company then stands in a line at the rear of the stage and individuals step forward. They pair off and face one another, holding the other partner's hands. But instead of an embrace the touch develops into arm wrestling. The men leave and the women cluster in the center doing deep knee bends and flexing.

The men return to carry the women off in high lifts, but a moment later one returns to take up the aimless whirling again. Soon all are engaged in it, and by chance one woman ends up with one man but they separate, and the dance concludes with each whirling and whirling and whirling.

The feeling of the piece is of lonely youth searching and not finding. The crossings of the men and the woman are encounters that could as easily have transpired between molecules rebounding from one another. There are no

* Originally *Session '58.*

lasting commitments, and the only recourse is to turn and turn, looking in all directions, waiting for something to develop while being very energetic as one waits.

CHOREOCHRONICLE
OF ANNA SOKOLOW

1934

Death of Tradition (with Jane Dudley and Sophie Maslow)

1935

Strange American Funeral

1937

Excerpts from a War Poem
Façade—Esposizione Italiana
Four Little Salon Pieces
Opening Dance
Slaughter of the Innocents
Speaker
Satiric Suite (with Jane Dudley, Sophie Maslow and William Matons)

1939

Ballad in the Popular Style

1940

El Ranacuajo Pasaedor

1944

Songs of a Semite

1951

The Dybbuk

1952

A Short Lecture and Demonstration of the Evolution of Ragtime as Presented by Jelly Roll Morton

1954

L'Histoire du soldat
*Lyric Suite

1955

La Primavera
*Rooms

1956

Poem

1957

Le Grand Spectacle

1958

Session '58

1960

Esther the Queen (tv)
Opus '58

1961

Dreams

1963

Suite No. 5 in C Minor
Opus '63

1964

Forms
The Question
*Session for Six

1965

Ballade
Odes
Opus '65

1966

Time + 6
Night

1967

Déserts
Memories

1968

Tribute
Time + 7
Steps of Silence

1969

Echoes

1970

The Dove
Magritte, Magritte

1971

Scenes from the Music of Charles
Ives

1973

Three Poems

1974

Come, Come, Travel with Dreams
A Cycle of Cities
Ecuatorial
Homage to Federico García Lorca

1975

Ride the Culture Loop

n.d.

Untitled Work
Two Pioneer Marches
Anti-War Cycle
Case History No. —
The Celebrations
The Song of Songs
Forces in Opposition

GLEN TETLEY

After military service during World War II, Tetley began his dance training with Hanya Holm, receiving a scholarship to do so. He continued with his college studies and also aided Holm as an assistant in staging several Broadway shows, including *Kiss Me, Kate,* and he danced in her company for five years. He also studied ballet with Margaret Craske and Antony Tudor concurrently, which explains the ease with which he creates dances in both the balletic and modern dance styles. He toured abroad and in the United States with John Butler's modern dance company and American Ballet Theater before he decided to pursue his own independent career.

His first independent program was performed in the spring of 1962, and in the fall he was invited to join the Netherlands Dance Theater. With the exception of a brief return to the United States in the late 1960s to re-establish his own touring company, he has lived in Europe working as a choreographer with a series of companies including the Royal Danish Ballet, the Royal Ballet, and the Batsheva Dance Company. Most recently he has become the artistic director of the Stuttgart Ballet.

PIERROT LUNAIRE

Choreography by Glen Tetley. Music by Arnold Schönberg. Scenery and costumes by Rouben Ter-Arutunian. First performed at the Fashion Institute of Technology, New York, N.Y., May 5, 1962, by Glen Tetley, Linda Hodes, and Robert Powell.

The dance is cast in the form of a game, but it is a most serious game, a game of life with its emotional entanglements. It was the first piece that Tetley created after he decided to form his own company, and it reflects his dual concern with tradition and his desire to find a contemporary expression for archetypal characters. In a program note he explained: "In the antiquity of the Roman Theater, began the battle of the white clown of innocence with the dark clown of experience. Pierrot and Brighella are their lineal descendants, and Columbine their eternal female pawn."

A white trapeze and supporting structure occupy the center of the stage. Pierrot, in white, gambols around the structure and slowly descends toward the stage. One is convinced of his total remove from the world as he mimes being overwhelmed by the fall of a leaf. Columbine flashes past and jolts Pierrot, who clings to his scaffold and waves playfully as she writhes. She sways provocatively past and draws out a line of washing which she attaches to the scaffold, indicating a certain domesticating interest in the innocent Pierrot. He assumes such an interest and approaches her amorously. She slaps him and leaves. He is annoyed but misses her.

When she returns in a long nightgown and a bedcap, he is entranced, but then Brighella enters and Columbine leaves. Pierrot returns winsomely to clambering around his scaffolding. The intriguer Brighella follows him, and they have a combative skirmish in which Brighella produces a sword. He teaches Pierrot how to use it and then stabs him and ignores his death throes to retrieve Columbine, who wears a suggestive red dress but covers her features with a white veil. She and Brighella obviously understand one another, as the hopeless Pierrot does not.

He attempts to dance with her, but Brighella and she attach elastic bands to him and make him into a caricature of a puppet. After he collapses, Brighella strips him of his jacket and trousers to draw them on himself. He and Columbine frolic and then climb to occupy the tower. Pierrot recovers and runs around distraught but then returns to assume his previous place. Brighella returns his white hat to him, but all has been spoiled. He throws it away and ends a victim, suspended between them.

The use of traditional and stock theater figures has the advantage of familiarity, as far as audiences are concerned, but has the difficulty of making a new statement with them. In this piece Tetley produced an excellent work that drew cleverly on the conventional figures and made their triangular relationship a viable and moving drama.

MYTHICAL HUNTERS

Choreography by Glen Tetley. Music by Oedoen Partos. Scenery and costumes by Anthony Binstead. Lighting by Haim Tchelet. First performed by the Batsheva Dance Company in Tel Aviv, Israel, December 1965, by Rena Glück, Rina Schenfeld, Ruth Lerman, Ahuva Inbari, Galia Gat, Oshra Elkayam, Moshe Efrati, Ehud Ben-David, Rachamin Ron, Shimon Brown, Dani Binstead, Moshe Romano.

The dance has a timeless aspect, and one could even believe its locale to be underwater. There are no clues as to its historical setting. It merely presents us with the doing of a seriously motivated but insular group of men and women partaking in some birth ritual that is cyclical.

Four men with long poles enter in silence and move purposefully but calmly. A woman crouches on stage and then rises, to be carried off limply by the four men, who hoist her over their heads. The ceremonial of birth is first accomplished. A second woman enters and occupies the same spot and performs a solo that has the sense of an initiation ceremony. Three men carry on three women and then a fourth woman grabs the fourth man, who is alone. The woman in the center is still outside the concern of the group.

The first woman returns on the shoulders of a man with a large arc of transparent tubing in each hand, and these are grasped for a moment by the woman in the center. The woman leaves, followed by the other woman.

The men return to take the girl in the center with them. She becomes the object of their interest. Two men fight among themselves and then a net is thrown over the woman and she is trapped into the cycle. She is carried off. When the men return, both the first and second women are on their shoulders, and each has two of the long transparent arcs of tubing, and the stage is visited by a third woman entering the cycle and beginning her solo dance.

Tetley is facile with movement invention and is drawn to long developing themes in much of his work. He hates to be hurried and delights in spinning out his dances to create a feeling of being outside time. It always seems as if there is plenty of time for still another elaboration of the theme, and so a dance about cyclical regeneration is extremely congenial to him.

CHOREOCHRONICLE
OF GLEN TETLEY

1962

Birds of Sorrow
Gleams in the Bone House
How Many Miles to Babylon
*Pierrot Lunaire

1964

The Anatomy Lesson
Sargasso

1965

The Game of Noah
*Mythical Hunters
Fieldmass

1966

Chronochromie
Ricercare
Tehilim

1967

Dithyramb
Freefall
Ziggurat
Seven Deadly Sins

1968

Embrace Tiger and Return to
*   Mountain*
Circles

1969

Arena

1970

Field Figures
Imaginary Film
Mutations (film inserts by Hans
   Van Manen)

1971

Mutations (full version)
Rag Dances

1972

Laborintus
Small Parades
Strophe-Antistrophe
Threshold

1973

Der Wandlebare Garten
Gemini
Voluntaries

1974

Tristan
Rite of Spring
Stränder
Stationary Flying

1975

Daphnis and Chloe

JOYCE TRISLER

As a native Los Angelina, Trisler studied with local teachers Carmelita Maracci and Lester Horton. The latter made an indelible impression on her, and she is one of the leading exponents of the Horton technique. She had exposure to Antony Tudor and Robert Joffrey in New York when she attended the Juilliard School of Music Dance Department.

She joined the Horton company in the early 1950s and appeared with it in its last East Coast tour. After leaving the Horton company she became a member of the Juilliard Dance Theater during the latter half of the 1950s, and with its dissolution she formed the Trisler-Wilson Company with John Wilson.

She began designing dances in the mid-1950s, almost always for companies which were not her own, and has continued to do so, working currently with the Alvin Ailey American Dance Theater, for which she created *Dance for Six.*

DANCE FOR SIX (NEW VERSION)

Choreography by Joyce Trisler. Music by Antonio Vivaldi (two concertos from La Cetra). *First performed at the Ninety-second Street YM-YWHA, New York, N.Y., February 22, 1969, by Jane Honor, Dimitra Sundeen, Rita Resnik, Haruki Fujimoto, Daniel Maloney, and Lar Roberson.*

The piece, simply a design for three couples, has a smooth, creamy texture to its movement. It does not strive for dramatic statement, although the encounters of the dancers have an understated dramatic content.

The three men and three women at the rear of the stage are frozen in gently athletic poses. When the music starts they move down toward the audience, turning repeatedly and contracting their torsos. The flow of the dance has begun. At the end of the first movement all rush off, leaving a couple together, and quietly a second woman joins. They all stride around and do attitude turns in formation. There is a sense of celebration for the sheer pleasure of moving to Vivaldi's lively music.

The men enter and one leaps powerfully to the side; a girl enters and is partnered carefully and considerately by another man. The lilting music carries the dancing on and on into other casual and beautiful formations. A man alone walks in a circle and two men and a woman join him. She runs to one who takes her extended arm and swings her to the side in a circular dip so that her ear skims the surface of the stage. It is dazzlingly dangerous especially in the context of the even-tempered flow that has marked the dance. The three men stand in a line and as she walks past the first, he lifts her, and she continues to stride in the air as she is set down. The other two repeat the "walking on air" lift, and then they carry her off.

In another duet the woman reclines and the man assists her up. He lies on his back and she balances on his drawn-up knees and outstretched arms. They go off and another man completes a series of intricate steps involving long leaps. A second man leaps across, followed quickly by two women and another man. They all join him in dancing the delicate step. One woman appears to flirt momentarily and then go off.

For the conclusion the three couples occupy the stage. First two of the dancers start a step moving from side to side, and then three of them do it and the whole group joins. The dancers then form themselves into the grouping that began the work, each balancing on one foot.

Trisler created a dance that would in ballet be known as a *ballet blanc,* that is, a piece which is costumed in white but which emphasizes dance movement most strongly and does not have any elements of dramatic characterization impressed on it. The piece is best seen with a strong cast of virtuoso dancers when it becomes a seductively appealing vision of movement seamlessly spun out.

CHOREOCHRONICLE
OF JOYCE TRISLER

1956

Playthings of the Mind

1957

Journey

1958

Place of Panic
Preludes
The Pearl

1959

The Bewitched
Theatre Piece

1960

Nite Life
Bronx Zoo
Primera Canción
Dance for Percussion

1961

Bergamasca
Écossaises
Brandenberg Concerto

1964

Ballroom
Dance for Six

1968

King Arthur (p)

1969

*Dance for Six (new version)
Peer Gynt (p)
La Strada (mc)

1970

Look to the Lilies (mc)

1971

Beatrix Cenci (opera)

1972

Ambassador (mc)

1973

Beatrix Cenci (opera, new
production)

1974

Rite of Spring

1975

Four Temperaments
Death in Venice

JAMES TRUITTE

After he had had a successful career as a show dancer, Truitte decided that there was a great deal that he did not know about dancing and wanted to study seriously for an extended period. Accordingly, after the conclusion of a national tour of *Carmen Jones* in 1947 he asked Janet Collins, a former teacher, whom he should approach for instruction. Her answer was Lester Horton, who maintained his theater and studio in Los Angeles. Truitte remained with Horton as a student and dancer until Horton's death in the early fifties. Out of the dancers of that company Alvin Ailey formed his own group, and Truitte was a featured soloist until his retirement from active performing. He also functioned as company *régisseur* for many years. He taught at the Horton School and, among other assignments, at the Alvin Ailey City Center Dance Theater School and the Cincinnati College-Conservatory of Music. He received a John Hay Whitney fellowship to record the Horton technique.

VARIEGATIONS

Choreography by James Truitte. First performed at the Henry Street Settlement Playhouse, New York, N.Y., December 5, 1958, by Joyce Trisler.

A great teacher can have a profound influence on a dancer's career, and Truitte has gone out of his way to acknowledge the effect that Lester Horton had on his. In addition to preserving the Horton technique in as pure a form as he learned it, Truitte has also given lecture demonstrations and choreographed pieces that seemed as much designed as a homage to Horton as to having their own independent life. This one ranks among his best.

The dance starts and continues as a progression of movement exercises that are taken from a Horton class. The "deep floor vocabulary" has the woman standing and then sinking to the floor, where she rolls and tumbles. The woman becomes a kind of abstracted and almost impersonal instrument as she works through the "studies for percussive stroke," "pelvic lift balances," and "dimensional tonus." Her long white dress blossoms out to the sides as she leaps, tucking her feet under her, or again swirls out in a shell-like whorl as she moves rapidly into a series of dashs on the diagonal. Throughout one feels the elastic tension of great and sustained strength and control. Nothing is forced and everything flows without stress.

When the Alvin Ailey company made its first visit to London on a European tour in 1964, Truitte presented this work to familiarize the audience with the technique that played so important a part in his creative life and that of the Ailey company. It is not a dance that tells a story other than that of technique exercised for its own logic unadorned by a story or plot line. In its way it is an expression of delight in controlled movement such as one might encounter in Harold Lander's *Etudes* or any ballet constructed on classroom technique.

CHOREOCHRONICLE
OF JAMES TRUITTE

1955

   Introduction to the Dance
   Miss Salome

1956

   Mirror, Mirror

1958

   With Timbrel and Dance Praise
     His Name
   Two Spirituals
   The Duke's Bard
  *Variegations

1960

   Bagatelles

1971

   Guernica

1975

   With Timbrel and Dance Praise
     His Name (new version)

n.d.

   The Mole People (mp)
   The Sins of Rachel Cade (mp)

NORMAN WALKER

When one sees the work of Norman Walker, one is immediately aware that the "war" with ballet is over. He combines elements of ballet and modern dance skillfully and shows that he has trained extensively in both disciplines. He studied ballet with Robert Joffrey, Fernand Nault, and Valentina Pereyaslavec and modern dance with May O'Donnell, Gertrude Shurr, and at the Martha Graham school. He is a graduate of the School of Performing Arts and the City College of New York.

He first appeared with the May O'Donnell company in the early 1950s and formed his own company in 1961. He has created over fifty works in the twenty years that he has been actively choreographing, and these include pieces for his own company, which he maintained until 1971, and other companies. He has been commissioned to create dances for the Boston Ballet and the Batsheva Dance Company of Israel, of which he was the artistic director for several years. He was appointed to the staff of the Harkness Ballet in 1974, a company that he has created seven ballets for. He has appeared frequently at Jacobs Pillow as a performer and as a member of the staff and is currently a member of the Department of Performing Arts at Adelphi University.

MEDITATIONS OF ORPHEUS

Choreography by Norman Walker. Music by Alan Hovhaness. First performed at Philharmonic Hall, New York, N.Y., May 19, 1964, by Norman Walker and Cora Cahan.

Among the most widely adapted myths for dance presentation, the story of Orpheus and his doomed Eurydice must rank as one of the most suitable. It has the form of a *pas de deux* and lends itself to treatment both as a duet and in expanded versions. Walker chose to set it as a series of flashback episodes in the mind of the grieving Orpheus.

The man meditates on the past and thinks first of the love that he and Eurydice shared. She joins him and they wrap themselves in a joyous and ardent skein of movement that seems to envelop them like a benign cocoon. Then the man recalls her in his imagination as she must be, caught behind in the kingdom of the underworld. She is in funereal black as he seeks her, and there is again the tragic glance which must be the instrument of their separation. He recoils from the loss which the infatuation of their previous entanglement virtually foreordained. One can almost feel that the strings of Orpheus' lyre are strands of fate as well, for at the end Eurydice finds herself tangled amid them as Orpheus drapes himself in mourning cloth and returns to his solitary sorrow.

Walker's talent for the sinuous duet reached a peak in this piece, which he originally conceived for himself and Cora Cahan. It had both an exquisite lyricism and a tense dramatic sense that made the fate of the doomed couple poignantly real.

CHOREOCHRONICLE
OF NORMAN WALKER

1956

Four Cantos from a Sacred Will

1960

Baroque Concerto
Variations from Day to Day
Terrestrial Figure

1961

Cowboy in Black
Prussian Blue
Splendors and Obscurities
Crossed Encounter
In Praise of . . .

1962

Clear Songs After Rain

1963

Enchanted Threshold
Reflections

1964

*Meditations of Orpheus
Ritual and Dance
The Testament of Cain
Trionfo di Afrodite
Figures and Masks

1965

The Night Chanter

1966

A Certain Slant of Light
Night Song

1967

Baroque Concerto No. 3
A Broken Twig
Eloges
Passage of Angels

1968

Illuminations

1969

L'Enfant et les sortilèges
Baroque Concerto No. 4
Illusive Image
Kleediscopic

1970

Spatial Variations on a Theme
by Benjamin Britten

1971

Baroque Concerto No. 6

1972

Mahler's Fifth Symphony

1973

Three Psalms
Lazarus

1974

Ceremonials
Ballade

n.d.

Contrasts
Drifts and Dreams
Prussian Officer

JUDITH WILLIS

Being born in Evansville, Indiana, gave Judith Willis the opportunity to study with Sybil Shearer at one point in her career and opened up a world of eccentric humor to her. She had been raised in Evansville and had been sent to study dance at several camps and summer schools which offered courses in dance instruction, such as National Music Camp, Jacobs Pillow, and Colorado College. When she entered high school she began to travel regularly to and from Chicago, where Shearer had a studio, and found herself influenced by Shearer's highly idiosyncratic approach to dance.

Willis attended freshman year at Northwestern University but transferred to the Juilliard School of Music in 1960 and graduated in 1963. She and two other students, Art Bauman and Marcia Lerner, formed a short-lived touring company, but then they went separate ways. Willis continued making concert appearances, presenting her own works and dancing with other companies. She did not try to form her own company but joined the faculty of Teachers College in New York City and continued to create her works at a measured pace. She has tended to be inactive in recent years.

SONGS FOR YOUNG LOVERS

Choreography by Judith Willis. Set to a tape collage of popular songs. First performed at the Ninety-second Street YM-YWHA, New York, N.Y., May 8, 1965, by Sara Rudner, Carla Maxwell, Laura Glenn, Ann Mittelholzer, Edward Effron, Edward DeSoto, Daniel Lewis, and David Earle.

The setting for the dance is a high school prom with all of the young men and women decked out in their best. The music is a collection of popular songs, but there is an undercurrent of competitive tension that the protagonists try to hide.

"At the time I first choreographed it I was deeply involved with the songs it used, wanting to find the very best examples of the strange deflected mirrors of those eras the songs provided. So I used 'Falling In Love with Love' sung with great guttural elegance by Della Reese, and Ruth Etting and Russ Columbo from the twenties singing 'Every Little Breeze' and 'You're My Everything' and those urbane, glorious and offhand gems from the thirties and forties like 'Small Hotel', 'Blue Room', 'That Old Black Magic', 'My Romance.' There was one modern rock-soul piece included by James Brown, used as contrast, grinding, loud, inarticulate and funny. Lots of 'Yeah, yeah, yeah . . .' After all, it was the heyday of the Beatles.

"The dance was about falling, being pushed, leaning, lunging, being knocked down, resisting gravity. It was also about relationships and how our view of what makes up a loving couple changes. I was interested in the romanticism and nostalgia with which we view the past, and how that affects what we perceive as reality in present-day relationships. The movements and the relationships change from sweetness and rapturous meetings and partings, to isolation, domination, general combat, or ritual. There is a lot of running and chasing, a lot of violent encounters, a knock-down, drag-out fight with judo flips and all the rest between a boy and a girl in silence, a male solo full of isolated strivings, for contact, a ritualized minuet for three couples employing karate chops in three-quarter time etc. . . ."

There is little to add to the choreographer's own words except to say that it is a dance that has met with great audience enthusiasm wherever it has been shown, by making social dancing a witty, overt, sexual combat zone.

CHOREOCHRONICLE
OF JUDITH WILLIS

1962

Beyond these Windows

1963

Poor Valley
Quintet
Trio
Quartet

1964

Syllogism

1965

*Songs for Young Lovers

1966

Gifts
Locales (I–IV)
Locales (V–VII)
Locales (VIII)

1967

116th Street Strip

1969

Last Dance
Approaches

1972

Staying On
Rolling

Freedom
and New Formalism

With the same enthusiastic disregard for tradition that drove the founding generation to revolt from Denishawn, the latest generation of choreographers has abandoned its predecessors. It was a break that was as radical in its way as anything that had been done by the founding generation. By the decade of the 1950s colleges and universities throughout the country had established departments in which dance could be taken for degree credit. There were regular concerts given by the major modern dance companies in various parts of the country and many of them had been sent abroad as good-will gestures through the efforts of the State Department's cultural touring program. In the 1930s those modern dance companies which toured the college circuit had to perform for the most part in gymnasiums, since dance was offered initially as part of the physical education program. But by the fifties numerous universities had constructed new theaters in which the companies could perform.

Although the Bennington College Summer School of the Dance had not been revived after World War II, its successor, the American Dance Festival, could be found at Connecticut College in New London, where each summer, starting in 1948, a six-week summer program was offered that was patterned on the Bennington model, and regular performances were given by the major modern dance companies. A decade after its establishment the directors of the school set aside a special evening for the work of younger choreographers. It did not replace the major companies' evening, which was Saturday, but it was the less desirable Monday. It was, however limited, an attempt to provide an outlet for newer creative energies in the context of the established pattern. In New York City, where the Ninety-second Street YM-YWHA, under William Kolodny, had long been host to modern dancers, many of the newer choreographers presented their work. There were few other places with the respect that the "Y" commanded. There were so many calls for use of the Theresa L. Kaufmann Concert Hall, though, that it was decided to establish a jury to judge new work at an audition before the "Y" would let the house be rented by the aspiring choreographer. Thus it was that the major outlets for modern dance work were administered closely by the previous creative generation, which was interested in seeing its tenets perpetuated and not repudiated.

One of the few substantial theaters that were hospitable to new work was the Henry Street Settlement Playhouse, with Alwin Nikolais as its resident director since the late 1940s. Nikolais had been a student at the Bennington College Summer School of the Dance in the late thirties and was particularly attracted by the work of Hanya Holm and later studied with her in the summers at Colorado College, where she maintains a summer program. When he was appointed to the playhouse, he found it had deteriorated from its past renown, and he set about rebuilding it physically and also re-establishing its reputation. He succeeded and by the middle 1950s had begun to produce a body of work that was recognizably new and different.

Having placed himself apart from the preceding generation, he naturally attracted other choreographers who were dissatisfied with the existing situation and who wished to perform their own works. Thus it was that Paul Taylor performed his first work there, and James Waring created several pieces which were first seen at the Henry Street Settlement Playhouse. Waring went on subsequently to establish a series of programs at the Master Institute on Manhattan's upper West Side and then eventually, in the early 1960s, to perform at the Living Theater. Alternative performing areas were being opened up, but there was such a crush of new choreographic energy that there were not enough of them to accommodate it. Merce Cunningham's studio had been a choreographic workshop and the students, many of whom had studied at the Cunningham dance studio for technique as well, wished to have performances in an area large enough to accommodate all those who wished to attend. The studio was not that large, and the students auditioned for use of space at Judson Memorial Church on Washington Square South and were accepted.

The search for alternative performing areas of necessity pushed many of the newer choreographers outside of the usual theatrical ambiance. Some remained loyal to the proscenium arch theater, but one of the characteristics that distinguish the newer choreographers is a willingness to perform almost anywhere without the resources of the standard theater. The founding generation, no matter how much it disliked what Denishawn was offering the public in the theater, did not turn its back on the theater as the natural place to present dance. The newer generation demonstrated a willingness to dance on roof tops, in parks, on city streets, in parking lots, in churches, or on an excursion boat circling Manhattan island as well as in the traditional theater.

In questioning the primacy of the theater, the younger choreographers were in effect questioning the ways in which theatrical space affected the design of a dance. The standard theater presents motion to an audience with a strong frontal design. Because of the space the dance is meant to be seen from straight ahead. The parts of the dance which transpire closest to the center of the stage are usually the most important. In the ballet the leading dancers of a company appear in center stage most often, and the less important tend to spend proportionally more time along the sides and back of the performing area. To a great extent the founding generation of modern dance, while rejecting the styles and manners of other serious theatrical dance traditions, accepted a good many of their conventions.

When the frontal aspect of creating a dance was rejected, then there was no reason to place the most important dance action in a central and frontal position on the stage and the whole of the performing area could be used. Some choreographers used this liberated space on conventional stages, and many others decided that with dance liberated from its frontal orientation it could happily be presented in almost any area upon which one could dance. The move to alternative areas begun modestly in the 1960s became a commonplace choice for choreographers in the 1970s. Once the newer choreographers had broken with the strict rules imposed by the conventional theater, many of them elected to work both within and without the proscenium stage, depending upon the given situation and the suitability of the spaces available.

It was a situation that was to be repeated with many of the customs that had been thought to be unchangeable. The newer choreographers changed the ground rules, created striking dances, and then sometimes returned to making dances under slightly altered forms of the "rules." Costuming suffered a fall from grace among many who danced in normal everyday street wear instead of theatricalized garb. Stage make-up was discarded by many, although some kept it and others returned to it periodically. The necessity of music was challenged and many choreographers discarded it entirely for many of their dances. Other choreographers kept it but only as one element in a dance that contained sound, motion, and theatrical decoration. It did not by any means dominate the production or dictate the actual rhythm of the dancing. It was an accompanying sound, pleasant or not so pleasant, depending on the listener's taste.

The most serious challenge to traditional and established custom was made over the style of movement, or whether, for that matter, one had to move at all or train as a dancer to consider oneself a dancer. It was claimed that any movement selected by a choreographer to complete a dance design was made "dancing" by the fact of its selection. There was no reason to make an artificial distinction between the act of raising an arm as if to throw something and the elevation of the arm in a recognized and circumscribed "dance" manner. Both were equal and one was to be preferred to the other only if it more completely suited the choreographer's needs and not for any inherent beauty that it might possess. It was the test of practicality applied where previously only professional aesthetics had been used as a yardstick.

In each of the preceding modern dance generations the need for dance technique had been seen as an absolute necessity. But if it were true that one gesture was the equal of another, then it was also true that acquiring a specialized technique was not strictly necessary in order to participate in a dance. And if the dance were created for the average person without technical training, then one did not need specialized training to perform it. Often forgotten at the time, was that possession of a technique enabled the dancer to have a wider choice of dances to perform, though a dance for the untrained was possible and frequently was made by this generation.

What eventually resulted from the ferment was an attitude toward dance that was markedly less formal than that of previous generations. Dances could be made without special costuming, designed for outdoor areas and not stages, to be performed by people with no particular dance training and without the benefit of dramatic lighting effects, and they frequently were, during the middle and late sixties. Once valid dances had been made under such seemingly adverse conventions, many of the choreographers again began to look for the widest possible use of the conventional stage again. It was a return to the theater but a theater whose customs were no longer as narrow as previously conceived, a place where the rules had been stretched to include the experimentation of the group that followed the founding generation.

MERCE CUNNINGHAM

Merce Cunningham was among the first to challenge the conventions of the founding generation of modern dance. His own career started on the West Coast. He was born in Centralia, Washington, and showed an early interest in dance instruction which was centered on popular forms, including tap, a style for which he retained a great fondness. At Cornish School of Fine and Applied Arts, in Seattle, he continued his studies and became exposed to the musical ideas of John Cage, who was on the faculty in the late thirties. One summer he attended the dance session at Mills College, in Oakland, and danced in Lester Horton's *Conquest*. The following year, in 1939, the faculty of the Bennington College Summer School of the Dance, including Martha Graham, was resident at Mills College, and Cunningham was invited to join the Graham company in New York for the fall season. He was the second man to join her company.

He remained with the company until the mid-forties and created many roles, including the Revivalist in *Appalachian Spring,* the Acrobat in *Every Soul Is a Circus,* the Christ figure in *El Pentitente,* and a sprightly solo "March" in *Letter to the World*. It was in this last role that great use was made of his nimble and high jump. He began to experiment with his own choreography at Bennington College, where he co-choreographed three works with Jean Erdman, a fellow member of the Graham company. Subsequently he created solos for himself and formed an artistic alliance with John Cage as his musical director, one that persists to this day.

He formed his own company after leaving the Graham company and his work was increasingly marked by its new approach, which was not dependent on the accepted need for story, character, and dramatic mood. He was interested in pure movement and its inherent possibilities. In 1947 he created a ballet, *The Seasons* for Ballet Society, the precursor of the New York City Ballet, and during this time he also taught a modern dance class at its official school, the School of American Ballet. His first major season with an expanded company of his own took place in the early fifties at the Theatre De Lys, in Greenwich Village.

He undertook a world tour in 1964 that began in Europe and concluded in India. He introduced the idea of chance determination in which parts of a dance would be ordered according to random methods and even sequences of movements selected according to the toss of a coin. His method of dance composition in which the scenic designer, the composer, and the choreographer each worked independently of one another, knowing the climate of a dance but not its particulars, attracted advanced painters such as Robert Rauschenberg, Jasper Johns, Robert Morris, Andy Warhol among others and advanced composers Christian Wolff, Morton Feldman, Earle Brown, Gordon Mumma and Conlon Nancarrow, to name but a few. Each of the three elements of a dance united by mood and duration came together as an entity after each of the parts had been completed separately.

The Cunningham Dance Studio has over the years attracted some of the most promising students in modern dance, and at its present location in Westbeth on Manhattan's lower West Side it serves also as a showcase for experimental dance, theater, and music.

SUITE FOR FIVE IN SPACE AND TIME

Choreography by Merce Cunningham. Music by John Cage. Costumes by Robert Rauschenberg. First performed at the University of Notre Dame, South Bend, Ind., May 18, 1956, by Merce Cunningham, Carolyn Brown, Viola Farber, Remy Charlip, and Marianne Preger.

One of the results of Cunningham's forward-looking career has been to open up creative possibilities for other choreographers. Many young choreographers have been quick to seize on the new freedom of stage space and the ideas of chance and random activity having a part in dance and to use these ideas naturally but without direct attribution to Cunningham's influence. One of those who admire his work profoundly is the extremely talented Twyla Tharp, who as a homage created a dance tribute to Cunningham, a set of variations based upon the trio in this piece. She called it *After "Suite."*

"At Random" begins the piece and is a quiet solo for a man who moves spiritedly after the initial silence and then bends forward to the ground. A woman follows with a similarly calm solo, "A Meander," in which she almost seems like a woman regarding herself in a mirror and striking poses as the lights go down. The trio for two women and a man is called "Transition" and finds one woman to the rear of the stage while the two others are forward, closer to the audience. The woman close to the audience runs off, and the woman upstage whips her arms around, and again the lights are dimmed. When they come up the man poses, leaning on the two women for support. They separate and act independently of one another.

"Stillness" is the second solo for the man who opened the piece. Again he is tranquil in his movement, doing no more than wandering easily around the stage. He is joined by the woman who did the second solo, and together they dance that duet "Extended Moment," which incorporates gestures from each of their solos and contrasts them. He develops a jolly, humorous persona while she emphasizes the more meditative side of the duet. She leaves and he works through a strong, violent sequence in "Excursion," extends a hand out toward the audience, and bows his head. The whole company joins in the finale, "Meetings," where each passes along in his or her separate orbit for the most part, although there are meetings and momentary alliances, but then the women move to one side and are looking up as the men exit.

Cunningham, who tends not to be a wordy man, preferring to let his dancing speak for him, usually includes the following program note for performances of this work: "The events and sounds of this dance revolve around a quiet center, which, though silent and unmoving, is the source from which they happen." It makes one think of Elgar's *Enigma Variations,* which has a counterpart theme that is not heard but is a very real part of the work.

COLLAGE III

Choreography by Merce Cunningham. Music by Pierre Henry (excerpts from Symphonie pour un homme seul). *First performed at the University of Pittsburgh, Pittsburgh, Pa., April 21, 1958, by Merce Cunningham.*

Cunningham was introduced to the *musique concrète* of Pierre Schaeffer and Pierre Henry by Leonard Bernstein at a concert that the conductor was giving at Brandeis University. Bernstein chose excerpts from *Symphonie pour un homme seul,* which was composed directly on magnetic tape, and because of the novelty of the score he wanted to play it twice. Cunningham composed a solo for himself and then created a dance for his own highly trained company and the students of Brandeis who wished to participate. The latter were given everyday gestures as their part of the dance so that they would not be intimidated and could participate fully in the event. Subsequently he created another solo for himself, which he designated as *Collage III.*

He is dressed in street clothes, jacket, shirt, and trousers, and slowly circles, punctuating his walk with little jumps. He removes his jacket and then takes a balletic formal stance at the center of the stage, placing his feet tightly together. He opens his arms and legs outward with a strong, easy command of the technique, then swings his legs from side to side in a contrasting impish movement.

He then appears to be a man beset, scanning with his eyes rapidly around the empty space. He becomes more careful and almost guarded in his movements and then begins a rousing variation to counter the feeling of malaise, but then runs off shaking his head from side to side as if saying, "No!"

One of the strongest dance technicians of his generation, Cunningham has never stressed the showy aspects of dance for their sake alone, but it is a distinct treat to see him as a soloist commanding the stage with his performing presence. The piece is a very personal one and very moving, as it explores the fate of a man alone with his craft and his tools of space, to be meaningfully traversed in a given time.

ANTIC MEET

Choreography by Merce Cunningham. Music by John Cage (Concerto for Piano and Orchestra). *Scenery and costumes by Robert Rauschenberg. First performed at Connecticut College, New London, Conn., August 14, 1958, by Merce Cunningham, Carolyn Brown, Viola Farber, Marilyn Wood, Judith Dunn, and Remy Charlip.*

Because of his formidable reputation as a serious, uncompromising, and advanced choreographer, many are surprised at the number of humorously light dances that Cunningham has created. This one is among his best.

Four women and two men enter. One man walks on a diagonal with his girl and looks enviously at her. He offers a bunch of flowers and she ignores him. He exits. A moment later he returns with a bentwood chair strapped to his back. A door on wheels follows him across the stage. He opens it and there is his girl in a mammoth muumuu. He kneels and she sits in the chair and they banter as best they can. She leaves and he is alone and rubs his hands with glee and cavorts with three mini-skirted women. His girl returns and does catch-up movements to duplicate everything that they have done.

The man returns without the chair and does a series of large balletic forward kicks very rapidly with a smile, then leaves with his legs a bit twisted. Two women mime throwing things at one another and spin into a balletic mode of moving. They stop and relax into normal posture. One bends and the other braces herself on her as one might on a ballet practice barre. The two men cavort like burly dock hands wearing sweat shirts covered with tattoos. Both collapse as they shuffle away, and then one drags himself off only to return to retrieve his friend.

One woman wearing sunglasses is brought out and deposited, then the others enter with sunglasses and all do a round of elegant poses linked with sudden little turns. In the next episode the first man desperately tries to put on a sweater which seems to have more than the usual number of sleeves but no hole to put one's head through. The women in voluminous white dresses circle and simper as he struggles. They cup their hands to their heads and leave and he finally does the same as well.

One woman sits at a table near the edge of the stage and the other man enters to remove it. She gets up and does a short, rapid sequence of small steps. The first man returns in white coveralls and launches into a soft-shoe routine with relaxed confidence and then wanders off. The four women return in their original costumes to parade in front, while the two men leap frantically in the background.

The dancers constantly look startled as they meet one another, almost as if they never expected to see another human being, and the piece develops as a wacky flirtation dance. The men are always being driven to some feat or another, and the women are studiously decorative. It has the zaniness of slapstick farce and a lovely warm ambiance.

NIGHTWANDERING

Choreography by Merce Cunningham. Music by Bo Nilsson. Costumes by Nicola Cernovich. First performed at the Kungliche Teatern, Stockholm, Sweden, October 5, 1958, by Merce Cunningham and Carolyn Brown.

In Cunningham's long career one of his most valued collaboraters has been Carolyn Brown. In addition to being a superb technical dancer with elegant bearing and precisely articulated gestures, she also has an excellent visual memory and has functioned as the *régisseuse* of the company during her association with it. It is difficult to assess her exact contribution to the developing body of work that Cunningham has produced with Brown in the company, but she has always been his most resilient and compliant dancer in picking up on his choreographic suggestions and fleshing them out to his satisfaction. Finding himself at an engagement in Copenhagen with her and having to create a dance on short notice, he decided to make a duet for them. Three days is an awfully short time to complete a dance, but undoubtedly the task was facilitated greatly by her responsive intelligence.

The first thing that strikes one about the dance is its primitive costuming, which suggests early cave dwellers. He wears a rough, shaggy sleeveless vest and she a furry long garment also without sleeves. While the textures and the appearance of the costuming appear rough, the movement is lyrically smooth. The course of the piece reflects support on his part and dependence on hers. They run rapidly around at one point and then he pauses and she luxuriously stretches her body back to back with his, or at another point he arches his body upward and she reclines easily across him as he rocks back and forth.

The dance pairs two of the finest performers in the world, picking up and playing off each other's strength. He is the motive energy of the pair and she translates the power into exquisite pictures.

CRISES

Choreography by Merce Cunningham. Music by Conlon Nancarrow. Costumes by Robert Rauschenberg. First performed at Connecticut College, New London, Conn., August 19, 1960, by Merce Cunningham, Carolyn Brown, Viola Farber, Marilyn Wood, and Judith Dunn.

An unusual aspect of the dance derives from the elastic bands that dancers wear around the waist or one arm. At times one or another of the dancers will join another by slipping a hand through the band and effectively linking the two. In this situation they have to move together, but in others the dancers reflect each other without the linkage.

A man and a woman stand on opposite sides of the stage facing one another. He bows to her eccentrically, touching various parts of his body as he acknowledges her presence. She responds with an equally quirky arabesque and he approaches her, turning and rolling his head while keeping his torso quite still. Three women enter as he flexes his arms above his head. Two of the women are joined with an elastic band and they kneel and lie down as the third continues to move, only to return, striding deliberately. All do individual variations and then exit.

One by one the women return to run or stand and extend one leg. The man dashes out to grasp one leg then releases it to watch while kneeling. Two other women dance similarly before all leave. The three women return to course about in little semicircles, and the man returns to catch another woman, who is bending backward, and he assists her in a backward walk. He offers her his elastic band and she grasps it behind her head, and both whirl to the rear of the stage. Their duet begins with falls and displays an almost classical adagio. A slow passage of walks is punctuated by lifting the heels from the floor periodically and then developing into a series of turns. Two of the women join hands and leap up and down in unison.

The man makes a slow, crablike crossing of the stage to the woman he first bowed to. He grasps her hand and one extended leg as she hops into the wings. All enter singly to perform solo variations of hops and form a rough circle in the center of the stage. The man returns to the center of the stage with one of his hands trapped beneath the elastic band around his own waist and turns frantically from one to another as if faced with an extremely difficult choice. He rejoins the first woman and slides his arm beneath the band circling her upper arm and assists her in sliding off.

The crises all seem to be of a technical humorous nature, such as trying to find suitable ways to dance while linked. He has wedded both classically balanced, almost balletic movement with odd asymmetrical gestures. It is as if the dance existed at two levels at the same time: one showing polite reserve and then another pragmatic set of movements designed to solve particular problems and commenting wittily on the process. In his autobiography Cuningham wrote: "One of the special characteristics of this dance was due to Viola Farber [the first woman]. Her body often had the look of one part being in balance and the rest extremely off."

AEON

Choreography by Merce Cunningham. Music by John Cage (Atlas Eclipticals with Winter Music, *electronic version*). *Scenery and costumes by Robert Rauschenberg. First performed at La Comédie Canadienne, Montreal, Canada, August 5, 1961. First performed in the United States at Palmer Auditorium, Connecticut College, New London, Conn., August 17, 1961, by Merce Cunningham, Carolyn Brown, Viola Farber, Judith Dunn, Marilyn Wood, Remy Charlip, Shareen Blair, Valda Setterfield, and Steve Paxton. First performed in New York City at Philharmonic Hall, August 13, 1963.*

The dance celebrates an epoch that is not placed in any time but almost seems to be the story of man and woman throughout time. The strict definition of the word as given in the dictionary is that it denotes a long but indefinite period of time, usually thought of in thousands of years. The dance is full of elaborate stage effects including exploding flares, and a large smoking machine which travels across in the air while some of the dancers lie prone in the darkness. Because of its complexity a shorter version and an even shorter touring version of the piece were prepared which did not contain all of the effects or the movement.

The piece opens with all the dancers onstage and two dazzling flares fire off. One man begins to move, then the dance is picked up by two women and the other men, and all are moving in place. The last two women to begin now switch places and six of the seven start skipping while the other eventually joins and all go off. The flash seems to announce some cataclysmic event such as the beginning of animate life. A brief duet has one man carrying a woman from place to place, pausing, and then they leave. All the women run around and are joined by the men wearing ruffled leggings. One of them makes an approach to one of the women, and it is like a comic version of an eighteenth-century gallant pressing his suit. Various men take turns in presenting themselves but leave, and the women leave as the smoking machine makes its crossing of the stage.

A man returns without the leggings and does a proud roosterlike dance and is joined by a woman. Together they dance a jazzy variation. Other groupings succeed them: two trios of a man and two women; first one group falls and then the other, and then they both collapse together. A single spotlight now illuminates the stage, and one man walks just outside of its glare. When the lights illuminate the rest of the stage, he joins one of the women who enter with three others and a man. All of the women leave as the third man enters, and these three walk, pausing from time to time to clasp a foot. A woman with a colorful cloak enters and is carried off by one of the exiting men, the last of whom duck-walks off making gestures of combat like a Japanese warrior.

All return to dance a variation again in place as at the opening of the piece, whipping arms about, and then the men separate from the women. All leave except a man dancing alone, as another man and a woman enter and cross from time to time flashing stroboscopic lights from their wrists. Again there is a period of romantic ardor as a man in leggings dances, followed by a woman who rides out on the back of another man. The chap in leggings ties a string of tin cans to her, suggesting a honeymoon trip. She immediately has an argument with the man bearing her, and he leaves in a huff. The rapid-fire encounters continue until one man is left dancing with the women, and they leave and he leaves to conclude the piece.

This dance and others show Cunningham's mastery of entrances and exits. He uses the disappearance and reappearance of his dancers with consummate artistry, always bringing an element of surprise to the dance. One can never anticipate precisely who or what will be the next to appear from the wings. In this case he gave us the battle of the sexes with wit, humor, and a dazzling array of technical stage machinery and fast costume changes.

WINTERBRANCH

Choreography by Merce Cunningham. Music by La Monte Young (2 sounds, April 1960). Costumes by Robert Rauschenberg. First performed at the Wadsworth Atheneum, Hartford, Conn., March 21, 1964, by Merce Cunningham, Carolyn Brown, Viola Farber, Barbara Lloyd, Albert Reid, and Gus Solomons, Jr.

The dance has been a puzzle and problem since it was first performed. It is a good dance, but it is difficult to enjoy at first viewing because of its unusual setting and musical accompaniment. At one performance an outraged man seated near me shouted angrily that he wanted the lights turned out, which were shining across the audience and momentarily dazzling some. In subsequent performances the lighting design was modified and various other of the stage elements were changed. The setting which I enjoyed the most was at the Brooklyn Academy of Music, and the description follows the details of that series of performances.

The stage area is in dusky shadow, and one perceives the dancers and the décor as one might peering around in early evening. One black curtain hangs straight and squarely down, while its mate is drawn up partially into a full, rich, romantic curve: a suggestion of male and female. The dance commences in absolute silence and pencil-thin shafts of light cut through the gloom; someone crawls along the back of the stage in a sack. A woman stretches near the edge of the stage, and two men enter to carry her to the rear of the stage, where she again stretches. A man and a woman dance together and then topple to the ground. (There is a general feeling of energy running down as all of the people in the dance tend to go earthward at some point or another in the course of the piece.) He rises and assists her to her feet and she slides back and he drags her off. Another couple does a lackadaisical duet.

At this point the sound begins. It consists of two sustained tones, one low pitched and the other high, and both are amplified greatly, and the dance picks up to a frenzied pace. All of the dancers wear sweat shirts and pants and have black smudges applied beneath their eyes; one man wears a black skullcap. The woman who stretched in the first part of the dance now reclines on a cloth, and two men grab the ends and drag her off. Three couples dance duets in which one of the partners falls and the other supports her. One girl arches backward with her arms above and to the side and begins to teeter, and her partner bends beneath her and catches her so that she slides off his back to the floor. One couple remains, as the other exits, to whirl and tumble rapidly. Others return, two men lift a woman; one supports the upper body as the other supports her legs. At the rear of the stage a strange little machine with winking lights begins to make slow progress across the stage from the right to the left. It looks like a cartoon version of an official police car with its flashing red light on the top. The company masses and is covered with a large cloth by one woman and crawls off en masse as she does a slow bump and grind in the center. All return to lie prone as the performance ends.

Interpretations of the piece have ranged from a plea for racial understanding to an interpretation of a shipwreck. Reactions have been violent at times, warm at others, and quietly hostile at still others. The loudness of the score at times provokes anger and the intermittent flashing of the lights bothers others, but the mystery of the gloomy setting is probably most disquieting. It is a dance which provokes a sense of uneasiness. It is certainly not pretty in any conventional sense, but it has a sincerity and an integrity that make it one of Cunningham's most intriguing dances.

VARIATIONS V

Choreography by Merce Cunningham. Music by John Cage. Film by Stan Van Der Beek. Distortion of television images by Nam June Paik. Electronic devices by Billy Klüver and Robert Moog. First performed at Philharmonic Hall, New York, N.Y., July 23, 1965, by Merce Cunningham, Carolyn Brown, Barbara Lloyd, Sandra Neels, Albert Reid, Peter Saul, and Gus Solomons, Jr.

Always receptive to the new and newer, Cunningham has been in the forefront of those choreographers willing to use the latest in stage properties and décor. In this case five magnetically sensitive poles are the pylons around which the dance develops. As the dancers pass near them their bodies break electromagnetic fields which cause changes in the electronic score accompanying the dance and the slide projections and films which provide its background.

The dance contrasts slow, ordinary, paced gestures such as sitting and walking with high velocity dancing. A man first walks across the stage alone carrying a plant in a small clay pot and places it down at the edge of the stage. Another man and a woman walk on as projections show a dance studio and a locomotive, and she promptly stands on her head as he raises and lowers her, tugging on her upraised legs. The first man returns to dance among the poles; his partner walks slowly on and places a pot with newspapers in it next to his plant. Their duet is followed by a series of solos for three men, while three women also do solo variations at another part of the stage. The films at one point show bicycles as the men do imaginary pedaling in the air.

Dancers enter and leave the performing area with a zestful enthusiasm, in contrast with some of the slower walking paces of the earlier section. The first man sees his partner smash his flowerpot and replant the plant in her own pot, carefully arranging the leaves. He does a series of exercises on an electronically sensitive mat. The costumes of the dancers change as the dance moves along. The women appear at one time in fast sleek bathing suits and flesh-colored tights and then at another in street clothes. The pace accelerates as the dancers dash across from one side of the stage to the other and then abruptly two of the men stop to sit and watch the others dance. Then all join in unwinding a long cord which is pulled into a large zigzag shape that they weave up and down, and then all dash off. There is a momentary pause, and then suddenly the first man returns, and this time he is riding a bicycle that has a small air horn attached to the handle bars. He wheels in and around all of the poles, breaking the magnetic fields and causing changes in sound and sight while tooting his little horn.

The dance has an ironic twist to it when one thinks of the simple act of walking which opened the dance and the unusual (onstage) act of bicycle riding to conclude the dance. In between, of course, there has been a great deal of easily recognizable "dance" movement, but Cunningham also draws our attention to other types of movement which can function equally well and humorously in a dance.

HOW TO PASS, KICK, FALL, AND RUN

Choreography by Merce Cunningham. Music by John Cage (readings from his book Silence, *later including readings from his* A Year from Monday). *First performed at the Harper Theatre, Chicago, Ill., November 24, 1965, by Merce Cunningham, Carolyn Brown, Barbara Lloyd, Sandra Neels, Valda Setterfield, Albert Reid, Peter Saul, and Gus Solomons, Jr.*

Playful is the word one thinks of in connection with this dance. There is in addition to the playful frisky movement of the dancers themselves a playful performance by John Cage, who reads anecdotal stories from his book *Silence*. This is the sound accompaniment to the dance and consists of one story per minute. Cage smokes, sips at a fine vintage champagne, and sometimes is joined by a second reader, David Vaughan. The stories are light and humorous in tone. The dance requires no special décor, and the costumes are very simple black tights and solid-color sweaters.

On a brightly illuminated clear stage a man jumps on exuberantly, flings his arms outward to the side, and twirls. Two other men take up a stance that suggests Indian wrestling. A couple of women run between the men; another woman is lifted high. One feels as if there is an elaborate game of "tag" being played. The whole pacing of the first part is fast; women pick their way across the stage, looking carefully where they place their steps; a man and two women leap in short, bouncy jumps. Then there is a pause in the frantic activity.

Slower-phrased gestures replace the energetic ones, falls are performed by the various couples, and then all sit in a semicircle. Runs begin and the first man repeats part of his opening solo, the group forms a large cluster which revolves upon itself, and then all scatter. The first man remains in the center, skittering and raising himself on the balls of his feet as the others move to opposite sides of the stage, and the curtain falls on a scene of activity.

Cunningham explained that the reason he created the dance was that he was a practical man of the theater and had to have a simple piece; simple in the sense of costuming, lack of décor, and necessity for special rehearsal time. It would of course be an easy piece to tour, but more than that it is an example of his puckish humor given an expansive and enjoyable outing.

PLACE

Choreography by Merce Cunningham. Music by Gordon Mumma (Mesa, for Cybersonic Bandoneon). *Scenery and costumes by Beverly Emmons. First performed at the Fondation Maeght, Saint-Paul-de-Vence, France, August 6, 1966, by Merce Cunningham, Carolyn Brown, Barbara Lloyd, Sandra Neels, Valda Setterfield, Albert Reid, Peter Saul, and Gus Solomons, Jr.*

This is an odd title for a dance that seems to be about no particular place, but then it could be anyplace. It is also unusual in that it respects the traditional conceptions of theater space. The center of the stage is the most important part of it, and the most important actions occur there and the dance always develops forward toward the audience. Usually Cunningham allows his dances to transpire over the entire surface of the dance space, but in this one he chooses not to. The music has a menacing drone.

A man enters a totally deserted area and performs a short, cautious solo as if seeing strange territory for the first time. Suddenly he is joined by a woman, then three others; all are costumed in industrial weight transparent plastic subtly tinted blue, pink, green, and yellow. The others leave and he partners the first woman. They separate and he goes to the rear of the stage, where two small geodesic lights sit on a length of cloth. He lights the smaller of the two and rubs his shin reflectively as if meditating about an old hurt.

He kneels and slowly draws the cloth toward him. The others dance farther down the stage closer to the audience. He lights the second lamp. He stands and makes crisscross motions with his hands as if to ward off something, almost like a man brushing away annoying gnats or trying to get rid of troublesome thoughts. He is somberly clad in black, and the other men and women are in colored costumes. His second solo finds him still alone and isolated. The men and women change partners and carry through a rather cool series of duets like mating automatons. The man in black dances alone again, and while the others involve themselves with one another he tends the two lamps. The women drop one by one and are carried off by the men. When they have all left, the man in black walks forward to look around him at the deserted area. He returns to his solitary life, and this time he half slips into a plastic bag and wriggles, thrashing, along the floor. It is not clear whether he wants to be wholly in it or free from it, but the curtain descends as he is still thrashing.

The dance has a futuristic look in its see-through plastic costuming and geodesic lights and makes one feel very lonely and abandoned. The man tending his lights seems intent upon preserving something in the midst of this alien atmosphere, but at the end even he is driven to some display of emotional desperation as the last of the coolly distant inhabitants has left. He is not of like temperament and yet they both dwell in the same place virtually side by side, separated by an invisible wall of exclusion.

RAINFOREST

Choreography by Merce Cunningham. Music by David Tudor. Scenery and costumes by Andy Warhol. First performed at the Upton Auditorium, Buffalo, N.Y., March 9, 1968, by Merce Cunningham, Carolyn Brown, Barbara Lloyd, Albert Reid, Sandra Neels, and Gus Solomons, Jr.

There is no rain to be seen or heard in the piece, and the "forest" is a cluster of inflated pillow shapes, but there is a strong feeling of a jungle setting in the choreography. Some of the silver pillows are filled with helium so that they float in the air above the dancers, and others are just tossed casually on the stage, to be moved by the breeze of the dancers passing. They provide a changing and playful backdrop to the somewhat animalistic dance. Just before the first performance the designer Andy Warhol went around from dancer to dancer cutting little holes in the costumes so that the dancers would appear to be somewhat ragged in contrast to the smooth, shiny pillows.

Three figures are seen standing as the light slowly brightens. A man and a woman are close together and another man stands some distance away. All weave their arms and swirl in place. It appears as if they are stretching, suggesting the first movements of the day. The man and the woman now start to snake around one another; the movement is young, strong, almost rough. The first man leaves, and the one in the background moves forward to dance with the woman, after which they lie together.

A third man enters and together he and the other man push the lying woman to the edge of the stage. The man most recently arrived does a fast and assertive solo which attracts the woman, and they go off together. The second man stands and a second woman dashes on briskly and engages in an athletic romp with him, after which they go off together.

A third woman begins a proud, vital solo that attracts the attention of the first man who has returned. He joins her and creates the impression of a warrior, during which she leaves and he follows, to leave the stage bare of people but full of the slightly rocking and swaying pillows, serene as ever.

The dance is like a representation of life in a primitive society where relationships are simple and somewhat brutal. The suggestions of rooting and cavorting that are in the piece contrast wonderfully with the almost antiseptic décor, suggesting cave men in a computer era.

CHANGING STEPS

Choreography by Merce Cunningham. Music by Christian Wolff. First performed at the Brooklyn Academy of Music, Brooklyn, N.Y., March 22, 1973, by Merce Cunningham, Carolyn Brown, Barbara Lias, Julie Sukenick, Brynar Mehl, and Robert Kovich.

This exceptionally fine dance is a rarity in that it does not have a part for the choreographer himself. Ordinarily one expects to see him in each work, but this one was created for the members of his company and represents a beautiful and lean demonstration of Cunningham's style of movement as designed for others' talents, not just his own.

A man enters and performs a slow sequence of Adonis-like poses that are classically clean and leaves after a few thrusts and leaps. A woman lyrically bends forward and backward, dancing lightly on the balls of her feet. A second woman dances a solo, entering the spot just vacated by the other. She turns and strikes balances and then exits. There is an utter simplicity in the way that the dancers execute the steps and then just leave without a hint of dramatic or emotional coloring to the dance.

A series of solo dances by men and women ensue, and then two men enter with a woman for a trio in which they cradle her in their arms. Two women and a man prance side to side in unison and separate to do solo variations, skittering and leaping off. Three women slide into splits and hold the position while two men leap across their outstretched legs like sword dancers avoiding sharp blades. They turn and assist the women up, and then all cluster into a cozy group huddle and collapse. The energy of the dance is high, and the physical look that the dancers have makes it appear as if almost the whole dance is being done on the tips of the toes.

A couple dances together, he presenting a strong, solid appearance while she does little fluttering foot movements. It is almost as if they are sketching out the movement for a duet rather than dancing it full out. A second couple almost appears like a pair of tap dancers doing a team routine, at the end of which he lifts her on his shoulder and carries her off. A man forms the secure center of a trio in which two women turn and depend on him.

Each sinks to the floor from time to time but revives, and all exit, turning rapidly.

A man lies prone with his palms flat on the stage and rests his chin on them. A woman sits on his shoulders, and as he rolls over she cuddles comfortably close to him. They perform a romantic duet just rolling and then conclude by returning to the opening pose. Another couple flirtatiously romps across the area, running hand in hand back and forth. Another man enters to do an exaggerated version of ballroom dancing with his partner. A second girl tags along with them, inserting herself between them at one moment or just fluttering around at another, like a persistent little sister. She tires and dashes off to do her own solo variation but collapses. The couple has pity and includes her in the dance, and all exit together. Two couples enter and form a tight circle and create a miniature world of gestures, all working very closely to one another, passing and repassing one another in a highly compact area, bringing the dance to its triumphant finale.

It is the lean economy of the piece that gives it its extreme delight. One feels that the choreographer has taken every unnecessary or extraneous movement out of work and kept only those absolutely essential steps required to accomplish his design. It is spare but not desiccated and has a taut richness that marks it as one of his finest dances, almost a distillation of one whole aspect of his talented career.

CHOREOCHRONICLE
OF MERCE CUNNINGHAM

1942

Seeds of Brightness (with Jean
   Erdman)
Credo in Us (with Jean Erdman)
Renaissance Testimonials
Ad Lib (with Jean Erdman)
Totem Ancestor

1943

In the Name of the Holocaust
Shimmera

1944

Triple-Paced
Root of an Unfocus
Tossed as It Is Untroubled
The Unavailable Memory of
   Spontaneous Earth
Four Walls (dance play)
Idyllic Song

1945

Mysterious Adventure
Experiences

1946

The Encounter
Invocation to Vahakn
Fast Blues
The Princess Zonilda and Her
    Entourage

1947

The Seasons
The Open Road
Dromenon

1948

Dream
A Diversion
Orestes
The Monkey Dances

1949

Effusions avant l'heure (Games)
Amores
Duet
Two Step

1950

Pool of Darkness
Before Dawn
Waltz
Rag Time Finale

1951

Sixteen Dances for Soloist and
    Company of Three
Variation

1952

Suite for Six Short Dances
Excerpts from Symphonie pour
    un homme seul

1953

Suite by Chance
Solo Suite in Space and Time
Dime a Dance
Septet
Untitled Solo
Fragments

1954

Minutiae

1955

Springweather and People

1956

Galaxy
Lavish Escapade
*Suite for Five in Space and Time
Nocturnes

1957

Labyrinthian Dances
Changeling
Picnic Polka

1958

Suite for Two
*Antic Meet
Summerspace
*Nightwandering
*Collage III

1959

From the Poems of White Stone
Gambit for Dancers and
    Orchestra
Rune

1960

*Crises
Hands Birds
Waka
Music Walk with Dancers

1961

Suite de Dances
*Aeon

1963

Field Dances
Story

1964

Open Session
Paired
*Winterbranch
Museum Event No. 1
Cross Currents
Museum Event No. 2
Museum Event No. 3

1965

*Variations V
*How to Pass, Kick, Fall, and Run

1966

*Place
Museum Event No. 4

1967

Museum Event No. 5
Scramble

1968

*Rainforest
Walkaround Time
Gymnasium Event No. 1
Gymnasium Event No. 2
Gymnasium Event No. 3
Museum Event No. 6

1969

Gymnasium Event No. 4
Gymnasium Event No. 5
Canfield
Theater Event

1970

Tread
Second Hand
Signals

1971

Loops

1972

Borst Park
TV Rerun
Landrover

1973

Solo
*Changing Steps
Un Jour ou deux

1974–75

Events to No. 140*

* These were collages of movements from repertory dances.

ERICK HAWKINS

Erick Hawkins had an unlikely background for dance, as he was a Harvard graduate who had majored in Greek. On trips to New York he encountered, almost by chance, recitals of European expressionist dancers such as Harald Kreutzberg and Yvonne Georgi. He enrolled at the recently established School of American Ballet after graduation. In a few years he was invited to become a member of the American Ballet, and he also danced with Ballet Caravan, both of which companies were forerunners of the New York City Ballet. Ballet Caravan began its first season with performances at the Bennington College Summer School of the Dance, where he encountered Martha Graham, and two years later he became a member of her company. He was the first male dancer to join her company and she created a wide range of roles for him. Foremost among these was as her partner in *American Document*, the Husbandman in *Appalachian Spring*, the Ringmaster in *Every Soul Is a Circus*, and He Who Beckons in *Dark Meadow*.

They were married in 1948 and separated in 1950, at which time Hawkins began a new direction in his own choreography. While he was with the Graham company his works, such as *John Brown*, tended to be involved with intense dramatic incident, but he altered his choreographic approach subsequently to stress the calm flow of movement and created works such as *Eight Clear Places, Here and Now with Watchers*, which are ceremonial and suggest the unhurried passage of time that one encounters in the theater of the East.

Almost from the beginning of his independent career, Hawkins has collaborated with composer Lucia Dlugoszewski, who has provided him with many original and haunting scores using percussion instruments of unique sound and design as well as traditional orchestral instruments. Hawkins is doctrinaire in his insistence upon live musical accompaniment to his dances, and also that each dance requires its own original musical composition. His dances are recognizable for their often symbolic and surrealistic décor and costuming, and many of these striking designs have been created by Ralph Dorazio.

Hawkins involves himself in all aspects of a production from the initial choreographic preparation to the particulars of costume design. His pieces are meticulously finished and have a precise fastidiousness. His studio has attracted a wide variety of students, some of whom have continued to explore his creative direction in their own work and others who have made personal use of the technique but whose choreographic products do not bear the shaping traces of Hawkins' own dances.

HERE AND NOW WITH WATCHERS

Choreography by Erick Hawkins. Music by Lucia Dlugoszewski. Costumes by Ralph Dorazio. First performed at the Hunter College Playhouse, New York, N.Y., November 27, 1957, by Erick Hawkins and Nancy Lang.

In a way this dance may have been the most important one that Hawkins has ever made. When it was given its premier performance he had been working on it for over two and half years and it clearly indicated his own individual creative direction. During the time he was with the Martha Graham company his pieces showed a marked influence of her work, but in *Here and Now with Watchers* he subsumed the Graham aesthetic into his own and made a definitive personal statement. It also marked a significant musical collaboration between composer Lucia Dlugoszewski and himself that continues to the present. It has elements of ritual, humor, and mystery presented with flowing, nondramatic movement having the flavor of Eastern ceremony.

The dance is a series of solos and duets having surrealistic titles such as "The," which opens the piece. The man and the woman each carry large openwork wings which look like delicate xylophones and they each have a large black rosette attached to their torsos. They present themselves almost like participants in a primitive religious rite as they walk, tilt backward, and peer at one another.

"Inside Wonder of Whales (says my body of things)" develops through elaborate nuances of arm and hand gesture, and in the following solo the man turns and sinks and recovers again, giving one a strong sense of a body engaged in a relentless war against the downward tug of spent energy. There is the suggestion of excitement, of triumph over adversity as there is suggestion of joyous pleasure in others of the sections.

After the first five sections the work develops a greater emotional weight as the tensions and accommodations of the man and the woman reach a greater expressiveness. They are lyrically and warmly together in "Multiplicity," and the man, with a red spot on his nose and a dome-shaped hat, is humorously coy in "Clown Is Everyone's Ending." The final love duet, "Like Darling (shouts my body and shouts itself transparent)," is an exploration of male/female poetic eroticism and a fitting culmination to the preparatory portions that preceded it.

A program note prepared by Hawkins describes the intent of the piece. "In the choreography itself far below the level of words I would like to show the miracle of two people, the perfection of the one beside the perfection of the other and the poetry of the space between them. For the man and the woman I would like to discover as many levels of movement as a live person can imagine from the gentlest opening of the mouth, the fastest blink of the eye and the tiniest wiggle of the toes, to the strangest leap and the deepest mystery of the spine."

8 CLEAR PLACES

Choreography by Erick Hawkins. Music by Lucia Dlugoszewski. Costumes by Ralph Dorazio. First performed at the Hunter College Playhouse, New York, N.Y., October 8, 1960, by Erick Hawkins, with Barbara Tucker, Kelly Holt, and Kenneth LaVrack. Subsequently reduced for two dancers.

Hawkins grew up in Colorado and before he started his dance career went searching through the state for Indian dances to "see and feel if a grown man could dance without being a fool." He obviously found what he was looking for, and he also has always shown a special sensitivity for natural phenomena, many of which he also encountered in his home state. This dance is a celebration of nature and man's awareness of it told in highly stylized movement and costuming.

The "North Star" is the first section and a woman maneuvers a large black screen with a four-pointed star on it around the performing space. A series of crystalline tinkling sounds accompany the progress of the screen before it disappears into the wings. A man enters with a rusty red sheath on his left arm and a leafy green one on his leg. Across his face, masking the profile, is a narrow block of wood with five curved, protruding tines. It is "Pine Tree," and he turns slowly and stamps his feet looking like some emerging half-human, half-grotesque creature. It is a ritual circling and acknowledging all points of the compass, in which one has the feel of a solidly rooted being that also displays little surface shudders, much as a tree will shake in the wind.

In "Rain Rain" the woman enters, carefully bearing a tall, crooked pole with feet, which she places down accompanied by a sound that is like heavy rain on a roof. As she bows and dashes away, the little pieces of wood in her hair clatter lightly. In a long, vertically striped robe the man moves across the stage with tiny steps and cupped hands. He jumps in place and wiggles down to the floor before bowing stiffly from the waist and carrying the crooked pole off with him. He is followed by the girl in a swooping solo designated "Sheen on Water," in which she does rapid little turns and outlines "S"-shaped curves before turning to back off.

The "Inner Feet of the Summer Fly" has a dry, humorous quality as the man wanders from side to side in a large square black costume that brushes the floor. He is restlessly active, pausing at one spot before passing on to the next. She enters with a square headdress that has bouncing metal rods extending out of it like a long plume and walks determinedly in a circle as the rods sway. Her hands are agitated, and the sound of the score suggests dry rustling. She is in white, as is suitable for "They Snowing." The final section of the dance, "Squash," suggests a fertility rite for crops. Each wears a small white mask. At one point he has a stick attached across his shoulders with a small flag dangling down at either end. At the end he enters in a striped, tightly fitting body suit with a squash shape covering his head and covers himself with long vines as he lies down. After rising he jogs a moment and then exits.

The piece has a zany logic that brings the costuming, movement, and music together in a way that almost defies logical analysis. It is a meditation on states of nature which is at one moment very strange and at another very clear and obvious. The two dancers don't really try to be pine trees and snowstorms but provide movement correlatives for what these states of nature might be like. The piece is inventive and so varied that it is a bit of a surprise to realize that it has a small cast of two.

CLASSIC KITE TAILS

Choreography by Erick Hawkins. Music by David Diamond (Rounds). *First performed in New York City at the ANTA Theater, October 26, 1972, by Nada Reagan, Carol Conway, Erick Hawkins, Beverly Brown, Natalie Richman, Lillo Way, and Robert Yohn.*

Sometimes an artist will devise a piece for the sheer playfulness of a single idea or the delight that comes from a simple motion. One has the feeling that Hawkins seized upon the floating and darting look of flying kites with accompanying streaming tails and just wanted to translate it into a dance for the fun of it. Whatever the motivation the piece has a humorous lilt that makes it a pleasure to watch.

The stage is carefully set with eight sculptured seats for the dancers. The first to enter are four women who approach the seats and one by one settle themselves. Then two men follow; one sits and the other walks ceaselessly around as if being driven along by the singing David Diamond score. He is joined by the second man, and then various of the women scamper up to course through the area in solo variations. They are all like happy zephyrs.

All of the women join in a group, and then two pair off to do a dance, and one presses her palm to her forehead as if in a gentle transport of enjoyment. The lead man stands off to the side, observing for a time as if he were directing the ecstatic couplings and meanderings. Two men join a woman for a trio and a moment later there are two couples dancing. The women have a sweet melting quality as they move through the lighthearted design of the piece, swaying and dipping toward the ground, and all skitter together in formation at the conclusion.

In addition to its fluidity the dance has momentary dramatic encounters such as one might have during a barn dance when chancing upon a particularly winning partner. The piece is a hoedown of free and floating spirits sweeping joyously along while having a wonderful time. Hawkins has chosen to celebrate many natural phenomena and human involvements during his career and here has devised an appealing hymn to lilting movement.

GREEK DREAMS WITH FLUTE

Choreography by Erick Hawkins. Music by Claude Debussy, Ohana, Edgard Varèse, Alan Hovhaness, Matsudaira, and Jolivet. Scenery by Ralph Dorazio. Costumes by Raya and Tad Taggart. First performed at the Solomon R. Guggenheim Museum, New York, N.Y., September 7, 1973, by Erick Hawkins, Cathy Ward, Robert Yohn, Nada Reagan, Natalie Richman, Kristin Peterson, and Cori Terry.

It was inevitable for a choreographer who was a classics major in college to select themes from Greek mythology for his dances. Hawkins' first such exploration was *The Strangler,* based on the Oedipus legend, and years later he created this dance, which is not so much a retelling of a particular myth as a celebration of classical antiquity itself.

A woman in a pleated gown and a laurel headdress flutters her fingers and prances in a dreamy, sensuous manner. The mood of her reverie is that of lighthearted abandon as she dances "The Nymph of the Grass of Meadows." When she has left, two men enter wearing extremely brief trunks, and one of them carries a small section of rail which he sets down. After the men three women follow, each bearing a gift. One has a piece of fruit, another flowers, and the third a white ring, all of which are presented for inspection. Each woman dances a brief solo, then all leave. The man by the rail flails his arms and pounces from side to side before carrying the section of rail off.

The "Year-Daimon" solo for the other man begins as he lowers a green and purple pillar to the floor and launches his body forward while making great circular designs with his arms. He throws a branch as if it were an arrow and after a moment inserts the branch into the toppled pillar at an angle and leaves. The first man returns to dance with the woman in the laurel headdress, and then the four women of the "Choros of the Daughters of Okeanos" enter, carrying a long, curved, horn-shaped object which they lower gently to the ground. Each of them wears a long white pleated shift, and their dance is a small celebration full of delicate little kicks and with swift darting to and fro before they carry the ceremonial object off. A "Satyr Play," by two bearded men, the traditional earthy comedy that concluded

Greek drama festivals, is the last portion. They construct a little hut of branches, leer and prance suggestively, and the romp ends with a shower of leaves strewn by the woman who opened the cycle of dances. Her gestures diminish in force as the lights lower, indicating the end of the combined ritual and revel.

In addition to its decidedly classical pattern the dance had an unusually clear story line, as one section combined with another to give a picture of an Arcadian society. In contrast to most of his other dances, Hawkins did not commission new music for this one but selected flute compositions from the existing repertory. The dance does not purport to have great emotional depth, but, as an idyl of the classical period, it has a great deal of charm.

CHOREOCHRONICLE
OF ERICK HAWKINS

1937

Show Piece

1940

Liberty Tree
Yankee Bluebritches

1941

Trickster Coyote

1945

John Brown

1947

Stephen Acrobat

1948

The Strangler

1953

Openings of the Eye

1957

*Here and Now with Watchers

1960

Sudden Snake-Bird
*Eight Clear Places

1962

Early Floating
Spring Azure

1964

To Everybody Out There
Geography of Noon

1965

Lords of Persia
Naked Leopard

1966

Cantilever
Dazzle on a Knife's Edge

1968

Tightrope

1969

Black Lake

1971

Of Love

1972

Angels of the Inmost Heaven
*Classic Kite Tails
Dawn Dazzled Dawn

1973

*Greek Dreams with Flute

1975

Meditation on Orpheus
Hurrah!
Death Is the Hunter

ALWIN NIKOLAIS

No modern dance choreographer has more command of theatrical excitement and expertise than Alwin Nikolais. He can and has created a world out of a handful of slide projections and colored lights. One is dazzled by the audacity of his patterns and colors and the intricate involvement of his dancers with the lighting designs and imaginative stage properties that they are supplied with.

His involvement with the theater began in Hartford, Connecticut, where he viewed many productions of drama and variety entertainment and tried to imitate them on his own. As a child, he experimented with making his own light-dimmer and later worked with marionettes. As a young man, he attended the Summer School of Dance at Bennington College and served in the Signal Corps during World War II. His first attempts at choreography were in Hartford, but when he left the Army he traveled to New York, where he found a comfortable niche teaching and designing productions at the Henry Street Settlement Playhouse.

His first works were for children and showed the direction that his work would ultimately take. In *Lobster Quadrille*, for instance, he had all of the characters dressed and costumed as snails, whitings, lobsters, and so forth with only Alice conventionally dressed. The people inside the constructed costumes only had legs or hands projecting. Subsequently, when he started to experiment with the dancers and lights, he often had them inside stretch jersey, among other things, pinching and pushing it into humorously grotesque shapes while being completely invisible themselves.

These pieces were startlingly different from anything that anyone else was doing and announced the mature phase of Nikolais' works. Today he is in demand not only in the dance world but also in opera, television, and film circles. He is recognized as a genuine pioneer in the use of lighting and materials.

He was most influenced by Hanya Holm, who was a pupil of the German expressionist dancer and choreographer Mary Wigman. And it is mainly through this teacher-pupil connection that expressionist dance had its strongest influence in the United States. Nikolais took the clean, almost machine-precise lines of dance movement that he admired and clothed them with his magic lights to create a theater of wonders that has his own special stamp but acknowledges his debt to the experimental work of the Bauhaus artists and artisans of Germany.

Nikolais takes the whole world of motion to work with and not just the emotionally stressed movement of violently motivated human beings. He is as intrigued with the lazy swing of a trapeze as he is with the passionate contortions of a traditional dance gesture and includes elements of both in his works. He represents the whole spectrum of nature in his dances and refuses to limit himself to the narrow range of human emotion that totally engages other choreographers. It has caused some, unjustly, to characterize his work as being somewhat alien to personal expression. It is merely a widening of the viewer's focus to encompass a full range of phenomena that includes man but is not wholly dominated by him and in a larger view of the planet, with its massive oceans and microscopic worlds, it might be a more accurate one at that. Whatever the contending philosophies, though, no one denies the unique excitement of Nikolais' theater magic.

IMAGO

Choreography by Alwin Nikolais. Scenery and lighting by Alwin Nikolais. Music by Alwin Nikolais and James Seawright. First performed in West Hartford, Conn., February 24, 1963, by Murray Louis, Gladys Bailin, Bill Frank, Phyllis Lamhut, Peggy Barclay, Albert Reid, Raymond Broussard, and Roger Rowell.

The piece is undoubtedly Nikolais' most widely known dance theater work. When he created it, Nikolais went back to his native city, Hartford, to give it its premier performance, and then he presented it in a six-week season at the Henry Street Settlement Playhouse starting the following month. In subsequent years he has presented other full seasons devoted to it and also embarked on a six-week national tour with it. It is subtitled *The City Curious,* and it certainly has a strange and wonderful collection of inhabitants.

The group looks like a gaggle of busy robots in Regency striped costumes and small cylindrical hats. The accompanying sound resounds like a cosmic Ping-pong game as they scurry along and at one point go into a rocking tilt from side to side, almost to the point of unbalance. The five women in the second dance wear flowing overblouses on top of their leotards and perform a perky and cute dance that suggests little static flashes on a video screen. They are succeeded by five men who move like ponderous links in a long genetic chain. They each have long extensions which lengthen the reach of their arms, but they are covered by their costumes so that they seem like real appendages with flat discs at the ends. They place these together and almost seem to be communicating with one another through them. The projection of an enlarged cobalt blue crystal makes this appear to be a glimpse into a submicroscopic world of creatures or elements. The climax of the first act is a dance for the men and women between the lines of elastic tapes stretched from one side of the stage to the other. They are almost like notes cavorting on a musical staff.

The start of the second act reveals three men who attract and repel tiny pennants, seemingly hanging in mid-air, as they move. The pennants are actually attached to the men by black cords which transmit their movements to the bits of cloth almost by magic, and the pennants playfully respond. The woman who follows them dances her solo in bursts, starting and stopping abruptly like some molecule in a vast solution. Two men then pursue another woman in a trio that has her trapped and unable to escape their attentions, since they envelop her by forming a little enclosure with their arms and two little objects that look like rolling pins. All simply enact individual roles with a kind of deterministic resignation. Some people are pursued and some are pursuers; that is the way things are. The act continues with a male variation that has an assertive but mechanical quality to it, and concludes with the entire company in a small frenzied dance. All wear loosely fitted, cover-all shrouds that enclose the arms, and they gather together only to explode apart periodically. They react to one another like elastic spheres, rebounding in an endless but stimulated cycle of random encounters.

A projection of dark blue chunks on a light blue background forms the setting for the male-female duet that opens the final act. The man's costume is bright blue and hers is pastel blue. Their dance together is a touching assertion of individuality in a world that seems to be comprised of faceless and strictly reactive creatures. But it is essentially a futile gesture in an indifferent world. The company enters smoothly in small groups, moving as if they were rolling on wheels rather than taking steps. Beautiful projections in varying colors fill the wall behind them. Three men carry on little constructions with colored circular sheets of gelatin. Later three of the women hold the sheets over their heads like glamorous umbrellas. All slip out of their shrouds and run frantically in place, facing to the left, and then make a climactic bow toward the direction of a powerful explosion sound.

Imago is one of Nikolais' most brilliant pieces and would probably be mentioned by many as his most powerful dance work. It is a full evening piece that never flags in its invention and spectacular display of lighting design. It is Wagnerian in the sense of a *Gesamtkunstwerk*, in which music, motion, and lighting are all brought together by one artist to express his idea. Nikolais' remarkable talent operates in this dance at the peak of his capability.

SANCTUM

Choreography by Alwin Nikolais. Music, costumes, and lighting by Alwin Nikolais. First performed at the Henry Street Playhouse, New York, N.Y., February 20, 1964, by Murray Louis, Phyllis Lamhut, and Bill Frank, with Raymond Broussard, Susan Buirge, Ann Carlton, Mimi Garrard, Raymond Johnson, Roger Rowell, Olga Zampos, and Diane Black, Joy Boutilier, Debby Gerson, Janice Gottbetter, Meikle Guy, Donna Kerness, Sheila Mason, Peggy Novey, Wanda Pruska, Kaiya Schoonmaker, Spencer Snyder, and Albert Wunder.

In terms of a dictionary definition a sanctum is a sacred or private place, a study or private room where one is not to be disturbed. In dance terms it is a striking panorama of a man's descent from a secure observatory into a world and then a retreat from it.

The man swings lazily from a trapeze while the members of the company are prone on the floor beneath him. He reaches down to them as they start a group calisthenic exercise, and eventually drops down to join them and disappears in the center. The first collective dance finds them all encased in stretchy cloth ovals which they open and close like giant wombs. The second group dance features large silver poles which are manipulated up and down as the dancers weave in and out of each other. These collective dances are followed by solo variations, two trios, and a duet. One man suggests a primitive tribal dance, and a woman is comically seductive, flashing through sequences of social poses. Two men and a woman shamble through a mildly brutish social dance, while another dance shows a man driven by relentless staccato music, struggling against it and being slightly comic in his efforts. A couple finally manages to dance together, and he prances with glee as she is attracted to him. Their mating dance is a series of frantic leaps and clutches. When joined by another man of more primitive impulses she goes off with him at first but returns, and the entire company reassembles for the dance that concludes the first act. The dancers with poles form a large circle around the others, who freeze in position like a collection of statues.

The opening of the second act reveals a brilliant collection of five square enclosures. Each contains a man, and its moveable roof and stationary floor are connected at each corner with elastic cords. The men are trapped in a humorously flexible cage that is a real trap. They struggle to escape, but after all their pushing and twanging the boxes return to their original shape with the men still securely penned up inside. Women parade back and forth with banners, and when they are finished the men and the enclosures are gone. The group goes into a mob dance in which it becomes obvious that their visitor is literally the odd man out. He doesn't want to be absorbed into the faceless crowd and continually tries to exert his individuality, but they close in on him, and when they release him he looks like a dehumanized puppet. The next series of dances pause to display various striking movement effects such as a "soft-shoe" duet for two men supporting themselves from two suspended trapezes. The final dance of the act is a grotesque duet for two puppetlike figures, a man and a woman, who are observed by the rest of the company. They are manipulated by their attendants, who try to make them embrace passionately, but they topple without the support of the attendants. A little girl sits alone on a stool observing both the puppets and their masters with some skepticism. The attendants give the puppets Punch and Judy style paddles and accidently they knock one of the attendants flat. The observing group laughs and the puppets smash them as well. The little girl cheers them on and she is smashed as well, and the two puppets are last seen pounding away at one another.

The final act reveals two giant folded panels facing one another within which men and women meet. The rest of the company is on the outside staring at the construction, which unfolds to an almost upright position. Lights are cast on the outside and trios of dancers circle it. The visiting man enters the interior and seems revivified by the passage. The whole company seems charged with energy, and then all crowd into the interior of it, and the visitor returns to his perch, but this time he has the exhausted droop of one who has been pushed beyond his strength. At the beginning he was reaching down to the group and now its members are stretching out to touch him.

The piece suggests a whole universe of people roughly divided into two groups, male and female, brutish and intelligent, bystanders and participants, all of whom are ceaselessly passing from one state of agitation to another. It is not a happy universe, though it is presented with great humor at times and some of the movement has a special poignancy. The man on the trapeze begins in curiosity and ends in utter exhaustion like one who has passed through a whole lifetime from birth to death.

TOWER*

Choreography by Alwin Nikolais. Costumes, sound, and lighting by Alwin Nikolais. First performed at the Tyrone Guthrie Theatre, Minneapolis, Minn., December 10, 1965, by Phyllis Lamhut and Murray Louis, with Bill Frank, Raymond Broussard, Susan Buirge, Carolyn Carlson, Ann Carlton, Mimi Garrard, and Raymond Johnson.

The technical finish of all Nikolais' dances marks his works with a special sheen. They are all supremely professional in their polish and attention to detail. In this work he has provided each of his dancers with a single and identical prop, a small section of metal fence which is shaped into a variety of structures and culminates in a large tower constructed right onstage.

The eight men and women in the group enter, and each has a length of rail tucked under one arm. The score develops in bursts and clusters of sound and the dancers respond with frenzied activity when prodded by the electronic music. During the moments of relative quiet the dancers pause from their energetic activity and straddle, lean on, or balance against their individual sections of rail. They talk in an unintelligible babble, reminding one of a thousand back-fence conversations all jumbled together. No matter what the situation, though, relative quiet or the activist sound of the score, each is bound to his or her section of fence. It goes where they go, whether they hold it up in front of their faces like a giant window or place an elbow casually upon its top rung. The person and the prop are wedded.

During one pause for the group a man emerges to chase after one of the women. It is a comedy duet that relieves the relentless group activity. When it concludes, all of the members of the group cluster together, forming an enclosure with the fence, but ironically there does not seem to be room for all those who want to huddle collectively inside, and periodically one or another is propelled outside, since it is just too crowded. After a momentary scramble the person pushes back into the group, and someone else pops out from another part of the mass.

The group then makes a collective effort to rear a magnificent structure, using all of the sections like building elements in an Erector set. The pieces are locked into one another as the men and women scamper happily around, obviously pleased with the progress of the tower. A second and smaller story is placed on the first, and two men climb up to add yet another portion. Several of the dancers run in a circle carrying large banners as the final pieces are being put into place. Flags are passed up to be affixed to the top, and all come down to chatter happily about what they have created and are now

* First performed as Part Three of *Vaudeville of the Elements.*

affixing streamers to. The moment of triumph, however, is threatened as a flash and an explosion send the whole structure tottering as they run to it.

Tower suggests a contemporary tower of Babel, yet another futile effort of man's ambition to be greater than he is or to reach further than he is innately capable of. The suggestion is made that there is an irresistible determinism to all such activity. Each has a building section which logically should be joined to other such sections, but when they are, some unperceived power intervenes to bring it all back to its basic units again. The implication is a melancholy one, but the gorgeously presented action of the dance tends to conceal it.

TENT

Choreography by Alwin Nikolais. Music, costumes, and lighting by Alwin Nikolais. First performed at the University of South Florida, Tampa, Fla., June 1968, by Murray Louis, Phyllis Lamhut, Carolyn Carlson, Michael Ballard, Emery Hermans, Gale Ormiston, Wanda Pruska, Sara Shelton, Robert Soloman, and Batya Zamir.

Unlike most contemporary choreographers, Nikolais has found it congenial to work on evening-long theater pieces, and some of his most successful productions have been three-act dances. He has also created shorter works such as this one, which is dominated by a large circular white tent that is an active participant in the dance.

A long, folded, limp white cloth is carried on by the men and women of the group, each of whom supports a small section of it. They open it and let it settle flat on the stage; it has a large circular opening in the center. Individuals move to the center to do a variation alone or to dance with another person, and then all ceases as long lines are lowered from above. These are clipped onto the cloth, which is drawn up into a tent shape to hover above them. The dancers flutter beneath it like a disturbed hive or a swarm of insects, and the tent descends slowly to still them. One man stands to dance in the circular opening. Others appear, doing simple repetitive gestures; there is the feeling of a collective assemblage which has been disturbed in some way.

The tent is drawn up into little peaks though it lies mostly on the floor. The dancers appear wearing fringes of silver streamers which extend down to the ankles and take positions near one of the peaks, which rears up and settles down periodically as an individual moves toward it. During the dance they make hissing noises, suggesting the situation of a snake charmer and his sinuous partner. Then all disappear beneath the tent, and suddenly facial masks rise upward through small vents in the cloth attached to dancers' extended legs. It is like a grove of swaying stalks with heads again suggesting a reptile movement or a many-headed monster like a Hydra. The tent itself appears to have a collective personality that is greater than any of the individuals that go to make it up.

When the tent lifts and pauses above them, the men and women seem naked and vulnerable, and stripes of colors are projected on them. They are on their own, and their couplings and uncouplings have a desperate and somewhat hopeless quality to them. The tent begins a slow pulsing motion up and down above them, and they prostrate themselves as it settles down to cover them like a blanket of snow over the individual features of a landscape.

The effect of the tent is somewhat chilling. It is not subject to the people who carried it on but has a life of its own which is all consuming. By the end of the piece it has become the master and its bearers have become servants and attendants subsumed under its sheltering embrace. A classic case of the creature turning upon its supposed master.

CHOREOCHRONICLE
OF ALWIN NIKOLAIS

1936

Choreography for Sabine Women
Choreography for World We Live In

1939

Eight Column Line

1940

American Greetings
The Jazzy "20's"

1941

Opening Dance
American Folk Themes
Pavanne
Evocation

1942

War Themes
Metamorphosis
Popular Theme
Barber of Seville (opera)

1947

Ten Maids and No Man (opera)
†*Fable of the Donkey*

1948

Romeo and Juliet
Princess and the Vagabond (opera)
Dramatic Etude

† Indicates a Children's Theatre production.

1949

Extrados
†Lobster Quadrille
†Shepherdess and the
    Chimneysweep

1950

Opening Suite

1951

†Sokar and the Crocodile
Heritage of Cain
Invulnerables
†Starbeam Journey
†Indian Sun

1952

Committee
Vortex
†Merry-Go-Elsewhere

1953

†St. George and the Dragon
Masks, Props and Mobiles
Aqueouscape
Noumenom Mobilus
Forest of Three
Kaleidoscope
Farm Journal
Devil and Daniel Webster (opera)

1954

†Legend of the Winds

1955

Village of Whispers

1956

Kaleidoscope (revised)
Prism

1957

The Bewitched
Runic Canto
Cantos

1958

Mirrors (improvised concert)

1959

Allegory
Finials
Web
Kites
Ritual
A Time to Dance
Seascape
Totem
Paddles
Kaleidoscope (revised for tv)

1961

Stratus & Nimbus
Illusions

1962

Totem (revised)

1963

*Imago

1964

*Sanctum
Totem, the World of Alwin
    Nikolais (mp)

1965

Galaxy
Vaudeville of the Elements
    *Tower—third section

1967

Somniloquy
Fusion (mp)
Premiere
Triptych

1968

Costume and Environment
   Exhibit
*Tent
Limbo

1969

Echo

1970

Structures

1971

Scenario

1972

Foreplay

1973

Grotto

1974

Scrolls
Temple
Cross Fade

1975

Tribe

PAUL TAYLOR

Paul Taylor began his dance career during his college years. He was first an art major at Syracuse University and a member of the swimming team. His broad athletic physique brought him to the attention of the Juilliard Dance Department when he presented himself at a dance audition. Prior to leaving Syracuse he had joined an undergraduate dance class but arrived essentially untrained. He received scholarships for study at the Juilliard School, the Martha Graham School, and the Metropolitan Opera Ballet School. While studying he worked after hours as an assistant to Robert Rauschenberg and Jasper Johns, who were at the time doing window displays.

Taylor first danced with Pearl Lang's company and Merce Cunningham's company in 1953. His own choreography appeared in 1955 in a concert at the Henry Street Playhouse, and since then he has created dances steadily. Rauschenberg created many décors and costumes for him, among which *Three Epitaphs* is outstanding by the aptness of its glittering black costuming by Rauschenberg and Taylor's poignantly witty choreography. During the years between the mid-fifties and early sixties Taylor danced with the Martha Graham company. He found himself portraying the roles of Aegisthus in *Clytemnestra,* Hercules in *Alcestis,* as well as dancing other major roles in her conventional mode, while he was himself creating vanguard dances to telephone time signals in *Epic* and heartbeats in *Panorama.*

He formed his own company in 1961 and created the pivotal piece *Insects and Heroes,* which bore elements of both traditional and experimental approaches to dance design. He has toured abroad extensively at major European festivals and staged his *Aureole* for the Royal Danish Ballet, where it is currently in repertory. George Balanchine, of the New York City Ballet, created a solo for him in his *Episodes* and he has created a solo for Rudolf Nureyev for a television special. Nureyev is an outspoken admirer of Taylor's work and has appeared with the company as guest artist in New York, Mexico City, and London. Taylor's first full-evening work, *Orbs,* was created for the Holland Festival in 1966. Its décor and costumes were created by Alex Katz, who has frequently worked with him achieving brilliantly matched décors and dances. Taylor's choreography is a beautiful blend of athletic energy and humor which frequently occupies the ambiguous middle ground between tragedy and comedy.

EPIC

Choreography by Paul Taylor. Set to recorded telephone time signals. Lighting by Robert Rauschenberg. First performed at the Ninety-second Street YM-YWHA, New York, N.Y., October 20, 1957, by Paul Taylor.

Taylor reduced a critic to complete silence (no mean feat) with the concert in which this piece appeared. The critic was the late Louis Horst, who was a devoted partisan of modern dance but simply could not comprehend what this or other pieces on the program he saw were all about. In his magazine, *Dance Observer,* he printed probably the most famous of all contemporary dance reviews. It consisted of the name, date, and place of the concert followed by a quarter column of blank white space and signed at the bottom with his initials, L.H.

A man stands in a trimly tailored business suit with a white shirt and a fashionable, striped narrow tie. His shoes are highly polished, he is clean-shaven, and his hair is tightly trimmed. He is the paradigm of a conservative businessman. Suddenly a voice is heard announcing time signals such as one might hear from the telephone time service. It is the start of the dance. Throughout as the man performs tight, restrained squiggles of movement extracted from daily gestures, the voice continues to intone the passing of time. He makes a slow, deliberate progress across stage, sketching and indicating gestures removed from their ordinary context in five broad groupings. The time signals and the dance conclude together.

Taylor said that it was the most difficult dance that he had ever done, since he had to rely on his own complicated system of counts without receiving any clues from the accompanying sound. He raised the everyday gesture to the level of art by transporting it to a performing situation. It was the sort of thing that is accomplished when a painter makes a collage out of the scraps and bits of everyday material. It was a dance that preceded public acceptance by several years and predated some of the most radical dances being done as much as ten years later.

THREE EPITAPHS

Choreography by Paul Taylor. Set to American folk music. Costumes by Robert Rauschenberg. First performed at the Festival of Two Worlds, Spoleto, Italy, June 8, 1960, by Paul Taylor, Akiko Kanda, Mabel Robinson, and Kathleen Stanford.

The piece began life as *Four Epitaphs* and was danced twice, once with bright illumination and the second time with low-level lighting. Robert Rauschenberg, who designed the striking costumes, remarked that one didn't "know whether it was the saddest or the funniest thing you ever saw." In recent years it has been trimmed to three sections, but it still has its uncertain piquancy.

Two figures stand; one is large and male; the other is small and female; both droop like marionettes with the strings gone slack. Both are identically costumed in black with head coverings that completely mask the features. Tiny reflectors are affixed to the headpieces. They look like slag in human form dotted with shiny bits of mica. The smaller one tags after the larger form. He is the object of her mute admiration as he leaps upward or shambles off with hands drooping. She follows docilely behind, knees flexed and head tilted to look at him.

The dance develops in a series of crossings that have a curiously two-dimensional quality, as if the performers are moving in grooves incised on the stage. Even a backward sag wearily admitting his lassitude fails to discourage her rabid and fixed attention. The early jazz music is vaguely funereal in its insistent thump. Three other figures gather together to gabble with propeller sweeps of their forearms at one point. At another time four of them form a diagonal line to cross the stage. One detaches from the rest of the group and appears center stage alone as if to finally break out of the humorous rut all are stuck in, but after a moment of preening decides that there is nothing to say or do and with only a pause shambles off in dejection. The piece closes with no resolution of their irresolution, except that the large figure slumps in resignation at the clumsy dogged attention of the tiny one.

The piece has been one of Taylor's most popular since it was introduced. It has both wit and pathos, a potent combination.

JUNCTION

Choreography by Paul Taylor. Music by Johann Sebastian Bach. Scenery and costumes by Alex Katz. First performed at the Hunter College Playhouse, New York, N.Y., November 24, 1961, by Paul Taylor, Maggie Newman, Linda Hodes, Dan Wagoner, Elizabeth Walton, and Elizabeth Keen.

Taylor often prepares elaborate program notes to go along with his dances and almost always scraps them or pares them down to very brief statements such as the one attached to this dance, which informs the audience that the piece transpires as pedestrians cross at the intersection of Tranquil Street and Turmoil Boulevard.

A solo cellist sits at the rear of the stage with a music stand in front of him. Just behind him is a series of stark vertical lines which portion off the wall into a series of identical bars, almost like a cage. The dancers are in brightly colored costumes of varied colors. The pace of the dance almost seems to exist outside of the rhythm of the music; where it is slow the movement is rapid, and slow where the pulse of the music is lively.

The eight men and women move with a feeling of solemnity in their parades and then crumple abruptly into crouched positions. The women take turns standing and dismounting from the back of one crouched man. At one point carpets are rolled out and the dancers seriously walk along them. The carpets are then rolled up and not seen again. A white tablecloth is folded in half first by one couple and then passed to another couple for an additional fold, and the tiny result is placed on the waiting arms of one woman who solemnly bears it off. One man carries out a woman in his arms. She sits as if in a chair with her heels tucked under her, staring straight ahead. He passes her to a second man and leaves in the opposite direction, and the second man in turn passes her to a third, who carries her off. The dancers form two diagonal lines which intersect like a giant "X" as they walk past one another without touching and continue in opposite directions. A woman stretches her arms out over a fallen man lying face down. The music concludes with a lively gigue, and the dancers move slowly and beautifully against its seductive pull.

The dancing moves so consciously and deliberately against the flow of the music that it sets up a special tension all its own, almost like a declaration of independence. At one point between movements the dance continues through the silence. The austerity of the Bach unaccompanied cello was paralleled by the calm, self-contained decorousness of the dance, with its alternating moods of tranquillity and turmoil.

INSECTS AND HEROES

Choreography by Paul Taylor. Music by John Herbert McDowell. Scenery and costumes by Rouben Ter-Arutunian. Lighting by Louise Guthman. First performed at Connecticut College, New London, Conn., August 18, 1961, by Paul Taylor, Linda Hodes, Dan Wagoner, Maggie Newman, Elizabeth Walton, Elizabeth Keen, Sharon Kinney, Renee Kimball, and Daniel Lewis.

The summer of 1961 found three major companies in attendance at the American Dance Festival at Connecticut College: that of Merce Cunningham, the most radical; José Limón's, the bastion of tradition; and Paul Taylor's independently in between. Each of the choreographers gave the first performance of a work (Limón actually did two), and each advanced his own creative cause but none more so than Taylor, who presented one of the pivotal works in his career. The piece was actually presented with different décor and more dancers at its premiere, but the description follows the revised version, which has been performed most frequently in the subsequent years.

Six bare bulbs dangle at the ends of their cords. Three men and two women stand underneath five of them. Individually the dancers reach up and switch on the light directly overhead. Something that looks like a caricature of a cactus with floppy, shiny spikes enters with rapid little steps. The five men and women look at it apprehensively. The first man begins to dance alone, then one of the women moves out to do her solitary variation. One by one the three others follow, and all are quite obviously alone seeking something or someone.

With inquisitive gestures they wander among one another, touching and patting as if to assure themselves of the others' basic friendliness. Then the second man, emboldened, prepares to combat the strange, menacing creature. To reassure himself, he pounds his own body before approaching the creature, but the engagement with it suddenly develops in a confusing manner, and he and the first man are contending with one another instead of the thing and they flap their elbows in and out like angry, stumpy wings. The creature bangs a triangular object, throwing them all into a spasm of uncontrolled twitching, except for the first man, who has left. As the men and women grapple and clutch into contorted groups, the creature scoots around observing the results of its work and then goes off.

When the creature has left the four men and women unwind from their twisted positions and dance happily but are frozen again when the first man returns on the run. He is pursued by the creature, and they are unable to help him. He must face it alone, which he does after coursing through the immobile quartet several times. When defied the creature is thwarted and leaves. It returns once more to try to cow the rest, but the four vanquish it. When it returns for the last time, it draws a checkered tablecloth out of an aperture, indicating its expiration as a terrorizing influence, and occupies the empty place underneath the sixth bulb; joining the group, and shedding its spiky outer garment.

Taylor is fascinated by the junction of two types of behavior and shows an almost romantic infatuation with the interpenetration of independent but related spheres of activity. Here he showed that two modes of behavior can inhabit the same personality, that of great bravery and that of immobilizing fear, and that transformation takes place through courage, while terror inhibits growth.

PIECE PERIOD

Choreography by Paul Taylor. Music by Vivaldi, Telemann, Haydn, Beethoven, Bonporti, and Scarlatti. Scenery and costumes by John Rawlings. First performed at the Hunter College Playhouse, New York, N.Y., November 8, 1962, by Paul Taylor, Bettie De Jong, Elizabeth Walton, Renee Kimball, Sharon Kinney, and Dan Wagoner.

Writing to his audiences in a program for one of his seasons, Taylor warned them that his intention was not to "present literary messages," recalling the movie star Humphrey Bogart's comment that his "message is nothing you could send by Western Union." He simply encouraged viewers to view his pieces as "food for the eye," suggesting that their enjoyment would be found there and not through excessive thinking about them. In an amusing way the title of this dance implies the same thing in the sense of *Piece* (dance) *Period* (end of report), but it also slyly tells the viewer that the episodes are all set in the style of some historical period.

The first episode is a male solo depicting a wandering troubadour with a multicolored costume and a lute. He is an entertainer but a tired one, and hints of his weariness keep peeping through his very accomplished routine, suggesting that he could perform it in his sleep. He is succeeded by four women in black Spanish-looking costumes and a fifth woman in blue contemporary dance costume. The four sweep past and appear scandalized by her lack of a concealing, floor-length dress. They surround her and bend her backward, then suddenly the woman she was bent across slips out and all surge out, leaving the chastened woman in blue.

A second man in knee breeches and a white powdered wig and white gloves stomps in, driving his fists up and down. He is a dynamo of virile activity, battering the very air into submission, and he leaves still pounding and striding. Piquantly a bucket is lowered to the center of the empty stage, and a woman with a large flower in her hair espies it. Doing the natural thing, she breaks into a solo variation that suggests a frolicsome milkmaid. An interlude follows this fourth episode as a woman places four buckets in prearranged places. She has the air of a ballerina but unexpectedly breaks out of her reserve and tears through the space collecting them again fervidly, and delightfully returns to her chaste ballerina pose just before vanishing.

Three women in long, rich-looking dresses with ruffles around the neck enter and demonstrate an extreme delicacy of hand mime, delineating a variety of domestic and maidenly tasks. Their unison precision makes them like a humorous team of housewives trained for the stage. A chandelier constructed of Ping-pong balls is lowered from above but continues down and down until it hits the stage, where it collapses into a pathetic little heap from its former grandeur. Four women walk on, each in a shorter nightgown, to strike attractive poses, giving one the strong suspicion that one of them is drunk. The manly gent in the wig appears and the women jostle one another vying for position to be seen. The troubadour appears again, offering a résumé of his solo, and all of the sequences seen are represented by a parade of the various characters.

The dance is a delightful display of blackout sketches aided and abetted by brightly witty stage properties and costumes. It is a form of dance that Taylor has made from time to time with unfailing success. He has a showman's eye and sense for the right balance of incongruities, and the choreographer's skill to provide each of his performers with a telling roster of gestures.

AUREOLE

Choreography by Paul Taylor. Music by George Frederick Handel. Lighting by Thomas Skelton. First performed at Connecticut College, New London, Conn., August 4, 1962, by Paul Taylor, Elizabeth Walton, Dan Wagoner, Sharon Kinney, and Renee Kimball.

Among the scores of dances he has created there is none more popular with audiences than this simple and joyous dance for two men and three women. All exist in a world that is full of light and playfulness. Their relations with one another are always just a moment away from the friendly lilt of laughter and are expressed with great tenderness.

A man standing in the center of the stage cradles a woman in his arms, while two other women stand at either side of the stage. It is they who move first, prancing toward the center and away again. The man sways from side to side, sets her down, and all bound on toes and leave. The man returns and is followed by the women, and all shoot their arms upward in a happy, broad, flapping motion that recurs again and again as if the dancers were flying in some giddy atmosphere. He kneels momentarily and is flanked by two women, swaying their hips. He turns first to one, making a soft pushing motion with the flat of his hand, and then to the other like a man undecided over an impossible choice of delectations. The three women at another point hop up and down ecstatically, and the man makes a rapid series of turns in a squatting position, and all line up in a diagonal to walk calmly off.

The second movement brings on a second, bare-chested man to do a weighty and solitary adagio variation in which he leans yearningly forward and then stands to extend one leg behind him and reach out to one side. He pauses to stand with his arms and legs extended rigidly in the form of an "X," as if at some crossroads, and then begins his lonely meditation again. The first man and three women enter and remain crouched to one side, awaiting his decision. He helps one woman up and then circles the area and exits, leaving them to leap happily. One woman makes little undulating curves with her hands as her hips sway playfully. The roundelay of three women and one man has varieties of groupings with quick-stepping exits by the women and bounding, mock-heroic jumps by the man as he leaps and then in mid-air tucks his feet up under himself. The feat, repeated many times, is both impressive and funny, but then the whole feel of the movement combines a feeling of physical good humor.

The duet between the second man and one woman follows. They lean from side to side and he supports her attentively. The first man and another woman circle the two at a distance as he carries her toward the audience and then lets her slide softly to touch her feet to the floor. The second couple embraces briefly and exits. The duet ends with the woman cradled in his arms.

The exultation of the first movement returns in the conclusion as all bound and rebound happily with their arms paddling through broad arcs. Each of the men and women crosses the stage and exits, only to reappear a moment later running with the same headlong abandon and finally joining in a lively parade behind the second man as he leaps diagonally across the stage to exit.

The lift and joy of the piece move it to the fore in the canon of Taylor's work and would have to be listed as among the finest achievements of dance theater in the twentieth century. Taylor's own company has presented it to varieties of audiences, and the Royal Danish Ballet includes it in its repertory, as does Rudolf Nureyev with his concert group. One can only marvel at its simplicity and beauty.

SCUDORAMA

Choreography by Paul Taylor. Music by Charles Jackson. Scenery and costumes by Alex Katz. First performed at Connecticut College, New London, Conn., August 10, 1963, by Paul Taylor, Elizabeth Walton, Dan Wagoner, Bettie De Jong, Sharon Kinney, Renee Kimball, Twyla (Tharp) Young, and Ceulah Abrahams.

The word is one coined by Taylor to describe this panorama of scuttling and scudding human forms which are backed by a dark back cloth, with wisps of clouds suggesting a stormy sky. The program note is a verse from Dante's *Inferno:*

> What souls are these who run through this black haze?
> And he to me: "These are the nearly soulless
> whose lives concluded neither blame nor praise."

Eight prone figures are seen as the stage lightens. A man in a checked jacket attempts to rouse his partner, who is just too limp to stand, and he wanders away. Others begin to stare, and one has the impression of an outdoor party the morning after. He removes his coat and crawls off. Four women, three in black with oversized clerical collars, stir themselves into a short, jazzy variation, and one crawls away as if injured. The man returns stripped down to a plum-colored body suit, and pulls a beach towel off the injured woman and flails it in the air as three other women also swing their towels overhead. He puts it down and the woman falls on it and is pulled off.

A second man in a jacket enters with a woman in solid yellow. They throw a towel over the three women in black, the three then heedlessly throw a towel over him, and all lie down. The man rises and steps across their bodies, when a whistle sounds and they are galvanized into a short, twitchy variation as before and then leave. The man in plum strides on with a woman in black clinging to him, and they lie in an "X" sprawl on the stage, to be joined by the second man with a girl across his shoulders, and these two collapse on top of the other pair. A third couple joins the heap, and then the cluster begins to revolve with a spastic energy and then halts. All separate and move hesitantly around as if on the point of hailing someone and then thinking better of it. The atmosphere is dark with suppressed feelings, veiled hostility, and indecision.

A woman in red stands in the center of the stage while three women circle; one wears a sweater, another a jumper, and a third a raincoat. These three appear like aspects of the center girl's life, perhaps schooling, motherhood, and a career. They fall outward, to remain prone while she dances. When she falls they leave.

Merce Cunningham.   PHOTO BY JACK MITCHELL.

James Waring in Tambourine Dance from *In Old Madrid*.

Erick Hawkins in *Eight Clear Places*.   PHOTO BY TED YAPLE.

Paul Taylor and Eileen Cropley in *Aureole*.   PHOTO BY KENN DUNCAN.

Paul Taylor and Company in *Orbs*.   PHOTO BY JACK MITCHELL.

(LEFT TO RIGHT) Roger Rowell, Ray Broussard, Murray Louis, Bill Frank, Albert Reid in Alwin Nikolais' *Imago*.   PHOTO BY ROBERT SOSENKO.

(LEFT TO RIGHT) Ray Broussard, Phyllis Lamhut, Murray Louis in Alwin Nikolais' *Sanctum*.   PHOTO BY SUSAN SCHIFF FALUDI.

A woman in yellow enters as if to join the woman in red, but she just cartwheels past. The man in plum leaps out at her, and others natter about her prissily crossed hands. Again one feels the tug and pull of understated hostility that is the power that drives this social group round and round. They have stripped off their street clothing and now are all in solid colors. The man in plum draws the red woman to him and forces her to dance. While they are together another couple crawls across the back of the stage. The woman in red slips away; the man in plum crawls jerkily away. The stage is ready for its final confrontation as six men and women come on, bent over and covered with the brightly colored beach towels. As they meet in the center they recoil and fall away from one another.

The dance starts with inert forms and progresses through slow to frenzied action, but all is tinged with futility. The characters are exposed in their basic coloration and also in their civilized trappings, but nothing seems to make any difference to their relationships; they are repelled by one another almost to the same degree as they are driven to fraternize with one another. The dance is not a pretty one in the conventional sense, but it does have a grimly realistic sweep and shows another side of Taylor's imagination, that of the darker-toned relationships that are as much a part of a society as the lighter ones.

ORBS

Choreography by Paul Taylor. Music by Ludwig van Beethoven (Quartets Op. 127, No. 2; Op. 130; Grosse Fuge, Op. 133). Scenery and costumes by Alex Katz. First performed at The Hague Opera House, Holland, July 4, 1966, by Bettie De Jong, Dan Wagoner, Carolyn Adams, Daniel Williams, Molly Reinhart, Jane Kosminsky, Janet Aaron, Eileen Cropley, and Paul Taylor.

This was the first full-evening dance that Taylor ever attempted, and he succeeded in working with music of impressive depth and framing a parallel structure of gesture that was not intimidated by its accompaniment. As in other pieces that he created he began this one with music different from that that was finally used. He started the first rehearsals with Vivaldi's *The Seasons* before he switched to the Beethoven string quartets.

The opening tableau shows the sun surrounded by all of the planets and moons, each in its proper positioning in a balanced universe. He clashes the heels of his hands together as a signal for movements to begin and reigns benignly over the whole assemblage. He is a divine figure, paternalistic and kind.

In the "Venusian Spring" he draws apart pairs of planets and shapes, the men and women around one another, in an instruction of the arts of love.

He leaves them to work out their own particular relationships, and one couple is the young frisky earth duo, while another is a more mature and dignified couple. But both are racked from time to time with the torments of the unleashed passion.

"The Martian Summer" is dry and enervating. The couples draw themselves along as if almost too wearied to do anything else. The moons flutter around them like a swarm of angry gnats at one point and at another thread their way around the prone forms of the planets as they lie exhausted. The sun has returned to them at the beginning of the section with a mask of his own features affixed to the back of his head, giving him a Janus-like ability to face in both directions at once. It is he who can initiate actions that cause the seasonality that rules the lives of the planets and their satellite moons.

The beginning of the second section is costumed entirely differently. Where previously the dancers wore timeless designs of varying colors that did not suggest any particular culture or location, now they wear street clothes that might be seen in any middle-class or "average" community which does not tend to extremes of fashion. The men wear dark suits with white shirts and ties, and the women wear simple dresses and modest hats. The scene is the here and now and not the immense void of the universe. The sun has become a preacher, the planets a wedding party, and the moons are adoring attendants. The best man, of course, cannot find the ring and the groom is nervous. The bridesmaid weeps and the bride is ecstatic while the attendants beam. The celebration of the union turns into a drunken brawl, and the preacher pinches one of the bridal attendants. The large silver arc which showed an ascendant half during the first of the work now is seen only as a diminishing quarter.

The "Terrestrial Autumn" is succeeded by the "Plutonian Winter," and the dancers reappear in their first costumes. It is a time of cold; they stand immobilized by the chill and rub their bodies meditatively, indicating both a feeling of icy cold and a declining sense of their own vigor. The seasons have come full sway, and decline necessarily follows growth. In a burst of high energy the piece concludes with a life-affirming group dance that leaves all happily prancing.

The idea of changes that occur naturally and with a purposeful direction had appealed to Taylor strongly, and when designing this dance he tried to show the relations of the changes throughout the whole system. In a program note which he later decided not to use he explained: "It is a fact that the seasons of planets change according to their orbit around the sun. Such changing seasons are also true of our human solar system." The dance expressed it even more effectively.

PRIVATE DOMAIN

Choreography by Paul Taylor. Music by Iannis Xenakis. Scenery and costumes by Alex Katz. Lighting by Jennifer Tipton. First performed at the City Center Theatre, New York, N.Y., May 7, 1969, by Paul Taylor, Carolyn Adams, Daniel Williams, Cliff Keuter, Janet Aaron, Eileen Cropley, Karla Wolfangle, and Senta Driver.

Taylor has been particularly lucky in his choice of artistic collaborators, especially with painter Alex Katz, who has demonstrated again and again a special sympathy for his work. In the case of this dance he provided a radical décor of dark cloth panels which hung across the front of the stage, effectively segmenting the stage into selected viewing apertures. He also designed swimming suits for the dancers, a shiny surfaced greenish-silver for the women and black trunks for the men. The result was to create an aquarium-like effect.

The company engages in random coupling, and one or another poses in an aperture looking hungrily around. One woman starts moving on a diagonal path while the others move laterally to designated places. Another woman is carried on, passed to another man, and placed down. When all have reached their appointed spots, the women begin a soft, sensuous swaying from side to side. They leave while one man moves through a powerful solo suggesting a robust lifesaver, hero-of-the-beach type, furthering the undercurrent of narcissism that flows through the dance.

When the others return he stretches himself and leaves them spread out through the area, each very self-absorbed and paying little attention to anyone else. The women wriggle invitingly. A man walks among the five and selects one of them to carry off. The others continue as before, and he edges back toward the activity. Another man leaps and circles energetically. The focus of the dance ranges back and forth and from side to side as first one couple draws attention to itself and then another. Dance events do not occur in a straight line sequence of one to another but coexist at the same time. The men and women move to the front periodically like fish swimming up to the wall of a tank and then recede. A man dances with a woman, another man dances with two women, still another trio sensuously undulates. One woman has a long solo after which she sinks onto a cluster of other dancers. All of them scatter and circle, returning to distribute themselves in the three apertures where they stand staring outward.

The cooler greenish lighting at the rear of the stage, which becomes slightly warmer in tone as it approaches the audience, combined with the bathing suits gives the dance the distinct feel of transpiring under the surface of the water. The casualness of the dancers and the transitoriness of their engagements have the random profligateness of a species providing for its survival without much thought about the individual needs of its members. In such a deterministic scheme one can scarcely speak of eroticism, but yet the dance has a strong element of sexual electricity.

CHOREOCHRONICLE
OF PAUL TAYLOR

1955

Jack and the Beanstalk
Circus Polka
Little Circus

1956

The Least Flycatcher
Four Epitaphs
Untitled Duet
Tropes
Obertura Republicana (with Remy Charlip, Marian Sarach, David Vaughan, James Waring)

1957

The Tower
Epic
Events I
Resemblance
Panorama
Duet
Events II
Opportunity

1958

Rebus
Images and Reflections (full company version)

1960

Option
Images and Reflections (duet)
Meridian (trio)
Meridian (full company)
Three Epitaphs
Tablet
Rebus (second version)
The White Salamander

1961

The Least Flycatcher (new)
Fibers
Insects and Heroes
Junction

1962

Tracer
Aureole
Piece Period

1963

La Negra
Fibers (tv version)
Poetry in Motion (with Katherine Litz)
Scudorama
Party Mix
The Red Room

1964

Duet

1965

Dances (with music by Corelli)
Post Meridian (The Red Room)
From Sea to Shining Sea

1966

*Orbs

1967

Agathe's Tale
Lento
Public Domain

1969

*Private Domain
Duets from Work in Progress
Churchyard

1970

Foreign Exchange

1971

Big Bertha
The Book of Beasts

1972

Guests of May
So Long, Eden

1973

Noah's Minstrels

1974

Sports and Follies
American Genesis

1975

Esplanade
Runes

JAMES WARING

Despite his reputation at one time of being an *enfant terrible* dedicated to breaking down the conventions of establishment dance, Waring has spent an extensive amount of time working with classical ballet companies as well as small modern dance groups. He began his own dance study in California and continued it in New York after his military service during World War II. His wide-ranging interests include serious work as a collagist even prior to his choreographic emergence, and even today he is liable to describe the appearance of a projected dance piece in graphic painterly terms.

Because of his interest in painting, he has been his own most sympathetic costume and set designer and has produced scores of costumes that rank with the best work to be seen currently on the stage. He is a teacher of some distinction, and in addition to the numbers of his pupils who have entered modern dance companies one has danced with the Bolshoi Ballet and has become a member of the Joffrey Ballet. In the late 1950s he produced a number of programs which featured works of young choreographers, such as Paul Taylor, as well as his own. At the same time he formed his own company and presented dancer-choreographers Lucinda Childs, Aileen Passloff, Deborah Hay, Arlene Rothlein, and Yvonne Rainer among others.

When he decided to abandon the role of company organizer, he continued with his choreographic work for a variety of other companies, including the Manhattan Festival Ballet, the international concert ballet couple Bruce Marks and Toni Lander, the New England Dance Theater, the Netherlands Dance Theater, and the Pennsylvania Ballet. In addition to his sense of classical structure he has a quick wit, and the combination has graced some of his most beautiful pieces such as *Poet's Vaudeville* and *Spookride*.

Waring's nostalgia for the past is often seen in his work, and he has even re-created a turn-of-the-century operetta with fine sense of period style. His titling of dances is often whimsical, such as *Pumpernickle and Circumstance* or the florid *Purple Moment,* and his quick intelligence often detects the incongruous at serious moments. It is one of the characteristics of Waring's pieces that they often slide from high seriousness to high spirits in the twinkling of a single gesture. When he created *Amoretti,* using the balletic vocabulary of movement, he turned a simple rearward hop in arabesque into a backward escape by the male who kept his partner "covered" with fingers pointed as pistols.

Waring has been receptive to a wide variety of influences and lists among them the ballets of George Balanchine, primitive art, and the performing magic of ballerina Alexandra Danilova, whose ability to create period style he admired fervently. He has created works for large companies and individual artists with equal facility. Most recently he has been working as artistic director with the New England Dinosaur, a modern dance company resident in Boston. Prior to his sudden fatal illness in 1975 he was on the staff of the University of Maryland at Baltimore.

POET'S VAUDEVILLE

Choreography by James Waring. Music by John Herbert McDowell. Scenery by Charles Stanley. Words by Diane di Prima. First performed at the Judson Memorial Church, New York, N.Y., August 25, 1963, by Fred Herko, Arlene Rothlein, Lucinda Childs, James Waring, and Deborah Hay.

Waring's passionate interest in all aspects of theater has made him attempt a variety of presentations for his works. In this one he takes a traditional form of popular entertainment and strings the various segments together with knowing artfulness.

The banging of a drum from the rear of the audience announces the arrival of the participants in the dance. It immediately reminds one of the old theatrical custom, used by strolling players, of drawing attention to themselves by beating a large drum in a public square. The musicians, two instrumentalists and a singer, pass down the aisle, as do the three female and two male dancers. It is a festive entrance, and the musicians arrange themselves on stage as two of the dancers erect a large banner that reads "Poet's Vaudeville" in large letters.

After a moment's silence two of the women begin a happy, lighthearted duet that is immediately followed by a bizarre tango. In "The Seasons" section individual variations limn the seasonal mood and drift of one atmospheric climate into another, and at the end of the "winter" segment all of the dancers are momentarily frozen in place. They then launch into a robust cakewalk that completely chases away the chilled aura of the season's conclusion.

The singer moves to the center of the stage and projects a rousing rendition of an old song which Waring dedicates to the music-hall performer Harry Langdon in a program note. At its conclusion the dancers in a muted, serious mood dance and then depart, ending the presentation.

The piece is a brilliant combination of dance, song, and pantomime accompanied by cello and assorted toy instruments. It has a fantastic aspect in its blending of the most childlike simplicity and sophisticated attitudes toward performing. It is as if the company is both seriously presenting an entertainment and at the same time standing aside as if to say they are aware of themselves creating roles. It is magically poetic in its daring and touching in its alternating of tough and tender moods.

DOUBLE CONCERTO

Choreography by James Waring. Music by Johann Sebastian Bach. Scenery and concurrent events by George Brecht. First performed at the Judson Memorial Church, New York, N.Y., May 19, 1964, by Arlene Rothlein, Lucinda Childs, Deborah Hay, James Waring, Fred Herko, and Gary Gross.

Some of Waring's most intriguing pieces were created with the collaboration of artists interested in a form of collage theater known as "happenings." Waring did each of several of his dances by designing an over-all plan for the work in which he would create the dance movement, and his associate would design some dramatic incident. One of the most facinating was this one.

The rear of the stage is divided into two distinct portions. On the left two chairs flank a small table. At some remove five simple chairs stand in a row facing the audience. A couple in street clothes sit at the table and wash their hands in a bowl. Afterward the same water is poured into the drinking pitcher. Quietly and individually the five dancers have walked out to the performing area to stretch and limber up in clear view. This exercise is part of the piece, which in effect begins before the audience is even aware of it. Throughout the couple in street clothes performs tasks, while the dancers listen to the music of Bach and create a lyrical counterpoint to the humdrum, everyday movements of the couple. The chairs that the couple occupy are stark black or white and the dancers chairs are floridly colored.

As the music begins the dancers join one another in a suite of dances, first a quartet of three women and one man, then a solo dance for another man, and the two men join for a duet. This is followed by a duet for two women and concludes with another quartet. The couple in the meanwhile go about furnishing their area as if it were a house, putting up a wall fixture, decorating the table, and the like. Periodically one of them tears a strip from a large cloth and stashes it away. The dancers have seated themselves and individually bob up to do a solo variation. The man in street clothes produces a gun and shoots his mate and she in turn stabs him with a knife. They smile at one another inanely and do a snatch of a social dance. It is after all part of their lives to express such hostile feelings and they take it as calmly as all of their other activites.

During the slow movement the dancers yawn and flutter their fingers in front of their mouths, while the couple puts on winter headgear; he a ski cap and she a kerchief. She claps her hands and he removes his cap and ties to a chair, a black tape that stretches down, and he does the same with two other tapes.

In the final movement a woman cuts these tapes with scissors and the dancers slap the floor with the flats of their hands. The everyday couple tears off another piece of the cloth. The lights in the theater come up as the music finishes. The dancers march down to the front of the stage and sit. They rise one at a time and go to shake hands with the couple and go off as the man is wound with the torn strips of cloth.

The contrasting movement patterns emphasize the isolation of one group emotionally from the other. The couple ignores the music and reacts only to ugly sounds like the ringing of a doorbell, while the dancers create sweeping designs in space. The couple eventually imprisons itself with the artifacts gathered by their mundane activity, while the dancers exit leaving a bare, uncluttered space and the lovely memory of their dancing.

AT THE CAFE FLEURETTE

Choreography by James Waring. Music by Victor Herbert, additional lyrics by Arthur Williams. Costumes by James Waring. Scenery by John Wulp. Lighting by Teresa King. First performed at the Judson Memorial Church, New York, N.Y., February 11, 1968, by Catherine Lloyd, Ann Danoff, Teri Loren, Richard Colton, Gretchen MacLane, Edward Barton, Deborah Lee, Christopher Lyall, and Arlene Rothlein; and by singers Nancy Zala and David Vaughan; pianist, Al Carmines; and waiter, Bryan Hayes.

The subtitle for the dance reads: "A Garland of Songs and Dances for Vernon and Irene Castle." Waring is fond of dedicating his dances and in this tribute honored one of the greatest of the ballroom dance couples. The music is all selected from operettas written by Victor Herbert, and the ambiance is one of friendly nostalgia.

The setting is a small cafe, and a man and woman begin with three songs: "Jeanette and Her Little Wooden Shoes," "Romany Life," and "Falling in Love with Someone," which comprise the overture and set the scene for the first dance. It is "Estrellita," a trio for three beautiful women in lush feather headdresses who move about in a decorous and lonely fashion. During their dancing the waiter opens a bottle of champagne for the singers and serves them as they observe from their table.

A bundle of energetic leaps and bounds is the person of Punchinello, who immediately follows the three maidens. A couple performs a *morceau caractéristique* in "Panamericana," during which they portray an enchanted couple with a South American sway. There is a studied undercurrent of animosity between them, which adds to the piquancy of their performance and leads one to think that they are not all that they represent themselves to be. True love is not their motivating drive.

The second couple is all sugar and spice, and he delicately catches a kiss from the air and carefully tucks it away in his pocket. He wears tails and she a hobble skirt as they waltz to the duet from *Sweethearts*. The final specialty is an "Oriental Dance," in which a sexy woman with finger cymbals and shaking hips entrances the patrons of the cafe. She is joined by all of the dancers, who strut out to the "March of the Toys."

The vintage atmosphere of a popular entertainment bill is both cherished and kept at wry arm's length by Waring, who masterfully captures the era and teases it a bit. He obviously cherishes the past but embraces it with a knowing wink. It probably never was entirely the way that it is presented, but then one always is fond of dreams even while realizing that they are dreams.

SPOOKRIDE
(VERSION II)

Choreography by James Waring. Music by Frédéric Chopin and Ezra Sims. Costumes by James Waring. Scenery including filmed segments by Joseph Keller. Lighting by Malcolm Waters. This work was performed at the Walnut Street Theater, Philadelphia, Pa., in 1970 by Carolyn Anderson, Wendy Barker, Kathleen Callaghan, Svea Eklof, Laura Gurdus, Linda Keeler, David Kloss, Carmela Martinelli, Gary Masters, Rudy Menchaca, Gary Moore, and Marjorie Philpot (members of the Pennsylvania Ballet). The first version of Spookride *was given at the Massachusetts Institute of Technology, January 1969.*

After its first appearance Waring decided to revise the work for a larger ensemble of a dozen dancers. In it he combines everyday movement and balletic steps and also the work of the nineteenth-century composer Chopin and the contemporary Ezra Sims.

A recording of an orchestral selection is heard, followed by a burst of applause after which a pianist enters to bow repeatedly. There are four chairs and two white screens standing at the rear of the stage as the dozen dancers enter. They dance in a rapid series of combinations and then the "heroine" reclines at the center of the stage, and one man, the "hero," steps over her and arches his arms and body in a striking attitude. Another woman goes to her and draws out a lifelike replica of the ballet character Dr. Coppélius, then a film of a girl dancing is projected along with portraits of film stars, including Marlene Dietrich. The dancers do individual pirouettes and exit. One woman walks with a box.

Four women enter at each side and stand in parallel files; the first man poses in the space between the two lines. Three men stand off to the side, and the first woman on the right begins a short dance, after which she climbs on the back of one of the men, then goes and tilts the head of one of the other women. All walk momentarily and then exit.

A man leads on three women in line like three noble goddesses. His attitude is stiff and militaristic at first and then becomes sinuous. He strikes a pose and holds it. The women come to him and he launches into a ritual of arm crossing and knee flexing. They all go to the rear of the stage and march down toward the audience like a small disciplined band. The women shuffle forward and he bounds around as their leader. All freeze in position. The women point and then separate. He manipulates a screen down toward the audience, and one woman circles him as he does. She grasps the side of the screen momentarily, lets go, and all go off.

When the group reappears it is with a picnic basket and a tablecloth, and they all congratulate one another effusively, shaking hands. The men form an "X" formation in the center and the women stand in pairs to the sides. One woman throws herself into the male group and the others mime shocked horror as she dances a rote of stock balletic phrases humorously and is gallantly manhandled by one of the men.

In the succeeding section the group is once again armed with props, balloons and an arrow, and one man wears a cowboy hat with a length of rope, and another has boxing gloves and a robe. The balloons pop one by one, the boxer feigns fighting, and the whole looks like a scene from a silent-film comedy. They retire. Two formations of dancers enter, and in one the women circle their arms about each other's waist. One man leaps and turns softly between the lines, then turns each of the women, one after another, in one formation. All leave except one woman who dances with him a duet that features arabesques for her and small leg beats for him. At its conclusion she rejoins her formation.

The spell of the classical dancing is broken and replaced by the women engaging in social ballroom dance, while the man mimes giving another a haircut. A film of sheep being shorn appears on the screen. Others run in place and a woman peels a banana. When the tasks are concluded they leave.

In the final portion the dancers dash helter-skelter across the stage, breaking classical poses with little waggles of the hips and hand flutterings. The line of dancers extends across the stage, the music and tape sound blend, two women sit in a chair, and two men shake a third.

The humor of Waring's piece arises from his sense of incongruity, and in this work he alternates mime passages that border on the absurd with pure dance passages that find themselves slipping from an elevated mood to one of less serious import. It requires performers both with the technical skill to dance the classical repertory and the insouciance to leave that special training behind when ordinary representational mime is required.

CHOREOCHRONICLE
OF JAMES WARING

1946

Luther Burbank in Santa Rosa

1948

Dances for Noh Play (by Paul Goodman)

1949

Duet (suggested by Poe's *The Fall of the House of Usher*)

1951

The Wanderers

1952

The Prisoners

1953

Pastorale
Lamento
Burlesca

1954

Frieks
Three Pieces for Solo Clarinet

1955

Intrada
Largo
Little Kootch Piece
Jeux d'enfants

1956

Duettino
Adagietto
Pieces and Interludes
Fantasy and Fugue in C Major
Suite
Obertura Republicana (with
    Remy Charlip, Marian Sarach,
    Paul Taylor, David Vaughan)
Phrases

1957

Humoresque
Poeta Nascitur
Ornaments
Dances Before the Wall

1958

Octandre

1959

In the Mist
Pyrrhic
Corner Piece
Extravaganza

1960

Peripateia
Tableaux
Gossoon (revised)
Landscape
Lunamble
A Swarm of Butterflies
    Encountered on the Ocean

1961

Dromenon: Concert for Music,
    Dancers and Lights (dedicated
    to Ruby Keeler)
Little Kootch Piece Number Two

1962

Two More Moon Dance, with
    Radio Music as an Overture
Dithyramb
Exercise

1963

Bacchanale
At the Hallelujah Gardens
Divertimento
*Poet's Vaudeville

1964

*Double Concerto
Stanzas in Meditation (in four
    parts, titles by Gertrude Stein)
Rondo in A Minor and Fugue in
    C Major
Panacea

1965

Three Symphonies
Tambourine Dance
Musical Moments
In Old Madrid
Andante Amoroso and Adagietto
Minuet, Gigue, and Finale
*Three Dances from Triumph of
    Night: Scenes for a Masque*
*La Serenata in Maschera: To
    Pietro Longhi*

1966

*March: To Johann Joachim
    Kandler*
The Phantom of the Opera
Mazurkas for Pavlova
Northern Lights
*Good Times at the Cloud
    Academy* (with Deborah Lee
    and Irene Meltzer)

1967

Arena
Salute
Musical Banquet
Well . . . . . Actually (with
    Remy Charlip and John
    Herbert McDowell

1968

Spell
Winter Circus
Amethyst Path
*A Waltz for Moonlight
    Comedians*
**At the Cafe Fleurette*
An Oriental Ballet
Seven Poems by Wallace Stevens
Polkas and Interludes

1969

Revision of Mazurkas for Pavlova
*Dance Scene, Interlude, and
    Finale*
Spookride
Beyond the Ghost Spectrum
Purple Moment (dedicated to
    Joan Blondell)
Pumpernickle and Circumstance
Amoretti

1970

**Spookride Version II*
Purple Moment (new version)

1971

Variations on a Landscape

1972

An Eccentric Beauty Revisited
*Twelve Objects from Tender
    Buttons*

1973

32 Variations in C Minor
Feathers

1974

Moonlight Sonata
Scintilla

1975

A New Life

Freedom and
New Formalism
(Second Generation)

TOBY ARMOUR

As a child, Armour was not destined to be the dancer in the family by her parents; instead her sister was sent to take lessons. While growing up in New York, however, Armour went to a performance by Martha Graham, and it made her want very much to be a dancer. She enrolled at the Graham studio for serious study and for the next several years took class there and also at the Merce Cunningham studio as well as with James Waring. She was quickly introduced to performing and danced with a number of companies in the late 1950s and early sixties, including those of Midi Garth, Paul Taylor, James Waring, and Aileen Passloff. She left New York and lived in Paris for several years, during which time she studied ballet with Egorova and gave several recitals including solos done for her by Taylor and Waring. She had begun to choreograph her own pieces and had presented many of them at Judson Memorial Church in New York when she returned to the United States, although she was living in Boston. There she formed her own resident company, the New England Dinosaur, which tours and performs regularly in the region.

HEADS

Choreography by Toby Armour. First performed at the Cubiculo, New York, N.Y., July 23, 1973, by Toby Armour.

Though she has used all sorts of stage properties in her dances, such as life-sized puppets and gorgeously lush costumes, Armour decided in this solo to strip the dance down to its barest essentials. She costumed herself in black, used no props, and did not move from the place that she seated herself at the beginning of the work. It emphasized the mime aspect of dance movement.

The entire stage area is darkened; a bright spotlight illuminates the face and shoulders of a woman. Her arms cross her chest, and her hands are draped over her shoulders. She is absolutely still. Then she begins to animate her features and her hands. They express first one side of a conversation as she listens and then the other side as she responds. She uses a wide range of expression and shows at times frivolity, negative interest, anticipation and boredom. It is a frantic exchange at one moment and then a slow banter at another, and during it there is no sound and no motion other than the flow of facial gesture. To conclude, she stretches as if waking from a sleep.

The idea of creating a dance that does not involve broad rapid movement is a dangerous concept. One constantly runs the risk of alienating an audience or simply losing its interest through sheer boredom. It was a risk taken and survived by Armour, who has presented the piece often to raptly attentive audiences.

CHOREOCHRONICLE
OF TOBY ARMOUR

1962

Solo
Godmother

1963

Last News of a Morning Cruise

1964

Group work

1965

Solo
Duet
Tango Family

1966

Fragments of Minor Murder

1967

Largo
Runway
Reveries of a Solitary Walker
Relámpago

1968

Props
Quartet
Anti-Matter
Visions at the Death of Alexander

1969

Pastorale

1970

Brick Layers
Abalone Co.
Interlope

1971

Ethnic Dance
*Holiday Time at Stanley
    Brown's*
Ruby Turnpike
*Solo (A Time for Silence and
    Watching)*

1972

Dinosaur Love
Social Dancing

1973

*Heads
Elliptic Spring
Where the Wild Things Are

1974

Black Breakfast
Heads cont.

1975

Adagio

ART BAUMAN

Exceptional patience and painstaking labor are the tools that Bauman uses to create his dances. He has even gone so far as to tape-record his own monologues and then analyze them for thought and speech patterns. He is able to work on dances and break them down into individual discrete units and then reassemble them for the final performance with the utter confidence that everything will fit since he has planned it all out on paper ahead of time.

He studied ballet in his native Washington, D.C., and later studied modern dance and composition at the Juilliard School. He has held a variety of jobs both administrative and managerial in the dance field in addition to his own performing and choreographing. In recent years he has tended to cut down on his own performing in favor of creative work. He has been associated with Dance Theater Workshop as a member of its board and one of its choreographers since the middle 1960s. In its loft he has created some of his most successful works, including his solo *Dialog,* and a quartet, *Burlesque/Black & White.*

BURLESQUE/BLACK & WHITE

Choreography by Art Bauman. Set to a tape collage. First performed at the Dance Theater Workshop, New York, N.Y., February 12, 1967, by Tina Croll, Marcia Lerner, Nancy Topf, and Art Bauman.

This piece, like others that he did at the same time, was designed to take maximum advantage of the performing space available to him. It was a long, narrow loft area which Bauman decided was particularly suitable for collage pieces, which could be assembed like so many successive "photographic" segments.

A large plastic sheet is seen in the center of the space. There is some struggling activity, but the identity of the covered cluster of people is hidden until, one by one, three women struggle out to look at one another. They are newly hatched from their somewhat strange cocoon and wear only simple black slips. A blackout ends the section.

When next seen the women are still in their slips but walking around with a preening strut and vying with one another for position at a mirror to strike fashion model poses. As they promenade they are accompanied by the sounds of traffic noises which are interrupted by the crashing sound of a shattered mirror. In the next segment the narcissistic competition is escalated as they each begin to dress themselves, drawing clothes from a large plastic bag. They mime elaborate application of make-up.

In the following tableau a man sits in a chair reading a newspaper as a woman sinuously undulates to popular rock-and-roll music. He glances at her from time to time but does not move to join her. She breaks off her dance but returns to its insistent beat and then collapses.

A party scene follows in which the man sits with his back to the audience while holding a drink and smoking with sophisticated ease. One of the women approaches him and swivels his chair to the front. He wears a blank mask. Compulsively she alters the position of his chair, turning him like a compass needle trying to gain some reaction from him but does not.

The final "snapshot" reunites the three women in slips posing as if on a television screen as advertising messages are heard. They offer their beautiful sexy selves as endorsements for varieties of products, and the screen suddenly goes dark. When the lights go up a moment later, the women line up to pose for the camera with broad smiles firmly in place and the piece ends with a flash.

The work has a satiny surface glamour that cloaks the loneliness of the three women who work their way through this "burlesque" that is the story of their lives. They cannot interest the men they come in contact with and end up living just for the image that they can project. Ultimately they become a photograph, strikingly posed but still a flat, lifeless photograph.

DIALOG

Choreography by Art Bauman. Music by Michael Czajkowski. Film by Kirk Small-man. Still photography by Edward Effron. First performed at the Dance Theater Workshop, New York, N.Y., in 1967, by Art Bauman.

This was the last of the "photographic" pieces that Bauman made, and in some ways it is the most striking. It is a solo, and prior to assembling the elements of the dance Bauman prepared decks of cards noting intriguing bits of movement down on each. From these he developed the final work.

A man, wearing the anonymous businessman's suit of correct but undistinguished cut, stands holding a telephone. A voice addresses him, asking him to resubmit some report figures. The demanding voice begins to lose its aural focus and becomes a simple, insistent sound without any precise verbal formation. Behind the man a film shows long and deserted corridors in a large office building as well as moving but equally empty escalators. The man begins to jog in place, holding tightly to his attaché case.

Now we see him in the film wearing the same clothes that he has on. He is obviously caught on an endless and exhausting treadmill. The voice reasserts itself to demand work from the man. Abruptly the large word "Stop" is flashed on the screen, but the man cannot stop; he continues his restless activity, running in circles and pausing to measure unseen things. The voice now demands that he send the report that has been requested, and we see a life-sized photograph of the man frozen in his earnest haste. It topples forward and concludes the unequal *Dialogue* between him and the unseen but insistent voice.

The image of a man caught up in the coils of a demanding and unrewarding system of work has rarely been presented with such imagination and technical finesse. For along with Bauman's imaginative conceptions comes a technical sense that relentlessly polishes each element of a dance until it becomes one neat and smooth unit.

CHOREOCHRONICLE
OF ART BAUMAN

1962

Journal

1963

The Time of Singing
Desert Prayer
Barrier
Break Forth into Joy
Nocturne

1966

Errands
Headquarters
Periodic

1967

*Burlesque/Black & White
*Dialog

1968

Relay
Chances

1969

Sketches for Nocturne

1970

Approximately 20 Minutes
Processional Hymn, Sermon,
    Sanctis & Recessional

1971

Dancing in Sheep Meadow
DTW Improvisation Group
Materializations

1972

Dancing in the Cathedral
A Dance Concert for Radio
You are Here
A Movement Project

1973

Dances for Women
A Piece About Pieces
Mute Piece (with Anthony
    LaGiglia)

TRISHA BROWN

A native of the West Coast, Brown went to college at Mills and after gradu-ation taught dance there. She has taught at a variety of other places, includ-ing Reed College and New York University. She studied composition with Ann Halprin in San Francisco and with Robert Dunn in New York.

She was one of the founders of the Judson Dance Theater and has presented her work there as well as at other Off-Broadway theaters. Her work has a strongly physical side to it, forsaking neatness when necessary to project the force and weight of gesture. All during the sixties she worked with a loose association of other dancers and choreographers to realize her work, and it was not until the seventies that she decided to establish her own company. Since that time she has toured extensively. She has shown a predi-lection for unusual spaces to display her dances and has developed quite freely and happily outside of the traditional theater in museums, art galler-ies, and across roof tops. Her choreography tends to be unisex in its basic as-sumptions, treating men and women equally as functioning dancers without any hint of emotional encounter.

PLANES

Choreography by Trisha Brown. Music by Simone Forti. Film by Jud Yalkut. First performed at the NYU School of Continuing Education, New York, N.Y., October 22, 1971, by Carmen Beuchat, Trisha Brown, and Penelope.

One of Brown's creative concerns throughout her career has been the in-terplay of dancers and gravity. To push her explorations to the extreme, she has used elaborate machinery at times to suspend dancers off the floor and enable them to walk around walls. In this dance she had a white wall con-structed with large circular holes cut in it. A faintly bluish light was pro-jected on the wall, shaped like a single frame from a moving picture.

Clinging to the wall are three climbers. They use the holes as handgrips to assist them in moving over the surface of the wall. They are roughly in the center of the wall, and two begin to move upward while the other descends. They "walk" across the face of it and then hang upside down. Two of them wear costumes that are all black on the back and white on the front, and the third is just the opposite.

As they move slowly, one's sense of space perception changes so that they appear at times to be "walking" across a ceiling and at other times to be climbing a sheer wall, and at other times one has the feeling of being above

them and looking down. Their motions are all done with great deliberateness, having a slow-motion look that one associates with deep-sea divers
or the weightless maneuverings of space travelers. The accompaniment to
the piece is a rushing sound that is heard from time to time, and at another
point a voice intones a single note. The piece can hardly be said to begin or
end, it is more like the restless molecular activity that goes on continually
whether one is watching or not.

The piece is decidedly tranquil in its presentation and lends itself to spec-
ulative reverie. The dancers appear to be superhuman at times and less than
human at others. They are governed by rules that exist outside of our own
but show us motion that is quietly purposeful even if its intent remains
somewhat shadowy.

ROOF PIECE

*Choreography by Trisha Brown. First performed in SoHo (South of Houston
Street), New York, N.Y., June 24, 1971, by Trisha Brown, Eve Poling, Liz Thomp-
son, Carol Goodden, Sylvia Whitman, Nanette Seivert, Valda Setterfield, David
Gordon, Douglas Dunn, Emmett Munay, Sara Rudner, Nancy Green, Elsie
Miranda, Suzie Harris, and Carmen Beuchat.*

As attuned as she is to the simple repetition of movement, it was only natural that Brown would create a piece that involved repeating precisely the
gestures of another dancer. What made the dance extraordinarily effective
was the decision to place it on the roof tops of selected buildings in lower
Manhattan and have the dancers pass the motion from one to another
across a half mile by means of human links.

The fifteen men and women of the work are each stationed atop a long
chain of buildings with irregular intervals between them. Some of the
spaces are relatively short because the sight lines are restricted, and others
are longer because one has an uninterrupted view. The dance begins with
one woman sending her movement semaphore of bends, twists and arm rotations from the top of 420 West Broadway.

She can be seen by only a few of the dancers, all of whom wear brightly
colored clothing for best visibility. When the first woman has completed her
variation, she stops, and the second person in the chain picks it up and
passes it along to the third, who repeats it for the next person in line, so that
for the bulk of the dance most of the performers are waiting for the gestures
that they will transmit.

The sequence is carefully kept intact as it is passed southward along the
line until it disappears out of sight. Then with all of the dancers facing
south the movement sequence begins to return as it is passed from one unseen person at the end of the line back to its source at 420 West Broadway.

The sight of the movement coming back from the distant and unseen end of the chain was eerie, almost as if one were receiving a radio transmission from outer space. The feeling was heightened because of the peculiar remoteness of the world of the roof tops. Below in the street people were attending to their daily business while above and unnoticed a dance was going on.

ACCUMULATION, PRIMARY ACCUMU-LATION, GROUP ACCUMULATION

Choreography by Trisha Brown. First performed together at the Sonnabend Gallery, New York, N.Y., March 27, 1973, by Trisha Brown, Carmen Beuchat, Carol Goodden, Penelope, Gail Swerling, and Sylvia Whitman.

These three pieces are all related in the basic premise of adding motions to one another to create an entire sequence of movement, and so it seemed logical to present them together as Brown has in her concert work. Because she is not particularly concerned with creating dances which have to be seen on a conventional stage, Brown often gives her concerts in gymnasiums, museums, art galleries, and public spaces, once even floating on rafts in a pond. In the spring of 1973 she offered a full day of performance at the Sonnabend Gallery in lower Manhattan, and these pieces were given at her last concert of the day.

In the first solo a woman stands with her elbows tucked into her sides and her forearms aimed to the front. The thumbs of both hands are extended upward and then are turned downward to point at one another as she rotates her forearms a quarter turn inward. She then twists them outward so that the thumbs point off in opposite directions. Her arms move forward and then back, she drops her arms to face the palms outward to the front and then slowly begins to involve the rest of her body in the motion with a leg extended to one side. The hand and arm motions continue as she adds new motions. She steps forward and back and then adds a little roll of the shoulders and soon has built up an entire combination from the simple impetus of the first small twisting movement.

The "Primary Accumulation" begins with a woman lying on her back with the length of her body facing the audience. She lifts one arm straight up from the shoulder and the other just from the elbow. With a small twist she draws the knee of one leg up and with another extends her other leg straight up. Then she lets the limbs return to the rest position. She clenches her fist slightly and runs her hands across her body just like the adjusting motions of a sleeping person. She bends her head up and looks at her feet and half twists her body to present her back to the audience and then lies back. She spreads her legs in a wide "V" and snaps them together again.

Still lying down, she rotates so that she is seen at a variety of angles including a feet-first vertical position, and then she returns to the horizontal to conclude.

For the "Group Accumulation" five women stand, all costumed in the same simple coveralls. Each has a separate variation which lasts half a minute and is timed with a monotonous ticking of a metronome. There are thirty separate motions to be executed, allowing only a second for each. One starts with a slight rocking, another bends an arm across her face and tilts forward, the third puts her hand across her chest and the fourth begins by thrusting a hip to the side. Rapidly each adds the rest of the motions. The "leader" has a variation that begins with the words "Start over!" And she repeats them each time she gets to the end of her variation and begins from the top again. The whole group has a syncopated look to it, although the dancers do not consciously try to play their motions off one another's responses.

One sequence has a stamping, assertive character, another suggests weeping, a third, simple determination, and another a kind of lyric dancy quality. The sequence does not change, but by facing in different directions as they do them the dancers change the look of the piece. After several repetitions the piece ends with a little flourish.

The simplicity of the gestures employed draws one deeply into thinking about the development of movement. One is made aware of the adjustment of the human body to compensate for any motion and how these can be linked up to create a dance variation. The movements are not given any particular dramatic emphasis but are just allowed to emerge and display themselves without any special heightening or addition of emotional stress. They are quite ordinary, but their repetition and development reflect a conception of dance that is not at all ordinary.

CHOREOCHRONICLE
OF TRISHA BROWN

1961

Untitled

1962

Trillium

1963

Lightfall
Untitled Duet
Part of a Target

1964

Target
Rulegame Five

1965

Motor
Homemade

1966

Inside

1967

Skunk Cabbage, Saltgrass and
Waders
Medicine Dance

1968

Snapshot
Ballet
Falling Duet
Dance with the Duck Head
Sky Map
Yellow Valley

1970

Man Walking Down Side of
Building
Clothes Pipe, the Floor of the
Forest and Other Miracles,
Dance for a Dirty Room,
Everybodys Grandmother's Bed,
The Costume, Adam Says
Checkered Sea
Leaning Duets
The Stream

1971

Walking on the Wall
Leaning Duets II
Falling Duet II
*Accumulation
Rummage Sale and the Floor of
the Forest
*Planes
*Roof Piece

1972

*Primary Accumulation

1973

Accumulating Pieces
*Group Accumulation
Roof and Fire Piece
Spanish Dance
Structured Pieces
Figure 8

1974

Drift
Spiral

1975

Pamplona Stones
Locus

PAT CATTERSON

One of the most advantageous things about having dancing parents is that one absorbs the ambiance of performing without any conscious effort. Catterson's parents were a ballroom dancing team and opened a studio in Indianapolis, where she took her first lessons in acrobatic and tap dance and formed a miniature team with her brother. She continued class all the time that she was going through high school and then decided that she wanted to be a clinical psychologist. She enrolled at Northwestern University, which also had a strong theater department, and continued to take class at Gus Giordano's studio in Chicago. She graduated with her degree in psychology but had received a scholarship to study at Connecticut College's Summer School of the Dance as well. She took composition class with Bessie Schönberg and started to design her own pieces, and in 1968 she showed her work at Clark Center for the Performing Arts in New York. A serious knee injury kept her inactive for over a year, and she created a full-evening program in 1970 at Judson Church, which launched her independent career. She has appeared with James Cunningham and Yvonne Rainer and gives lessons in tap at her own studio and Dance Theater Workshop.

BLEECKER TO WEST 80TH AND EPILOGUE

Choreography by Pat Catterson. Music by Fernando (Subway Composition) *and Syntonic Research, Inc.* (Environments). *First performed at the Judson Dance Theater, New York, N.Y., December 9, 1970, by Pat Catterson, Larry Comer, Billy Siegenfeld, Ruth Barnes, Lee Harper, and Clarice Marshall.*

A bad knee injury forced Catterson to restrict her performing for a year prior to the concert in which she presented this piece. During that time she worked with dance therapist Frances Cott, masseur Ben Benjamin, and physician Jack Davis, all of whom received program credit with thanks for their help. While she was strengthening herself she had a great deal of time to think about her work, and the concert made for an impressive debut.

A woman does a solo to the sounds of a subway journey and is joined by a man and another woman. One woman twitches her shoulders and the other strides around. The three are spread around the outside of the area. Suddenly they all bend forward and rush to the center and are joined by another man and woman who join them in a crouch. They form a tight, compact mass. The dance movement goes and stops, as does the accompanying sound track. There are the stations where people board and exit, and there is the actual traveling which takes place between the stations. During the traveling sections the dancers move in groups, and at the stations individuals perform solos. There are repeated falls and the dancers rise to fall again. The movement has a crabbed and tight look, suggesting an urban lack of space. The group tumbles and shoves; these are the subway games that people play. Each person tries to retain some individuality in the midst of the restless, surging mass. To conclude, they all step over a fallen member of the group and dash to the outer edges of the performing space. They run back to the center, tumbling the last few feet like an implosive concentration of particles.

In the epilogue all have left, and a solo woman turns and tumbles in patterns that suggests the spiral swirl of a snail's shell. It is a beautiful sequence and is accompanied by the sweet sound of waves crashing and birds twittering.

Catterson's rough and tumble energy was sensitively modulated in the final solo, which was offered as a contrast to the violent thrashing of the previous section. It was a pastorale as opposed to an urban stress situation. Movement and music underlined the differences strongly.

CHOREOCHRONICLE
OF PAT CATTERSON

1968

$(5+1)=(1+5)$
Tubes

1969

Ground Row

1970

This Door Swings Both Ways
*Bleecker to West 80th and
*   Epilogue*
Warm-Up for Judson Church

1971

Roof Piece

Yvonne Rainer's Trio A
*   Backwards*
Like as Not (with Douglas Dunn)
I Will I Williwilliwilliwill
Post Roof Piece

1972

Shoes and Hair in White II
Does Anybody Else Remember
*   the Banana Man?*
The Relay
Purple (with film by Abe
   Likwornik)
Biographies

1973	1975
Previews and Flashbacks (with film overview by Abe Likwornik)	*Yes No Noisy Show* *Serial I* *Serial II*
Someone Old New Borrowed Blue	

REMY CHARLIP

There is scarcely any job either onstage or off connected with dancing that Charlip at one time has not done. As a dancer, he appeared with Merce Cunningham for eleven years (designing costumes during eight of them) until he decided to establish his own choreographic career. In addition to creating works for himself, such as *Meditation,* he designed two beautiful solas in *April and December* in a balletic style for Aileen Passloff as well as imaginative group works such as *Clearing.*

He has shown a great interest in children's theater and was one of the founders of the Paper Bag Players. He has written a small shelf of children's books and was honored by an exhibition of plates and drawings from a book on Harlequin at the Library and Museum of the Performing Arts, Lincoln Center. He was awarded an Obie for his direction of the Off-Broadway production of *A Beautiful Day.* He choreographed the Living Theater's first production of *Dr. Faustus Lights the Lights* and several others. He designs costumes, décors and occasionally writes a brilliantly perceptive piece of dance criticism when he has the time.

MEDITATION

Choreography by Remy Charlip. Costumes by Remy Charlip. Music by Jules Massenet. First performed at the Penland School of Crafts in 1966 by Remy Charlip.

In addition to his work as a dancer, Charlip has also collaborated extensively with various drama groups as a director. While highly trained in razor-sharp movement, as is anyone who performs, for over a decade, with Merce Cunningham, Charlip also has developed a dramatic side to his own work that can be seen in this little vignette of a solitary man.

The man is soberly and sensibly dressed. There is nothing excessive about his clothing. He wears conventional trousers, a shirt, and a tie. He is, however, driven by inner feelings that challenge his conventional status. His lips tremble slightly and he looks around him agitatedly to see whether he is observed. He reaches out and withdraws quickly. His life seems to be a constant fight between desire and imposed restraint. He struggles to express his feelings but is terrified of his own immoderate passions. We leave him still tormented by his internal upheaval.

One is reminded of T. S. Eliot's *The Love Song of J. Alfred Prufrock,* in which the repressed hero wonders whether it would be acceptable for him to do something as daring as to roll his trousers up or to eat a peach. Anything out of the ordinary is a threat to his whole carefully constructed life.

CLEARING

Choreography by Remy Charlip. A selection of Eskimo and Pygmy music. Costumes by Remy Charlip. First performed by the Dance Circle of Boston at the Massachusetts Institute of Technology, 1967, by Toby Armour, Cynthia Full, Claire Mallardi, Elizabeth Martin, Anne Tolbert, and Marlene Wallin.

Charlip's dances all have the feeling of a snapshot perception that has to be worked out in economical movement. He rarely allows himself the luxury of a really long dance and depends instead on concentrating the most into a restricted time.

The friendly country sound of birds twittering fills the air as the six women of the dance walk on. They are wearing long orange shifts and seem like votaries of one deity or another. They circle the area slowly and then link arms to form a long "buggy whip" chain.

They loosen the "links" of the chain and cluster in the center in a tight circle as African chanting is heard. Slipping from the circle one at a time, the women pass to the center of the ritual circle and begin to rock ecstatically back and forth. After each has performed the rite, they form a line and shuffle forward slowly.

The comfort of the circle formation draws them again, then five separate themselves to line up in a file as the sixth woman dances around with a stone in each hand. A child's tiny voice is heard and all scatter on curving tracks and are gone.

One has the feeling of being present at the birth and then dissolution of a society. There is no panic to be felt, however, merely the fulfillment of an inevitable occurrence. One has the sense of a primitive resignation.

CHOREOCHRONICLE
OF REMY CHARLIP

1949

Drama in Ex Libre

1951

Dr. Faustus Lights the Lights
Falling Dance
Dialogue Between the Manikin
    and the Young Man

1952

Crosswords for Cunningham
    Company

1953

Exquisite Corpse No. 1

1954

Exquisite Corpse No. 2

1956

Obertura Republicana (with
    Paul Taylor, Marian Sarach,
    James Waring, David
    Vaughan)

1959

Cut-Ups

1960

Scraps
Tonight We Improvise

1961

Group Soup

1962

Fortunately
Man Is Man

1964

Patter for a Soft Shoe Dance
December
Leonce & Lena
Sing Ho! For a Bear (mc)
April

1965

A Beautiful Day (mc)
Dance for Boys
April and December

1966

Jonah
*Meditation
Theater Songs of Al Carmines
    (mc)
The Sneaker Players
The Tinguely Machine Mystery
More, More, I Want More

1967

Etude
Between the Black and the White
    There Is a Rainbow
*Clearing
An Evening of Dances, Plays, and
    Songs
Variety Show
A Re-examination of Freedom
I Ching Poem for Johnny
I Am My Beloved (with Aileen
    Passloff)
Concrete Rainbow
Bertha
Well . . . Actually (with James
    Waring, John Herbert
    McDowell) (mc)
Celebration of Change

1968

Sayings of Mao Tse Tung
Differences
Meditation (second version)
Celebration
Untitled Play
Green Power

1969

Hommage à Loie Fuller
Happy Is the Man in Whose
    Hand Line Meets a Line (with
    Burt Supree and June Ekman)
The Red Burning Light
Dark Dance
Yellow Umbrella Dance

1970

Biography
Faces
Under Milkwood (p)

1971

Secrets
The Book Is Dead

1972

Dance
Instructions from Paris

1973

Quick Change Artists
The Moveable Workshop
Mystery Play (p)

1974

Thinking of You Thinking of Me
Le Cahier vierge
Arc en ciel
Mad River

LUCINDA CHILDS

It seems ironic that, among a group of total individualists such as choreographers, the one word that seems best able to convey Childs's special quality is "individual." She follows her own logic and her own drummer even through the midst of a crowd of others doing intriguing and somewhat similar things. She was a dance major at Sarah Lawrence College, where she graduated in 1962. In the same year she attended class at the American Ballet Center and the Merce Cunningham Studio in New York. She became a member of the newly formed Judson Dance Theater and performed off and on within its framework for the next six years. She has choreographed sparingly but effectively, always at her own pace and with her own particular style of unhurried detachment. At one point she retired from active performing for several years to acquire a master's degree in education. When she received her degree she returned to begin teaching in her own studio, and she appeared at the School of Visual Arts as well, as a guest instructor. In addition to her early dance training she has also studied the Alexander technique.

CARNATION

Choreography by Lucinda Childs. First performed at the Institute of Contemporary Arts, Philadelphia, Pa., April 24, 1964, by Lucinda Childs.

During the early part of her career Childs seemed to have a special need to work with domestic tools in impossible situations. It was never entirely clear whether she was using them or they were using her but the result was a piquant and often amusing series of encounters.

The woman sits atop a kitchen table and places an ordinary colander on her head like a particularly outrageous and unsuitable hat. Mistaking it for her head, she begins to place large hair curlers on its tiny pronged metal feet. She takes the small sponges normally associated with household chores and stuffs them into her mouth. She is either incredibly inept or diabolically clever and in the twinkling of an eye jumps down from her perch, tosses all of the bits and pieces she has been manipulating into a blue plastic bag, and firmly jams her foot in on top of them.

She abandons all of that to do a headstand while deeply involved with a sheet that has two socks attached to it. It is the *Götterdämmerung* of a housewife gone mad and yet through it all she retains a personal distance from whatever it is that she is doing. She does a back flip onto a plastic bag and stares about with a glaring expression. She starts to cry, then stops and returns to her deadpan normal expression.

One almost has the feeling that the woman and her artifacts have been placed together by some malevolent force that enjoys the incongruity of their encounter. She methodically destroys them as operative objects but then weeps at having done so and maintains her ambiguous relationship to them. In a way it is an apotheosis of her entire relationship with dance and situations, embracing and holding them at arm's length at the same time.

CHOREOCHRONICLE
OF LUCINDA CHILDS

1963

   Pastime
   Three Piece
   Minus Auditorium Equipment
     and Furnishings
   Egg Deal

1964

   Cancellation Sample
  *Carnation
   Street Dance
   Model

1965

   Geranium
   Screen
   Museum Piece
   Agriculture

1966

   Vehicle

1968

   Untitled Trio

1973

   Untitled Trio (revised)
   Particular Reel
   Checkered Drift
   Calico Mingling

1975

   Duplicate Suite
   Reclining Rondo
   Congeries on Edges for Twenty
     Obliques

JAMES CUNNINGHAM

With a background as diverse as Cunningham's is, it is not surprising that his dances take the unusual configurations that they do. He is a native of Toronto, where he first became interested in dance and drama. During his college years he also studied and performed and, when he left school, moved to London to work in the theater. At the time he studied voice and directed several productions for the London Academy of Dramatic Arts. While in London he created his first dances and then in 1965 came to the United States to take up intensive dance study at the Martha Graham School.

He started to work seriously toward creating his own company and establishing his own special blend of theatrical dance. His mature works combine both words and motion. He is an accomplished monologuist and at times in his works will insert passages of declamation for himself and elements of song for others as well as himself. His exceptionally supple body has an elasticity that is truly remarkable, and, like most choreographers, he is the best interpreter of his own works. He has a special facility for involving audiences in his dances, which often conclude with a session of group dancing. He does not insist that anyone join him, nor does he badger the reluctant. He simply invites participation and has had tremendous success in having audiences move from their accustomed place in front of the footlights to the performing area to dance freely and unself-consciously. He makes dancing a very natural and enjoyable activity.

DANCING WITH MAISIE PARADOCKS

Choreography by James Cunningham. Film by John Atkin. Costumes by Bill Florio. First performed in New York City at the NYU School of Education, September 20, 1974, by Barbara Ellman, William Holcomb, Lauren Persichetti, Ted Striggles, Linda Tarnay, and James Cunningham.

Paradox is a concept that Cunningham likes to toy with, and parody is one way in which he examines seemingly irreconcilable elements. It sometimes backfires. He is fond of doing parodies of classic ballets such as *Swan Lake* and including little excerpts from them in his own pieces. The reception is usually warm and full of laughter. Unexpectedly facing an audience in Alaska at one time which had no familiarity with the original, his parody was mistaken for the real thing and no laughter eventuated, merely a slight contentment among the audience that it had now seen a true excerpt from the original. No one knows who the Maisie of the title is, nor is it ever explained, but then it doesn't really matter.

Six men and women in white sheets sit in a circle and chant and then rise to walk in a circle. Their sheets float out behind them when they begin to run, and they flap them like capes before rushing off. A couple in animal masks tussles and rolls offstage as a woman with mask and parasol strolls on. She moves it up and down as two others lunge and parry with one another. She begins a vamp routine to the music "Hey, Big Spender." What began as a quiet incantation almost religiously ritualistic has become a madcap circus. A man with a rabbit mask dashes out with an attaché case and removes a telephone from it. Threatened by the vamp, he takes a pistol from the case and shoots her, then places a timid, victorious foot on her fallen body.

A man dressed as a cowboy and a businessman chop and slash at one another as a man in a wedding dress enters to grasp one of them and talk about the joys of impending marriage. Suddenly "her" monologue churns up family memories and the businessman collapses when she reveals her love for the dog film star Lassie; the cowboy collapses. Suddenly a woman in a dog costume leaps onto the stage to dance a romantic duet with the "girl" in the wedding dress.

A new set of characters emerge in paradoxical dress, such as a girl in a baseball uniform riding a bicycle. After the sound of a car crash she falls off. A couple in white tunics circles her as if they were angels. They roll her off as the sound of "Whistle While You Work" is heard. Two dancers in tiger masks are tamed by having a flower tossed to them. A man enters in a military uniform and hangs the jacket on the back of a chair before putting himself through a stiff regimented drill during which he salutes and kicks viciously at an imaginary enemy as he shouts "trained to kill." He is obviously under severe pressure and collapses in his chair.

An elflike person enters in a leafy costume looking like the *Specter of the Rose* from Fokine's ballet. The creature tidies the military man's socks and slips his shoes out of the way before waking him. Then the creature leaps and prances with abandon as the military man watches dumfounded. He is irresistibly drawn to this fey figure and also wants to kill and destroy it. He joins in the graceful dance for a time, but then, when the Specter leaps into his arms, does an abrupt about-face and shreds the petals from the Specter's flower. The creature staggers and slips away, just managing his famous last leap. The military man stands and has a rabbit mask slipped over his head, a jacket thrust on him, and a necktie, and an attaché case. He has become the torn and tormented man in another guise, feeling tenderness but fearing to express it. The cowboy joins him and they do feats of strength. They are both vanquished by a tough-looking little woman who arm-wrestles the cowboy and punches the rabbit. Other confrontations with men as women, women as men, and all as animals transpire until all enter with white sheets, then doff them to do a unison sidestep and bow off.

The dance plays with the ideas of gender identity, male and femaleness, strong, weak, and a dozen other polarities that spring from sex differentiation. The mood is manic, and the dance is never at a loss for another confusing confrontation. It brilliantly mixes recitation, dance, song, and mime for its effects.

CHOREOCHRONICLE
OF JAMES CUNNINGHAM

1968

Father Comes Grandly Down and Eats Baby

1969

Lauren's Dream (with Lauren Persichetti)

1970

Junior Birdsmen
Lions and Roaring Tigers
Evelyn the Elevator
Mr. Fox's Garden

1971

The Clue in the Hidden Staircase

1972

Treasures from the Donald Duck Collection

1973

Everybody in Bed

1974

Apollo and Dionysus: Cheek to Cheek
*Dancing with Maisie Paradocks

1975

The Ham Show: Isis and Osiris (with Lauren Persichetti)

n.d.

Skating to Siam

LAURA DEAN

The fascination of hypnotic movement has been harnassed by Dean into a series of utterly absorbing dances that are designed around simple movement patterns which are repeated steadily until they completely absorb the interest of the viewer. Individual excerpts from them would tend to look totally incomplete, since their effect is dependent on incessant reassertion.

Dean was born in New York and studied with a wide variety of teachers and schools, beginning with Lucas Hoving and including the School of American Ballet, the American Ballet Center, and the Martha Graham School. She graduated from the School of Performing Arts and has appeared with several companies, such as those of Paul Taylor, Paul Sanasardo, Kenneth King, and Meredith Monk, before assembling her own performing group in 1971. She began to choreograph in 1966 and has made several tours of the United States and Europe, appearing frequently with composer Steve Reich, who shares a similar interest in the aesthetic possibilities of repetition. Her dances are usually performed in a clear and bare space, not a proscenium stage, and are costumed in white for the most part and illuminated with simple white light.

SQUARE DANCE

Choreography by Laura Dean. Music by Steve Reich (Phase Patterns). *First performed at the Loeb Student Center, New York University, New York, N.Y., April 27, 1973, by Janis Beaver, Judy Clark, Laura Dean, Bekka Eastman, Kathy Johnson, and Cathy Kerr.*

The dance has six dancers who stand in a square, hence the title of the piece. Like all of Dean's work it is simple and depends upon continued repetition of its movements to make its effect. Despite the apparent ease with which the steps are assembled, their relentless repetition makes great demands on the dancers' stamina.

The music which accompanies the dance is hypnotically repetitive but does have different "phases" to which the dancers respond with large directional shifts. As the dance begins the six women are dressed in simple white shirts and slacks. Two of them stand together at a spot which is the rear left corner of the square. A single woman stands at the front left corner, and two women stand at the front right corner. The formation is completed by a solitary girl at the rear right corner. Thus the "two women" corners are diagonally opposite, as are the "one woman" corners. This will always be the case as the dance progresses.

As the repeated pounding of the music begins, the six women bounce up and down in place energetically. In a few moments the "extra" women on two corners move in opposite directions. The one from the rear moves directly forward to join the woman on the front left corner, and at the same moment the woman on the front right corner moves to the rear right corner. When both have arrived, all the women half turn to the center of the formation and approach it with the same bouncy step they have been doing in place. They sweep their arms forward and cluster tightly at the center while waggling their hands up and down, after which all return to their starting corners.

The "extra" women switch corners again, this time traveling in exactly opposite horizontal directions across the rear and across the front so that the formation is as it was at the beginning. They repeat the diagonal bouncing dance to the center and back again. They return to the center and burst outward into two parallel lines of three dancers each while keeping up the rhythmic jogging step that is the basic energy step of the dance.

Suddenly they break from that step and begin to turn and turn and turn in place. The music stops and they continue to turn at a decreasing rate until they all stop and the dance is over.

Dean's dances have a special fascination all their own and are extended in duration for the most part. This one has the fascination of borrowing a title that brings thoughts of folk dancing to mind but turns out to be literally dancing in a square. Like her other works it bears patient observation so that its mood of controlled change can exert itself.

CHANGING PATTERN STEADY PULSE

Choreography by Laura Dean. Music by Tim Ferchen (Clave). *First performed at the Loeb Student Center, New York University, New York, N.Y., December 8, 1973, by Janis Beaver, Barbara Chenven, Laura Dean, Marcos Dinnerstein, Andrew Floud, Dakota Jackson, Diane Johnson, Pamela Kekich, Pedro Lujan, Edward Marsan, Lee Wasserwald, and Kathleen Weir.*

Dean used one of the most primitive accompaniments possible to pace the progress of this dance, and that was the rhythmic clapping of two blocks of wood. The very simplicity put one in the ambiance of an older, less complex society, where relationships were governed by quite recognizable rules of behavior.

Two rows of dancers face one another across a gap that is empty except for a musician clapping two blocks of wood together. Two lines of six men and six women oppose one another, and all are dressed in white shirts and trousers. The two rows of dancers are at the farthest end of the performing space. Individuals move out from opposite lines with a short, hopping skip and bounce toward one another at the center of the space, where they circle one another and then return to the line one slot down from the one they had just left. Since every other person moves out to the center to perform this chaste proto-mating dance and then returns one space farther down the line, the whole group progresses along the length of the hall by little stages. It is like seeing a giant weaving machine propelling itself along as the various members continue to repeat the same little circles at the center and then return to the outside lines. When the entire space of the hall has been traversed the dance is over.

The men and women never touch one another as they circle at the center, but there is a feeling of social ritual being carried out. Except that this social ritual has been stripped to its basic anatomy; almost abstracted to the inexorable tracery of tiny particles about a nucleus. Like all of Dean's dances it takes time to develop and patient observation to derive the maximum satisfaction. What could be tiring after five minutes of repetition is fascinating after twenty.

DRUMMING

Choreography by Laura Dean. Music by Steve Reich. First performed at the Brooklyn Academy of Music, Brooklyn, N.Y., April 3, 1975, by Laura Dean, Joan Durkee, Sarah Edgett, Susan Griss, Greta Holby, Diane Johnson, Kathy Kramer, and Dee McCandless.

The simplicity of the title scarcely prepares one for the variety and movement complexity of the dance as it was given by the eight female dancers who realized the work in its first performance at the flexible LaPercq Space above the foyer of the Brooklyn Academy of Music. As is Dean's custom, she costumes her dancers in simple white blouses and trousers and eschews romantic lighting in favor of simple white illumination. The musicians, led by composer Steve Reich, move from one set of percussion instruments to another while the dance is going on. There are small drums, marimbas, and glockenspiels, two sopranos and a piccolo player.

The dancers occupy the area in front of the audience in an open formation with three women in the front row, two in the second, two in the third, and one in the fourth and last row. Each is spaced well away from the others, and all begin slowly marking time in place. They accelerate and drift backward to form a line at the rear. A group separates to move forward in unison then to the side and back. The remaining dancers do the same, and the momentum of the movement is now suggestive of an American Indian ceremonial dance reflecting the quality of the drum sound. The dancers move like the shuttle of a giant loom. Side by side all are at the front and step to the left, swinging their arms forward and back almost as a skater would.

They form a horizontal line at the rear again then move into two parallel vertical columns, rolling their hands rapidly over one another and kicking out toward the facing dancer. The pace has accelerated considerably from its slow start, and the front dancers from each column detach themselves and spin while moving upstage, to be followed by all the others who reconstitute the horizontal line again. The ends of the line curve forward to form an upside-down "U," and the dancers separate into the opening formation.

To conclude the first section, all spin in place after forming a circle around one woman in the center who is also spinning.

The quality of the music for the second section is the more mellow marimba sound, and the movement slows to turning rather than the more energetic spinning. Two of the women orbit the woman in the center, and all are circled by the remaining five dancers, who sidestep gently around the three. The woman closest to the woman at the center moves more rapidly so that she is at the opposite end of the circular orbit made by the second satellite dancer at times and at other moments passes her and is at the same hour point on an imaginary clock. The pacing is beautifully sustained, and one is dazzled by the inevitable symmetry. Two more women are drawn into the tighter orbits, and the three remaining continue to circle and turn. All weave small patterns of simple gesture with their arms, bend forward, straighten up, and open out.

The metallic jingling of the glockenspiels announces the third movement, which again finds all of the dancers in the opening formation. They turn and then in unison weave to the rear of the area with small shuffling steps in "S" patterns, conjuring up images of delicate Chinese clockwork dolls. The strict ground-hugging steps used to move from one formation to another are broken by small leaps in which they cross and uncross the legs at one point. They return to the delicate shuffle to re-establish the opening formation. After a series of turns, all step to one side and bounce, giving the impression of tap dancing. The pace slows as all sway in place.

All of the instruments announce the fourth and final section. Again the dancers accelerate, turning first in one direction and then the other, waggling their shoulders, making one think of the formation dancing of a large musical review. The gestures have great verve but are presented with an innocent reserve. Hopping turns precede a small series of kicks forward, and the piece concludes with the dancers turning in place and then all stop together.

Playing with the various timbres of the percussive sound, Dean created the most ambitious of her group dances. The whole was like an unrolling scroll of movement telling the same story of group reliance, compacting and dispersing smoothly, but performed with a variety of accents. The work lasts slightly over an hour without pause but passes incredibly rapidly as one is drawn into the intricate and ever-changing patterns of the calmly self-composed performers.

CHOREOCHRONICLE
OF LAURA DEAN

1966

3 Minutes and 10 Seconds

1967

Christmas Piece

1968

Theatre Piece
Life Is All Around You
Red-White-Black
No Title

1970

At Alan Saret's
An Hour in Silence

1971

Bach Preludes
A Dance Concert
Stamping Dance

1972

Quartet Squared
Trio
Circle Dance
*Square Dance
Walking Dance

1973

Jumping Dance
*Changing Pattern Steady Pulse

1974

Response Dance
Spinning Dance

1975

*Drumming

WILLIAM DUNAS

The earliest modern dancers all started out as soloists, and many pursued their entire careers as solo artists. Dunas is a bit of a throwback to those independent days of yesteryear and has concentrated for the most part on solo dances. At one time he eschewed even sound accompaniment of any kind. In an ear-shattering reversal later in his career he had an accompanist beat on water-filled bottles with a spoon that produced sound close to the threshold of pain. He has also used narration of texts of his own devising, and even some music from live radio. He was born in New York and attended C. W. Post College and Brooklyn College. He is interested in acting and the fine arts as well as dance and studied all of them at one time or another. Among his dance instructors were Alfredo Corvino, Mia Slavenska, Don Farnworth, and there were periods spent at the schools of Paul Sanasardo, Merce Cunningham, and Daniel Nagrin. He has been artist in residence at the University of Wisconsin and taught at New York University's School of the Arts.

WAIL

Choreography by William Dunas. Music by John Cage, John Coltrane, Pierre Schaeffer and Pierre Henry, and Krysztof Penderecki. Lighting by Gary Harris. First performed at the Cubiculo, New York, N.Y., March 3, 1969, by William Dunas.

Alone among concert dancers, Dunas designs solos for himself that are long, intense meditations which occupy his entire program. He does not offer a bouquet of dance vignettes but creates a whole dance that cumulates at times with crushing emotional effect. While he will include passages of lyrical dancing in his pieces, he is most interested in dramatic impact and presents his movement with a maximum emotional weight. This dance is one of a series exploring a vein of desperate loneliness.

A man wearing a green union suit sits and eats a piece of bread, and the lights go out. When they come up a moment later, he is facing a wall, then walks in a half-circle to face another wall. He closes his eyes and leans his head back. He falls prostrate and remains so for a moment then rises to skip in a circle. Advancing toward the audience, he puts his fingers in his mouth then walks away to squat at the rear of the stage. When he advances again, his body convulses and his head shakes in a violent gesture of negation. He falls again but then rises to return to his skipping, and a foolish smile creases his face as he walks in a circle. The lights go out.

In a moment three cones of light illuminate the stage and he coughs violently and then begins to laugh to himself; there is a tinge of hysteria to it. In another blackout sequence he says, "One," then reels off a few sentences of description and says, "One," again. A moment later he is seized by a ghastly discordant rendition of a rock-and-roll tune. He shows a horrible enjoyment of it while lying on his back. One has the feeling of being in the presence of a demented imagination.

When the lights come up again he gulps water from a glass and breaths loudly. In the next episode he relates, "I scratched her." "She laughed." "I stood up." "She slapped me." "I licked her." "She cried." A moment later he is prone and howling in torment. Next he sucks greedily on a cigarette. Nothing that he does has any modulation or reserve in it, he is a man on the edge and seizes nourishment and pleasure as best he can and when he can. There may be no tomorrow!

He relates, "They picked me to play the yellow rose of Texas." "They made me a long dress. They sang and I skipped." The whole stage is illuminated with a dusky light. He lies on his back collapsed and draws his legs up and moves to a half crouch but tumbles back. He manages to stand and run in a circle. Repeatedly he falls but rises to continue and then falls and slithers away. In the final tableau he walks and says, "In the name," kneels, and continues to walk. At the end the lights are fully on and he frenziedly leaps and throws his arms violently around until the lights are blacked out for the final time.

The dance has a desperate air hanging around it. It is not pretty in the conventional sense but radiates a powerful integrity. We are being shown an inner landscape of anxiety which has been stylized for the stage but still has a raw, painful energy. Dunas toned down the starkness of his solos in succeeding years and introduced elaborate collections of ritual objects and props which gave a slightly surrealistic look to his dances, but this early example of his work shows him and his struggle with special clarity.

CHOREOCHRONICLE
OF WILLIAM DUNAS

1968

Gap
X
Express

1969

*Wail
Wax
Ajax

1970

Job
Bojo

1971

Bad
The Rite
The Trip
The Site
A Poor Fool

1972

The King Is Dead
From Fool to Hanged Man
Our Lady of Late
The Time of Your Life
The All the Same Faces Affair
To Love Us Is to Pay Us
The Children's Crusade
Go Directly to Jail Do Not Pass
 Go

1973

I Went with Him and She Came
 with Me

They Saw the Marching Band
 Go 'Round the Grand Stand
The Kids at Four
Gap (revival)
The Great Birthday Party &
 Exercises for the Rocker
Eclipse

1974

The Trust
Five Quartets
An American Landscape

1975

Story, An American Narrative

JUDITH DUNN

At the center of the formation of the Judson Dance Theater in the early 1960s, Dunn had emerged from years of professional performing and touring with Merce Cunningham. Her husband, musician Robert Dunn, was invited to give a course in dance composition at the Cunningham studio, and she was his assistant in this and in the subsequent courses which he gave at her studio in lower Manhattan. Dunn's own performing had previously occupied most of her energy, and it was only after she had left the Cunningham company with its heavy touring schedule that she had sufficient time to create her own pieces, which were marked by an offbeat, almost dadaesque sense of humor. She began to show her work during the early years of the Judson Dance Theater in collaboration with others and finally on programs of her own. She began to work with jazz musician Bill Dixon and formed a company with him and currently is artist in residence at Bennington College.

ACAPULCO

Choreography by Judith Dunn. First performed at the Gramercy Arts Theater, New York, N.Y., June 30, 1963, by Lucinda Childs, Judith Dunn, Alex Hay, and Deborah Hay.

Dunn's physical control is such that it permits her to start a gesture in one direction and then seemingly without effort change it unexpectedly so that it ends up traveling at an unexpected and novel tangent which colors the whole preceding phrase. She has experimented with all sorts of movement and time durations, and this piece toys with the idea of delayed reactions.

A woman on a chair begins to rise, twist, and sink back. A man walks over to stand near the chair expecting to catch her. At an unexpected time a few moments later she topples off the chair into his waiting arms. In another episode a woman sits expectantly and calmly in a chair waiting for something or someone. Another woman begins to move toward her taking tiny steps, stalking her with great care as an attacker might track a victim in a cartoon. The tension mounts as she approaches, and then when she is within striking distance she produces a comb and begins to run it through the seated girl's hair. The seated woman emits a long drawn out "Ou-u-uch."

One has the feeling of events that are transpiring without any order based on the usual cause and effect procedure. The simplest actions are drawn out to super-slow-motion speed and occur over unexpected distances almost as if one had begun to stretch time and space like taffy. A woman enters to play a round of cards but is wheeled in instead of walking. Her partner accepts it all as being part of the natural order and deals the cards with a kind of "Alice in Wonderland" confidence. Another woman irons a dress carefully, except that she is wearing the dress instead of spreading it on a board.

Dunn toys with and exploits audience anticipations. She knows that audiences will expect the usual so she always gives an unusual twist to the events that she produces. She causes one to see things in a fresh way. Her special manner of displaying slowed motion anticipated and excelled the more publicized and grandiose practitioners of this mode of theater, of joining episodic events and stretching time.

CHOREOCHRONICLE
OF JUDITH DUNN

1963

Index (mp)
Speedlimit
*Acapulco
Motorcycle
Witness I
Witness II
Astronomy Hill
Airwave

1964

Natural History
Before Any Beginning
Last Point
Official Doctrine (mp)
Three Dances (mp)

1966

Quipus
The Grocery Bag Bursts and the
    Oranges Fall to the Floor
West Orange Lecture
Dew Horse
Pomegranate
Motorcycle
Ground Speed
Solos

1967

The Improvised Piece for Helen
    Alkire
Nightfall Pieces (I)
The Goucher Lecture
Nightfall Pieces (II)
Workprint
Papers
File Box Piece

1969

A Concert of Improvisation I
A Concert of Improvisation II

1970

Relay

1971

Day One
Day Two

1973

1972–73 (Day Three)

1974

Life Dances

VIOLA FARBER

Stylistically Viola Farber's work belongs to the sharp and precise movement that is most often associated with Merce Cunningham. To it she brings a humorous, bounding enthusiasm that is definitely a personal contribution of human warmth. She first studied music at American University in Washington, D.C., and later attended Black Mountain College in North Carolina, where John Cage and Cunningham with Robert Rauschenberg and M. C. Richards created the first "happening." She joined the Cunningham company in 1953, leaving after twelve years to establish her own company. At this time she began to create her repertory. In addition to study with Cunningham she has also studied with Katherine Litz and Margaret Craske. Her own reputation as a teacher is high, and she has taught at the Cunningham studio, the London School of Contemporary Dance, as well as at her own school. She has created works for the Repertory Dance Theater of Utah and Manhattan Festival Ballet. In 1971 she and her husband, Jeff Slayton, were awarded the gold medal for expression and creativity at the Ninth International Dance Festival in Paris.

NOTEBOOK

Choreography by Viola Farber. Sound arranged by Viola Farber. Read by David Vaughan. First performed at the Judson Memorial Church, New York, N.Y., September 12, 1968, by June Finch, Margaret Jenkins, Cathleen Powers, and Dan Wagoner.

In his book *Changes: Notes on Choreography*, Merce Cunningham took time out to praise Farber's special dancing quality. She obviously made a great impression on him and vice versa. She has taken the Cunningham style of fast, razor-sharp movement and adopted it to her own ends, adding the unusual little twists and quirks that give the work her own personal stamp.

One hears the unmistakable sound of a police whistle, and three women and one man walk out to the center of the performing area. They cluster together and act worried then walk back and forth agitatedly. They run and two escort another. They yell from time to time with frustration. A reader declaims platitudes periodically during the course of the dance. "A stitch in time saves nine." After he states, "Don't look a gift horse in the mouth!" the women look around and stare intently. After "Birds of a feather . . ." all leave one by one until there is only one girl alone. The others drift back.

The man brings on a chair and tries to find a comfortable sitting position but cannot and leaves to partner one of the women. Her twitchy movements put him off. He looks at another bounding woman and just leaves. When he returns the women are interested but he fidgets and leaves. The stream of platitudes continues unabated. While the women rush on and off the man sits in the chair and watches. He tries to partner the same woman as before, but it just doesn't work out. He reclines on the floor and she bends over him to try this awkward but moving duet. "Adversity makes strange bedfellows." In the concluding sequence of the dance they crawl off then all return and the women fall and twitch. The man runs from one to another straightening them up. He returns to the chair while the three do a short precision variation in unison, and two of the women leave. His girl falls and he lifts her.

The last words of the narrator are "If the shoe fits, wear it!" It seems a fitting conclusion to the somewhat desperate situation the four find themselves in. In effect they have one another for good or ill and they may as well try to make the best of it. Farber's wry fatalism attempts no prediction.

ROUTE 6

Choreography by Viola Farber. Set to Longines Radio Favorites. First performed at the Brooklyn Academy of Music, Brooklyn, N.Y., April 21, 1972, by Viola Farber, Andé Peck, and Jeff Slayton.

This is the sort of dance title that has a most baffling import, since the dance itself has absolutely nothing in it to suggest automobile travel, the open road, or highway touring. It is a trio for two men and one woman with humor, sadness, and touches of isolation in the course of its clean design.

The musical accompaniment of the dance is the rather lushy orchestrated selection of semiclassical compositions entitled "Longines Radio Favorites." The romantic "Journey into Melody" begins, and the three dancers make their entrance striding and balancing purposefully on one leg. They move in relation to one another but stay in their own small orbits, giving one the feeling of chaste reserve.

"Seems like Old Times" fills the air, and the two men and the woman cluster tightly near one another. One by one each collapses in turn and is caught by another with care and firmness. They separate again and traipse off on isolated paths rotating their arms windmill fashion.

A bouncy selection has one of the men stepping on smartly alone, and then the three become involved again. The woman strikes a pose and the two men pick her up and carry her as if she were a statue. They then adopt a languid and sophisticated appearance but break out to run and skip like kids at play. There is a hint that they are not so completely carefree, however. The music continues for a moment after they leave.

Farber's dances have a lean and somewhat odd elegance. *Route 6*, for instance, is a game of some sort that has an import more weighty than just the winning of a frolic. The frolicsome elements are there and readily observable, but one has the feeling that the players know something that the spectators are not aware of. It doesn't really matter but does give the work an added resonance.

CHOREOCHRONICLE
OF VIOLA FARBER

1965

Seconds

1966

Surf Zone

1968

*Notebook
Time Out
Legacy
Passengers
Excerpt

1969

The Music of Conlon Nancarrow
Duet for Mirijam and Jeff
Quota
Passage
Standby
Tristan and Iseult
Pop. 18
Pop. 11

1970

Tendency
Area Code
Curriculum
Co-op
Window

1971

Survey
Patience
Mildred
Five in the Morning

1972

Default
*Route 6
Dune
Poor Eddie (1972/73)

1973

Soup
Spare Change

1974

Willi I
Some of the Symptoms
Dinosaur Parts
No Super, No Boiler
Defendant

House Guest
Temporary Life
Working Dance
Duet for Susan and Willi

1975

Motorcycle

LAURA FOREMAN

Foreman is almost as well known for her sponsorship of others' work as for her own. In 1964 she founded Choreoconcerts in order to provide choreographers a framework in which to present new dances without having to prepare an entire program of their own works. It was and is a form of instant repertory, and usually three or four new works are presented on each program.

She re-established a dance department at The New School, which had been a bastion for modern dance in the thirties, and she teaches regularly as well as creating her own works. She retired from actual performance relatively early in her career and has confined her energy to designing works exclusively since the late sixties.

Her main interest is in producing dance theater events that incorporate elements of dramatic incidents, "happenings," dance, and sometimes singing. Her husband, John Watts, is a composer who frequently prepares scores for her works.

A TIME

Choreography by Laura Foreman. Set to a tape collage by John Watts. Films and slides by Lynda McNeur and Stan Summers. Environments by the Third Eye. First performed at St. Luke's Auditorium, New York, N.Y., February 25, 1968, by Charlotte Honda, Margot Parsons, and Betty Steinfeld.

One of Foreman's preoccupations is time, its passing and its recapture. At times it appears that her entire career is a meditation on the nature of time. She is constantly dredging up radio or video scraps that set a particular era in sharp focus, the way that an issue of an old magazine can bring back a whole world that might have been forgotten. In this dance time is passing.

A woman wearing a patriotic costume of a red leotard, a blue skirt, and white tights is turning and spinning like a leaf in the corridors of time. The music has a metronomic beat with its little bell like clinks. She slows her turning and the stage is blacked out. When the lights come up she propels herself across the stage on her back while two other women spin around. The woman in the center vibrates her pointed fingers, suggesting a machine gun. The music is a music appreciation of Beethoven's "Eroica" Symphony, and the commentator solemnly announces that its whiplash sounds shattered the eighteenth century. Immediately real whiplash sounds are heard.

The three women enter and disappear then rock from side to side and swear silently at the audience mouthing the words. Then they begin role playing; one pretends to be a big doll asking for "Mama," another points at the audience, and the third sings a popular song from the thirties. They leave and films are shown of them running in a studio. When they return the first woman stares out at the audience, peering between her legs and gurgling vacantly as an orchestrated version of one of Satie's *Gymnopédies* is played. A stroboscopic light flickers on and off, catching her and the two other dancers frozen in poses as they perform a dance phrase involving jumping and laughing. The music and lights go off and two of the women leave, but films of them are projected as the remaining woman spins and then halts.

The dance jumbles time present and time past in films with a deft hand. The dancers seem like dizzy kids frolicking in a world of what was and what is without any real comprehension of the nature of the game. With Foreman there is always humor and always anxiety, and the balance remains uncertain. One is literally not sure whether to laugh or to cry. It probably depends on one's mood in any given performance.

SIGNALS II

Choreography by Laura Foreman. Set to a score for ARP Synthesizer. Text by John Watts. Costumes by Alice Schwebke. First performed at the Washington Square Methodist Church, New York, N.Y., March 26, 1971, by Esther Chaves, Christian Singer, Sean Singer, Dana Wolfe, and Catherine Rowe (singer).

Choreographers often make do with the talent that is available to them at any given time, but in a rarely imaginative leap Foreman selected two small boys without dance training and included them in a dance that she put in motion with two other, highly trained dancers and a singer to make a cleverly evocative piece.

Two small boys wearing dance belts rush out to run after one another in a mock chase. They giggle as they run, imparting the light feeling of fun that they must experience as children in the sheer enjoyment of moving. One catches the other and they clasp arms around each other. At an invisible signal they break and resume the game of fleeing and catching, finally exiting after filling the performing space with laughter and good spirits.

A singer begins a recitative of instructions from official bodies such as the fire department, the post office, and other such structured bureaucracies, warning the public about regulations and signaling their intent. After a short blackout the lights reveal a woman doing a series of deep bends slowly and carefully changing places and altering her feet to correspond with the basic positions of the classic ballet. She extends her leg then walks forward in a crouch to a point closer to the audience, where she tumbles on back and extends both legs upward in a "V" shape. She rises and repeats the series of bends she first performed. Again there is a blackout, and the singer begins another recitative about the fiber content that should be found in a particular garment.

When the lights come up another woman in point shoes picks her way across on a diagonal and a bell tinkles lightly inside a pregnant bulge under her leotard, and the singer concludes with a recitative on unsolicited pornographic mail.

Despite the varied combination of elements in the dance the theme of signals of one sort or another dominated. Whether it was the overt vocal warning or the game of catch and release with its own private rules, the structure of communication was established.

CHOREOCHRONICLE
OF LAURA FOREMAN

1961

Evocations
New Dance
Divided
Lyric Dances

1962

Last
Sound Piece

1963

Improvisation Suite
Seasonals

1964

Memorials
Expiations
Freedom Suite

1966

Study I
Study II
Film Dances

1967

Solo Suite
Study (for solo figure/film)
Experimentals
Media Piece

1968

Events
Group Dances
Pulses
Media Dances
Games
*A Time

1969

Study (for group/film)
perimeters

1970

Signals
Epicycles
†*Untitled*

1971

glass and shadows
Laura's Dance
Commercials
*Signals II

1972

still life
lecture-dem
Spaces (*Collage I*)
Spaces (*Collage II*)
Environments
songandance (*section 3*)
MARGINS

1973

Performance
Spaces (*Collage III*) Originally
   titled WESTELEVEN
Spaces (*Collage IV*)
Locrian
SONGANDANCE (complete
   three-part work: still life,
   lecture-dem, songandance)

1974

postludes
à deux
city of angels

† This piece was *really* meant to be untitled, only a blank space was shown where the "title" would have appeared.

SIMONE FORTI

There is a feeling of naturalness about all of Forti's works in the sense that they resonate or tune themselves in accordance with natural processes such as rolling, falling, and the like. She was twenty-one and living in San Francisco in 1956 when she first began to study dance. Instinctively she sought out Ann Halprin, whose unconventional dance school and performance group drew inspiration for much of its work from observing natural process.

She moved to New York four years later and began to study at the Martha Graham School and at the Merce Cunningham studio, neither of which was much to her liking. The movement had too much of a disciplined "artificiality" to it to satisfy her. She began to attend "happenings," participating in several, and was invited to devise some movement pieces for a series in 1960 that was sponsored by composer LaMonte Young. It was her first complete concert of her own work, and it had a great effect on the imagination of many young choreographers who were dissatisfied at the time with more formal dance movement. For the next fifteen years she taught, traveled, and produced an occasional concert, always drawing sustenance from natural process. In Rome once she patterned her dances after the movements of animals she observed in the zoo.

HUDDLE

Choreography by Simone Forti. Costumes were self-determined by the participants and consisted of casual street clothing. First performed at a loft on Chambers Street, New York, N.Y. in the spring of 1961. The names of the performers are not available.

Among the pieces that made up her first full evening was this physically demanding and amusing work. The whole program was called *Five Dance Constructions and Some Other Things* and was given in a loft on Chambers Street. The unconventional location and space were a function of the difficulty in obtaining any other space and also reflected a desire to break with the physical limitations of a conventional proscenium arch theater. The dance is designed for a half-dozen people.

The piece begins as a mixed group of men and women walk to a designated spot and cluster together in a tight circle facing inward. Casually but firmly the individuals place arms about each other's shoulders and waist, drawing themselves closely together. The dome-shaped huddle is structurally very strong.

One or another of the group detaches himself or herself from the mass and begins to crawl slowly and carefully over the outside of the huddle, ascending, crossing the top, and descending on the other side, without hurry. The person rejoins the structure once again, linking arms around the nearest waist and shoulder. Another person makes the same climb until everyone has had a chance. One readily gets the feel of the strenuous physicality of the effort and is intrigued with the skill of the climbers at finding footholds and grips that are secure but also do not dislocate someone's nose or painfully twist an ear.

In some performances the piece has been made participational when sympathetic members of the audience join one of the original huddlers and form another huddle of their own. With the right type of audience there can be a yeastlike expansion of huddles. Like many of Forti's works this one is designed to give people the feel of their own bodies and put them in touch with the physicality of movement without any effort to dazzle with technical virtuosity. In their way her pieces are instructions or teaching assignments almost more than performing vehicles but yet retain a theatrical coloration.

CHOREOCHRONICLE
OF SIMONE FORTI

1960

See-Saw
Rollers
Platforms

1961

*Huddle
Hangers
Herding
From Instructions

1967

Face Tunes
Elevation Tune No. 2
Cloths
Fallers

1968

Bottom

1969

Sleepwalkers
Throat Dance
Accompaniment for LaMonte's
   2 Sounds and LaMonte's 2
   Sounds

1971

Slantboard

1975

Idea Warehouse Performance

n.d.

Censor
Over, Under, and Around
Book
Two at Once

DAVID GORDON

A gentle voice and a gravely gentle sense of humor distinguish Gordon, and it only seems fair to allow him to speak for himself in this autobiographical sketch which he composed in the middle sixties.

"David Gordon began dancing with James Waring. Continued dancing with Merce Cunningham. Went to Connecticut College summer dance school on scholarship and continued studying with Merce Cunningham. Began studying with Martha Graham and Louis Horst and stopped immediately and stopped dancing with James Waring. Rehearsed once with Merle Marsicano and began dancing with James Waring again and stopped. Began studying composition with Merce Cunningham and with Judith and Robert Dunn. Began dancing alone and with Valda Setterfield and married her. Began dancing with Yvonne Rainer. Hopes to stop all this dancing soon."

He hasn't stopped dancing, thankfully, and has continued to prepare pieces of his own as well as working with the co-operative "Grand Union" company.

RANDOM BREAKFAST

Choreography by David Gordon. Music, a tape collage. Costumes by David Gordon. First performed at America on Wheels (skating rink) in Washington, D.C., May 9, 1963, by David Gordon and Valda Setterfield.

Though he has created a variety of dancers, the duet seems to appeal to Gordon and to draw out the best from him. Most frequently his partner has been his wife, Valda Setterfield, who has a polished comic charm and together they project a world of zany incongruities.

A woman, glamorously dressed, comes on to do "The Strip." She is earnest and begins to grind through her routine, shedding an article of clothing here and there with casual professionalism. Something, however, is subtly wrong. She has the detachment that an actor might have playing the part of a character in a play that he stands apart from. At the end of her routine she flounces off with her silly little fringed G-string flapping.

A man enters in a striped polo shirt to explain in words and motion how to put together a "Prefabricated Dance." It is a do-it-yourself instruction in both words and motions. He stresses the need for an exciting entrance and runs in circles from time to time to break up the sections of the dance. He repeats movement variations the audience will become familiar with and feel comfortable with, and verbally suggests that the budding choreographer do things that the audience will understand.

At the same time he is explaining how to make a dance, the woman is performing "The Seasons" on another portion of the stage and ends up taking a nap on the floor in her fur coat and bikini bathing suit. The "Lemon Hearts Dance" is a flamenco number that the male dancer storms his way through.

The woman reappears dressed as a traditional nun. She is full of joy as she moves happily around the stage. All of her movements speak of her contentment and confidence in the basic rightness and fitness of things. She places a box on the ground and in an abrupt change of character blurts out a jumbled string of swearwords, picks up the cake from the cakebox, and slams herself in the face.

The finale finds the man with a top hat perched on the back of his head in a spotlight smiling. He moves from side to side and slowly away from the audience with the smile never leaving his face. The sound is Judy Garland singing "Over the Rainbow," and the low-key movement and high-key smile seem to be perfect commentaries on the song.

As in other works Gordon takes a variety of situations and satirizes them with a mixture of sounds and motions. He has a glorious sense of deadpan humor and always manages to blunder through with his aplomb intact although the scrutinized subject is often the worse for wear.

CHOREOCHRONICLE
OF DAVID GORDON

1962

Mama Goes Where Papa Goes
Mannequin Dance
Helen's Dance

1963

*Random Breakfast
Honey Sweetie Dust Dance

1964

Silver Pieces (Fragments)

1966

Walks and Digressions

1971

Sleepwalking
Liberty

1972

The Matter

1974

Spilled Milk (solo)
Spilled Milk Variations
    (grouped solo)
Chair, Alternatives 1 Through 5
One Act Play

ANN HALPRIN

As a young dancer in New York, she was traditionally schooled in mainstream modern dance, that broad spectrum of techniques which developed out of the Graham-Humphrey-Weidman experimentation of the thirties. Her first dances were designed in this vocabulary. She moved to San Francisco after marriage to Lawrence Halprin, the environmental architect, and joined Welland Lathrop, a former Graham dancer in the Halprin-Lathrop studio.

She began to evolve from the strict discipline of her early training and to develop a more direct relationship with space and nature in the course of the fifties. One of her favorite teaching assignments for students is to tell them to study some natural object in direct line of sight from the outdoor platform where she is conducting class. Among the odder choices was one made by sculptor Robert Morris, who espied a rock and crumpled to the ground and tried to balance himself on one point as it was. For Halprin such a choice was neither good nor bad; only the result of the creative exploration counted. Her pupils number in the hundreds, and one thinks of James Waring, Simone Forti, Yvonne Rainer, Meredith Monk, and Trisha Brown among others. She early pioneered the use of nudity in modern dance and encountered some severe legal harassment in the beginning. Subsequently as nudity became commonplace she performed in major theaters without disturbance. Her force as a teacher is to open pupils' eyes to creative possibilities.

PARADES AND CHANGES

Choreography by Ann Halprin. Music by Morton Subotnick. Costumes by Jo Landor. Lighting by Patric Hickey. First performed at the Hunter College Playhouse, New York, N.Y., April 21, 1967, by Karen Ahlberg, Todd Bryant, Ann Halprin, Michael Katz, Morris Kelley, Daria Lurie, Nancy Peterson, Kathy Peterson, Joseph Schlichter, and Peter Weiss.

It would be impossible to give a description of the definitive version of this work since it changed from performance to performance. The only thing that one can do is talk about the particular evening that one viewed it. That evening for me was April 21, 1967. The company had toured Europe and appeared "naked" on Swedish television among other places and had a scandalous reputation that helped make its New York performances complete sellouts. The furor over nudity completely overshadowed the experimental aspect of Halprin's work, although not for the artistic community which turned out in force to see the concert.

The first part of the dance finds eight performers walking out on stage in street clothes and then standing to stare at the audience. Then slowly and deliberately, very slowly and very deliberately, they begin to remove their clothes, one item at a time, looking like moving statues as they are doing it, until they are nude. They then put their clothes back on with the same deliberate speed and strip once again. The very deliberateness of the action served to underscore the nudity when achieved, since it was so clearly a conscious, deliberate choice. Two assistants roll out huge sheets of brown paper and the dancers in the nude embrace and crumple large sections of it. It becomes like an adult play environment as they walk, stop, squat, crumple, and finally gather up all of the scraps and one by one drop off the stage into the orchestra pit out of sight.

The second portion of the work is completely different. Halprin begins the section alone and enters in a baggy pants costume with a prop bag out of which she pulls a variety of objects, slips into oversized shoes, does a shuffling little dance, chews gum, lies on her back, and at one point blows on a police whistle. She has an English policeman's hat on. Suddenly everyone else appears wearing white trousers and shirts. Some appear out of the orchestra pit, others crawl up the aisles, and a man lets himself down from the balcony by means of a rope ladder carrying a suitcase. He presents it to Halprin onstage, and she begins to dress herself in the colorful clothes that it contains.

A second squadron of dancers appears in black jackets, which they tear off, and cavort wildly around the stage, leaping, falling, and twitching. As all of this continues, a platform is pushed across the back of the stage behind a light gauze curtain, and Halprin is disrobing on top of it. Wooden platforms are dragged onstage and the dancers hop and pound on them, yell at the audience, and then freeze as a silhouette of Halprin sitting in a bathtub appears on the gauze curtain.

The piece was just about as riotous and confusing as it sounds. It was a burst of animal energy and as such made a strong impact. It was also daring, so much so that there was some fear that the police might arrest the performers, despite the fact that the presentation was being made at respectable Hunter College, a major educational institution. To forestall any difficulty, a conspiracy of silence greeted the premiere and none of the daily newspapers which would normally print a review the next day did so. Each waited until two days later after the second performance was over before printing a notice. By the time the police issued a warrant, the company had left town.

CHOREOCHRONICLE
OF ANN HALPRIN

1955

The Prophetess
Steig People

1957

Birds of America; or Gardens
Without Walls

1961

The Flowerburger
Four-legged Stool

1964

Procession
Esposizione

1967

Parades and Changes

1969

A Ceremony of Us

1971

Animal Ritual
Ceremony of Signals
West/East Stereo Boou'la bo'ici
  bo'ee
Initiations and Transformations
(with Dance Workshop)

ALEX HAY

As a painter, Hay has drawn on the everyday world of common objects for his subject matter from a standard brown paper bag to a shiny toaster. He is a meticulous craftsman, and his pieces, both graphic and performing, have a surface finish and polish that are technically impressive. While the major thrust of his career has been as a painter, he became interested in dance through his wife Deborah, who studied at the Henry Street Settlement Playhouse and toured with the Merce Cunningham company.

Hay's naturally athletic build was suited for the climbing and tumbling that he used in his dances. In the early 1960s, when he first began to create his works, he was associated with the Judson Dance Theater, which often appeared at Judson Memorial Church in lower Manhattan. Subsequently he showed pieces in varieties of locales, none of which were conventional theaters. In recent years he has tended to show less and less interest in choreography, but his works made a strong impression in those rebellious years when new styles of movement were first challenging the old canons of modern dance tradition.

LEADVILLE

Choreography by Alex Hay. Set to a voice/sound tape collage by Alex Hay. Scenery, costumes, and lighting by Alex Hay. First performed in New York City at the First New York Theater Rally, Eighty-first Street and Broadway, spring, 1965, by Alex Hay.

The television studio at Broadway and Eighty-first Street in Manhattan has seen a wide variety of theater productions from "Sesame Street" to forgotten soap operas, but never so unusual a collection of pieces as were included in the "First New York Theater Rally." This was a collaborative effort by dancers and painters to show off the range of new dances and approaches to theater that had occupied their energies for the previous half-dozen years. Hay presented the premiere of this dance.

A man is seen perched atop a long silver pole. He is wearing a silver costume and silver body paint with a tape recorder strapped to his back, giving the impression of being a robot. Slowly he begins to descend the pole and to approach the ground. A measured countdown of intoned numbers is heard as he nears the audience's level. When he plants his feet on the ground securely, he begins to walk slowly forward toward the audience. The feeling is absolutely eerie like the approach of a being from another planet.

He gropes and tests the ground tentatively as a voice from his tape recorder intones the deliberately spaced words "I . . . wish . . . I . . . were . . . a . . ." The intervals between the words are filled with the sound of rushing feet. The man himself advances with tiny jumps. Suddenly a popular song, "Red Roses for a Blue Lady," is heard and he breaks into a cumbersome social step, extending his arms as if to grasp a partner though he is alone. There is a trail of brown recording tape pouring onto the floor from the point that he began to step forward from the pole. There is no pickup reel, and the silver-plated man is bleeding sound before the audience's eyes. He moves forward again and then with a fierce pride drops to his knees and makes a traversing movement with his extended arm as the clatter of machine-gun fire is heard. By the time the last bit of tape is expelled he lies prone and inert.

The piece had a strong emotional wallop as the creature expressed a wish to be a "mountain" or a "mesa" while hopping forward. He came into the audience's world from his perch, announced his aspirations, but was forced to dance, and then expired leaving an exhausted trail of recording tape.

CHOREOCHRONICLE
OF ALEX HAY

1962

   Rafladan (with Deborah Hay and
     Charles Rotmil)

1963

   Prairie

1964

   Colorado Plateau
   Rio Grande

1965

   *Leadville

1966

Topsoil
Field Calling
Talk, Listen, Do

1967

Grassfield

1970

Beach Description

1971

Ann Brinstein
Breakfast

1973

Earshot Argument

DEBORAH HAY

As a child growing up in Brooklyn, Hay was given her first dance instruction at the age of three by her mother. She began teaching the child tap dancing. Years later, after Hay had studied at the Henry Street Settlement Playhouse, had performed with the José Limón company at Connecticut College, and toured with the Merce Cunningham company, she choreographed a tap dance in one of her own pieces and dedicated it to her mother. It was a sweet, sentimental gesture coming in the midst of the extreme experimental movement that she was involved with.

Hay first approached dance with a highly disciplined and dedicated professionalism, which she was later to abandon in favor of a more natural style of movement. She gradually began to use fewer and fewer professionally trained dancers in her pieces and recruit performers from whatever group she was among. In recent years this has meant a commune group for which she devised protofolk dances to be done by the group. While simple technically they are extremely pleasant to do and display an intelligent ordering of elements. Though she rarely makes concert appearances, she has written a book describing ten of these circle dances with instructions as to their performance. Throughout her career she has been concerned with threads of communication between people in moving situations, and the book seems to be another message sent out over her creative lines.

WOULD THEY OR WOULDN'T THEY?

Choreography by Deborah Hay. First performed at the Judson Memorial Church, New York, N.Y., November 10, 1963, by Alex Hay, Deborah Hay, David Lee, and Yvonne Rainer.

The title vaguely suggests the classic male musing about an unknown female, and the dance intriguingly sets two men who are not trained dancers to working with two women who are. The dress for each is street clothing.

With a stirring peal of march music two men crawl out with two women hanging on them. The men go off to stand on their heads inside a trapezoid pipe construction while the women run off to dance alone. The men hang on a heavy rope as long as they are able. They are motionless except for a slight, uncontrollable swaying motion. The women, on the other hand, are full of dancy, saucy motion and perform around them. When their strength gives out, the men fall to the floor. The women stop dancing and sit crouched with their knees up.

In the next portion of the dance the men become the active ones and the women remain immobile. In turn the women call the men by their first names. At the summons the man goes to the woman, picks her up, still in the crouched position, and deposits her at another point in the room. The men retire to lie head to head and butt one another a bit, rise up, and jostle again, while the ignored women dance pretty little figures alone. At the start of the dance the women were dependent burdens to be dragged around and then insistent burdens demanding to be carried, and finally are just pushed out of the men's consideration all together. They perform their actions inside the "fortress" of the pipe construction while the women make little pathetic flying motions outside like moths at a lantern. Throughout the men have not shown the slightest interest in the women as persons. To conclude, all grasp one of the pipe sections and hang side by side slightly swaying.

There is an air of quiet and intense desperation in the work that is covered by the cool, dispassionate performing level at which it is conducted. The women's voices do not even betray a hint of emotional interest in the men whose names they call. One is reminded of the phrase "quiet desperation."

TEN

Choreography by Deborah Hay. First performed at the Anderson Theater, New York, N.Y., April 4, 1968, by Suzanne Brockman, Christos Giankos, John Griefen, Helen Harrington, Tony Holder, Mimi Miller, Forrest Myers, Steve Paxton, Edwin Schlossberg, and Simone (Forti) Whitman.

In the spring of 1968 an adventurous entity called "Midsummer Inc." presented a series of dance concerts at the Anderson Theater in lower Manhattan. The moving force behind the group was Christophe (De Menil) (Thurman) Marca-Relli, who had sponsored a series of experimental events the previous summer in Easthampton, Long Island. With an advanced taste for graphic art she displayed an understandable enthusiasm for vanguard choreographers and asked Hay to do two concerts.

The stage is traversed by a horizontal metal pole four feet above the floor, confining the colorfully dressed rock musicians to the back quarter of the stage and freeing the dancers to work in the front portion. A vertical pole rises from the center of the stage and disappears upward into the flies. There are three groups of performers: a couple, a trio of women, and five men. All are dressed in white, contrasting sharply with the musicians. Each group has to stay together but can perform any series of exercises that it wishes to do at the signal of anyone of the group. If the horizontal pole is used by the person who wishes to become the leader, then all others have to replicate his stance farther along the pole. If the vertical pole is chosen as the starting point, then all of the others have to attach themselves to the person in front of them in a chain of links as identical as possible. It is a game, and the performers are like bits of sentient cork bobbing around in the din-filled sea of sound created by the amplified musicians.

The dance tested their ability to signal to and communicate with one another to the utmost. It was relatively easy to pick up the visual cues by glancing right and left, but dissolving a chain emanating from the vertical pole was accomplished by a shout from the last person to form a link. The shout was often difficult to hear.

The dance had a rowdy charm of tracking, stalking and playfulness, and Hay repeated it successfully in several places, including a gallery in Rome. It was a piece that came halfway in her emergence from disciplined traditional dancing to the open, freer form that her work was to assume in its participational phase, dances that are really more like classes than performances.

HALF-TIME

Choreographed by Deborah Hay. First performed at the Whitney Museum of American Art, New York, N.Y., February 24, 1969, by Carol Alexander, Winnie Bellaar-Spruyt, Sylvia D'Arcangelo, Tina Girouard, Helen Harrington, Deborah Hollingworth, Haru, Joan Jonas, Julie Judd, Epp Kotkas, Gina Kravitz, Jane Lahr, Jean Lawless, Barbara Lipper, Jane Marasco, Susan Marshall, Karla Munger, Debra Pelletier, Kate Rediker, Carol Ross, Dorothy Sibley, Leni Silverstein, Susann Weiner, Rima Wolff, and Wendy Ann Yujuico.

One of the liveliest buildings in New York is the Whitney Museum of American Art on Madison Avenue. Its exterior façade is plain and broken only by a couple of large windows that protrude like eccentric bay windows, and inside it has broad, unbroken expanses of floor space. The floor is stone and the ceilings are high and the white walls set off anything that they enclose. It was in one such gallery that Hay decided to display the beauty of twenty-five women, all of whom were asked to dress as they would when attending an art opening, traditionally a time for bright-colored and festive clothing.

The dance is delightfully simple, consisting of columns of women moving to and away from one another, sometimes toward the audience and at others away from it. Small clusters break off to gather at various sections of the room, and climactically all spread out into a huge wheeling circle.

The movement is flowing and lyrical, and there is no feeling of urgency or hurry connected with it. It is a languid demonstration of beautiful women in easily made and easily unmade formations.

The "art scene" in New York is one that Hay was familiar with through her husband and their close relationship with Robert Rauschenberg, among others. Artists and dancers had worked together from the beginning of the 1960s, so the idea of using friends, female artists, and wives of male artists in a citadel of art sounded like a logical art crowd activity. The result was a stunning, joyful, and sensuous celebration of female beauty.

CHOREOCHRONICLE
OF DEBORAH HAY

1962

Rain Fur
5 Things
Rafladan (with Alex Hay and
    Charles Rotmil)

1963

City Dance
All Day Dance
*Elephant Footprints in the
    Cheesecake* (with Fred Herko)
*Would They or Wouldn't They?
    (renamed *They Will* [with Fred
    Herko], 1964)

1964

All Day Dance for Two
Three Here
Victory 14

1965

Hill

1966

No. 3
Serious Duet
Rise
Solo

1967

Flyer
Group I

1968

Group II
*Ten

1969

*Half-Time
*20 Permutations of 2 Sets of 3
    Equal Parts in a Linear Pattern*
*Deborah Hay with a Large Group
    Outdoors*
*26 Variations on 8 Activities for
    13 People plus Beginning and
    Ending*

1970

*Deborah Hay and a Large Group
    of People from Hartford*
20 Minute Dance

1971

Deborah Hay and "The Farm"

1972

*Wedding Dance for Sandy and
    Greg*

ELIZABETH KEEN

As a child, Keen took ballet class but did not find herself committed to dancing as a career. During her second year at Radcliffe College she decided that she did want to study dancing more seriously and transferred to Barnard College in Manhattan. She studied through the rest of her college years and upon graduating became a member of the Tamiris-Nagrin company. After leaving it she joined the Paul Taylor company for a year's touring.

She began to have the desire to create her own pieces and so left to work privately. Her first works were presented at Judson Memorial Church in the early sixties. She has been a restless experimenter, trying various combinations of film, movement, voice recitation, jazz, and nearly everything else one can think of to shape her dances. She is strongly attracted by drama and has worked to devise movement for several Off-Broadway productions. She has also worked with neighborhood groups in presenting street theater.

In her best works there is a wry irony that draws smiles as well as grimaces, and she has a wickedly deft sense of humor. There seems to be no space too difficult for her to consider as suitable for dance. In addition to working out of doors, she has used conventional theater space and even a roof top as locales for dances. Everything is grist for her choreographic mill.

QUILT
(REVISED)

Choreography by Elizabeth Keen. Set to traditional music. Costumes by William Burdick. Quilts by Sarah Freidman, Sarah Kurshan, Davidson Lloyd, Barbara Roan, someone in northern Vermont, and Beverly Emmons' great-grandmother. Film by Kirk Smallman. First performed at the Judson Dance Theater, New York, N.Y., February 13, 1971, by William Burdick (guest artist), Blondell Cummings, Elizabeth Keen, Anthony LaGiglia, Davidson Lloyd, Paula Lucas, Anne Maybury, Laura Powell, Barbara Roan, Debra Austin, Thomas Cahill, John Tarrell, Jim Frost, Renee McCoy, Frank Pastritto, Linda Pernise, Sharon Powers, Richard Schmonsees, and Ricardo Velez; and by guitarist John Orlando and lutenist Laura Spiegel. An earlier version was presented at the New School for Social Research in 1970.

The décor for the dance was one of the prettiest that ever was seen at Judson Memorial Church and consisted of a half-dozen original quilts of varying sizes affixed to a long white curtain. In addition there were color projections of quilts.

Two horizontal rows of three dancers each roll slowly forward like a giant log as bagpipe music is heard. A trio of two women and a man enter to do a jig at the center and also to create a series of hand gestures that suggest knot tying. They are joined by those who rolled forward.

A lute and guitar player enter. The lute player is seated on the back of one of the dancers who rolled forward. After a brief musical interlude they leave and a mature couple enters, then a younger couple, and then an even younger pair. It is a parade of generations as each moves toward and then away from the audience. They join hands in a circle and then separate to do a folk dance. There are traditionally costumed dancers and those in contemporary jeans and solid-colored shirts. The traditional do a short jig, and then those in jeans take over to sweep to and fro. They do playful things, athletic little jumps, and then a sewing gesture that ties them all together. After this has been accomplished one man calls for scissors and all go off.

The three who did the original jig return to do a reprise variation. A couple in "mod" purple enters to try to embrace one another, but each breaks away from the arms of the other. The jumble of clothing styles and the colors are a patchwork quilt of dazzling energy rivaling the real quilts on the walls. All are joined together, the older couple leading the assemblage in a minuet. The floor is dappled with moving colors and concludes with the dancers all joining hands.

One of the nicest things about the dance was the way traditional dances, carefully reconstructed, were joined with contemporary choreography. The ages of the performers ranged over several decades reinforcing the inclusiveness of the dance's intent. Even the quilts themselves were a mixture of contemporary work and traditional. Keen stitched the whole together imaginatively and with great discretion and wit.

POISON VARIATIONS

Choreography by Elizabeth Keen. Music by Gwendolyn Watson and Joel Press. First performed at the Manhattan School of Music, New York, N.Y., April 9, 1970, by Elizabeth Keen, Laura Pawel, Ted Striggles, and Davidson Lloyd.

During one season Keen was working at Stratford, Connecticut, and began speculating about the character of Hamlet's mother, the Queen. "What if the Queen were really an accomplice to the plot to murder her husband and not an innocent bystander?" Keen took the idea and made a short dance episode in which poison is poured in the ear of another while the Queen is present. The section was included in the final dance, which was expanded to include a variety of episodes in which people turn on one another with harming intent which stops well short of murder.

The four dancers, two women and two men, enact various ambiguous situations that may or may not have serious import. In one section they display a plastic body petulance by holding the configurations that result from stamping a foot on the ground. In another section a warmly sexy woman dances while the other three make hostile chops and thrusts at her without her being aware of the activity behind her back. A man furtively strings an imaginary bow and another raises an arm as if to strike her.

The last variations of the dance contain some of her most felicitous movement inventions. A trio of two men and a woman perform a series of involved supports and lifts for one another that suggest beautiful shapes rather than individuals dancing. They assist one another and the center of their attention is on what they are doing, with scarcely a thought as to why they are doing it. Even when a particularly complicated lift is missed, they smoothly press on. In the final segment the two men assume the positions they had in a variation at the start of the piece which involved a series of falls and catches. This time, as one man launches into a forward fall expecting to be caught, the other man steps indifferently aside and the man slams down prone. Blackout!

The acid wit of the piece is carried in a cradle of headlong movement that tumbles its performers from one situation into another with scarcely any time for a respite. It is amusing to see the dancers co-operate with one another at one moment and then at another decline to offer the needed support. The resulting pratfall is funny, but the abandonment has an element of the tragic. It is the interplay of the two that gives the piece its special force.

A POLITE ENTERTAINMENT
FOR LADIES AND GENTLEMEN

Choreography by Elizabeth Keen. Music by Stephen Foster. Costumes by Whitney Blausen. Lighting by Jim Harrison. First performed at the City Center Downstairs, New York, N.Y., February 15, 1975, by Janis Ainsley, Jennifer Donahue, Dalienne Majors, Avi Davis, Michael Rivera, and Ted Striggles.

The advent of the two-hundred-year existence of the United States as an independent nation has unleashed an incredible amount of patriotic energy. The Bicentennial celebrations began officially the year before the actual anniversary and Keen was one of the early starters. She first showed this humorous dance to the lovely airs of Steven Foster's songs in February, almost a full year before the Bicentennial was to tune up to its full pitch.

The dance is for six couples and the costuming is period American of the nineteenth century. The men wear trousers, full shirts, and striking suspenders, and the women full ballroom gowns with pantaloons underneath. The couples form tableaux and melt from one to another; the men appear to talk and the women whisper. A couple dances a romantic duet that starts with backbends to the floor and ends with her carried off languishing. The "Regret" of the second movement is poignantly obvious as the couple just never seems to be on the same track. When he kneels she is standing, and vice versa.

The full company returns to join together in a jolly, hearty dance that is sweetly jingoistic and simplistic in its attitudes, but then the whole of the dance plays unashamedly on the nostalgia for the settled order of an older time and also rags it a bit at the same time. This is followed by a period of adoring glances and furtive touches of the hands to the song "Beautiful Dreamer." The touch of the adored's hand more often than not sends the adorer fleeing in the opposite direction, and one man who secures his adored turns to lead her away and finds that she has slipped his arm for another. The three women join together, dance delicately in unison, and then humorously reveal that they are not completely ethereal as they become relatively athletic. The men follow with a fist-clenched dance that boosts the virtues of sobriety.

A woman enters with two men and she flirts with them in turn to the song "If You Only Had a Mustache." One of them actually does and steals her away. A man finds himself being berated by a woman because he is late home. She storms at him but underneath does not really mean all of the things that she indicates by her accusing gestures. Their reconciliation is capped by a lift in which she appears to be as light as a feather. The company returns individually, one man attends a woman, and another man taps him on the shoulder with a flower, using the gesture one would at a social dance when cutting in. At another point two women cry, a third extends her foot, and a man places a rose between her toes. Soon dancers are producing roses unexpectedly and continuously. One woman steals around and gathers them in a humorously greedy manner and sweeps around with two handfuls at the conclusion of the episode. The final section finds the couples doing a social dance and then forming several tableaux as they had at the beginning.

The tongue-in-cheek dance is one that is awfully difficult to sustain successfully throughout its length. Keen manages it marvelously in this work, which combines the innocence of another age with the knowing irony of a later age. She is able to celebrate the way things were and also to wittily point out some of the flaws in bygone attitudes. The competition between individuals was just as fierce then, but there was an overlay of manners which kept the raw nerves sheathed rather than allowing them to be exposed. One laughs and one winces a little as well.

CHOREOCHRONICLE
OF ELIZABETH KEEN

1962

Dawning
Sea Tangle
The Perhapsy
Match

1963

Bird Poem
Blinkers
Reins
Formalities

1965

Suite in C Minor
Red Sweater Dance
One X Four

1967

Scanning
Short Circuit
Stop Gap
Rushes
Attics
Recipe

1968

Sub-Sun
Everyman

1969

Point
West Side Story (mc)
Mime Hamlet (p)
Mr. Estaban (p)

1970

*Poison Variations
The Train (Irish epic)
Quilt
On Edge

1971

*Quilt (revised)
Parentheses

1972

Act Without words, No. 2
Tempo
The Unravish'd Bride

1973

Mini-Quilt

1975

Open Parenthesis
Pale Cool—Pale Warm
Close Parenthesis
Dancing to Records
*A Polite Entertainment for Ladies
*   and Gentlemen*

CLIFF KEUTER

There is a touch of antic madness about Keuter's work that makes one think of surrealist theater. He is enormously fond of using all sorts of props, and one of his favorites is the plastic brown helmet liner that the Army uses to cushion soldiers' heads from their protective steel helmets. Keuter likes the way that they can be stacked and pushed around and the clattering noise that they make when tossed on the floor.

He was born in Idaho and had a country boy's upbringing, which included outdoor sports like fishing as well as the more conventional games that boys play. There always seem to be echoes of his childhood and young manhood running through his work in the form of footloose playfulness. His first dance training came in San Francisco, where his family moved, and he studied with Welland Lathrop, who taught composition as well as technique.

Keuter later moved to New York, where he studied with Helen Tamiris and Daniel Nagrin and was eventually taken into the Paul Taylor company. He toured with it for two years before deciding to leave and establish his own performing ensemble. Since that time he has made regular appearances and has created the repertory of his company.

THE GAME MAN AND THE LADIES

Choreography by Cliff Keuter. Music by Ezra Sims. Scenery by Tom Gardner. Costumes by Cliff Keuter. Lighting by Nicholas Wolff Lyndon. First performed at the Minor Latham Playhouse, New York, N.Y., October 1969, by Cliff Keuter as the Man, *and Irene Feigenheimer, Elina Mooney, and Janet Aaron as the* Ladies.

This was the first dance that Keuter created for his newly formed company and was in its way a declaration of independence. It is based on human, indeed humorously tangled human, relationships, a subject that has been of constant interest to Keuter, and it sets one man into the midst of three women.

A man enters in swimming trunks. Two women loll around in bikini bathing suits. He looks at one and then another, they throw themselves at him and he tries to give his attention first to one and then another, but it becomes almost impossible and he pushes them away but at the same time runs a caressing hand along their bodies passionately. He then goes to devote his entire attention to reading a newspaper but interrupts it long enough to kiss one of them.

In the second portion a third woman joins and he and she worriedly and actively crumple newspapers and stuff them into each other's costumes so that they are puffed out. They embrace with a soft crumpling sound while the two other women frolic as they had done previously. One presents him with a broom and he grasps it firmly. Before he can do anything else, his partner places her hand on the handle above his, and then he does the same in the way that children will do in order to be the "top hand" on the handle and be able to choose teammates for a game. While the two dance the other women pick up the papers in the littered space and pluck the crumpled papers out of the couple's costumes.

The round of activity continues with the man continually indecisive about which, if any, girl he really wants to spend any time with. One of the women enters with a basketball beneath her shirt looking pregnant. He takes it away and treats it like a baby. He does a solo full of leaps and pounces. He wears a helmet liner, two of the women simulate gigantic breasts by inserting them beneath their shirts. He opens an umbrella and then partners two of them but can only give his full attention to one, and the other just hangs on, and then both slide off as he dons a stack of helmet liners and tosses one noisily over his shoulder into the wings. He is alone at last with his warlike gear.

Many of Keuter's dances show an indecisive man alternating between several women, unable to choose one or another. In this case he starts out looking like a beach boy or a lifeguard and concludes as a paramilitary figure, but throughout projects images of masculinity. Even though it is an undecided man, the game is still the pursuit of women. It is a game that all seem to enjoy, the pursued as well as the pursuer.

CHOREOCHRONICLE
OF CLIFF KEUTER

1963

Collapse of Tall Towers
Entrances

1964

Atsumori

1965

As It Was, Love
After a While, Love

1966

A Cold Sunday Afternoon, A
*   Little Later*
The Orange Dance
Now What, Love
White Shirt
Cross-Play
Hold

1967

Beyond Night
Eight

1968

Small Room
Dangling Man
Three-sided Peach Viewed
*   Variously Three Hours of the*
*   Day of the Plastic Garment Bag*

1969

*The Game Man and the Ladies
Letter to Paul
Dream a Little Dream of Me,
*   Sweetheart*

1970

Sunday Papers
Three for Four Plus One
Twice
Now Is the Hour in the Wild
*   Garden*
Crown Blessed
Bread, And the Proudest Man
*   Around*
A Snake in Uncle Sammy's
*   Garden*

1971

Amazing Grace
Gargoyles
Wood
Old Harry
Poem in October
If You Want Meditation, You
*   Have to Work for It*
Fall Gently on Thy Head

1972

New Baroque
I Want Somebody, Yes I Do
Match
Hold III
Poles
Passage
Cui Bono
A Christmas Story

1973

Unusual in Our Time
Musete di Taverni
Plaisirs d'Amour
Visit

1974

Restatement of Romance

1975

The Murder of George Keuter
Voice
Burden of Vision
Station

KENNETH KING

In college King majored in philosophy but was irresistibly drawn to dance. When he moved to New York in the early 1960s, he became part of an experimental group of dancers and choreographers which comprised Phoebe Neville, Meredith Monk, Gus Solomons, Jr., Elizabeth Keen, and Cliff Keuter. Frequently they appeared in each other's works, and though they shared a dissatisfaction with the then current trends in the dance world, each forged an individual creative path. King's work has tended to be highly cerebral and to exhibit an existential feeling of anxiety. His dance characterizations suggest a powerless loneliness, and his means of expressing this have been unique. At times he has remained rooted in one spot for the entire duration of the dance and at other times he has dislayed a hyperactive restlessness expressed frequently in relentless whirling. Toward the end of the sixties he began to work strongly with words and monologues, developing highly personal usages for syntax and spelling and also creating a series of alter egos. During one concert at which he was scheduled to appear he showed up disguised in a laboratory technician's coat and a mask and delivered a letter to the sponsor to say that he was being held prisoner and could not appear. The sponsor, who had never met him, was deceived. His work has become highly idiosyncratic, but the power of his early work clearly expressed his talent.

BLOW-OUT

Choreography by Kenneth King. Music by Mozart and Handel. First performed at the Judson Memorial Church, New York, N.Y., April 5, 1966, by Kenneth King and Laura Dean.

The piece was one of those imaginative assemblages that turned up with regularity on co-operative programs in the mid-1960s. Choreographers of a wide variety were trying out all sorts of creative approaches, some of which were unsuccessful and others of which were exceptionally well conceived. It was at such a concert at the Bridge Theater (now defunct) that I encountered a first, telling version of this piece. It was performed at the time in a solo version but was given frequently in its duet form.

A man in black leather with dark sunglasses sits in a chair at the center of the stage. His jacket is of the heavy black leather favored by motorcyclists, and so are his boots. He wears large leather gauntlets, and there are elastic lines running out from the end of each finger to anchor posts on the walls of the theater. His every gesture has a cosmic thrust, since he seems to occupy the entire space of the theater.

He tips back as one hears the "Gloria" from a mass. He is lost in a mental transport but rises when the sound is replaced by a single tone. He opens his mouth and small white cubes fall out. He begins to struggle in place, tugging and twisting, but he is caught in an elastic web. He drops to the floor with his mouth open in a wordless howl and spread-eagles himself on the floor in the same way that he stretched out his arms and legs when he was tilting back on the chair. It gives one the impression of a great interstellar tumble such as that taken by Lucifer in his fall from heaven.

The man rises and is changed, he seems more human scaled in his movements as he does a twitchy, flailing rock-and-roll dance to the "Alleluia Chorus" from *Messiah* and then concludes in a crouched, fetal headstand.

With his incredible performing presence King made this brief solo cosmic in its scope. He was the classic figure who at first is transported in the glory of still contemplation and winds up listening to the drumming of his own inner pulse and arrives at profane movement to sacred music. The fall from the one to the other took place in a short span and in a restricted space but was no less effective for its modest scale.

CHOREOCHRONICLE
OF KENNETH KING

1964

cup/saucer/two dancers/radio

1965

Spectacular
Self-Portrait: Dedicated to the
    Memory of John Fitzgerald
    Kennedy

1966

m-o-o-n-b-r-a-i-n and superlecture
Camouflage
*Blow-out

1971

Untitled

1972

Metagexis (Joseph's Song)
Anyone's Guest is Nobody's Guess
Patrick's Dansing Dances

1973

Inadmissleable Evident-dance

1974

Praxiomatics

1975

Battery

PHYLLIS LAMHUT

Born in New York on the lower East Side, Lamhut received her first dance training at the Henry Street Settlement Playhouse when it was directed by Alwin Nikolais. She was invited to join his company and was a featured dancer with it from its beginning in 1948. She remained with the company until 1969, when she left to pursue her independent choreographic career more intensively. She has been making dances almost from her first years with the Nikolais company, and continued when she joined Murray Louis's company. She has also studied at the Merce Cunningham studio and ballet with Zena Rommett and Peter Saul. Her special performing quality is revealed in her tough and very special humor. While working on her own choreography she continues to teach at the Louis-Nikolais Dance Theater Laboratory.

HOUSE

Choreography by Phyllis Lamhut. Music by Steve Reich. Scenery by George Trakas. Costumes by Frank Garcia. First performed at Barnard College, New York, N.Y., November 19, 1971, by Phyllis Lamhut, Donald Blumenfeld, and Rolando Pena.

During and after her long association with the Alwin Nikolais and later the Murray Louis company, Lamhut created pieces of her own, which she presented on full evenings of her own or on co-operative concerts. She is often thought of as a dancer with a special gift for comedy, which she has, but there is often a darker underpinning to her work which is expressed clearly in this work.

At the rear of the stage stands a tiny house with a large door. A big, blaring, jolly circus march is heard, and two men standing at the front of the stage lift up a large rectangular frame with a tissue stretched over it. Everyone waits expectantly to see someone come crashing triumphantly through, but nothing happens. A second march fanfare is heard and again nothing happens. A third strikes up but once again expectations are disappointed. Then a voice is heard to encourage the unseen performer, "Come out to show them." The phrase is repeated over and over again and finally a woman steps out of the little house.

She does not release the door handle and steps quickly back inside. She opens the door again and steps out and again decides that she does not want to leave her secure home and darts back in, closing the door. The voice which has been repeating the encouragement to "Come out to show them" has now been electronically blurred so that it is almost a pure rhythm devoid of sense. She comes out and closes the door with some determination. She parts from the house and runs in small circles, waving coyly from time to time, and then retreats inside but leaves the door open, though she pulls it shut a moment later. On her next venture out she does a headstand against the door and says, "No! No! Yes! Yes!," suddenly rights herself, pulls it open, and shouts inside. She stands with her back to the audience making her hands tremble and shrieks. She breaks away to run up and down, crossing and recrossing the stage area, and breaks into a fixed purposeful jog in a circle and crashes through the tissue to lie flat, spent. The two men who held the frame carry it off and dismantle the house and remove it. There is nothing left except the woman lying alone on the stage.

The piece began with the expectation of spectacular feats delivered with an almost garish flourish. When nothing happened that remotely resembled a spectacular presentation, the irony of the ordinary contrasted with the theatricalized began to be demonstrated. The dancer did not want to leave the shelter of the dwelling but was coaxed out and then used the last of her energy to make the circus leap through the tissue. The setting was decidedly unusual, and Lamhut's lean economy of gesture was wonderfully effective in presenting the tragic humor of the work.

CHOREOCHRONICLE
OF PHYLLIS LAMHUT

1950

Nostalgia

1951

Incantation of Greed

1952

Annoyous Insectator

1953

Theme and Variations
Periphery of Armor
Cameo

1954

Lady of the Aviary
Interlude

1955

Hex
Clock
Gemeni
Loreli
2 Dances

1956

Stick Figure
Sleep
Lament
Tragedienne
Ritual

1957

Reverie
Excursion
Coif
Suite
Willow
Trifoliate

1958

Unmirrored

1959

Hands
Lavella
Cebrina
Ceremonial

1960

Pastel

1961

Herald
Fanfare
Portrait
March

1962

Trilogy
Tocsin

1963

Group
Shift
Recession
Touch Dance

1964

Computer Piece

1965

3 Dance Movements
Ostinato
Fickle Idol

1966

Viods
Monody
Incidentals

1967

Come on and Trip

1969

Space Time Code

1970

Big Feature
Extended Voices

1971

*House
Area I
Field of View
Act I

1972

Congeries
Scene Shift
Two Planes
Dance Hole

1973

Terra Angelica
Z Twiddle
OTD (*Off Track Dancing*)

1974

Medium Coeli
Late Show
Country Mozart

1975

Theatre Piece (Untitled)
Solo with Company (Work in
    Progress)
Hearts of Palm
Conclave

MURRAY LOUIS

After service in the Navy during World War II, Louis began his college studies at San Francisco State, but left after the first year to return to his birthplace, New York. While in San Francisco he had the opportunity to study with Ann Halprin and during the rest of his college career, at New York University, he studied with Alwin Nikolais at the Henry Street Settlement Playhouse. After graduation he joined the staff of the Playhouse and has worked with Nikolais steadily ever since, although he formed his own company for independent touring.

He has choreographed regularly for the concert stage since the mid-1950s and has appeared frequently on television with the Nikolais company and with his own dancers. In addition he has produced a series of films illustrating his own approach to technique and choreography. His touring has carried him throughout North and South America as well as Europe, the Middle East, and the Far East. As a performer, he is unique in his muscular control. He is able to produce spasms and ripples of movement seemingly without any overt anticipatory preparation and then allow them to subside just as quickly and without any apparent effort. His sense of comic timing is extraordinarily precise, neat, and pertinent.

JUNK DANCES

Choreography by Murray Louis. Tape collage of popular and operatic music. Décor by Robert Wilson. First performed at the Henry Street Settlement Playhouse, November 11, 1964, by Murray Louis, Phyllis Lamhut, Susan Buirge, Ann Carlton, Mimi Garrard, and Janet Strader.

When the score card of enduring dances has been compiled, there will certainly be an entry for this work. It has been of the favorites of the Louis repertory since it was first performed in 1964. It has an urban setting of such distinguished squalor that it immediately brings a smile to one's face. Here is the underside of the sophisticated world where ordinary citizens live and buffet one another according to the programming provided by the latest in advertising suggestions.

A fireplug and a trash can stand down near the front of the stage and a tenement wall is the backdrop. The man of the house wears a jaunty straw hat and sips beer from a can while resting one foot on a table. Three windows with shades pierce the wall. The mistress of the house is a mass of flossy clothes. The window shades are lifted to reveal legs of other dancers and they start a short variation. A happy popular tune is heard, the man dances a solo, and then his wife displays herself in full control of this faded ambiance of proletarian elegance.

Four women enter twirling brooms as they stare straight ahead, seemingly with most of their attention on an unseen television set. The man and wife return: he wears a top hat and velvet evening clothes, she is a blousy glamour girl in a gray leotard with an outrageous corset stitched on it. Their duet is like a tintype version of a popular dance. It is a contest of will for domination, and between punching him she bats her huge, overlong eyelashes. He is almost driven to punch her back but gives her a big kiss and they part.

The women return with gayly colored shopping bags containing assorted clothes and dress themselves in a parody of show style as the wife plants paper flowers in an outrageous pot. During their first "broom" interlude the wife "laid" a box of cornflakes like a chicken, and now she returns, mouth moving silently a mile a minute, to perform a solo detailing the difficulties of her day with excerpts of household work actions. When her husband returns, he somehow manages to catch his arm awkwardly inside one of the legs of his tights. She secures an awful yellow tie around his neck and ties a sexy scarf around her own leg. He is now thoroughly cornered, and the other women enter to festoon him with boxes of food and washing products and finally slip a construction like a Christmas tree over him that has flashing red lights on it. He is completely trapped.

The piece cleverly polarizes the role of provider and providee. He is the poor unthinking husband who was happy at the beginning of the piece sipping his beer in humble contentment, but by the end of the piece has been thoroughly locked into his role as worker and wage earner whose job it is to fill up their lives with the objects that advertising suggests are necessary for gracious and not so gracious living. She meanwhile concentrates on her assigned role of glamour at any cost. It's a parody of married life but close enough to cause a certain discomfort through the laughter.

CHARADE
(CHIMERA)

Choreography by Murray Louis. Music by Alwin Nikolais. Scenery and costumes by Margo Hoff. First performed at the Henry Street Settlement Playhouse, New York, N.Y., February 25, 1966, by Murray Louis.

Louis is undoubtedly one of the most talented dancers of his generation, possessing a supple muscular control that enables him to move in such a way that parts of his body seem independent of one another. This solo, which he created, takes full advantage of his special talents.

Toward the rear of the stage a large cloth is hung with three apertures in it. The first is dome shaped and the height of a man; the second has a similar shape but only reveals the body from the waist down; and the third is a small circle at head height. Behind it a figure is costumed from ankles to eyes in stretch jersey which is bulged out at odd places through the placement of his hands inside it. He moves across behind the cloth from the largest opening toward the smaller, and the audience sees less and less of him until only his face appears in the circular hole. He is like a mysterious creature of unusual conformation and imperceptibly slow locomotion.

He appears now in front of the cloth in a costume covered with triangles and does a twitchy little introduction to his solo, which suggests an ordinary person and not an exceptional creature at all. He brushes himself and dusts off imaginary lint, he mimes throwing a ball, and then begins to include motions that suggest the partially glimpsed movements of the first portion inside the stretch jersey. He moves behind the cloth as if he wants to hide. The audience sees an arm or a leg in a momentary flex or stretch. He reappears in the same costume to dance again, but this time in more flowing and expansive gestures, but before he returns to the security of the cloth he makes a little drumming motion on his forehead as he had done in the previous "everyday life" solo. Succumbing to an inner uge, he goes back behind the cloth to perform the variation he did in the stretch jersey but without the protective sheath.

The dance suggests varieties of role playing and the ways that people go about disguising themselves from others and perhaps themselves. Beneath the surface of anyone, the dance suggests, there lies a whole unknown world if one could only penetrate to it.

HOOPLA

Choreography by Murray Louis. Set to traditional music played by the Lisbon State Police Band. Costumes by Frank Garcia. First performed at the Brooklyn Academy of Music, Brooklyn, N.Y., January 26, 1972, by Murray Louis, Michael Ballard, Anne Ditson, Les Ditson, Helen Kent, Robert Small, and Marcia Wardell.

The music used is that of a Portuguese police band, and the title is an old stagecoach drivers' expression to get teams of horses moving. Colloquially the term indicates great excitement, and the piece has a great deal of that. It is a series of skits in outrageously clever costumes backed by marvelously evocative slide projections.

The melodious blare of the overture announces the beginning of the show as three men and three women do deep knee bends while large playing cards are projected on the screen behind them. They unfurl small banners with illustrations of circus scenes. A man walks on encased in a large tube of cloth from neck to ankles, and they decorate him with the banners as if he were a kiosk. They line up and pose for the audience's attention like extravagant performers, and suddenly they produce little pennants with such words as "Amazing" and the like. They then unfurl a long cloth with people's shapes painted on it except for the heads. They each select a particular shape to go with a face and stand behind it in a line. They leave, followed by the man in the cloth tube who spins off in a pretty blur of flying pennants. The whole feeling of the work is silly good fun like a real circus.

The man returns and after slipping out of the cloth tube does a long, slow solo, climbs back into the tube, and exits. A ringmaster appears, making great leaps and flourishes, and is joined by two women in fluffy caps. They are succeeded by a man in a safari outfit complete with pith helmet who carries a tiny folding chair and a miniature whip with which he attempts to tame a three-headed creature who slithers along and blithely ignores him. The creature is made up of three dancers, each encased in a long tube, and the ends of the three are secured. The creature undulates like a caterpillar and nearly turns itself inside out before it leaves. The man in the safari jacket returns in a costume with a large star on the chest and dances an athletic duet with another man and they seem like two acrobats.

They are followed by three women and two men with capes, masks, and toques all in black. These are the magicians, and they suddenly begin to produce small objects, a scarf, an egg, and a bird, then smoothly create the setting of a puppet theater with their cloaks. They swirl from place to place doing more conjuring tricks, and then they dash away. The next skit has a flower growing rapidly out of a box at the center of the stage, and the man who brought out the box feels threatened. He hefts an ax and takes a mighty swing to dispatch it but the flower ducks and survives. Following this are the tumblers in a beautifully designed adagio in which one woman is manipulated and never allowed to touch the ground by her two attendants. The long robes of the costumes are wonderfully decorative. A man in a dazzling silver suit does a happy, exuberant solo, and then in the finale all of the creatures of the circus take part in the concluding parade.

Louis discovered the music while on tour in Portugal and decided that it would make a fine accompaniment for a dance. He then made a splendid one in which he displayed his mastery over witty, eccentric movement. The series of skits and crossovers dissolve and flow into one another so that it almost appears as if one is at a three-ring circus, there is so much activity. It is a bit of a shock to realize that it was all done by just seven dancers.

CHOREOCHRONICLE
OF MURRAY LOUIS

1953

Opening Dance
Little Man
Antechamber
Star Crossed

1954

Affirmation
For Remembrance
Courtesan
Family Album
Martyr
Triptych

1955

Piper
Court
Dark Corner
Monarch
Night
Polychrome
Man in Chair
Figure in Grey
As the Day Darkens
Small Illusions
Frenetic Dances
Belonging to the Moon

1956

Suite
Incredible Garden
Corrida
Harmonica Suite (Reflections)

1957

Journal

1959

Entre-Acte

1960

Odyssey

1961

Calligraph for Martyrs

1962

Facets

1963

Interims
Suite for Divers Performers

1964

Transcendencies
Landscapes
*Junk Dances
A Gothic Tale

1966

*Charade (Chimera)
Choros I
Concerto
Illume

1967

Go 6

1969

Proximities
Intersection

1971

Personnae
Continuum
Disguise

1972

*Hoopla
Dance as an Art Form

1973

Index . . . (to necessary neuroses)

1974

Porcelain Dialogues
Scheherezade, a Dream

1975

Moments

JOHN HERBERT MCDOWELL

Among those composers most associated with the vanguard dance movement, McDowell is by far and away the most prolific, having created over a hundred scores for his own and other choreographers' works. He began composing tape scores in the late 1940s, and though he has worked with live musicians in the intervening years, the bulk of his output has been for electronic reproduction. His interest in theater has been constant, and he himself took movement courses for some years though no formal dance instruction. In the early 1960s, when the burgeoning Judson Dance Theater was the cutting edge of advanced modern dance, McDowell was encouraged to try his own hand at movement direction as well as musical composition and in a few years produced a small and fascinating body of work. He has worked on a sustained basis over a number of years with James Waring and Paul Taylor as well as literally dozens of other choreographers. In recent years he has confined his theatrical activities to music, but one never knows when he may feel the choreographic impulse again.

DANCE IN TWO ROWS
(VERSION III)

Choreography by John Herbert McDowell. Lighting by Jennifer Tipton. Costumes were chosen by the dancers. Music by John Lennon and Paul McCartney. First performed at the Judson Memorial Church, New York, N.Y., by Toby Armour, Jennifer McDonagh, Gretchen MacLane, Phoebe Neville, Arlene Rothlein, Elaine Summers, Jennifer Tipton, Margaret Wise, Edward Barton, Rethal Bean, Cliff Keuter, Larry Rée, Arthur Williams, Charles Stanley, and David Tice.

There is a mad vivacity to McDowell's works, a feeling that the choreographer will try anything just for the sake of it. It's all true. During one concert McDowell had himself hurled bodily onstage to demolish a property when he landed on it. It was a dance called *First Act Finale*, which was actually set to the second-act finale of *Die Fledermaus*. Behind the laughter there is a serious intent, although the message is always manically sugar coated.

The dance begins with the men and women of the piece standing in two horizontal rows, one behind the other. The rows are parallel and remain so as the performing group steps from side to side. The assortment of costumes runs from that of a mailman to a transvestite man in a ballerina's tutu. It is a vision of individual sensibilities run riot. The logic of the piece is that each of these performers has been allowed to dress as some fanciful person that intrigues him or her.

All of the performers sing in a low, mournful voice a popular song by the Beatles called "You've Got to Hide Your Love Away." The rendition that they give is like a dirge compared to the peppy original. Watching carefully over the two rows of performers as they step out to do individual variations is another performer in his very favorite dress-up costume, a mailman who reads others' letters. An attractive woman demurely dresses as a girl scout. One man in white tie and tails breaks free to bound around with his tambourine before being drawn back into line. The male ballerina is regally aloof, while another man looks like an escapee from an old horror movie in boxer's shorts and a mask, and still another shows an elastic, gymnastic bounce with an auto horn. One of the women preserves a style of dance reminiscent of the "moderne" movement, and another just sings. After each has had a turn the dance is over.

Everyone is inhibited from expressing some private desire by social pressure and McDowell made a dance out of freeing people. He has adapted the work to the people who were available to him at a given time, and of the groups that I have seen this was my favorite, as it contrasted dream and repression most charmingly.

CHOREOCHRONICLE
OF JOHN HERBERT MCDOWELL

1961

Prelude and Dance

1962

February Fun at Bucharest

1963

Auguries

Eight Pas de Deux, Pas de Trois
and Finale

First Act Finale

Dance in Two Rows (Version I)

1966

4 Minute Piece for 70 Dancers

1967

With Waterfalls and Dancing on
the Tables

Dance in Two Rows (Version II)

Well . . . . . Actually (with
Remy Charlip and James
Waring)

1970

*Dance in Two Rows (Version III)

1971

Tumescent Lingam

NANCY MEEHAN

If one had to name two states in the Union which have been exceptionally hospitable to dance, one would probably say New York and California. Nancy Meehan is a native-born Californian who has chosen to make her career in New York. She was raised in San Francisco and graduated from the University of California at Berkeley, and began her dance career in the Ann Halprin-Welland Lathrop dance company. She remained with the company for three years and presented her first independent dance works on Ann Halprin's Dance Deck Theater, which is located outdoors near San Francisco in Marin County. Meehan went to New York for further study at the Martha Graham School and also at the Erick Hawkins School. She was invited by Hawkins to join his company in 1962 and she remained with it until 1970. She then left to form her own company and school and since then has given regular concerts of her work. She was commissioned to create a new work at the American Dance Festival at New London, Connecticut, in collaboration with a contemporary composer in the summer of 1974.

WHITIP

Choreography by Nancy Meehan. Lighting by Chenault Spence. First performed at New York University, New York, N.Y., April 4, 1971, by Nancy Meehan, Kay Gilbert, Shelly Goldklank, Trude Link, Susan Lundberg, and Nina Sprecher.

As much as I had enjoyed the piece, its title was a complete mystery to me, and I went scurrying to the dictionary to see what enlightenment it could offer. The only entry was "whitetip," a species of hummingbird. That didn't seem exactly pertinent, although there were lots of swooping and dipping motions in the dance that could be considered birdlike. Talking with Meehan one day, I asked her about the title, and she told me that it was a nickname that she and her husband made up for a pigeon that used to perch on their window and that they were fond of until it flew away. Even without the solution the dance is a good one.

Six women in white leotards dash on in a series of arcs and then pause for a moment before hurrying off. They return in echelons of threes a moment later and then in a line at the rear of the stage that is formed as individuals complete a series of turns and link onto its end. The dance is unaccompanied and there is no sound as the women walk and then dash quickly into the wings out of sight.

One by one they come out to squat down and cross their arms over their faces. When all have entered the group rises and leaves, to reappear in a series of crossings, some of which are leaping and others in which the individual dashes out, pauses to rise on the ball of the foot, and then sidesteps off. The movement is fluid and subtly modulated, as individuals do their own variations. Two skip backward in a semicircle, and another balances on her palms and the balls of the feet; the group moves lightly to the side, swaying hands in the air, to absorb the remaining soloist. All move almost imperceptibly, turning their heels to the side together and then the toes. Individuals dash out of the line, leaping alertly, and then the group exits. As at the beginning they return for a brief passage in groups of three and then leave for the last time.

One can see the years of experience that Meehan had with the Hawkins company in her use of bodily flow, but to it she has added her own special energy that gives a sharp cutting edge to her pieces. The piece has a soaring momentum that is free of involved twists and turns but just seems to pour out easily and enjoyably.

CHOREOCHRONICLE
OF NANCY MEEHAN

1971

Hudson River Seasons
*Whitip

1972

Bones Cascades Scapes

1973

Live Dragon

1974

Bones Cascades Scapes (revised)
Split Rock
Yellow Point

1975

Grapes and Stones

MEREDITH MONK

When studying at Sarah Lawrence College, Monk was involved with a variety of interests, among which were dance and writing. She was unsure at the time whether she wanted to be a writer or a dancer and subsequently has shown a strong inclination for musical composition, even entitling one of her dance theater productions an "opera epic." It would be difficult to say which category she would feel most comfortable in, though she believes that her theater works are approached from a dancer's viewpoint. Among her teachers at college were Judith Dunn, a member of the Merce Cunningham company, and Beverly Schmidt, a former leading dancer with the Alwin Nikolais Dance Company. Monk appears to have absorbed ideas for movement and presentation from both and also from Ann Halprin, with whom she studied one summer. She has worked with both highly trained dancers and those with minimal dance training and has created movement suitable for each. She has created pieces for conventional proscenium arch stages and for outdoor locations that have been the size of several football fields. She was invited to appear at the Youth Pavilion of Expo '67 and has presented her work at the American Dance Festival at Connecticut College in New London. She calls her company, bound together by personal as well as professional ties, "The House" and augments its core of six members with students and interested others as required for individual concerts. She has a great feeling for individual performing spaces, exhibiting an almost cinematographic sense of production.

DUET WITH CAT'S SCREAM AND LOCOMOTIVE

Choreography by Meredith Monk. Sound by Daniel Zellman. Lighting by Stroblite Company, Inc. Photography by Charlotte Victoria. First performed at the Gate Theatre, New York, N.Y., October 26, 1966, by Meredith Monk and Kenneth King.

The classic duet is based on the interaction of a male and a female, and the music ordinarily characterizes each variation with strong, assertive sound for the man and sweeter, more lyrical music for the woman. Taking this convention to its logical extreme, Monk decided that the sound effect of a roaring locomotive would be an appropriate leitmotiv for the man and a howling cat for the woman. The duet was equally unconventional but logical as if two space-age toddlers had discovered the form for the first time.

The stage area is littered with a variety of objects: large blocks, stilts, small rocking half-cylinders with photographs of smiling mouths that are revealed as the dance progresses, and the two dancers move around in bright yellow togs. They first appear together on the stilts carefully picking their way amid all of the fastidious litter and then mount wooden platforms. They balance precariously on the half-circles and teeter from side to side after abandoning the platforms. They resolutely refuse to show any facial expression, although from time to time they tear masking strips from the half-cylinders to reveal smiling mouths as if to suggest an even more mechanical response to the situation, which is a matter of indifference to them.

From time to time the regular lighting of the piece is shut off and the stage is illuminated with eerie ultraviolet light which picks out details of make-up and costuming not previously visible. The smiling mouths of the rocking half-circles are an ironic accompaniment to the two as they proceed on their intended path performing tasks without wasting any time on emotional display. The contrast of the full-bodied performers under normal lighting contrasts with the spectral outlining that is visible under the ultraviolet light, the way a positive print of a photograph does with its negative.

Because of her intense theatrical sense Monk infused this detached and emotionally cool dance with the warm ambiance of theatrical magic. The couple performed in a way that was wholly strange in its particulars but followed the logic of the *pas de deux* for the man and the woman, which is at the heart of classical ballet. It could have been a shocking glimpse into the future.

16 MILLIMETER EARRINGS

Choreography by Meredith Monk. Set to taped voice by Meredith Monk. Cinematography by Kenneth Van Sickle. First performed at the Judson Memorial Church, New York, N.Y., December 5, 1966, by Meredith Monk.

One of the things evident from the earliest concerts of her work was that Monk was interested in theater spectacle. Even in a solo such as this she covered her stage with varieties of large wooden props, added film sequences, sang a simple melody, and linked all elements together with a dance impulse. She refuses to characterize her work further than to say that it is theater approached from a dancer's point of view.

A large white box, a steamer trunk, and a couple of chairs occupy the stage, and a woman is sitting in one of the chairs. She stands to reveal that she is wearing a brief bathing suit, dumpy house slippers, and a short net shift. Her voice is heard describing the physical aspect of the stage and its properties and then a dance. The woman responds with movements that are considerably less dynamic than those of the dance which she is describing. One could look at the descriptions of the set and the movements as theatricalized, heightened versions of the actual.

A film of the human body and slides from medical illustrations are shown on the side of the white box, and now one becomes aware of three simultaneous layers of sound: a speaking voice, a recording of the same voice, and the song, which consists of the repeated word "Nota." She wears a large globe over her head. Projected on it is a film of her face showing her repeating several hair-adjusting movements that she had just performed, once again offering an action and its recording at the dramatically emphasized level.

She wears a frightful red wig and seems like a tiny child and one hears the folk song "Greensleeves." A film of flames consuming a small unclothed doll is shown. The doll crumples and is slowly reduced by the flames. The woman is now inside the trunk, and as a film of flames is projected over it she stands nude and collapses slowly into it in a repetition of the doll's immolation.

The piece alternates between the presentation of the actual and the theatricalized version of reality and vice versa. One has the feeling of a witty game, an imagination at creative play picking over the bits and pieces of daily experience and expanding them to epic size so that they achieve emotional weightiness. In a way it had the effect of the camera close up creating "stardom" for actors and actresses by an intimate and overwhelming enlargement of ordinary unenlarged and unremarked-upon features.

JUICE

Choreography by Meredith Monk. Music by Meredith Monk, Janet Zalamea, and Don Preston. Scenery and costumes by Meredith Monk. Lighting by Beverly Emmons. First performed at the Solomon R. Guggenheim Museum, Minor Latham Playhouse, and The House, New York, N.Y., November 7 to December 7, 1969, by Dick Higgins, Madelyn Lloyd, Daniel Sverdlik, Meredith Monk, Monica Moseley (in the third installment), augmented by six other performers in the second installment, and seventy-four other performers in the first installment.

This was the largest scaled of a series of works that Monk created around the country in museums. It involved seventy-five performers and was given in three separate sections at three different sites, each of decreasing size. The first took place in the Solomon R. Guggenheim Museum; three weeks later on a regular proscenium stage at Barnard College's Minor Latham Playhouse; and the third, a week later at a loft on lower Broadway.

Before being admitted to the museum the audience sees a woman riding up and down in the street outside the museum on a white horse and then patrons are admitted and directed to sit in the center of the main floor with the broad spiral ramp ascending to the top level in a continuous spiral. Banks of performers dressed in white move to the edge of the ramp at various levels to allow themselves to be seen and, humming, retire out of sight. It is like the overture to an opera. Four performers in red costumes and body make-up enter the main level and begin a clomping walk to the top of the spiral. They are pressed closely together, and at each level they pause to separate and do a climbing or crawling exercise. Their ascent is interspersed with vocal music from individuals or groups both seen and unseen.

At various levels, three women in period costumes simply stand or turn slowly in place like mannequins in a window display. The first wears formal court dress and a white wig, the second is in an 1890s-musical costume, and the third in somewhat biblical dress. After the four red performers reach the top, one woman sings a song that resembles a muezzin's call. All of the performers in white, who had retired out of sight, reappear and rush down in a stream of running bodies to spread themselves around the first level rail-

Laura Dean and Company in *Changing Pattern Steady Pulse.*
PHOTO BY PHILLIP JONES.

Trisha Brown, Carmen Beuchat, Sylvia Whitman, and Carol Goodden in
Primary Accumulation. PHOTO BY BOYD HAGEN.

Rudy Perez in *Coverage*.   PHOTO BY HERBERT MIGDOLL.

Jan Van Dyke, Ted Striggles, Elizabeth Keen, and Louis Solino in *Poison Variations*.

Nina Wiener, Tom Rawe (obscured), Rose Marie Wright, Kenneth Rinker, Isabel Garcia-Lorca (back), Sara Rudner (obscured), and Twyla Tharp in *Eight Jelly Rolls*.   PHOTO BY TONY RUSSELL.

Lucinda Childs in *Carnation*.   PHOTO BY TERRY SCHUTTE.

James Cunningham
as the Specter of the Rose
in *Dancing with Maisie
Paradocks.*
PHOTO BY LOIS GREENFIELD.

Remy Charlip in *Meditation.*
PHOTO BY ANTHONY CRICKMAY.

ing. All stop as a man cuts some wood with an electric saw. A woman in black with a life mask of herself affixed to her stomach is carried to the second level, after which there is a blackout and the first scene ends.

The performers form living exhibits in the various niches and stair wells scattered throughout the museum, and the audience is free to wander among them. The audience freely looks and passes from one tableau to the next, observing this living décor. At a signal all the performers descend the spiral in a beautiful free run, cluster in the space the audience just vacated, and then exit.

The second part of the work consists of the four performers in red, along with a few property men and musician Don Preston. This portion shows the elements of the production on a reduced but still somewhat theatricalized scale. A reproduction of a painting suggests the real one in the museum, and the performers in red declaim personal histories in recitative fashion, whereas previously they were silent dancers. What had been a stylized hike up the ramp was now broken down into the component pilgrimages of four individuals. They play small improvisational games, feeding off their knowledge of one another's characteristic gestures.

The final section of the work is presented in a loft, and there are no live performers. The loft is decorated with the costumes and stage properties used in the other sections including a baby's hobbyhorse, recalling the real horse outside the Guggenheim the first evening. The red performers are present only by means of videotape monologues, which are repeated for the audience to listen to. These offer further autobiographical material in an even less theatricalized manner than the second section. After viewing the audience left.

The final section represented the complete compression of the performing material into the natural and untheatrical personalities of the performers from which the piece had developed. The full, somewhat allegorical and religious expansion of the group mystique had been presented in the Guggenheim, the transitional, partially staged, and partially improvised performance was seen at Minor Latham Playhouse, and the raw materials at the loft. It impressively combined its locales and the various stages of the creative transformation.

CHOREOCHRONICLE
OF MEREDITH MONK

1963

Me
Timestop

1964

Diploid
Break

1965

Cartoon
The Beach
Radar
Relache
Blackboard

1966

Portable
*Duet with Cat's Scream and
  Locomotive
*16 Millimeter Earrings

1967

Excerpt from Work in Progress
Goodbye/St. Mark/Windows
Blueprint
Overload
Blueprint (1)
Overload/Blueprint (2)

1968

Blueprint (3)
Blueprint (4)
Blueprint (5) Open House
Co-op

1969

Title: Title
Tour: Dedicated to Dinosaurs
Untidal: Movement Period
Tour 2: Barbershop
*Juice
Tour 4: Lounge
The Beach

1970

Voice Recital
Needle Brain Lloyd and the
  System's Kid
Tour 5: Glass
Tour 6: Organ
Tour 7: Factory
"Key"

1971

Tour 8: Castle
Vessel

1973

Education of the Girlchild
Paris/Chacon (with Ping Chong)

1975

Anthology
Small Scroll

ROBERT MORRIS

Originally a painter, Morris has made his substantial reputation as an artist by virtue of his sculpture. He had some early dance training but did not feel that he had any future as a performer, though his first wife, Simone Forti, felt that he had definite choreographic promise when they were in Ann Halprin's workshop in San Francisco. When they moved to New York, she was active in "happenings" and created a program of her own in 1961, in which she made a piece, *See Saw,* for him and Yvonne Rainer. With the advent of the Judson Dance Theater he began to work at choreography systematically and produced a variety of pieces at times with others and at times on his own. His performing was always strongly focused and powerfully direct, and it was a distinct loss when he abandoned choreography in the mid-1960s.

WATERMAN SWITCH

Choreography by Robert Morris. Set to a sound collage of music by Giuseppe Verdi and words by Robert Morris, and Leonardo da Vinci. First performed at the Judson Memorial Church, New York, N.Y., March 23, 1965, by Lucinda Childs, Robert Morris, and Yvonne Rainer.

The dance was one of the first from the vanguard group, centered around Judson Memorial Church, that became known to a wide public. It happened through a photograph of Morris and Yvonne Rainer which appeared in *Life* magazine showing them clasped in a nude embrace. The import of the piece was ignored because of the supposedly scandalous use of the bare body.

The celebration of the human body as an artistic subject begins with the two performers nearly nude and a third performer, a woman dressed in male clothing. She is an androgynous figure who throughout the piece is the intermediary between the couple. She moves the large gray tracks upon which the couple shuffles. She threads a string from one side of the performing area to the other and holds onto the middle of it as the two at either end relay little tugging signals to one another through her. At one point she holds a long pole with a red flag tied to the end of it and moves it around in a circle as the nude man runs after it. He pursues it so closely that it adheres to his body and covers him from the front like an Indian's breechclout.

Pressed closely together in an embrace, the couple itself is an androgynous mass since there never is a frontal exposure of sexual organs and the bare back is the same for both. The tracks determine the direction that the couple traverses. A sequence of photographs, from the Muybridge studies of motion, shows a man shot-putting and then the man does the same sequence of movement in the light of a projector beam. The man and woman shuffle slowly across the front of the performing area, and he allows a gush of mercury to flow down her back before they disappear. The woman dressed as a man strings the remaining cord back and forth across the performing area and then leaves as it vibrates in the empty space.

The whole dance was a flow of related but individual events, celebrating the nude human form, which created a collage of motion and then static representation of that motion. The roles of the male and the female reversed at times in the material that was danced and the indeterminate figure at the center remained enigmatic. It was gloriously imaginative in its thrust and pictorial invention.

CHOREOCHRONICLE
OF ROBERT MORRIS

1962

War (with Robert Huot)
New Poses Plasticues (with Jill
   Johnston)

1963

Arizona
21.3
Site

1965

*Waterman Switch
Check

JENNIFER MULLER

A graduate of the Juilliard School of Music, she began her professional career at the age of fifteen with the Pearl Lang company. From 1963 to 1971 she performed as a principal dancer with the José Limón company and assisted Limón in restaging his works for American Ballet Theater and the First Chamber Dance Company. She has also reconstructed several of Doris Humphrey's dances from Labanotation scores. In the late sixties she joined the Louis Falco company and remained with it as a dancer and choreographer for the next seven years. In 1971 she gave the first concert of her own work and three years later established her own company. As well as being a brilliant performer she has a substantial reputation as a teacher and has taught at Juilliard School, Sarah Lawrence College, and the School of Performing Arts in New York City. In addition to her own company, her dances are currently in the repertory of the Hartford Ballet, the Netherlands Dance Theater, and the Repertory Dance Theater of Utah.

NOSTALGIA

Choreography by Jennifer Muller. Tape collage by Burt Alcantara and Jennifer Muller. Costumes by Lois Bewley. Lighting by Richard Nelson. First performed at the Video Exchange, Westbeth, New York, N.Y., November 19, 1971, by Georgiana Holmes, Mary Jane Eisenberg, Jennifer Muller, and Erin Martin.

Some dancers have a special reputation as being "movers," indicating that there's a certain something natural and out of the ordinary about them. Muller is a "mover," and in the pieces that she choreographs she demands that her company members, whom she always designates as friends, also have exceptional performing skills.

Three women wearing platform shoes and print dresses come in to clump around. They look like the women that one might encounter in a picture of the 1930s in New York by painter John Sloan. They have a rough glamour. Completely isolated from them is an older woman in a black dress sitting quietly on a wicker stool by herself living with memories. The sound is that of the popular songs drawn from the decade of the thirties.

Their dancing has lusty fullness to it as they cavort and disport with the energetic abandon of youth. It is frolicsome, flirtatious and evokes a series of somewhat tarnished thoughts in the woman's mind. She rises, looks around, puts a hand to her cheek. At one point a bitterly amused smile appears on her face; she is the mirror of their movement, but only through small gesture and those impulses brought on by memory. The three are heedless of anything as they continue to dance individual variations to one tune after another. It is a variant of social dancing devised for solo presentation. Two of the women leave and the third continues on alone, finally slipping out of her print dress and leaving. The older woman goes to it and gathers it up.

The brassy movements of the three young women are expertly contrasted with the remote and slow movements of the older woman and together give the piece the bite of regret that make it so appealing. Being young is fun, and after one has been there it is hard to remember or believe that it really happened and is over. One finds oneself fingering relics of the time to make it live again.

CHOREOCHRONICLE
OF JENNIFER MULLER

1965

  Braided

1966

  Waiting

1969

  Eve d'Autun

1970

  More Than Sixty Places (an Indispensable Handbook for Students, Now out of Print)

1971

  Sweet Milkwood and Blackberry Bloom
  *Nostalgia
  Rust (Giacometti Sculpture Garden)
  Stravinsky Cantata

1973

  Tub

1974

  An American Beauty Rose Speeds
  Biography
  Between Me and Other People There Is Always a Table and a Few Empty Chairs – C.H.
  Winter Pieces/Oranges

1975

  Intermission Piece No. 1
  Intermission Piece No. 2
  White

PHOEBE NEVILLE

When she was fifteen years old, Neville began to take dance class with Joyce Trisler. Up until that time she had had no formal training and almost immediately had the misfortune of dislocating her kneecap, which required an operation. Two years later in 1958, she spent three weeks studying during the summer at Jacobs Pillow, where she saw Daniel Nagrin performing. She was attracted to his work and in the next few years studied with him and joined the Tamiris-Nagrin company. She presented her own work for the first time at a young choreographer's concert at Clark Center for the Performing Arts in 1961 and joined the co-operative Studio Nine two years later in the company of other young choreographers who decided that it would be cheaper to share studio expenses. She became involved with the Judson Dance Theater and worked with Kenneth King and Meredith Monk in particular for the next several years along with others such as Carolee Schneemann. While she danced in others' works, she continued to create her own pieces and began to present evenings of them. In addition to her formal dance training, which included ballet, she was deeply influenced by ethnic dance studies and the fluid Chinese exercise regimen of *tai-chi*. She has steadfastly maintained her deliberate pace of creating dances and showing them only when she felt that they were ready for public inspection. In the process she has created a repertory of small, jewel-like pieces.

MEMORY

Choreography by Phoebe Neville. Sound score by Philip Hipwell and Phoebe Neville. First performed at the Cubiculo, New York, N.Y., in 1972, by Christopher Beck, Philip Hipwell, and Phoebe Neville.

The dance is one of the most unusual and intimate undertaken by Miss Neville, who traditionally has worked on a small personal scale. It is divided into seven parts, each of which is illuminated by some type of flame carried and manipulated by the dancer.

In the first section the darkened stage is suddenly brightened by a small flame in the palm of the dancer's hand. She wears an asbestos mitt and a scarf covers the lower part of the face. She moves as if hypnotized by it, transferring it from one gloved palm to the other while staring at the flickering movement of the flame. She reclines, stands, and extinguishes it. With its light gone the stage is dark. A man bearing two candles walks on. He wears a long robe and looks like a votary of some kind. He faces forward at center stage and moves the candles close to his cheeks, then behind his head and around again to illuminate his face. It is a prayer offering of subtle mystery. Bringing both candles together in front of his mouth, he softly breathes them out. In the third section a woman dressed in a costume reminiscent of that of a harem dancer manipulates a single candle in a cup-shaped vase casting large shadows on the walls as she performs her private devotion. She finally bows her face close to it and banishes the flame with the merest puff as from a kiss. In the ensuing darkness one hears strong footsteps, and suddenly a match flares to illuminate the walker's way for a moment before it goes out. The steps are heard again and another burns for a moment before the darkness returns. The gesture is repeated twice more before the traveler walks off in the gloom.

As he exits a woman runs joyfully on, turning and dashing in the light sparks given off by a hissing firework. Her movements are almost driven by the light that one sees them by. A man holding a candle to light his way walks on, followed by another figure, a woman also in a long robe, who dogs his steps and eventually snuffs out the candle he holds so dear. At the conclusion a woman in plain farm clothes sits at a table and lights a hurricane lamp and sits thinking. Slowly the faint sound of birds twittering is heard and a pale blue light begins to illuminate the stage. Both the light and the sound intensify, and it is clear that the night and its episodic illuminations are over. It is a woman in the light of day thinking back over the events, trying to decide what they meant or perhaps whether they ever happened at all in her dreams.

Despite its episodic nature and lack of a consistent sound accompaniment, the piece has a graceful symmetry and balances the nighttime whispers of the unconscious mind with the daytime activity of the awakened consciousness, analyzing and trying to understand the images. The fitful sounds that are heard in parts of the dance remind one of low groaning and at times whistled breathing, but ultimately they remain unidentified background sound. The dance calls for exceptional intensity from its performers to make the most of its spare but judicious gestures. It shows Miss Neville at her mysterious but quietly eloquent best.

TRIPTYCH

Choreography by Phoebe Neville. Music by Meredith Monk (Under Street, Fat Stream, Do You Be from Key). *First performed at the Cubiculo, New York, N.Y., in 1973, by Phoebe Neville.*

Having worked happily with Meredith Monk in a variety of concerts, Neville decided that she would like to create a dance using three of Monk's wailing chants. She obtained three of them, and each accompanies one of the movements to the dance, which is a solo of unusual design and great power.

A woman is alone and her eyes are shielded by a red blindfold. She struggles as if in a harsh, constricting bind. She constantly collapses upon herself and ultimately ends spread-eagled on the floor. The lights go out.

The second movement has a lyrical meditative sound, and the woman in a sweat shirt leans up against a wall with her back to the audience. She slowly rolls around to face it and then ducks her head. She braces herself against the wall with the back of her neck and shoulders and then straightens up. She now leans her stomach against the wall then arches her body and braces herself with one hand. There is an irresistible attraction to its firm obdurateness and, to complete the section, she flattens herself against it and tilts her head to look upward as if in supplication or perhaps weariness. The dim light is extinguished.

She returns to the center of the space as an overhead spotlight encircles her kneeling form. She clenches a rubber snake in her teeth and moves slowly to the intermittent burst of the chant. She stretches her arms slowly and then closes them again and, bending forward, allows the rubber snake to fall from her mouth.

There is a surreal atmosphere to the work as it presents three aspects of life in its discrete units. The constant thread seems to be a restless seeking of someone or something which always remains out of sight and out of reach. As is her custom, Neville firmly pares away anything extra in the way of movement flourishes in order to present her work with the lean economy that she finds congenial. Each piece has a precise place and is made to slip smoothly into the whole pattern.

CHOREOCHRONICLE
OF PHOEBE NEVILLE

1962

Of the Dark Air

1963

Remnant

1966

Terrible
Move
Ragaroni
Dance for Mandolins

1967

Mask Dance
Eowyn's Dance

1968

Nova
Light Rain (with Philip Hipwell)

1969

Edo Wrap (with Philip Hipwell)
Ninja
Caryatid
Termination

1970

Terminal (with Micki Goodman)
Untitled Duet

1971

Memory (solo)

1972

*Memory (complete)
Night Garden
Triptych (*Panels I and II*)

1973

*Triptych (complete)
Passage in Silence
Solo

1974

Cartouche
Ladydance
Canto

AILEEN PASSLOFF

Her career combines the roles of performer, teacher, and choreographer, and in each she has shown an individual approach. She slips nimbly from idea to idea in her pieces and has created a dance for herself and a pencil and another for two female dancers with two neutral benches. In the midst of such unconventional creativity she found time to dance two beautifully sensitive and balletically styled solos, *April* and *December*, designed for her by Remy Charlip. She has worked with James Waring and seems specially sympathetic to his combination of the serious and the comic in a single dance. Her own wide repertory of dances includes both larger-scaled works and solos, and she maintained her own company for ten years. While she concentrated on concert dance, she did not exclude drama, and she appeared in several Off-Broadway plays and musicals, including Al Carmine's *What Happened* and David Ross's production of *The Dybbuk*. In addition to teaching in her own studio she has taught at the Master Institute in New York and at Bennington College.

A DREAM UNDER A BLACK HAT

Choreography by Aileen Passloff. First performed at the Cubiculo, New York, N.Y., June 7, 1971, by Aileen Passloff.

Although she has created varieties of dances for large and small numbers of performers, Passloff has always brought a special touch to her own solos. These have customarily had a degree of oddness to them, either in the movement design itself or in the setting and costuming. Often they have had a pastoral quality.

She enters as if exploring the space. She runs her hand along the brick wall along one side and then the other. The feeling is that of a stranger entering an area and attempting to orient herself. As the dance progresses she becomes visibly fonder of the space, placing a kiss in her palm and touching the flat of her hand to the floor. From time to time she stops and cocks her head slightly as if listening to something, and then frames, almost sketches, a configuration in the air in front of her, like an explorer marking distinctive points of a landscape for mapping and familiarity. There is a growing air of mastery and ease in her feeling about the place. She has entered as an outsider but now feels much more comfortable. At the end she removes the soft wide-brimmed hat and looks back to the space in friendly fashion before leaving.

The dance also has the suggestion of a painter encountering a landscape, trying to fathom its organization and slowly coming to feel at ease with its particular atmosphere. The velour hat makes one think of the nineteenth century by its texture and styling and the battalions of young artists similarly attired trekking out to explore for themselves the difficulties of framing nature for pictorial representation.

CHOREOCHRONICLE
OF AILEEN PASSLOFF

1950

Prism

1951

Duologue

1953

Wing Song

1956

Intruders

1957

At Home
Dust

1959

Sarabande
Tea at the Palaz of Noon
Arena

1960

Cypher
Strelitzia

Battle Piece
Structures
A Dance of Sleep
Foam

1961

Phantoms on the Mudflats
Rosefish
Pagoda

1962

Asterisk
Glacier

1963

A Salute to the New York
    World's Fair
Pavilion
Tier
Boa Constrictor
Fandango
A Dozen Dances

1964

Unholy Picnic
Thanksgiving Dance for Joanna
  & Burt
Belissa in the Garden
Bench Dance

1965

Men's Dance

1966

Spanning
Waterwork
Crossover

1967

Dance from "Molly's Dream"
Duet from "Song of Songs"
Fauna
I Am My Beloved (with Remy
  Charlip)

1969

A Spike of Grain Bursts from
  Some Lips
Tarosh
Hopes and Fears
Moving Day

1970

Hans

1971

A Dream Under a Black Hat

1972

Struggle in the Doorway
Events from a Nightmare

1974

Entanglements

1975

Emergence

STEVE PAXTON

Steve Paxton has danced with a chicken, designed costumes for trees, and was an outstanding performer with the Merce Cunningham company. His background in dance started with an interest in gymnastics and developed into advanced dance training at the Merce Cunningham studio. As a performer, he had an enviable and electric stage presence, which won him a considerable reputation while with the Cunningham dance company but which did not satisfy his choreographic ambitions. Paxton believes that dance movement is to be found everywhere and in any person whether or not that person has had formal dance training.

This simple but profoundly revolutionary thought quickly drove Paxton into designing dances so radically removed from the dance tradition he emerged from that he became immediately controversial and has remained so ever since. For one dance he designed a visual score that consisted of pictures clipped from a soccer magazine and pasted up in sequences which the dancer had to try to imitate. In general the direction of his choreography has been away from that which a highly trained dancer can do and toward the sorts of movement which the average person can accomplish.

Paxton feels that the small amounts of performing energy which a mass of people can generate as individuals will cumulate in a performance to the type of theatrical energy which a trained dancer can create on his own. It is a theory which has caused him to design dance works for crowds of people and not for the disciplined few who constitute the professional world of dance. It is an audacious attempt to democratize what is and what perhaps must be a performing elite.

PHYSICAL THINGS

Choreography by Steve Paxton. Set to ambient sound of spectators passing through the interior of an inflated plastic tunnel and a collage of taped sounds. First performed at the 69th Regiment Armory in New York, N.Y., October 13, 1966, the first evening of Nine Evenings: Theater and Engineering, by Karen Bacon, Sue Hartnett, Margaret Hecht, Michael Kirby, Ted Kirby, Clark Poling, Elaine Sturtevant, David White, and others.

This work was the culmination of Paxton's "inflatable" series. It consisted of an enormous volume of plastic sheeting which was roughly designed in the shape of the digestive tract and was kept up by means of forced-air compressors. The performers were varied. There were a constant number of performers who were always part of the piece, carrying out simple tasks of sitting or making small movement tableaux, and in addition, the choreographer designated anyone who entered into the ambiance of the piece to be a performer as well. There were three sets of high school gymnasium bleachers set up at the exit of the piece, and those who had walked through could then sit there, so in actuality they had been part of the cast to those observing their passage from the outside.

Entering the long tube, walkers first marveled at the size of the air-supported tunnel that they were in, and then became aware of sounds coming from a concealed speaker. There was no set pace for passage through, and performers could take as long or a short a time as desired before emerging. In a way it mimicked the digestive process with its long tunnels leading to a large stomach-like area and away from it to the exit. At one point strollers encountered a small forest scene and then at the exit a long stool-shaped inflatable standing apart. In it were crouched figures in black costumes with irregular openings cut in their costumes, highlighting and isolating parts of the body that might not be looked at with much interest ordinarily, such as the leg from mid-calf to mid-thigh. At the exit transistor radios were passed out, and by standing at various points under a wire grid broadcasts of music or lectures could be picked up. After passage through the structure people could then enjoy watching others' behavior in the same circumstance.

Paxton abandoned using inflatable material after this piece and concentrated on bringing out the performance abilities of the average individual rather than the trained dancer. *Physical Things* was an experience that was marginally successful but demonstrated the possibilities of considering ordinary movement as spectacle and ultimately as a form of dance expression. People achieved a heightened awareness of themselves as they walked through the inflated tunnels, and that awareness did subtly and not so subtly alter their ways of moving.

SATISFYIN LOVER

Choreography by Steve Paxton. Set to ambient sound. Costuming consisted of street clothing selected by performers. First performed at St. Peter's Episcopal Church in New York, N.Y., 1967, by twenty-two men and women.

The components for this piece are variable, twenty-two to forty-two dancers, and any convenient space for them to walk across. Costuming is optional, and street clothes are the ordinary mode of dress. It is a work designed for anyone to perform and requires only that the individual walk across a designated space and then exit. There are three chairs placed at intervals along the way, and the file of walking people is behind them.

Various individuals are given the option of sitting in these chairs or just standing to stare at the audience for specified lengths of time. Otherwise the instructions to the participants are to walk across the performing area in as relaxed and as normal a manner as possible. When the last person has exited, then the piece is concluded.

One of the most fascinating demonstrations of how attention alters the stance of the individual is given in this piece. The piece also shows the great variety of walking stances which individuals have. These are indicative of a whole range of types from the exhibitionist to the most reticent, and it is from this multiplicity that the dance draws its energy. The parade of forty-two individuals creates a collage of walking habits that acquires an interest that the same motions unfocused by a performance frame would never have. It is, despite its casual nature, a performance at the border of the area where the everyday impinges upon the theatrical.

CHOREOCHRONICLE
OF STEVE PAXTON

1962

Proxy
Transit

1963

English
Word Words (with Yvonne Rainer)
Music for Word Words
Left Hand, David Hays
Flat

1964

Afternoon
Rialto
Jag Ville Gorna Telefonera (I Want the Telephone)
First (for Elaine)

1965

Section from an Unfinished Work

1966

Deposits
Earth Interior
A.A.
*Physical Things

1967

*Satisfyin Lover
Somebody Else
Love Songs
The Sizes
Walkin There

1968

State
Lecture on Performance (Beautiful Lecture)
The Atlantic
Salt Lake City Deaths

1969

Smiling
Liedown
Intravenous Lecture on Sponsors and Productions

1970

Untitled
Niagara Falls At

1971–75

Contact Improvisation

RUDY PEREZ

Rudy Perez came to dancing at a relatively late age, beginning regular dance training at the age of twenty-one. Prior to this he had interested himself in social dance, but with energy and drive he quickly developed his innate skills. Looking for a place in which to show his first works, he allied himself to the amorphous groups of dancers who were showing new work at the Judson Memorial Church on Washington Square in Manhattan.

Curious about all of the various aspects of theater, he also volunteered to assist with backstage production and has ever since produced his own tape music scores and frequently his own lighting designs. One of the great influences on his career was Martha Graham, at whose school he took class and whose own teaching impressed him with its dramatic power.

He himself is strongly muscled and has intense performing presence which dominates his work. His pieces are strangely outside of normal time in that they move at a deliberate pace that makes one very attentive to small detail. It is almost the sort of elastic time that exists in a dream. His vocabulary of movement consists of simple gestures forcefully projected, and his dances have a smooth, clean surface like highly polished stones.

COUNTDOWN*

Choreography by Rudy Perez. Set to two songs of the Auvergne, France. First performed at the Mary Anthony Studio, New York, N.Y., 1966, by Rudy Perez.

Countdown is a solo dance in two sections, and the musical accompaniment is two of the anonymous folk songs of the Auvergne. The first is lively and joyous in character and the second more meditative, but both having a definite lyrical quality. As the dance begins, the dancer is seen seated on a stool in a circle of overhead light. He puffs on a cigarette obviously lost in a tangle of thoughts and stares out but does not see anyone. All of his movements are done slowly, even the exhaling of smoke from his cigarette. It is a meditative moment touched with sadness as he puts his cigarette down into an ashtray and stands. He looks to his right and stretches out his arm but withdraws it and places his fingertips to his lips to blow a farewell kiss to someone or something that has departed.

Three long green streaks like stylized tears slash down one cheek. He seats

* Originally called *To Mary, With . . . ,* a title abandoned after the first performance.

himself, lowers his head into his hands; and as he looks up there are three freshly made streaks down his other cheek. Everything, however, is carried out in the calmest possible way. It is anguish but in slow motion. The concentration with which each movement is carried out makes the dance have an intensity that is incredibly strong. As the light dims, he has a final puff on his cigarette.

Countdown is a solo created near the beginning of Perez's career and is a piece that is close to the heart of his art. It is simple, intense, and requires a performing weight from its interpreters rather than great muscular facility. It is a curio in that it is a dance in which the soloist never moves his feet. The entire story is enacted within a small circle of overhead light and gives one the sense of an isolated moment of time in which human relationships are seen with a painful but insightful clarity. It neither clamors for attention nor departs from its own carefully designed trajectory. It is, in its scope, perfect for its economy of means and telling power.

TRANSIT

Choreography by Rudy Perez. Set to a tape collage. Film by Ed Seeman. First performed at the Cubiculo, New York, N.Y., January 26, 1969, by Barbara Roan, Anthony LaGiglia, and Rudy Perez.

The piece begins with a film, in this case shown as a negative image of three dancers, two men and a woman. As the film is being shown, one man begins to roll along the stage extremely slowly from the rear to the front on a diagonal. The woman crosses the stage also in slow motion, silhouetted by the images on the screen. The lights go on as the movie finishes and two crouch together in the center of the stage.

Suddenly in a complete contrast to their monumentally slow dance, the second man enters on roller skates. He swoops around and injects a quickened emotional pace as well as an increased speed into the dance. Before he arrived, it was in a limbo state, and now it has a new vibrancy. He halts momentarily and they stand on either side of him. Together the whole formation pivots, and then each peels off, led by the man on roller skates. They trot along behind him as he circles and performs. When he glides off they touch one another. He returns and they all go off together.

Even the film images have now changed from negative to positive. The man with the roller skates stands to one side and rolls his feet forward and back as if marching in place. He is marking time while the two others perform a duet. He stands in one spot, and she dashes around to stand in front of him. He in turn half-circles to place himself in front of her. It is the type of upstaging that one might encounter in amateur theatricals or in a child's game. It is play and also competitive action from which the second man is totally removed except that they all do dance together.

Now the two lie down side by side and restlessly bob up again. He begins to run and the woman bends to pick an imaginary bouquet. Each is doing some characteristic but faintly directionless gesture, just marking the passage of time without any particular direction, until the man on roller skates smoothly wheels back in.

As he pauses and begins to take off the skates, they stand far behind him and again revert to slow motion for their gestures as at the beginning, before the man with the skates entered. Now they approach him and each takes a skate to run it noisily back and forth across the floor. The second man stands behind them as they crouch and launch the skates into two separate tracks. A spotlight follows one, and as it slows to a halt we see the three staring at it.

One is constantly intrigued by the use of props in a Perez work, and none is more provocative than the pair of roller skates, which seem to convey the sort of power that one associates with the fairy-tale seven-league boots. They could enable a man to stride enormous distances in actual mileage, but these skates confer an artistic power. Where the dance and the dancers had been moving at a painfully slow pace, the entrance of the man skating enlivened the entire scene. Where there had been slow and almost planless activity, now there was a purposeful, unifying force to the activity. But it is not just the skates themselves that give the power; that can work only when the correct person wears them. One skate alone does not suffice either as the angry running back and forth of individual ones indicated. The mystery stands even to the end, where they all watch the skate come to a halt without its rider.

COVERAGE

Choreography by Rudy Perez. Tape collage by Rudy Perez. Projections by Phillip Meister. First performed at the Cubiculo, New York, N.Y., June 24, 1970, by Rudy Perez.

One of the strongest solos that he has ever created, it probably also was the most widely seen in abbreviated form. Making a guest appearance on the "Today Show" of the National Broadcasting Company, he prepared a two-and-a-half-minute version. It was very skillfully done so as to retain the tune. The tempo of the dance picks up, and he runs back and forth on a harsh abridgment. The basic decision to be made was how to show the enclosed world of the man being portrayed, since the dance in its longer form involved taping a large square area. For television Perez cleverly made him walk a straight line.

A man walks on very soberly and staunchly as one hears "On Top of Old Smokey," and he stops in three places as spotlights focus on him. The song is interrupted and a radical protest voice is heard. The man is being assaulted from two sides: his woman, who sings about a "cold-hearted lover," and the young voice demanding social change. The man is dressed in white workman's coveralls and a protective blue cap; the well-known "hard hat." He carries a large roll of gum tape, and as one hears the sound of a bagpipe march, he lays out a large square with the tape and secures it carefully. He then marches back and forth, quite comfortable inside his special zone.

He stops, moves to one side, strips off his coveralls, and removes his hat. All are placed carefully, and he then runs happily and energetically around the square. He is wearing red tights and and black trunks, which are quite a contrast to his outer clothing. He tumbles and frolics, covering the space in varieties of ways as slide projections show a stylized anatomical drawing of the human figure. But suddenly the march music is heard again and his buoyant leaps are stopped. He begins a heavy-footed dance to a rock music tune. The tempo of the dance picks up, and he runs back and forth on a long diagonal path and abruptly rolls up a blue tank-suit top that had been furled about his waist, and assumes a higher balletic body placement as he skitters happily through the space, changing directions sharply with ease and quickness. The free movement ceases, and he dons his coveralls again and his blue protective cap.

His movements now become lurching approximations of a stunted mechanical walk. He is like an automaton pushing one arm straight out as he sidesteps and then freezes in the military posture of attention. A woman sings a full-throated rendition of "God Bless America," supported by a big orchestral accompaniment. The man methodically begins to pick up the tape and remove any traces of the square. He returns to listen to the last bars of the music and respectfully removes his cap and protectively places it over his crotch.

The title suggests various forms of camouflage covering something that one does not want another to know about. It reflects some of the social upheaval of the 1960s but more importantly gives a character portrait of a man who is beset and afraid. To hide his own difficulties, he takes on protective coloration and the final gesture of the dance, combining an ostentatious patriotism with a gesture of self-defense, has the brilliance that only comes with great economy. When the dance was shown on television there were some protest letters.

LOT PIECE DAY/NIGHT

Choreography by Rudy Perez. Sound collage by Rudy Perez. First performed at Marymount Manhattan College, New York, N.Y., October 17, 1971, by Barbara Roan, Anthony LaGiglia, Wendy Summit, John Moore, Alice Coughlin, Raymond Johnson, Peggy Hackney, David White, Joan Schwartz, Daniel Press, Chip Largman, Rudy Perez, and more than thirty students of Marymount Manhattan College.

On a square section of earth from which the rubble had been cleared the dance begins as a man plants a small American flag in the center. He carries a portable television camera and points it at the flag as he backs away. The dramatic opening bars of Richard Strauss's *"Also Sprach Zarathustra"* indicates a historic event, but the happy swirl of over forty dancers who now occupy the area indicates that it is not a solemn one. They circle the flag and then stop, while a half-dozen of them dash in shallow arcs around the flag and then all stand on either side of it. They lean back and look up and all follow their example. Then each makes a large jump and runs to the far end of the performing area. They line up behind one another and slow-march across. As each finishes the run and jumps by the flag, he runs to join the end of the lengthening line. The breaking of formations and their reconstitution continue throughout the course of the dance.

As the line starts to turn toward the audience, each dancer does a little shuffle step to negotiate the turn. Then each does a staggering series of turns to get to the opposite side, where they stand facing a wall. The last girl walks across the area with careless ease, as a man with an unctuous official voice reads instructions for behavior during an atomic blast. The entire line begins to make halting progress across the space. Selected dancers drop to their knees while others step forward and squat. About half suddenly break away to run and turn so as to face the advancing group, but then rejoin it. The line divides to mime a gigantic tug-of-war, but dance music is heard and couples form to do ballroom steps. "War" has been replaced by "peace."

After a pause for "chatting" one man breaks out, doing a kicking step, and is followed by the rest. A half-dozen dancers run, leap, crouch, and then blend into the group, which is clustered together, doing a slow shuffling walk across the performing area. The first man circles the moving bunch jogging carefully while shepherding their progress. This is followed by a series of "follow-the-leader" variations in which the group takes its visual cue from whoever is out in front. When these are finished all sit on earth around the flag.

After a momentary pause individuals rise to dance their own little solos, and then the whole group begins hopping in place. The women clasp their hands over their breasts, and the men clamp their hands on their buttocks. It is like seeing a herd of modest kangaroos. After hopping all circle about and divide into two facing groups, one at either side. As a man describes the various types of birdcalls and gives examples of their whistles, the two lines intersect in a large "X" near the flag, as the individuals make the long diagonal, repeating the same step and turning continually. After concluding the crossing all form a tight group that mimes the motion of a locomotive.

Again one man breaks away and sets himself up as a mock police officer directing traffic with a whistle and hand signals. Dancers pass him doing swimming motions with their arms and pausing to balance on one foot. A children's song about washing in the bathtub is heard, and all mime the washing motions. Then, tiring of that, individuals make soap bubbles, another lights a cigarette, and all fall down to be revived by another social dance record. A small child walks over and removes the flag and then all begin ballroom dancing and members of the audience are invited to join them in the conclusion of the dance.

The work was one of several "people" pieces that Perez created for relatively untrained dancers. They are all structured to emphasize mass formations and have a general good humor to them. This one, like the others, such as *Monumental Exchange* in its various editions, showed Perez's ability to draw dance sense out of large groups without much formal training. As in all of his works he prisms the ordinary into a rainbow of meaning.

CHOREOCHRONICLE
OF RUDY PEREZ

1963

    *Take Your Alligator (Coat) with
      You*

1966

    **Countdown
    Fieldgoal
    Monkey See, Monkey Wha?
    Bang, Bang*

1967

    Center Break

1968

    *Topload-Offprint
    Loading Zone
    Loading Zone—Revisited
    Re-Run Plus* (revised *Monkey
      See, Monkey Wha?*)

1969

    **Transit
    Outline
    Match
    Arcade* (*Match,* revised)

1970

Annual
Round-Up
*Coverage

1971

Monumental Exchange
*Lot Piece Day/Night

1972

Asparagus Beach
Salute
Thank You General Motors
Steeple People
Lot Piece/Lawn 1971

1973

Running Board for a Narrative

1975

Parallax
Colorado Ramble

PILOBOLUS DANCE THEATER

This unlikely name was the designation chosen by two Dartmouth undergraduates, Robb (Moses) Pendelton and Jonathan Wolken, when they established this unique dance company in 1971. Subsequently it appeared as a quartet of men, the other two were Robby Barnett and Lee Harris, all of whom had received their dance training at Dartmouth under the guidance of Alison Chase. Most recently Chase and Martha Clarke joined the group, giving it a more traditional male-female balance.

The emergence of the company as a collaborative enterprise makes it radically different from any other performing troupe. The members create all of the dances themselves co-operatively and have displayed a fondness for unusual titling. The movement style is athletic and shows a sympathy for configurations that suggest gymnastics or tumbling. The dancers project strong and at times complex movement without any overt emotionalism, almost as if they were creatures and not people. Even in its most serious works there is usually a tinge of humor not far from the surface.

ANAENDROM

Choreography by Pilobolus. Music by Jon H. Appleton. Set designed by Lee Harris. Costuming and lighting by Pilobolus. First performed in 1972 by Lee Harris, Robb (Moses) Pendelton, Jonathan Wolken, and Robby Barnett. In 1973 two additional dancers were added, Alison Chase and Martha Clarke, and occasionally a guest arist, David Clarke, the dancer's seven-year-old son.

The titles of Pilobolus' dances are always something of a mystery; presumably they indicate something about the nature of the work, but it would take a scientist to know precisely what. It is much easier to watch and enjoy the works for their skillful blend of simple costuming and complex balances.

A wash of blue light forms the background to three wooden constructions. On the left is a box on stilts, in the center is a slowly revolving platform suspended by ropes, and on the right a box sits on the stage. Greenish light focuses on the objects. Suddenly a figure drops from inside the box on stilts and remains in his landing crouch. Another man gets off the twisting platform, and a third pokes his head out of the box. All have identical leotards and caps that cover the entire head. They make an apelike approach to one another and are joined by a fourth man. As they are assembling a second creature drops startlingly from the box on stilts and she joins them. They do a crab walk closely linked and appear to be like a large centipede.

Now they make themselves into a rolling line to transport her from one to another, the way one could move a large block of stone with logs. She gets off and places her palms flat on the floor and bobs her bottom up and down in a comical suggestion of a creature in heat. The male reaction to her is almost abstract as they shuffle to her for indifferent coupling. It is like watching the behavior of a clutch of anthropoids, it is so mechanical and impersonal. The quality of the humanoid movement also brings the humor to the piece. These are creatures like us and yet they are light years removed. It is the sort of innocent laughter that arises from watching the antics of inhabitants in a zoo enclosure. These creatures even shape hand pictures and at the end crouch tightly and bounce around like little cannon balls, then they twitch and scratch.

The muscular control that is demanded to keep up the various animal configurations is impressive enough in itself. What is even more amazing is how the members of the company never allow themselves to descend into mere whimsy but project the feeling of a real though strange community.

MONKSHOOD'S FAREWELL

Choreography by Pilobolus to tape collage. First performed at Connecticut College, New London, Conn., July 28, 1974, by Jonathan Wolken, Michael Tracy, Alison Chase, Moses Pendelton, Martha Clarke, and Robby Barnett.

The delight that viewers are likely to find in this dance is the same they would derive from browsing through a medieval manuscript. It is a curio that makes one think of fens and old castles, though there is nothing specifically programmatic about any of the sections. The whole piece, though, just has the atmosphere of a slightly mysterious other age where the chivalrous and the grotesque flourished side by side.

The dance begins with something resembling a joust. It starts simply enough but develops a variety of permutations requiring excellent balance, as one man, walking, holds another with his head pointed forward like a battering ram and his legs extended to the rear, and a woman balances by hooking her arms over those legs. Two such teams butt and stun one another. The two men who are contending have a slow-motion fist fight at another point and recoil from the simulated blows showing the physical changes that one is accustomed to see only by the slow-motion camera.

A man stands on one leg throughout a long solo in which he appears to be a curious water fowl, peering hither and yon and looking slightly silly. At another moment two women have a race with one another. Their means of locomotion are a team of men who kneel and crawl forward. Each woman has her own team and she appears to be striding as first one then the other man crawls forward with the woman keeping one foot in the middle of each man's back.

In "Lady Curzon Has a Hunch" the four men of the company shuffle around with hunched backs like friendly dullards. They are spurred into lumbering play by one woman, who cavorts mischievously and nearly dislocates herself in a jumping and falling-down solo that stirs everybody including the jealous Lady Curzon, who hauls her off like a misbehaving pet. When she leaves, the men are clearly dejected and place oafish but comforting hands around one another's shoulders. The concluding section finds the stage dimmed and three men leaning forward; each carries on his back another person who remains stiffly straight. It looks like the trek of a dying breed into oblivion.

The music selected for this piece was unusually effective in helping to create the proper mood. In the last section there was a suggestion of bagpipe music with its keening and lonely sound that was particularly appropriate. The piece was something of a departure for Pilobolus in that it played more explicitly on male and female roles and added a dramatic tension to the piece, which is a bit unusual in the muscular and humorous world that the company usually explores.

CHOREOCHRONICLE
OF PILOBOLUS DANCE THEATER

1971

Pilobolus
Walklydon
Geode

1972

Spyrogyra
*Anaendrom
Ocellus

1973

Ciona
Aubade
Syzygy
Cameo
Two Bits

1974

Pilea
Terra Cotta
Pseudopodia
*Monkshood's Farewell
Pilobolus and Joan (tv)
Triptych
Dispretzled

1975

Ciona (revised)
Alrone
Untitled

KATHRYN POSIN

Before she decided to establish her own performing ensemble, Posin appeared with a variety of other companies, including those of Anna Sokolow and Valerie Bettis, the short-lived but ambitious American Dance Theater at Lincoln Center and in the Dance Theater Workshop professional company. She was born in Butte, Montana, and grew up in Chicago. She received extensive dance training at Bennington College in Vermont before

settling in New York City, where she studied with Merce Cunningham and
Margaret Black.

Her college awarded her a choreographer's grant and she was the recipient of a Doris Humphrey fellowship from the American Dance Festival at
Connecticut College. She has taught extensively, including the Harvard
Summer School of Dance and the International Dance School in Bern,
Switzerland. In addition to working with her own company she has
mounted her works for a variety of other groups and has choreographed several Off-Broadway shows, including the rock musical *Salvation*.

THE CLOSER SHE GETS . . .
THE BETTER SHE LOOKS

*Choreography by Kathryn Posin. Music by Herb Alpert. Costumes by Kathryn
Posin. Lighting and scenic projections by Gary Harris. First performed at the
Ninety-second Street YM-YWHA, New York, N.Y., March 31, 1968, by Kathryn
Posin, Philip Johnson, David Krohn, Ray Cook, Elizabeth Whaley, and Irene
Feigenheimer.*

There is a certain type of loud, jolly, brassy music that seems designed to encourage people to spend money when they are in stores. Many supermarkets
have picked up the practice of broadcasting such music as people wheel
their shopping carts up and down the aisles of the store in the fond hope
that it will stimulate the acquisitive instincts of the customers. Posin took the
opportunity to use such music and shopping carts for a comment on the
relations between men and women in an acquisitive society.

The three men and three women in the dance are infected by the habits
bred from too much exposure to television commercials and too many advertisements of all kinds. Slides of shopping stores are shown as the six become
embroiled in a selection process that has little to do with human feeling but
a great deal to do with aimless "impulse" shopping. There are anxious encounters between them but the ultimately telling episode about contemporary relationships develops in a series of passages by the couples in which
they push one another about in wire basket shopping carts. The pushers
change from one to another with casual carelessness in the way that one
box of soap powder might be preferred to another and then a moment later
replaced on the shelf. Only in this exchange it is another person who is let
go. People, however, are utterly stripped of dignity, being heaped into the
carts like so many boxes and jars of one thing or another.

It's amazing to think that, with the prevalence of commercial messages,
both broadcast and printed, so few choreographers have taken the opportunity to make a social statement using them. Posin's wickedly keen and hu-

morous eye sharply framed the flummery in its ultimate aspect, as a measure of human behavior directed toward humans and not inanimate consumer items.

CHOREOCHRONICLE
OF KATHRYN POSIN

1967

Call

1968

Block
*The Closer She Gets . . . The
    Better She Looks
40 Amp Mantis

1969

Guidesong

1971

Days
Three Countrysides
Flight of the Baroque Airship

1972

Prism
Summer of '72

1973

Grass
Ladies in the Arts
Ghost Train
Bach Pieces (Solo "Ich ruf zu
    dir"; solo; duet; concerto)
Port Authority

1974

Nuclear Energy I
Children of the Atomic Age
Nuclear Energy II

1975

Nuclear Energy III
Street Song
The Waves

YVONNE RAINER

Among the generation of dancer-choreographers who rebelled against the conventions of the previous generation, none rebelled more completely or strongly than Rainer. She rejected "spectacle, virtuosity, the star image and any type of theatrical 'magic.'" She was left with the human body and its infinite possibilities for movement designs. The body was made to function like the good machine that it is, and not to divert energy into the projection of emotion or dramatic tension.

Rainer grew up in San Francisco and was involved with acting rather than dance until she moved to New York. In Manhattan she became interested in the ideas of John Cage and began to study dance with Edith Stephan. She later went to ballet class, the Martha Graham School, and the Merce Cunningham studio. James Waring included her in his company, and she began to perform publicly. She studied composition with Ann Halprin and with Robert Dunn. It was to find a performing space suitable for the last class of Dunn's course that made her and Steve Paxton approach Rev. Al Carmines to request use of the Judson Memorial Church. The favorable response was the beginning of the Judson Dance Theater, which was to become the focal point for vanguard activity throughout the sixties.

Rainer has taught at various colleges and appeared at the American Dance Festival at Connecticut College. She is an energetic polemicist who has written frequently on the state of dance and has made several films. She sometimes includes filmed segments in some of her dances.

TERRAIN

Choreography by Yvonne Rainer. Lighting by Robert Rauschenberg. First performed at the Judson Memorial Church, New York, N.Y., April 28, 1963, by Trisha Brown, William Davis, Judith Dunn, Alex Hay, Steve Paxton, Yvonne Rainer, and Albert Reid.

When the piece was first presented, it represented the most ambitious work that Rainer had attempted. It was designed to occupy an entire evening and was structured so that aleatory elements could take place if one of the performers called out a specific code letter or number. This was set within the over-all structure of the piece, which was preplanned. Despite its strongly antitraditional attitude toward shaping a dance, it did require the performing skill that one would bring to a more conventional work.

The six men and women start the dance with a diagonal walk across the performing space, keeping closely clustered. They walk to the back of the area and cross down again in a shallow diagonal, pausing at various points. Individuals or smaller groups now begin diagonal crossings breaking into leaps, hops, and detaching him- or herself from the group. At times one or another of the dancers goes to the side in an area outside of the active group and returns only when brought back by one of the dancers. Small games of passing and jostling each other are played by the dancers, alternating between the two actions.

Two women do a balletic duet. First each does an individual variation with the high open-arm look of ballet dancers. One of them punctuates her variations with bumps and grinds that suggest burlesque theater. Together they begin a series of poses that suggest modeling, and finally they crawl and tumble in a roughhouse fashion as the lights go down. In structure it suggests the adagio, variations, coda formula of classic dance, but in the performance it specifically is rendered as a species of calendar or poster art.

Five solos comprise the third portion of the dance, two of which are accompanied by the recitation of essays by Spencer Holst. The other three are not so accompanied except accidently if they are being performed while someone is dancing and reciting. The dancers in this portion have nothing to do with one another but simply execute their individual solos. When not performing the dancers stand casually by a police barricade which is moved to various points around the area during selected sections of the dance.

In "Play," the fourth section, dancers again call out instructions to summon others to join in. They are supplied with rubber balls by a man in the balcony, and the movement is fast and athletically snappy in its dynamics. The exceptions are those in which a performer stands doing nothing and looking relaxed or bouncing a ball. At another point clusters of dancers strike a pose together, and then the group is disassembled by the others who lift and carry them away like bits of furniture. A long erotic duet with sculptural poses and weighty lifts ends the section.

The final portion begins with all of the dancers lined up in a file on the left-hand side. Each begins to do small variations, passing to the right and then reversing back to a spot just short of the starting point. Eventually the whole group progresses to the right side and concludes the dance in the same order they had when it began.

It is difficult to relate the strangeness of the movement and the design of the piece to current practice, since current repertory includes much that was once considered outrageously revolutionary. These were trained dancers voluntarily choosing to function as athletes, citizens in the street, or audience members as they stood by the barricade, and also dancers. They stepped in and out of stage roles that were worn and doffed as easily as one might change hats. The movement, much of it raw and not polished, chaffed against the unusual strictures which ordinarily guided one's framing of a dance. It was blunt, honest, puzzling, at times wearisome and, most importantly, it was different. Different because it wanted to pose a direct challenge to custom and didn't have the time to be subtle or polite.

TRIO A

Choreography by Yvonne Rainer. First performed at the Judson Memorial Church, New York, N.Y., January 10, 1966, by Yvonne Rainer, David Gordon, and Steve Paxton. At its first performance it was called The Mind Is a Muscle, Part I, *but was subsequently changed.*

When she first created this dance in 1966, Rainer had no idea of how closely it would be identified with her or just how much use she would derive from it herself. She actually saw it as part of a larger work and called it *The Mind Is a Muscle, Part I,* but it has been excerpted so frequently that the piece has come to lead a life of its own. After coming back from a serious illness Rainer performed for the first time using *Trio A* but called it *Convalescent Dance.* She has taught it to hundreds of students and once told her own company to stop quoting it back to her in dances where members had a free choice for a variation. The dance has been performed by three people, as its title indicates, as a solo, and in relays of dance teams comprising ten dancers each. For simplicity's sake the description will be of the solo version.

A woman stands with profile to the audience and swings one arm across her stomach and the other simultaneously behind her. Smoothly swirling her arms, she joins hands and frames her head. The flow of movement continues in an unbroken and uninflected stream following the weight of the gesture rather than any emotional determinant. She taps one foot in a smooth arc and then the other, extends out to the side and makes tiny circling motions. Resting the weight on one leg, she lowers herself to the floor and then pushes herself up and kicks to one side; she stands to repeat the swinging motion of the arms that started the dance.

She sits and rolls over backward, rises to face away from the audience, wiggles a bit, and, turning in profile, she adjusts a little like an athlete ready to compete. She bends all the way forward, spreads her legs, and then drops into a squat to thrust a leg to the side. A sequence of rolling like a log is started, and she stops to offer a little spasmodic variation followed by bouncy leaps, and with her back to the audience she tilts her head to the left, arcs her body to the right, and concludes on the balls of her feet.

The piece is resolutely physical without any emotional overtones. No dramatic accents are used and the parts of the dance flow into one another without a break. It is this constant flow that makes it so enjoyable an exercise.

CHOREOCHRONICLE
OF YVONNE RAINER

1961

Three Satie Spoons
The Bells

1962

Satie for Two
Three Seascapes
Grass
Dance for Three People and Six
  Arms
Ordinary Dance

1963

We Shall Run
Word Words (with Steve Paxton)
*Terrain
Person Dance (from *Dance for*
  Fat Man, Dancer, and Person)
Room Service
Shorter End of a Small Piece

1964

At My Body's House
Dialogues
Some Thoughts on Improvisation
Part of a Sextet
Incidents (with Larry Loonin)
Part of a Sextet No. 2 (*Rope*
  Duet)

1965

Parts of Some Sextets
Partially Improvised New Untitled
  Solo with Pink T-Shirt, Blue
  Bloomers, Red Ball, Bach's
  Toccata and Fugue in D Minor
  (later, *Untitled Solo*)

1966

*Trio A
The Mind Is a Muscle (first
  version)
Carriage Discreteness

1968

Untitled Work for 40 People
The Mind Is a Muscle (final
  version)
Performance Demonstration No. 1
North East Passing

1969

Rose Fractions (with Deborah
  Hay)
Performance Fractions for the
  West Coast
Connecticut Composite

1970

> Continuous Project—Altered
>   Daily
> WAR

1971

> Grand Union Dreams
> Numerous Frames

1972

> In the College
> Performance
> Lives of Performers (film)

1973

> This is the story of a woman
>   who . . .

ROBERT RAUSCHENBERG

As a student at Black Mountain College, North Carolina, in the early 1950s, Rauschenberg was exposed to a variety of advanced theatrical ideas, including what is generally accepted as being the first "happening." When he settled in New York he became acquainted with Paul Taylor and began to work collaboratively with him, designing productions. After 1960, when they were no longer working together, Rauschenberg attended a composition course at the Merce Cunningham studio that was being conducted by Robert Dunn. He was encouraged to develop his own ideas choreographically and began to appear in his own pieces.

Like his paintings and constructions these pieces were a combination of elements with great and provocative diversity. As an early member of the Judson Dance Theater, he first showed his work there. In the following decade he continued to make pieces and also to become associated with the Merce Cunningham company as its designer. In addition to his dance pieces he also created "happenings" of a stronger dramatic character. He enjoys performing and has appeared in dances by Deborah Hay, Alex Hay, and Simone Forti as well as in his own. He was a prime mover in the "First New York Theater Rally," which he supported generously and later helped organize "Nine Evenings: Theater and Engineering."

PELICAN

Choreography by Robert Rauschenberg. First performed at America on Wheels (skating rink), Washington, D.C., May 9, 1963, by Carolyn Brown, Robert Rauschenberg, and Per Ultvelt.

In the early sixties an exhibition of painting and sculpture designated by the title "The Popular Image" was held at the Washington Gallery of Modern Art in the capital. As part of the show there were performance events scheduled, and Rauschenberg decided to make a dance. The performance area was to be a large indoor roller-skating rink, and Rauschenberg asked Carolyn Brown of the Cunningham company to join him along with Per Ultvelt in a trio. As a modern dancer Brown had infrequently danced in ballet shoes but had taken regular ballet class. Rauschenberg asked her to appear in blocked shoes, which would allow her to dance on full point.

Two men balancing themselves carefully kneel on axles with wheels at either end and make slow progress out toward the center of the performing space. They wear roller skates, but despite all of the wheeled locomotion their entrance has a somewhat laborious quality, though it is accomplished smoothly. When they reach the center of the area, they are joined by a woman in simple leotard and tights, picking her way in toe shoes.

The two men partner her in a version of a romantic trio from their somewhat hampered kneeling position. It is as if a pair of dotty, eccentric princes have chosen to honor the woman of their choice with hobbled but attentive support. She is gravely aloof throughout the *pas de trois,* during which she remains on point. She turns gracefully, stretches her arm and leg in a fluid arabesque, and accepts the assistance from her two kneeling partners. She then departs, elegantly picking her way out still on point. The two men, freed of their partnering work, rise and skate around in large circles. They each wear a small cargo parachute strapped to their backs and seem like some form of odd bird as they sweep ecstatically around.

The contrast of the wheeled freedom of the men once they have finished the classical trio remains vividly in the memory. Where they had been shackled to the axles and to her, they now flow around freely. Perhaps it is a comment on the role of the male in ballet, and perhaps it was intended only as a demonstration of wheeled locomotion and natural movement or the ungainly look of the pelican afoot and aloft. In any case it was striking.

CHOREOCHRONICLE
OF ROBERT RAUSCHENBERG

1961

   Collaboration with David Tudor

1962
   The Construction of Boston

1963

   *Pelican
   Prestidigitator Extraordinary

1964

   Elgin Tie
   Shotput

1965

   Map Room I
   Map Room II
   Spring Training

1966

   Open Score
   Nine Evenings: Theater and
     Engineering
   Statue of Liberty Happening

BARBARA ROAN

Among Roan's preoccupations is a feeling for individual idiosyncrasies, which has eventuated in a series of *Parades,* in which individuals are encouraged to portray some extravagant character. Roan herself has some of this extravagance built into her choreographic approach, which is at one moment highly serious and developed and at the next manically comic. Her dance background includes study with Erick Hawkins and a period of touring with his company. Among fellow members of that company was Rod Rodgers, who continued to dance with and choreograph for Roan after they had both decided to pursue independent concert careers. A major association for Roan was her long involvement with the dance company of Rudy Perez, where she was a featured performer and received roles that Perez had created for himself. She has toured widely with her own group and other companies and has been artist-in-residence at the University of Wisconsin. She has appeared with her company as part of the annual dance festival held at the Delacorte Theatre in New York's Central Park.

OCTOBER PARADE

Choreography by Barbara Roan. First performed at the Cubiculo, New York, N.Y., October 6, 1971, by Nancy Scher, Daniel Press, Irene Feigenheimer, Wendy Summit, Anthony LaGiglia, Dennis Florio, Alice Coughlin, Ellen Robbins, Barbara Roan, Joan Swartz, John Moore, Art Bauman, Ellen Jacobs, Jeff Duncan, Chip Largman, Bob Marinaccio, Connie Allentuch, Eddie Trieber, Amy Berkman, David White, Tom Clifton, and Diana Scott.

The small-town parade is a ritual familiar to everyone, and it seemed to offer unlimited dance possibilities to Roan. She first staged a version of the work in upstate New York and subsequently in New York City. Her happy innovation was to combine the elements of a circus parade with the stock characters that one might find in and around the performing world. The costuming was delightfully outrageous, and the performing energy was tumultuous.

A rousing march coincides with the slide projection of a majorette leading a brass band down a public street. A man walks out after the slide projection and carries a red, white, and blue pennant in his hands. To the sound of a patriotic speech he pulls it over his head, secures it, and walks off. A roustabout or workman sets up a ladder, climbs it, and then does the perfectly illogical thing and eats a sandwich. He watches the antics down below with some amusement and constant interest. Five dancers blowing ear-shattering police whistles enter and circle the area, and one wears a pair of hip waders. They are like jolly clowns, and when they leave the workman descends, folds his ladder, loads it on a small express wagon, and walks off.

Immediately five identical, quacking, pull toys are paraded around, followed by a series of individual variations. A man in a sailor hat bounces up and down slapping his chest; another in seventeenth-century costume drags around a quacky pull toy dog, to be joined by several others. A covey of dancers crawl in on all fours to bark and imitate dogs. The three-ring-circus aspect now takes over completely as a whole line of individuals move past the audience doing specialty acts. There is a woman with a large metal Coca-Cola sign that makes an unholy din every time she does an attitude on it. A couple holds a "Grand Opening" sign which tears in the middle. The first man with his patriotic pennant returns to promenade.

All of the exotics leave, and a woman in street wear slaps her forehead as if to wonder at all of the images and visions that she had just seen, and by contrast she dances in a self-contained and more conventional manner and leaves. The group sweeps the area once again and disappears, to enter a moment later. Each dancer places down a shoe, one directly in front of the previous one, and then circles around to pick up the last one and place it first and make the whole line of shoes describe a path. The line of shoes is then picked up individually and taken off. The company returns with hands linked to dance in a long serpentine. The second time around it is performed in march time, and the third time, backward.

Where they had laid down shoes the dancers now lay down a pattern of empty Coca-Cola cans very carefully in the shape of a rough "R." The woman in street clothes examines the line and leaves satisfied. The cast returns and gleefully demolishes the pattern by kicking the cans away. The dancers line up facing the wall along one side of the space and pass a whispered message from one to another. When it has been fully passed, all lie on their backs and weave patterns with their arms and stand to step elaborately backward and off. The man with the pennant is drawn around once more in the express wagon, and, to conclude, two men carry a banner that says "START."

The panoply of the circus is delightfully exploited by the piece, which has a wonderfully dizzy feeling of high spirits to it. It has been presented in many versions both outdoors and indoors and is never quite the same. This particular performance was given in October 1971.

CHOREOCHRONICLE
OF BARBARA ROAN

1968

Dog Run Entrance

1969

A Standardhighwaymileageguide
Driz...zle
Ocean
Pause
Prefix

1970

†Woolworth's I

1971

†Woolworth's II
*October Parade

1972

†*Woolworth's III*
Borrowed/Parts/Borrowed
Waystation/Truckers Only

1973

True Spirits (with Irene
    Feigenheimer and Anthony
    LaGiglia)
The Continuing Dance Exchange
    (with Irene Feigenheimer and
    Anthony LaGiglia)
45 Seconds to String (with Irene
    Feigenheimer)
Went (revision)

1974

Landmark—Showpiece
Range
Time/Still
†*Woolworth's IV*

† *Woolworth's* is a name Roan has given to any paradelike piece she does out of New York City that incorporates a large number of people.

MARIAN SARACH

Her training ranges all the way from modern classes at the New Dance Group to the study of ballet with Russian émigré teachers in Paris, and her choreography reflects the diverse strains of her training. Her first study was modern, and she was one of the early members of Dance Associates, which was founded by James Waring in the early 1950s to offer young adventurous choreographers an opportunity to create pieces and perform them without the restrictions that were imposed in other performing associations. She has created new works steadily from the early 1950s and was active in the Judson Dance Theater when it was established in the sixties. She lived abroad for several years in Turkey with her husband and took the opportunity to study ballet in Paris. She has performed with James Waring and with the Paul Taylor company and was an active member of the resident ballet company at the Brooklyn Academy of Music, appearing in opera productions as well as the company's independent dance evenings. She has taught privately and at the Educational Alliance, and was the assistant artistic director of the Contemporary Dancers of Winnipeg.

LUNAR LANDING

Choreography by Marian Sarach. Music by Jay Miller. First performed at the Cubiculo, New York, N.Y., June 26, 1972, by Marian Sarach.

The dance has nothing whatsoever to do with space travel, astronauts, or any type of galactic exploration. It is a witty solo that Sarach prepared for herself in the style of ironic wit that is her trademark.

She enters costumed in a riot of colors and bangles. Just before she appears there are cascades of arpeggios from a harp suggesting a personage of romantic leanings. Her entrance is made thunderous because of the wooden clogs that clatter on the wooden floor. She quite unromantically gets rid of them and then begins to leap and ricochet off the walls of the small enclosed space. She drops to the floor to wriggle and undulate.

She is wearing a rainbow-colored shift with one red glove and one green. She shakes her masses of bracelets furiously and frequently. She is a caricature of a houri as she switches from such coarse energy to attempt a yearning swoon inspired by the delicate harp music. She thinks the better of the swoon and is carried away with technical movement and quickly launches into a series of complicated movements involving fast whipping turns. She thinks the better of it all and slips back into her clogs. Her relatively silent exit is in contrast to the noisy entrance as she extends her arms forward with only the slight clashing of the bracelets heard.

The piece is delightfully witty as it presents a dancing-girl type coming to work with the heavy tread of any laborer. Her costume of course is more colorful, but then there are all sorts of work. She shows us masses of dance movement, only some of which are appropriate for a seductively alluring dance. The others are just technical feats that she does because she can do them, and is pleased with her skill. The alternation between the character and the performer behind the character is charming.

CHOREOCHRONICLE
OF MARIAN SARACH

1953–54

> *Mobile*
> *Bourée*
> *Aftermath*

1955–57

> *Nashki*
> *Triglyphos*
> *Desert Landscape*
> *Daphne*
> *Oberatura Republicana* (with
>   Paul Taylor, Remy Charlip,
>   James Waring, David
>   Vaughan)
> *Kinderscenen*

1966

> *Debussy Watusi*
> *Aerial Macabre*
> *Dulcimers, Sweet Tremors,*
>   *Nubian Drums*
> *Serpent Charmers*
> *Yesterday's Twilight Not Included*

1967

> *Intimations of Abracadabra*

1970

> *Etude for a March*
> *My Secret Life*
> *Facets*
> *Bread and Butter*

1971

> *Oriental Poppy*
> *Concertante*
> *Openers*
> *Celestial Vision*
> *Cambridge Memories*
> *Elements I and II*
> *Words for Bryan to Sing and*
>   *Dance*
> *Gaspard et Raina*
> *Marche*

1972

> *True Romance*
> **Lunar Landing*

1973

> *Earthly Pleasures and Heavenly*
>   *Delights*
> *Walk Don't Walk*
> *The Last Shimmy*
> *Eagles are Essential*
> *Cultural Exchange*
> *Coteau de Festin*

1974

> *O Canada*
> *Elegant Rag*
> *Sweet Swans*
> *Chocolate Soup*

1975

> *February Circus*
> *Saskatoon Pie*
> *Pastoral*

JOSEPH SCHLICHTER

Starting to study dance in college at Cornell University, Schlichter had to interrupt his training for three years to be a Navy pilot. He returned to study immediately after with Martha Graham, José Limón, and briefly Antony Tudor. He joined the Limón company and remained with it for three years. After leaving the Limón company he formed his own group, which was resident at Mills College on the West Coast, and began to do his own choreographic work in earnest. Movement motivation as well as the sheer exhilaration of dancing infused his choreographic efforts. On the one hand he could feel the rush of excitement generated when he walked down the face of a seven-story building tethered with a mountain climber's line in a Trisha Brown work, and on the other could create a dance composed of printed instructions asking individuals to perform spontaneously designed dance movement that would mirror the instruction. After a year he disbanded his own group and currently he is a psychotherapist using body movement.

FROM 1 TO 10 TO 7

Choreography by Joseph Schlichter. Tape music by Lee Haring, based on Claudio Monteverdi. First performed at the Gate Theatre, New York, N.Y., October 26, 1966, by Mark Gabor and Joseph Schlichter.

Plastic sheeting was one of the materials that received extensive use in the early 1960s and Schlichter made particularly good use of it in this piece. He created a sense of isolation by stretching it entirely across the front of the stage, sealing off the people behind it from the outside world.

A single figure enters. It is a man whose entire body is wrapped with vari-colored elastic bands. He walks in slowly and flattens his body against the sheeting facing the audience. A dark-garbed figure moves carefully up behind him and traces the outline of the man's body in black paint. The man leaves the sheeting with his outline upon it and begins to perform a series of dance variations. While he is doing this, the other man in the dark costume pads along after him and picks off bits of the rubber stripping. He reminds one of the little birds that walk along the backs of large animals and pick bits from their hides. In that case the bird is helping the animal, but there is an air of menace to the actions of the dark man.

Suddenly without warning he springs onto the man dancing and knocks him to the floor but then releases him. The man does not attempt to resist but exhibits a resigned passivity to it all; the picking and the assault as if they were the normal order of things. He returns to doing his lonely variation, and the dark man resumes his picking. It is obvious that the ending of the piece will be reached when he is picked clean and there is nothing left except the outline. The stage is darkened as the picking is still going on.

The absolute chilling menace of the simple picking gesture is hard to convey, but it was so relentless and so deliberate that one watched with attentive horror. It was like being present at the slow destruction of a fellow creature who was trapped with his destroyer in utter isolation. There was nothing that he could do and the encounter would run its inevitable course, and all that would be left of the colorful man was the bare faceless outline.

CHOREOCHRONICLE
OF JOSEPH SCHLICHTER..

1958

Ekstasis

1959

Cries

1962

Faces on a Coin
Period
Stones of Time

1964

Still
Psychodance

1965

Fugue for Three Marys

1966

Cube
*From 1 to 10 to 7

1967

Pump

BEVERLY SCHMIDT

As a former student and dancer with Alwin Nikolais, Schmidt shows the clean precision that has traditionally been a characteristic of students who shaped dances under Nikolais' benign but exacting standards. In addition to her work with him at the Henry Street Settlement Playhouse she also studied under his mentor, Hanya Holm, and for a year with her teacher, Mary Wigman, the eminent German expressionist choreographer and dancer.

Schmidt began her own creative career in the early fifties at the Henry Street Settlement Playhouse with works for small groups and occasional solos. Nearly a decade later she began to work seriously with combined film and dance productions and in the sixties achieved a notable work entitled *Duet for One Person (Blossoms)*. She has continued to choreograph and teach in the intervening years, and currently she is on the staff of the University of Illinois, Champaign-Urbana. Her work has a beautiful finish in its detailing and often has delicate touches of humor.

DUET FOR ONE PERSON
(BLOSSOMS)

Choreography by Beverly Schmidt. Music by Henry Purcell, Philip Corner, and Malcolm Goldstein. Film by Mario Jorrin. Conceived and directed by Roberts Blossom. First performed at Second City, New York, N.Y., May 27, 1963, by Beverly Schmidt.

The piece is an extraordinarily successful blend of film and dance in that it remains true to the spirit of each dicipline and makes imaginative use of the expressive possibilities of each. At times Schmidt performed the dance under the title of *Duet for One* but changed nothing other than the title.

On a large screen at the rear of the stage a dancer in a black leotard is shown in a filmed segment doing a series of turns and jumps in a practice studio. The film is in simple black and white. In the first live dance interlude, the same performer stands dressed as a small child. She has a large play hoop and a tall hat with a silly feather projecting from the top. She hops and skips in childlike fashion and from time to time attempts some of the steps that the filmed dancer is doing, but only manages to approximate them.

She leaves and returns as an adolescent girl, wearing a long, filmy dress, who has obviously acquired more of the dancing skill needed to be able to replicate the skill of the dancer in the filmed segment. This filmed dance goes on and on with a restless but yet slow-motion energy that suggests a time or a place that is not the here and now.

Suddenly the entire screen is covered with a color projection of a blossoming flower print pattern in red. The black and white film sequence is off, and the dancer herself has disappeared into the projected pattern. Then confidently and deliberately she reveals herself by stepping forward from the screen. She has been invisible because she is wearing a patterned dress just like the projected print. She steps back into the projected pattern and vanishes again. When she reappears she is wearing the identical costume as the dancer on film, and now as it unrolls again she joins in doing the same movement with precisely the degree of professional polish as the filmed dancer. She is in effect dancing with herself.

The floating motions of the screen dancer now appear as some sort of ideal performance toward which the live dancer was striving in her own mind and which was only visible to her own consciousness. No matter how tentative her first steps were she retained this image as her guide and finally blossomed into one who was able to live up to her aspiration.

CHOREOCHRONICLE
OF BEVERLY SCHMIDT

1953

Three Characters

1954

Interlude
Evil Eye

1955

Styx
Gigue
Last Flower
Six Miniatures
Beginning
Red Hoop
White Figure

1956

White Figure
Rite
Mobile
Penguins, Arise!
Caprice
Hymn
Rag
Premonitions
Magma
Droll Figure

1957

Idyll

1959

Crest
Wanderhythm

1960

9 Points in Time

1961

Aire
Black Traveler
Erg
Caper

1962

Pindaric
Mementoes
Prelude to a Masked Event
Chamber Dances

1963

*Duet for One Person (Blossoms)
Everybody
All

1964

With Gladys, et al.
Scene: Unresolved
Rocking Chair Dance
Poem for Theater No. 6
Florence, Italy

1965

Waltz
3 October Dances

1966

Moon-dial (with Aldo
   Tambellini)
Yes, Live Happily

1967

Movement Loops

1968

A Rehearsal for Michelangelo
Depot Soup
Kaleidoscope

1969

Patterns

1970

Yaxkin
Corolla

1971

A Long Walk
The Beginning of a Revolting
   Solo

1972

Dog
Requiem

1973

Moonlight Sonata

1974

Movement Loops with
   Bumbershoots
I Look Back, . . . I . . .
Flashback

CAROLEE SCHNEEMANN

As many other artists had approached the world of dance through the painter's theater events known as "happenings," so had Schneemann. When she heard about the composition classes being given by Robert Dunn that would eventuate in the creation of the Judson Dance Theater, she joined enthusiastically. One of her own first demands in a workshop was that everyone and everything in the room, including the radiator, be part of the dance. It reflected her total approach to the problem of moving within a selected space. She made her first real stir as a designer of human movement with the creation of *Meat Joy*, which was first seen in Paris and London before being performed in New York at the Judson Memorial Church. She presented some of her work at Pavillon de la Jeunesse, Expo '67, and spent three years abroad as a resident in London, where she published *Parts of a Body House Work*. She has made several films, worked in Dutch and German television, and has taught a course in film at the Carnegie Institute, Pittsburgh.

MEAT JOY

Choreography by Carolee Schneemann. Set to a tape collage of Parisian street noises and European popular songs. Lighting by H. Frederick Smith. First performed at the Paris Festival, Paris, France, May 29, 1964. First performed in New York City at the Judson Memorial Church, November 16, 1964, by James Tenney, Robert David Cohen, Tom O'Donnell, Stanley Gochenouer, Carolee Schneemann, Irina Posner, Dorothea Rockburne, and Sandra J. Chew.

The work so excited critic Susan Sontag that she saw it as the opening of a door for the future of the theater. It had an enormous vitality and outrageousness when it was first performed and quickly split audiences and critics wherever it was shown. Schneeman first presented the piece in Paris in the spring of 1964 and a few weeks later in London and at the Judson Memorial Church in New York in the autumn. While deploring the fact that the local customs demanded that performers wear clothes, Schneemann dressed everyone in the most casual clothes with very brief bikini bathing suits underneath.

The men and women performers can be seen at work making up in front of little cosmetic mirrors before the piece actually starts. As they are ready they move into the performing area and begin to engage one another in mild physical encounters, and one man stalks one woman in a large circle outside of the center of action. The performers begin to disrobe one another piece by piece and the striking man is overtly sexual in his predatory manner. Pots of paint stand around the area and huge piles of papers are pushed down from the balcony overlooking the space. Men begin to crumple the large sheets and the disrobing of all continues until everyone is down to small bikinis. The level of intensity of the encounters begins to escalate from the initial casualness. Two men drag two women over to the crumpled paper and tie them up in it and then bind themselves into the bundle and all roll around.

All are heaped up in the center, seemingly exhausted, when another brings out a huge tray piled with chickens, frankfurters, and fish which are thrown onto the pile of human carcasses. As the piece develops the men and women daub one another with the available paint and rub against one another to mix it. They haul the fish and chickens around with them through the encounters, which terminate after a while, and the piece is over, with the meeting ground looking like a littered social battleground.

The people at the conclusion looked as physically spent as the dead fish and fowl that they had manipulated. They had hauled at and tugged at one another like so many sides of beef being manipulated. It was not dance movement as conventionally understood, but it had the sense of movement that made it more convincingly kinetic than many other painters' attempts at dance theater. It had a sense of arranged pictorial tableaux, but it was a demonstration of physicality made with uninhibited enthusiasm.

CHOREOCHRONICLE
OF CAROLEE SCHNEEMANN

1956–58

Loving (with James Tenney)
Cat's Cradle (with James
Tenney)
White Eye (with James Tenney)

1960–61

Labyrinths

1962

Glass Environment for Sound
and Motion
Mink Paws TURRET
Newspaper Event

1963

Chromolodeon
Lateral Splay
EYE BODY

1964

*Meat Joy
Music Box Music

1965

"TV"
The Queen's Dog
Noise Bodies (with James
    Tenney)
Beast Event

1966

Water Light/Water Needle

1967

Snows
Night Crawlers
Ordeals
Snug Harbor

1968

Illinois Central
Illinois Central Transposed

1969

Nude Bride
Expansions

1970

Chicago Festival of Life in
    London: Thames Crawling

1971

Electronic Activations
Schlaget-Auf (Ein Gestalt)
Why We Run and Crawl
Rainbow Blaze

1972

Road Runners
Roller Moving Train Skating

GUS SOLOMONS, JR.

There was a long hiatus between the jazz and tap dancing lessons of his childhood and his sophomore year in college, when Solomons began to study seriously, but it did not prevent him from making a career in dance. He was studying architecture at the Massachusetts Institute of Technology at the time and managed to spend a great deal of time performing in amateur theatricals as well as taking dance training and still complete his degree program. After graduation he went to New York to continue study and appeared with a number of companies, including the Martha Graham, Pearl Lang, Donald McKayle, and Joyce Trisler groups. He began to do television work and then joined the Merce Cunningham company. When he left that company it was with the intention of organizing his own group and creating a repertory for it. His own performing has always been marked with a special crispness of attack, and his dances display an equal sharpness of design and detailing. In addition to his touring he has also prepared several television programs for Station WGBH in his native Boston, showing an imaginative use of the medium.

OBBLIGATO '69 N.Y.

Choreography by Gus Solomons, Jr. Set to voices from the 1930s and Bojangles Robinson. First performed at the Minor Latham Playhouse, New York, N.Y., fall of 1969, by Gus Solomons, Jr.

By affixing a date to this piece, Solomons places it precisely in time and encourages one to think of the conditions then prevailing that might have influenced the elements which went into the piece. It was a time when he had achieved his mature style, and yet it was set in another, earlier style of movement. Nudity was in the air and on many stages. Protest demonstrations were at their height, social disorder and civil injustice were handmaidens.

A man stands alone dressed in casual everyday clothes. He seems totally self-contained and unconcerned. The sound accompanying the dance is drawn from radio broadcasts of the decades of the 1930s and 1940s. The voices are strident, urging, and insistent by turns, but the man executes a tap dance, lightly crossing and recrossing the stage from one side to another as if nothing at all were happening. The pace is unhurried, and he appears only to be listening to the sound inside his own head, which blots out all the other voices clamoring for attention.

The parade of voices ceases and is replaced with dull, unimaginative jazz obviously adapted badly and commercially from original black musicians. The man ceases to move, his attention has been caught. He goes deliberately to the center of the stage, where he begins to remove layer upon layer of his clothing as the music continues to pour out. As each garment is laid aside, the lighting of the stage is turned down slightly so that as he approaches total nudity he becomes less and less visible and finally the stage is completely darkened.

The crisis which reached his concern was the music which was layers and layers of sensitivity removed from the accomplishment of the original musicians. As long as that had not been tampered with he could go along listening to the private sound in his own mind. When it was violated he stopped and began to peel back to basics.

URBAN RECREATION/THE ULTIMATE PASTORALE

Choreography by Gus Solomons, Jr. Lighting by Barry Suttin. Décor by Louis Pruitt. First performed at the Judson Dance Theater, New York, N.Y., May 4, 1971, by Margaret Beals, Randall Faxon, Jean Iams, Dianne McIntyre, and Gus Solomons, Jr.

When Solomons did this piece, he was infatuated with the motion of games and game time used to shape a dance. Of the pieces that he did, none emerged with a fuller, more satisfying shape than this one in which the women were regally proud in their carriage and the man was briskly efficient.

Nine square columns with a lightly rippled surface stand three rows deep and three rows across. Some of them have a hole piercing one side. Three women walk up and down the pathways inside the snug square that they form. A fourth woman circles outside the enclosure. One of the women inside does a back bend, leaning her torso out of the structure, and the leg of another appears at the same moment, projecting from the opposite side. Because of the columns the bodies of the women become bizarrely detached. They are dressed in black with a small necklace and look formally glamorous. Now they leave the maze one by one to join the woman who is circling outside.

Their large circling path is in sharp contrast to the rigid right-angle paths they had to take inside the rows of columns. One woman touches another and she heads into the columns. A man wearing three sets of suspenders affixed to his trousers appears and pushes one column out of the symmetrical cluster. One by one the columns are moved away from their confining pattern and pushed out of the dance. A woman dances alone and then the man returns with two of the women to do a brief trio. All now stomp around the space, turning periodically, with one arm extended upward and one leg thrust to the back. They join in a straightforward run, and the last of the columns is lifted out. The dancers alternate between walking at the periphery of the space to doing deep bends in the center.

The man dashes from one to another of the women touching them, and they skitter about in the center before lining up together at the side while he dances alone. They join him and all dance together, and then the women cluster together as at the beginning, although all of the sculptural columns have been removed, and they perform the variations that they did when only the little alleyways of the row of columns were available to them to move along.

Like most of Solomons' dances, this one was rigorously ordered in its dance organization, but the rows of columns gave it another spacial ordering which was fascinating to watch being used. The contrast between the strictness of the area inside the nest of columns and the free area was graphically emphasized as the dance broke out of the restrictive space into full freedom and then repeated its opening portion as if the restraining elements were still there. It combined the languid and the staccato, the elegant and the efficient securely.

CHOREOCHRONICLE
OF GUS SOLOMONS, JR.

1960

Etching of a Man

1962

Rag Caprices
Match
Fogrum

1963

Fast
The Ground Is Warm and Cool
Kinesia for Woman and a Man

1964

Four Field of Six

1965

Construction II (1959) and
*   Construction II½*

1966

Simply This Fondness

1967

Ecce Homo
Notebook
Neon

1968

Kinesia for Women
Kinesia No. 5
Two Reeler
City—Motion—Space—Game
Christmas Piece

1969

Phreaque
Draft Alteration
we don't know, only how much
*   time we have . . .*
*Obbligato '69 N.Y.

1970

A Dance in Report Form/
*   A Report in Dance Form*
Quad
cat⚹ccs70-10/13NSSR-gsj9M
Warm-up Piece

1971

> *Pyrothonium*
> *Patrol*
> *On Par*
> **Urban Recreation/The Ultimate*
> *Pastorale*
> *Title Meet*

1972

> *Beetcan Conserves*
> *Pocketcard Process No. 2*
> *Glandular Dilemma and Vision*
> *Masse*
> *The Gut-Stomp Lottery kill*

1973

> *The Son of Cookie Monster*
> *Brilllo*
> *Par/Tournament*
> *Yesterday*

1974

> *Chapter One*
> *Randdance*
> *Stoneflesh*
> *A Shred of Prior Note*
> *Molehill*

1975

> *Steady Work*

CHARLES STANLEY AND DEBORAH LEE

In and around the creative ferment of the Judson Memorial Church in the decade of the sixties informal creative alliances abounded. One of the most successful was that of Stanley and Lee. She had had some balletic training and he was most interested in dramatic movement as seen from a modern dance viewpoint. Stanley was also very active as a designer and was eventually cited for his skill with an Off-Broadway Obie.

Both had appeared in dances designed by James Waring, and showed a definite sympathy for blending movement, song, recitation, and exotic props together in unique combinations. From time to time one or another element would predominate, but audiences were always aware of the sense of total theater which infused their collaborations. Each eventually settled on a solo career when Stanley took over the management of the Cafe Cino after the founder's death.

BLACK AND WHITE AND SPARKLE PLENTY

Choreography by Charles Stanley and Deborah Lee. Tape collage by Charles Stanley and Deborah Lee of Gabriel Fauré and Richard Strauss music and spoken text by Paul Eluard. First performed at the Judson Memorial Church, New York, N.Y., October 16, 1966, by Deborah Lee, Arnold Horton, and Charles Stanley.

Of their various collaborations this piece is the most acutely balanced, showing the performers at the peak of their collective energy. It is quite unconcernedly outrageous, but the same time a totally engrossing piece of theater.

A tall, slender man elegantly dressed in top hat and tails enters the performing space and strides casually over to a spotlight mounted on a swivel bracket. He assumes command of the light with the casual skill of a stage electrician. A woman in a long, flowing dress dashes out, and he begins to follow her dance around the entire space while reciting a text by Paul Eluard suggesting that the woman and her movement are like the flight of a bird. His rich, caressing voice follows her as closely as the smoothly moving spotlight. She is quite clearly being celebrated as the epitome of graceful womanhood. Deftly he changes the colors of the light to match the poetical sentiments that he is reciting, and the whole lyrical dance is enhanced by its aural décor and illumination.

In the second movement a small, energetic man seething with excitement runs from side to side, pausing only momentarily to snatch up a bauble or a string of beads which he then drapes over himself. There is an evident intoxication with the whole gaudiness of the theater and its trappings. His eagerness in scooping up the trinkets and decorating himself, however, is so warmly presented that one feels a participation in some secular rite. To conclude the section, he runs down to the audience and offers random members small circular wafers as one would in a Eucharistic celebration.

The final movement brings the begowned woman together with the man who recited verses, only now he has left his top hat and tails and joins her, encased in a sequined sheath dress. A collage of sounds accompanies their sweepings through the space and suddenly the voice of Kate Smith is heard singing "God Bless America." He stops abruptly and begins a series of athletic exercises that seem to be the only appropriate response to such patriotic and stirring music. To conclude, both ascend a tall ladder from opposite sides, and as they approach one another the light following them narrows its focus to concentrate on their faces, moving closer and closer together. It leaves them in darkness and romantically fixes on a stained-glass window above their heads, where it continues to close until extinguished.

Though the piece only had a tiny cast, it seemed to be designed on the scale of a gigantic film spectacle. The elements, though incredibly diverse, were all tied together so securely so that one enjoyed the parody and also felt the stirrings of the originals. It was an extravaganza of the emotions both celebrated and laughed at, at the same time.

CHOREOCHRONICLE
OF CHARLES STANLEY AND
DEBORAH LEE

1964

Dance in a Black Dress (Lee)

1965

Mrs. Brown (Lee and Carol Marcy)
Evening Song (Lee)
Sandalwood (Lee)
Emma's Speech (Lee)

1966

Exclamations in a Great Space (Stanley and Lee)
Good Times at the Cloud Academy (Lee, James Waring, and Irene Meltzer)
Solo (Lee)
*Black and White and Sparkle Plenty (Stanley and Lee)

1967

Chance Openings (Lee)
Startled, The Dragon Uncoiled About the Billows (Lee)
Lola Montez (Stanley)
A Scarlet Pastorale (Stanley and Lee)
Opening July Fourth (Stanley)

1971

A Postcard from the Volcano— A Comic Postcard (Stanley)
Eroica! An Anti-Fascist Rally (Stanley)
Oboe Rampant (Stanley, McDowell, Bert Lucarelli)

1972

Past Image (Stanley)
Domination of Black (Stanley)
The Stream Has Shown Me My Semblance True (Stanley and Carolyn Lord)
Highways (Stanley)
Highways and Byways (Stanley)
Le Roi Soleil: A Personal Landscape (Stanley)

1973

Caligula (Stanley)
The Great American Pinball Machine (Stanley)
Thursday Night at the Fights (Stanley)

1974

The Twentieth Century Limited
Words and Images

ELAINE SUMMERS

The relationships between dance and film, dance and its environment have been of passionate interest to Summers, who founded the Experimental Intermedia Foundation to foster creative exploration in the field. She was born in Australia and conventionally reared, spending a good part of her childhood in Boston. She took dance as a child but did not begin a formal career until she had finished her studies at art school. She moved to New York and began to study at a variety of schools including the Juilliard School, the Martha Graham School, and with Mary Anthony and Daniel Nagrin. She became a member of the Janet Collins Dance Company and toured with it for two years. She began to attend classes at the Merce Cunningham studio in the early 1960s and became a part of the group of young dancers and choreographers who were to found the Judson Dance Theater at the Judson Memorial Church. She worked within this group for the next few years and then branched off to devote her full energies to the appropriation of unusual environments for dance with the use of film and slides.

COUNTRY HOUSES

Choreography by Elaine Summers. Set to words of Oscar Wilde, arranged by Robert Dunn. First performed at the Gramercy Arts Theater, New York, N.Y., August 1, 1963, by Edward Barton, Lucinda Childs, June Ekman, Ruth Emerson, Sally Gross, Deborah Hay, Al Kurchin, and Pira.

During the summer of 1963 the Judson Dance Theater was given the use of the oldest extant Off-Broadway theater in New York, the landmark designated Gramercy Arts Theater. It was the second full year of the Judson Dance Theater, and it was the first time that the company had the use of a conventional theater space. Summers' reaction was to expand her dance to include the entire house and not to confine herself to the designated performing area alone.

The long, narrow theater has a balcony covering half the orchestra, and a low balustrade runs across the front of it and into the proscenium arch at both sides. The arch itself is designed to look like the entrance to a gracious mansion. Along the sides of the orchestra several windows pierce the walls and the whole ambiance is that of a large house.

The performers are all dressed in white like the ghosts of people who might have inhabited such a house. They appear on the stage forming living tableaux of people in conversation. One woman hangs upside down from the proscenium arch reading selected texts by Oscar Wilde. Other performers move in the aisles of the theater and across the edge of the balustraded balcony. It is impossible to keep track of what everyone is doing at any given time, and in that way the piece gives one the feeling of being a participant in a large house party. Snatches of conversation rise from various portions of the theater and the accumulation of these isolated fragments hangs in the air like the specters of thousands of inconsequential conversations. The performers slowly and inconspicuously drift away.

The piece was a beautiful example of the imaginative use of an environment, and the theater became for a short time a real house, haunted by a ghostly party. There was no feeling of menace connected with it, however, any more than there would be in rummaging through the attic and discovering the artifacts of a past time.

CHOREOCHRONICLE
OF ELAINE SUMMERS

1962–63

Instant Chance
Newspaper Dance
Dance for Lots of People
Execution Is Simply Not
Dance for Carola
Suite
Walking Improvisation
Film Dance Collage
*Country Houses

1964

Fantastic Gardens

1965

Tumble Dance
Suspended Ring
Theatre Piece for Chairs and
*   Ladders*
Dressing and Undressing
To Steve with Love

1968

Walking Dance for Any Number
The Closer She Gets

1971

Jazz for a Lake and Trees
Floating Dance for Two on a
*   Raft in a Lake*
Celebrations in a City Place
Flashes

1972

City Light Signals
Energy Changes (Version I)

1973

Iowa Blizzard '73
Two Girls Downtown Iowa
Energy Changes (Version II)

1974

Intermedia Theatre Events

1975

Energy Changes (Version III)
All Around Buffalo
Illuminated Workingman

KEI TAKEI

On one of her many trips abroad Anna Sokolow spotted Kei Takei in Japan and recommended her for a Fulbright scholarship. Takei received the award and came to the United States in the late sixties to continue her studies and has remained ever since. Her studies have included instruction at the Martha Graham School, the Juilliard School of Music, the Henry Street Settlement Playhouse, and the Dance Theater Workshop. Out of it all she has evolved a type of dramatic theater dance which combines a sense of ritual along with a style of moving that is contemporary. She finds it congenial to work both with trained dancers and untrained performers, mixing them together and extracting the maximum impact from their individual skills. Since 1969 she has been engaged in the development of a long work in connected sections called *Light,* and at the present time has completed nine sections of it, though more can be added at any time.

LIGHT

Part I: *Choreography by Kei Takei. Costumes by Kei Takei. Lighting by Nicholas Wolff Lyndon. First performed at the Dance Theater Workshop, New York, N.Y., April 11, 1969, by Irina Compton, Elsi Miranda, Clara Scheffer, and Kei Takei. Part II: Choreography by Kei Takei. Music by Geki Koyama. Costumes by Kei Takei. Scenery by Ushio Shinohara. Lighting by William Lambert. First performed at the Cubiculo, New York, N.Y., August 3, 1970, by Carmen Beuchat, Anya Allister, Elsi Miranda, and Sheila Sobel. Part III: Choreography by Kei Takei. Music by Lloyd Ritter. Costumes by Kei Takei. Lighting by Nicholas Wolff Lyndon. First performed at the Dance Theater Workshop, New York, N.Y., November 7, 1970, by Carmen Beuchat, Elsi Miranda, Noemi Ramirez, Kei Takei, and Maldwyn Pate. Part IV: Choreography by Kei Takei. Music by Lloyd Ritter. Costumes by Kei Takei. Scenery by Maxine Klein. Lighting by William Lambert. First performed at the Cubiculo, New York, N.Y., December 18, 1970, by Carmen Beuchat, Elsi Miranda, Noemi Ramirez, Kei Takei, Maldwyn Pate, and John Wilson. Part*

V: *Choreography by Kei Takei. Music by Marcus Parsons III. Lighting by Technical Assistance Group (TAG). Costumes by Kei Takei. First performed at the American Theater Laboratory, New York, N.Y., July 26, 1971, by Lloyd Ritter, Kei Takei, and John Wilson.* Part VI: *Choreography by Kei Takei. Music by Jacques Coursil and Marcus Parsons III. Costumes by Kei Takei. Lighting by Vincent Lalomia. First performed at the Kitchen, Mercer Arts Center, New York, N.Y., December 16, 1971, by Kei Takei, Elsi Miranda, Noemi Ramirez, Carmen Beuchat, Pam Cruden, Blondel Cummings, Ching Valdes, John Wilson, Maldwyn Pate, and Lloyd Ritter.* Part VII (Diary of the Field): *Choreography by Kei Takei. Music by Maldwyn Pate and Lloyd Ritter. Costumes by Kei Takei. Scenery by Maxine Klein. Lighting by Edward I. Byers. First performed at the Auditorium of International House, New York, N.Y., April 20, 1973, by Carmen Beuchat, Sin-Cha Hong, Regine Kunzle, Elsi Miranda, Margot Crosman, Satoru Shimazaki, Maldwyn Pate, Lloyd Ritter, and Kei Takei.* Part VIII: *Choreography by Kei Takei. Music by Lloyd Ritter. Costumes by Kei Takei. Lighting by John P. Dodd. First performed at the Clark Center for the Performing Arts, New York, N.Y., January 12, 1974, by Frances Alenikoff, Maldwyn Pate, Kei Takei, Lloyd Ritter, and, Joe Ritter.* Part IX: *Choreography by Kei Takei. Costumes by Kei Takei. Lighting by Vincent Lalomia. First performed at the Brooklyn Academy of Music, Brooklyn, N.Y., March 1, 1975, by Abel, Amy Berkman, Richmond Johnstone, John de Marco, Elsi Miranda, Barbara Mitsueda, Wendy Osserman, John Parton, Maldwyn Pate, Joe Ritter, Lloyd Ritter, Joan Schwartz, Kei Takei, and John Vinton.*

When she began to choreograph the first section of the piece in 1969, not even Takei imagined that it would expand to nine sections which she would show as a single unit during a seven-hour concert, at the Brooklyn Academy of Music in the early spring of 1975.

The opening section has a woman squatting and rocking as four other women with large white bundles begin a journey, striding and turning without ever moving far from the spot that each started on. As in subsequent sections all of their costumes are white, giving a slightly haunted appearance to this pilgrimage. In the second portion two women with bundles are linked with a rope and circle about a woman who is trudging forward with her eyes fixed on something in the distance beyond her. They fall behind her and are drawn along in her slow but purposeful direction. Each of the sections is separated by a blackout which at times reminds one of the moment of darkness separating a series of slide projections. The work itself is so decorative pictorially that it reinforces the sense that one has of seeing panels of a decorative accordion screen that unfolds another scene in an almost endless series.

The central woman crouches as three blindfolded women and a man without a blindfold enact a series of encounters that range from the frustrating crash into a ladder into suggestions of sexual awakening. From time to time the light shines on the central woman as she observes. In the fourth part a woman assembles a large jigsaw puzzle and increasingly restricts the space available to the other dancers, who strut at times or frivolously twirl umbrellas. Inexorably they are crowded into the jail-like free area and the light goes out with them compressed into a fraction of the space they first had available. When the light rises on the next section a woman and two men are struggling to rise, but each keeps slipping downward as if the weight of life or experience had infected them with a chronic fatigue. Others join in the following section, which is like a bleak plane on which doomed armies contend.

The energy of the seventh section comes out with an almost rude vigor as the central woman strikes a stick on the floor and shouts orders that rouse the others into a tiresome effort to keep going. The women gather a harvest of balloons. In the eighth portion of the epic a man repeatedly throws himself to the floor with painful crashing leaps, and the central woman adorns herself with an ill-assorted cluster of clothing that almost renders her powerless to move, although she nevers ceases to attempt motion. The final section of the work shows people on a giant notebook. One leaf rests on the wall facing the audience, and the other stretches out toward the front of the audience. The dancers have become the tiny inhabitants of a giant ledger. A succession of men throw cloth balls through a hole in the upright page while announcing its purpose, and other dancers crawl through the loops of the spiral binding. A page is turned and another tableau takes place, and at the final page women with bundles leaking rice leave thin trails as they proceed on their forced and endless pilgrimage.

The nature of the piece is associational rather than a series of literal cause and effect episodes. Each incident has been selected the way a painter would add bits of scraps to a collage to achieve an over-all design. *Light* is a journey of a sensibility pouring over and sifting the scraps and shards of experience to assemble them in a subtly autobiographical whole. It is a journey of the creative intelligence.

CHOREOCHRONICLE
OF KEI TAKEI

1967

The Path
Search

1968

Voix/ko-e (with John Wilson)
Unaddressed Letter

1969

*Light, Part I
Mushihuzi

1970

Lunch
*Light, Parts II, III, IV

1971

*Light, Parts V, VI
Playing This Everyday Life

1972

Talking Desert Blues
Once upon a Time—A Journey

1973

*Light, Part VII

1974

*Light, Part VIII

1975

*Light, Part IX

TWYLA THARP

The torrential energy of Twyla Tharp is reflected in the inexhaustible invention of her dances, her own high-voltage performing style, and the sheer volume of dances she has created in the first ten years of her career. She is essentially a classicist in her concern with structure but has the rough-and-tumble approach to movement that one might encounter in a graceful athelete. The elements of the Tharp vocabulary of movement, as it is emerging, are strongly rhythmical use of the legs and feet and a throwaway, rambling look to the upper body that gives one the impression of a casual strictness.

Tharp began her dance training in Los Angeles, where she grew up and studied, in addition to ballet, modern dance, tap, and even baton twirling. Elements of all these disciplines have turned up in her works. She finished her formal education in New York City at Barnard College and studied with various dance teachers at the same time, including Erick Hawkins and Merce Cunningham. After her graduation she joined the Paul Taylor company and remained with it for two years. She began to create her own work in the mid-sixties, first with a small group of three dancers and subsequently with her own company of eight.

Her approach to choreography reveals a prodigious intelligence and a strong musical sensitivity. Her profound feeling for music and its authority caused her to abandon creating dances with musical accompaniment for a time so as to free herself from its influence. Her musical taste moves easily from popular to jazz and classical. She has worked with scores by Haydn, Ives, and Torelli as well as jazz pianists Scott Joplin, Willie "The Lion"

Smith, and Jelly Roll Morton, and the rock musicians the Beach Boys. Her guiding instinct in each case was to find the underlying structure of the music and use that as the basis for her movement designs rather than simply to reflect some of the music's surface color in gesture.

She has shown an openness to a wide variety of spatial situations for performance. During one day as part of an outdoor festival, she began at dawn with a trio across a lawn in Fort Tryon Park near the upper tip of Manhattan island, continued with a dance accompanied by a marching band at the lower tip of the island in Battery Park at midday, and concluded in the City Council's chambers in the evening. She has worked conventionally on a proscenium stage but has also found television studios congenial for her work. In addition to creating dances for her own company she has designed pieces for the City Center Joffrey Ballet, and American Ballet Theater.

RE-MOVES

Choreography by Twyla Tharp. Costumes by Robert Huot. First performed at the Judson Memorial Church, New York, N.Y., October 18, 1966, by Twyla Tharp, Margaret Jenkins, and Sara Rudner.

This was Tharp's first dance of special genius. Previously she had worked with the partitioning of space in one way or another, including a film dance, and she had experimented with varieties of music, most of which was popular. The inner fire for this piece was anger and it annealed all of the elements into a unified whole for the first time in her career. There was no music, costuming was severe, and the dance itself was walled off from the audience in selected portions. It wasn't easy to watch but it was special.

The three women in their demeanor are serious. Each wears a glove on one hand and leaves the other bare. One foot is sneakered and the other bare. Each carries a stop watch. A tiny triangle of white worn as a head covering suggests a nurse's cap. The dance is carried through first in straight lines up and down and then punctuated by a section of movement along a diagonal. All proceed as if programmed to do a job which they receive neither pleasure nor pain. At one point a woman walks inside a broad wheel up one side, across the front, and exits at the opposite side. At the end of the section the three reach downward and mime plucking flowers. On other occasions they allowed eggs to roll out of their palms and smash on the floor but in each case an organic growth was terminated.

The second portion of the work is not conducted with such severity and consists of a kind of tap dancing without the joy of such dancing but presented in a deadpan fashion with no overt show of emotionalism. Here again the movement is regulated into channels which emphasize right-angle directional changes like mechanical creatures moving along predetermined slots.

The third section is danced around the periphery of a large box about twelve feet high which prevents the audience from seeing any more than a portion of the dance. Since people are seated on three sides of the box, each group sees about a third of the dance, which is a series of twisting and turning moves that progress up from the back of one side, across the front of the box, and down the other side.

In the concluding section the box is removed, and the three women move with considerable vigor, contrasting to the deliberate slowness of the third section.

While this dance still depended on striking props for its realization, it also was a dance that had a dedicated movement impulse that was shaped and phrased in the manner that Tharp would continue to develop. It still has some specially strange visual effects such as a woman in the first section walking around the area inside the rim of a large wheel making right-angle turns and then exiting, but the vocabulary of movement that would come to be thought of as specifically Tharpian showed itself convincingly.

ONE TWO THREE

Choreography by Twyla Tharp. Costumes by Robert Huot. First performed at Hunter College Playhouse, New York, N.Y., December 1966, by Sara Rudner, Twyla Tharp, and Margery Tupling.

One of the severe problems for vanguard dancers in the middle sixties was that of using volumes of dance movement without falling into a reliance on the styles and formulas of previous generations. The movement had to be redesigned to take account of the varieties of ordinary gesture which had been brought into the newer dance structures and yet not become mired in spatial inactivity. This piece was one of the most important in that process for Tharp.

The trio finds three women identically dressed in white turtle-neck sweaters, black leotards and tights, and white sneakers. The impression is that of an austere and formal dancing lesson. The three extend a foot backward and then revolve on their own axes and close up their feet. They repeat the gesture in several directions. Everything is precise and exactly done, and they move toward the wings to exit. The curtain across the back of the stage is lifted slightly so that as the last woman exits the feet of the second woman are seen beneath the edge of the curtain, moving across the stage.

The first woman runs in long, sweeping circles and then hops and lands on both feet. She makes a sequence of emotive gestures then faces the audience directly and goes off. The second woman slouches like a primate. She arches arms and capers around. The feet of the third woman are seen moving beneath the curtain across the back. She enters the stage walking on her heels, while the second woman holds her hands clasped in front of her looking into the wings. The third woman suddenly has a spasm of movement but gives it up and goes out of character. She returns for a moment, slumps, and leaves. The first woman emerges and clasps hands behind her and turns away from the audience. The feet of the third woman are seen beneath the curtain.

The piece was lean and spare, tough minded, and was stylistically uncompromising. The women did not move with lyric grace but substituted forceful precision. One almost had the feeling of seeing a problem in trigonometry being demonstrated. On the one hand there was the classical tradition of what a trio should look like, and on the other the problem of expressing a classical form in a contemporary manner. In it Tharp began to cover space carefully, observing the rules as she understood them and reflecting the promptings of dance feelings that emerged as a form of twisting struggle. It would be a while before such stirrings would emerge easily, but a definite step had been taken.

FOREVERMORE

Choreography by Twyla Tharp. Costumes by Robert Huot. Set to two marching snare drummers. First performed at Midsummer Inc., Easthampton, N.Y., August 25, 1967, by Sara Rudner, Twyla Tharp, Margery Tupling, and Theresa Dickinson.

Dualities occur in Tharp's works with regularity. She effortlessly contrasts styles of movement, such as show dancing and ballet, or music of a classical composer with that of a popular writer. One of the first dances in which she overtly presented such a pairing was this dance, which was presented in a high school gymnasium which had a shallow balcony at one end. There were two sets of dance activities in this brief but telling piece.

Above in the balcony a tall woman wearing a black sheath dress walks along and then sinks to the floor out of sight but rises again a moment later to continue her progress back and forth. At the floor level are three other women dressed quite contrastingly in black sequined leotards and black tights looking like a chorus line out of a film spectacular. While the woman above puts up her hair languidly and lets it fall again as she passes from side to side, they step forward and back looking like hard-tapping chorus girls. From outside comes the sound of distant unseen drummers tapping out a regular march rhythm. The sound becomes louder and the three step out and around, return to their starting position, and repeat the sequence again.

Then they freeze. The woman above continues to adjust her hair, but the drumming sound has stopped, and in a last gesture she sinks out of sight.

The dance was barely four minutes long, but the strength of the contrasting styles of movement was so striking that the piece has a vividness usually associated with more elaborate dances. On the one hand there was the hard-moving line of chorines, and on the other the wilting, obsessively preoccupied maiden, and offstage the time being measured off by relentless snare drummers to whose different beats both the soloist and the trio were moving. And perhaps it would be that way forevermore.

GENERATION

Choreography by Twyla Tharp. Costumes by Robert Huot. First performed at Wagner College, New York, N.Y., February 9, 1968, by Sara Rudner, Theresa Dickinson, Margery Tupling, Twyla Tharp, and Carol Laudenslager.

Tharp's matter-of-fact description of this piece was that "it made us as strong as horses." After seeing it one could easily believe that it put terrific physical demands on the dancers, all five of whom were dressed in identically cut all-over body suits that bloused out at the trouser bottoms. There were, however five different types of fabric used, from the soft matte silver to a glittery, hard, metallic finished silver.

The woman in the softest silver lies on the floor as the dance begins and she stumbles and falls many times before assuming her confident upright place among the others. There is an insularity to the variations that they all perform and no feeling of warmth between them. One woman does a squatting walk that reminds one of Groucho Marx. The five never come into direct confrontation with one another or assist one another. The entire space of the huge gymnasium floor is taken up with them in their individual tracks. Periodically one or another will explode in a series of fast turns and a jump. There is a gradual opening up of the gestures which were restricted to begin with.

One or another slides or sits down and then with a start raises her torso. The pace of the dance begins to slow down as one woman does balletic attitudes, another stands still, and a pair do turns. Then suddenly the whole dance bursts open again and all are driven into another round of fast activity as if it were a dance of death that had to be participated in whether one wanted to or not. There is a hint of relentless spirits hovering over the piece, and yet one does not feel menaced in any way. It is almost as if one were observing the activities of knowledgeable, sentient beings who are slightly alien in their concerns. The woman with the shiny-finished suit falls; the others gather nearby and pose around her.

The dance keeps emotional involvement at arm's length and yet suggests the generative rise of one and the fall of a member of the older generation. The piece was sustained dance of pure movement that took up from where *One Two Three* left off and showed how far Tharp had come in her ability to energize a space with her own movement unsupported by any musical floor.

AFTER "SUITE"

Choreography by Twyla Tharp. Costumes by Robert Huot. Lighting by Jennifer Tipton. First performed at the Billy Rose Theatre, New York, N.Y., February 3, 1969, by Twyla Tharp, Sara Rudner, Theresa Dickinson, Margery Tupling, Sheila Raj, Graciella Figueroa, and Rose Marie Wright.

One work of art is often the best critical appreciation of another, more so than a verbal evaluation. In this piece Tharp was taking as a departure point Merce Cunningham's *Suite for Five*. She is an unabashed admirer of his work and in this piece offered him a homage and took the opportunity to increase her own mastery of dance form. All of the six performers are dressed in fashionably flowing beige jump suits.

The women enter and support one another in attitudes, then one steps back to look at the movement another is doing. Then she goes off pulling the first woman in the formation away in a turn. The dance begins to feed upon itself as the movement enchâinement develops. A small woman comes stamping on and off. Two other women return with her and do large leaps as if following the leader. The dancers, despite their brusque and energetic movement, remind one of something out of a fashion magazine. The small woman stands casually watching and doing extensions.

The second part of the dance is accompanied by the ticking of a metronome. Each of the six does her own individual variation, and then they begin to weave in and out of one another. They come to a halt and the beat slows down, and one leaves. The remaining five arrange themselves in a diagonal with a lone woman in the center and two pairs at the extremes. They move out of the straight line into a shallow circle and the slow ticking stops as two others leave. The three remaining do deep knee bends and rise on the balls of their feet. The others join and leaps are added to the selection of movements. A very slow ticking is heard, which accelerates slowly. All of the dancers find themselves being caught up in its beat. They are driven by it almost to the point of exhaustion, turning and looking upward with their heads leaning backward only at the end.

This was the last formally costumed dance that Tharp was to appear in for several years, as she turned her attention to working with larger groups of people in less formal performing spaces such as museums, exterior sites and the like. For her it was a significant advance in the sheer technique of moving dancers together without falling into the traps of conventional and perhaps even sentimental ways. In an advertising brochure she described the work in distinctly unsentimental terms. "Septet performed in three adjacent squares. As each section of the work is completed, it is immediately repeated in an adjacent square as a variant of itself (retrograde, shift of front, re-patterning) while the next section is being introduced. This procedure continues until the fifth section, where the movement has been distributed so that no one dancer will have a phrase intact. The sixth section, a trio, has one dancer performing a variant of her part in the fourth section, one dancer a phrase intact from the fifth section, and a third dancer shifting between unison in time and space with each of the other two through her own part of the fifth section, varied." It reads like a computer print-out but plays better than it sounds.

MEDLEY

Choreography by Twyla Tharp. First performed at Connecticut College, New London, Conn., July 19, 1969, by Sara Rudner, Theresa Dickinson, Margery Tupling, Sheila Raj, Graciella Figueroa, Rose Marie Wright, and students of the Connecticut College American Dance Festival.

In the summer of 1969 a new director of the American Dance Festival, Charles Reinhart, asked Tharp to open the festival with a new work, and she responded with this piece. It was a departure for both the festival and for Tharp. It was designed to be performed outdoors and to incorporate student dancers as well as Tharp's own highly trained professional company. For Tharp it marked a new working method; previously she had appeared in all of the dances that her company performed, and in this one she did not appear. Instead she worked from the outside making a dance that was designed to display each of her dancers in a special individual way, drawing on their quite different personalities. The tone of the piece contrasted strongly with most of her previous pieces which were computer accurate and cool surfaced. This piece was warm and also colorfully costumed. It was performed on the sloping lawn in front of the Lyman Allyn Museum on the campus of Connecticut College in New London.

The dance does not seem to have a specific beginning; it just grows organically from the outdoor space. As the audience arrives and individuals seat themselves, two of the dancers are already well into their variations. One wears ballet point shoes and is on a small, rigid square of board, and the other is closer to the audience, turning and sinking and rising slowly.

Four others join and begin to do individual variations by picking up and imitating gestures of the audience. They move farther and farther away from the audience, continuing their imitative gestures. The six women each perform variations; Sara Rudner hard working and technically delightful, Graciella Figueroa exuberant, Sheila Raj pixy quick, Theresa Dickinson dedicated and energetic, Rose Marie Wright long and elegant, and Margery Tupling strong and open.

They form a file and move forward and break apart to do supported falls. One woman leaves and the remaining women continue until there is only one left still dancing. She is like a spring lamb gamboling in a field, and when she finishes she joins the others. One breaks into a frenized sequence, and others add their own distinctive movements, which blend in a medley the way that distinctive voices can harmonize and enrich a song line. At the conclusion of the section three dozen student dancers break from the audience area, where they have been sitting unobtrusively as ordinary members of the audience, and join in line beside the six core members of the company. They copy the steps and gestures of each of the leaders of their particular line, who count out numbers like drill sergeants for this brilliantly hued augmented company.

The dancers separate into two large formations, one behind Dickinson and the other behind Raj, who move about demonstrating variations. The dancers all remain in place and imitate them. The energy of the piece is at its peak: one group is twitchy and quick and the other moves at a more laconic pace. All leave except for the core of six women and six others who do a parody of a class and a dance reconstruction demonstrating for one another as a kind of in joke. In the background all of the other dancers are scattered over the field like handfuls of multicolored marbles on green felt doing an adagio. Because of the slow-motion pace of the movement nothing at first is noticeable, but the look of the group alters imperceptibly. It is a dance of change without apparent transition. The sort of movement that one perceives in plants over a long period and particularly appropriate to the outdoor setting. As each finishes and leaves, the energy of the dance diminishes a little, more like the setting sun. As the audience leaves, a member of the company is still doing the adagio and is replaced at half-hour intervals by another member of the company until each has done it.

In addition to all of its special qualities involving growth, imitation, mirror images, and its wonderful locale, the piece also marked the first time that Tharp had included male dancers in any of her works. No special movement was created for them, but she would soon begin to turn her attention to the male dancer as well as the females with whom she had worked out her gestural vocabulary. *Medley* was a farewell and a fond one to the past and a turn to the future.

THE ONE HUNDREDS

Choreography by Twyla Tharp. First performed at the University of Massachusetts, Amherst, Mass., August 1970, by Twyla Tharp, Rose Marie Wright, Sara Rudner, Isabel Garcia-Lorca, Douglas Dunn, and student dancers.

During the early part of her career Tharp was not thought of as a choreographer with a sense of humor but rather as a strict and at times even harsh designer of dances. Everything that she seemed to do had a computer or seemingly computer-governed sense of proportion and style. It is to her credit that she was able to take such a complex set of variations and give them an amusing but logical twist.

Two women begin the dance by stretching and flexing. They make little jumps and move toward the back of the stage on parallel courses. There is a great deal of expressive movement for the upper body. The feel of the piece is quickness; one is bombarded by squiggles of movement. This first section consists of one hundred separate variations, half of which are done by one woman and half by the other.

Emerging somewhat from their self-centered focus, the dancers almost seem to court the audience, making a sketch of the "star" turn in tiny bursts of action which are not sustained, as nothing is in the dance. They lapse back into a reverie of flicks and twitches, including lots and lots of turns. The whole piece is compact but because it is performed by only the two women stretches out for some time. The second section is an exact duplicate of the first except that it takes less than half of the time to perform because the movements are parceled out to five dancers, each of whom does twenty. The final section sees one hundred dancers walk out and arrange themselves, and it takes about ten seconds to perform since all do one of the variations. When done, all simply leave.

The long buildup and the general repetitive scheme of the dance remind one of Ravel's *Boléro,* which builds and builds on the same thematic material and then concludes with a musical horselaugh. Tharp does not guffaw, but the incredible complexity presented by one hundred dancers, each doing a single variation, is comical. The dance is compacted to its maximum density and is in effect invisible although it is all there.

EIGHT JELLY ROLLS

Choreography by Twyla Tharp. Music by Jelly Roll Morton. Costumes by Kermit Love which he subsequently re-designed twice. First performed at the Delacorte Theatre, New York, N.Y., September 16, 1971, by Twyla Tharp, Sara Rudner, Rose Marie Wright, Isabel Garcia-Lorca, Mary Curry, and Naomi Cohen.

Among the most honored figures in jazz was Jelly Roll Morton, whose music Tharp admired exceedingly. For her, selecting a group of eight pieces became the means for creating a dance that was a homage to black music and a happy, nostalgic look at the style of the Roaring Twenties.

A woman stands alone in the center of the stage and makes tiny, almost casual flicks of her feet in one direction and then another, hardly moving from the place in which she is standing. A little later she begins to sweep one leg around in a funky, unhurried manner. Behind her two women march, after a fashion, back and forth with a hint of exaggeratedly stiff movement.

The woman is joined by one of the two who marched behind her in the first episode, and together they stomp and step in large, open strides suggesting tap dancing on the run. They flash a squiggle of hand gestures to one another then fold arms as they move around one another and clap hands in front and in back of themselves, suggesting a child's playfulness.

A hot white spotlight delimits an oblong area into which the second woman of the previous duet sidles. She weaves a pattern of expressive arm motions, shivers her shoulders slightly, and slides her feet along the floor in a way suggesting a social ballroom dance without a partner. It is a lonely but appealing solo.

The three women from the first section make a series of rapid dashes and retreats from the stage and then tumble and frolic around, when they decide to get out to the center of the space. One leaves and the two others toss themselves from side to side. The other woman returns and one of them leaves. The woman who returned is almost tremblingly stiff with her suppressed exertions. All are together for the final frantic trio, which ends with the smallest of the three being carried off.

She returns to tumble and stumble in front of a decorous group consisting of five women and one man, who provide a playful accompaniment to her slightly tipsy behavior. At one point they carefully step over her when she has fallen. She rises to stand among them as they loll their heads in unison and then leave. After one more tumble the section is over.

Five women stand in place as the man reaches with his arms and strolls in front of them. They are almost like a cluster of statues since they do not move from the place they occupy. Now he joins the group and one of the women takes his place. Then others successively come out to the front for a solo or a duet. At the end of the section they all cut loose a bit in unison and then freeze.

The woman who did the first solo struts easily back and forth in front of the group, who arrange themselves so as to mirror or underscore her languid gestures. The movement is slow and soulful, and they accompany her with the same casual but disciplined ease. In the finale all are on together doing fast individual variations, using frequent quotes from social dancing of the time, and then in a unison burst they turn the sides of their bodies to the audience, extend one arm straight forward and the other back, and all move toward the audience as if to say, "And there!" The group leaves and one woman rocks and sinks slowly down.

The costuming for the piece consisted of a stiff shirt front with a wing collar and a black bow tie. A black one-piece garment with flared trousers, a halter top, and highly polished black shoes completed the ensemble, giving the dancers a formal but also sleek look. The piece was a stunning evocation of the period, drawing on its mood and approach with affection and also with great intelligence. It was one of the pieces that made up a program broadcast on the British Broadcasting Corporation about Tharp, her work, and her company.

THE BIX PIECES

Choreography by Twyla Tharp. Music by Bix Beiderbecke. Costumes by Kermit Love. First performed at the IX International Festival of Dance, Paris, France, November 9, 1971, by Twyla Tharp, Sara Rudner, Rose Marie Wright, Isabel Garcia-Lorca, and Kenneth Rinker.

Tharp had been working with music of the twenties and the thirties, using the music of brass player Bix Beiderbecke, to represent a white feeling for jazz, and Jelly Roll Morton, to represent the black side of jazz development. The latter was celebrated in *Eight Jelly Rolls*. Talented choreographers have the ability to attract other talented choreographers, and such was the case with Tharp and Robert Joffrey, who saw this piece and invited her to create a work for his ballet company.

In the first section a woman in short pants with a ruffled shirt front and shiny black shoes is twirling a long cane as if it were a baton. She turns and moves from side to side and periodically drops her cane. Another is immediately thrown to her from the wings, where there is an inexhaustible supply. At the conclusion of her solo the stage is littered with them. She is joined by a woman in a short skirt who looks like a taxi dancer compared with the first woman, who reminds one of a show girl. After characteristic variations they dance together like a ballroom exhibition team. They are joined by a taller woman who is the central figure in their trio, and they float and hover around her as she progresses across stage. She is humorously self-contained and at one moment they hilariously celebrate and frame her by circling jumps around her. A woman in a satin jump suit enters; she is lean and elegant as she sleekly steps around in the front. The three others join and perform a casual high kick routine behind her. One is reminded again and again of show dancing but show dancing appropriated and grafted onto a rigorous structure as the dance moves from a solo to a duet to a trio then a quartet and ends with a man joining three of the women and replacing the first woman. All frolic energetically, and then he and the woman in the short skirt remain as the others leave.

The second section brings on an actress to recite autobiographical bits about the first woman and how she came to create this particular dance. In the meanwhile she is performing a short tap dance as the actress mentions that she had such lessons as a child. The second and third women enter, as does the man, and they all present a panorama of movements drawn from show dancing, the ballet vocabulary, and Tharp's own special style of twisting, squiggling modern dance steps. The actress comments on the similarities which exist between them all, noting that the terminology is different, but the dancers demonstrate that each system has evolved similar solutions to common problems. Again this is pointed out as the popular "I Want to Be Happy" is supplanted by a theme from a Haydn string quartet which had been adopted as the German national anthem. A series of falls and catches concludes the section. The narrator points out that there is nothing new, only new arrangements of familiar material, and that Haydn had not invented the famous theme but had drawn it from an anonymous folk source.

The last portion is accompanied by an arrangement of a traditional hymn, "Abide with Me," by Thelonius Monk. Three women (the second, third, and fourth) and the man cluster and perform excerpts of all that has gone before in a compressed space and shorter time, and we are presented with the final arrangement of the material.

The piece is a tour de force that is dazzling in its wit and invention. It was originally choreographed to Haydn and later adjusted for the Beiderbecke music. Throughout Tharp demonstrated an acute awareness of the nuances of style required for the various segments of show, classical, and modern dance. It was a piece that had elements of nostalgia, personal reminiscence, and technical demonstrations blended together. In effect the choreographer in the first section did the piece then in the second section explained how the piece was done and gave a demonstration of its composition and concluded with a restatement of the dance materials in highly compressed form. It was the final result and the process joined together as a single creation of ends and means.

DEUCE COUPE

Choreography by Twyla Tharp. Music by the Beach Boys. Scenery by United Graffiti Artists. Costumes by Scott Barrie. Lighting by Jennifer Tipton. First performed at the Auditorium Theater, Chicago, Ill., February 8, 1973, by Twyla Tharp, Sara Rudner, Rose Marie Wright, Nina Wiener, Isabel Garcia-Lorca, and Kenneth Rinker, and members of the City Center Joffrey Ballet: Eileen Brady, Donna Cowen, Starr Danias, Erika Goodman, Beatriz Rodriguez, Christine Uchida, Rebecca Wright, Henry Berg, Gary Chryst, Larry Grenier, Gregory Huffman, Robert Talmage, Glenn White, and William Whitener.

As a Southern California adolescent, Tharp grew up with the sound of the Beach Boys in her ears, and when she was invited by an Eastern establishment ballet company to do a dance for it, she decided to invade with West Coast energy. It is the understated tension of this outrageous invasion that gives the piece its special piquancy. She brought her own company to dance with the Joffrey Ballet and they were like a group of raffish hooligans turned loose in very polite society.

Three long white strips of paper extend from the floor and extend into the flies at the upper rear of the stage. A single woman dressed as a ballerina begins a slow variation using steps from the classical vocabulary beginning with *aile-de-pigeon* and eventually continuing through the whole alphabet by the time the ballet is finished. A man and a woman commence a short duet that also uses the classical vocabulary. Then suddenly the first sonic chords of the Beach Boys are heard in the title song, "Little Deuce Coupe," and the Tharp company begins a serial entrance across the front of the stage twisting and looking around repeating their variation as they begin to move upstage almost like the procession of the souls in the Kingdom of the Shades scene from Petipa's *La Bayadère,* but without such placid resignation.

The episodes follow one another with great rapidity, and while the modern movement of the Tharp company contrasts with the balletic movement of the Joffrey company, there are elements of similarity. They are not antagonistic but in reality complementary although the accents are different. A spirited duet accompanies "Honda II," in which the man and the woman compete violently with one another. It is not the competition of a man and a woman but a unisex demonstration of dancing prowess, and they nudge one another playfully as they part at the end of it. The clean white strips are now being decorated with wall scribblings by a half-dozen urchins who were selected from the hordes who compulsively scribble with spray paints on public surfaces. It emphasizes the anarchic element of the piece.

At the start of "Alley Oop" the ballet dancers are suddenly interrupted by the sight of several capering Tharp dancers with their knuckles trailing in the dust like genuine primates. The woman who danced the competitive duet enters with two men and strides back and forth across the front of the stage, giving strategic side kicks to coincide with rhythmic beats in "Take a Load off Your Feet." She reappears a moment later with a tall woman and frantically tries to keep up with her, collapses on her back, but is pulled up and out by the tall woman. In "Catch a Wave" the company does cross-overs, sliding as if surfing, and connecting all of the incidents are the balletic variations by the woman dressed as a ballerina. While she continues her strict alphabetical unfolding, a woman from Tharp's company does a slow, sensuous dance to "Got to Know the Woman." A mixture of women from both companies does a lament in "Don't Go Near the Water," one of the strongest and most inventive dances in the work. They deplore the defilement of the wilderness with exquisitely modulated grief. The upbeat sound of "Wouldn't It Be Nice" is used for a group of the ballet dancers predominantly, who sway and roll their torsos in a pastiche of sixties social dancing and ballet, and the entire company joins for the finale, which has a calmness and contrasting reserve with the ballerina as immaculate as ever. The huge paper strips full of graffiti which were created during the earlier part of the dance have been drawn upward, and only clear white paper is now seen as it was in the beginning.

The dance celebrated the fusion of traditional high art and the vigor of contemporary dance energy. The classic ballerina threaded her way throughout the piece as the other dancers were transformed from being either purely balletic or purely modern dancers into an amalgam of the two. The feeling of the piece was high, warm, and funny. Yes, it was an invasion but one carried out with great brio and with the knowing classic eye of Tharp, who recognizes that the evolvement of classic dance is a continuing process and not a dead, lifeless *fait accompli.*

CHOREOCHRONICLE
OF TWYLA THARP

1965

Tank Dive
Stage Show
Stride
Cede Blue Lake
Unprocessed

1966

*Re-Moves
Twelve Foot Change (retitled
  Yancy Dance)
Jam
*One Two Three

1967

Disperse
Three Page Sonata for Four
*Forevermore
One Way

1968

*Generation
Excess, Idle, Surplus
Group Activities

1969

*After "Suite"
*Medley
*Dancing in the Streets of Paris
  and London, Continued in
  Stockholm and Sometimes
  Madrid*

1970

pymffyppmfypnm ypf
Fugue
Rose's Cross Country
*The One Hundreds
Hour's Work for Children
*11 Minute Abstract, Repertory
  1965–70*

1971

*The History of Up and Down I
  and II*
*Eight Jelly Rolls
*The Bix Pieces

1973

*Deuce Coupe

1974

As Time Goes By

1975

Sue's Leg
The Double Cross

1976

Push Comes to Shove

JAN VAN DYKE

As a child, Van Dyke was taken to Germany by her parents and began her study of dance abroad. She continued when her parents returned to the United States, at a local school in Alexandria, Virginia. She attended the University of Wisconsin and graduated with a major in dance. She studied briefly with Alwin Nikolais in New York and danced one season in a summer stock company in Charlotte, North Carolina. The same year she studied with Ethel Butler in Washington, D.C., and the following summer attended the Connecticut College Summer School of Dance, where she received further instruction in the Graham technique from David Wood. She began to create her own pieces in 1965 and four years later moved to New York, where she studied intensively with Merce Cunningham and Viola Farber. At this time she began giving performances of her own work. She formed her first company in Washington and after its dissolution she did solo touring. In addition to teaching at her own studio she has taught at George Washington University, the University of Ohio, the University of Maryland, and at the summer school of the dance at Long Beach, California.

WALTZ

Choreography by Jan Van Dyke. Music by Johann Strauss, Jr. First performed at the Jewish Community Center, Rockville, Md., in 1973, by Jan Van Dyke.

The waltz has meant a variety of things to different societies. When it first appeared in the Austro-Hungarian Empire, it was considered a scandalous, roisterous, boisterous dance that came from gypsies gamboling down hillsides. It was definitely not considered proper social dancing, but Vienna became the home of the waltz and the waltz king was Johann Strauss, who wrote scores of them which to us appear to be the perfect romantic reflection of a bygone era of gentle manners and an aristocratically ordered society. They have nothing approaching scandal attached to them, and it was this romantic feeling that interested Van Dyke when she decided to do her own waltz solo.

A woman stands alone in the center of the stage with a spotlight creating a circle of light around her. Her back is to the audience as the lush orchestral sound of the *Beautiful Blue Danube* begins to fill the air. She stands quietly with her hands at her sides and then raises them slowly as if drawn up by the spirit of the music. She does not, however, make broad sweeping gestures but restrains herself.

Her dance consists of balletically influenced steps and poses mixed with her own expressionist gestures, but both are muted and subdued. She moves dreamily as if she were inside of the music rather than moving along its energetic surface. She is delightfully graceful and attractive and after the music stops she continues to move as if still feeling its special rhythm and only stops as the light begins to fade.

The understated nature of the dance is a delightful corrective to the many lavish and overlavish productions involving waltzes that are the usual rule. This is almost a meditation on the idea of the waltz and the society which produced it. There is no special necessity to bound and sweep along; one can sketch the movements and reflect their values just as well.

CHOREOCHRONICLE
OF JAN VAN DYKE

1965

Diversion

1966

Canto

1967

6 Sections of Orange
Dream Forcing
Solitude's Dance

1968

Rose Garden
Camp Lilies
Sisters
Jungle Perches
Hot Sleep

1969

I Am Waiting
One Potato, Two . . .
Backwater

1970

3 Ringling
Park Dance
Going On
Two

1971

Duet I
Duet II
Benches On and Off
Bird
Ready

1973

*Waltz
Park Dance II
Big Show

1975

Ella
Paradise Castle

1974

U.S. Lions
Ceremony in Six Acts

DAN WAGONER

Born in West Virginia, Wagoner had some training in dance. But only after he graduated from West Virginia University with a Bachelor of Science degree in pharmacy was he exposed to serious professional training. During his two years in the Army he continued to take dance instruction wherever he could. Upon his release from service in 1956 he was granted a scholarship to Connecticut College's Summer School of the Dance. This was followed by further study as a scholarship student at the Martha Graham School and then an invitation to be a member of the Graham company. He remained with it five years, eventually joining the Paul Taylor company to pursue his career there. With both organizations he was a featured dancer, and then in 1969 he established himself as a choreographer with his own company. Since then he has toured extensively in the United States and abroad.

DANCE

Choreography by Dan Wagoner. Set to march and country Western music. First performed at the Exchange Theater, New York, N.Y., November 3, 1972, by Dan Wagoner.

When the Exchange Theater in Manhattan's Westbeth, an artists' living and working residence, opened, Wagoner offered this solo as his part of the first night celebrations. It is a piece with a very personal intonation and expresses much about his feelings for movement and people. He created it by joining *Flag Dance* and his "washtub" solo from another work, *Cows and Ruins*.

The music which begins the piece is the heavily militaristic and stirring *National Emblem* march. The man who wears a paper Uncle Sam hat is driven to reflect the strong rhythmic cadences of the music as he moves around the area. He is a patriot but one whose heart is not really in his work. After obediently reflecting its pounding cadences he shows his own personal emblem as he breaks out a banner that has three hearts on it, and dashes around with it flapping.

The dance pauses for a moment as the man sits down and starts to talk in a quiet but earnest manner about the things that are closest to him, and he mentions a friend and two dogs that he is particularly fond of, while he washes his feet in a large galvanized iron tub. When he finishes he dries off his feet and the sound that now fills the air is a bluegrass tune, "Wildwood Flower." He rises and happily prances around to its more congenial beat and ends with a pleased flourish.

The dance shows a man serving conflicting demands of a society and his own personal feelings and is infused with the warmth of the latter. Yes, he can play a socially responsible role if need be, but he would rather be his own man and follow the dictates of his own inclinations. It seemed a very personal statement when it was performed and reflected the special quality of strictness and human concern that are always present in Wagoner's best work.

CHOREOCHRONICLE
OF DAN WAGONER

1968

    Flag Dance
    Dan's Rum Penny Supper
    Duet

1969

    Le Jardin au Monsieur McGregor
    Brambles
    Night Duet

1970

    Westwork

1971

    Iron Mountain
    July 13
    Cows and Ruins

1972

Numbers
Changing Your Mind
*Dance

1973

Broken Hearted Rag Dance
Meets and Bounds
A Sad Pavane for These
  Distracted Times

1974

Taxi Dances

1975

Summer Rambo

JAN WODYNSKI

Initially Wodynski wanted to be an actress, and before that she was very interested in high school athletics and was a member of the basketball and volleyball teams. When she graduated from high school she took a summer course at the American Academy of Dramatic Arts and that fall entered college. During her first year she took her first modern dance classes from Barbara Doerffer, a former member of the Charles Weidman company, and became thoroughly involved with dancing. After college she spent a summer at the Connecticut College Summer School of the Dance. She took a jazz class with Daniel Nagrin and liked the fact that he allowed for personal improvisation as part of the instruction. She studied at the Henry Street Settlement Playhouse with Alwin Nikolais and with Charles Weidman at his studio. She later joined Weidman's company and danced with him for five years. She formed her own company in 1969 and continues to work enlarging its repertory. She has taught at Jersey City State College and at Denison University, Ohio.

SUPERANTICS '70

Choreography by Jan Wodynski. Music by Alwin Nikolais. Costumes by Jan Wodynski. Lighting by Mike Wodynski. First performed at Jersey City State College, Jersey City, N.J., October 1, 1970, by Mike Wodynski, Bob Kosinski, Jan Wodynski, Donna Mondanaro, and David Monroe.

At one time Wodynski gave a concert subtitled "Experiments in Dance and Technology" as an expression of her interest in both dance movement and imaginative use of technical apparatus. Her husband Michael and she both dance in the company, and he is the technical director. They have both studied and worked with Alwin Nikolais, and the visual finish of their pieces owes something to his supremely professional, painstaking example. It also has a certain sympathy with Nikolais' sometimes puckish humor.

A lone man pushes a broom across the stage. He looks as if he is totally lackadaisical and is just marking time for want of something better to do. In complete contrast to him are three aggressive and assertive men dressed in outlandish skullcaps and capes, suggesting comic-book heroes with supernatural strength and power. As he looks on, the three begin to string ropes across the stage like a network of cables.

Striding along beneath the ropes, they move hand over hand as if they were suspended by their powerful arms and crossing the area in mid-air. Periodically they turn to the audience and flash dazzlingly self-conceited smiles to show their prowess and to take the opportunity to flex their muscles. The first man continues to push his broom. Two women suddenly appear to totter around like frivolous creatures, and as they weave around they bump into the strong men. Completely ignoring the men's antics, the two women produce clothes and appropriate the ropes as they hang washing on them, bursting the dream bubble of the men.

Back-yard washing lines were far more common years ago than they are now, but the humor of men fantasizing themselves into supermen as they perform a mundane task of stringing such a line has an immediate appeal. The women of course know nothing of the inner thoughts of the men and deflate them with unconscious and witty ease.

CHANGEOVER

Choreography by Jan Wodynski. Music by Mike Wodynski. Costumes by Jan Wodynski. Lighting by Mike Wodynski. First performed at the Cubiculo, New York, N.Y., January 15, 1973, by Kathy Eaton, Joanne Edelman, Julie Maloney, Idelle Packer, Madeleine Perrone, and Linda Ravinsky.

Among the pure dance works that Wodynski has created, this one for six women has an attractive and witty flow of movement. It provides moments of humor and also precise unison passages. The finish of the piece is clean without any baroque trim but sets about its course like a well-machined engine with all of its gears meshing smoothly and efficiently.

Six women enter and three of them retire to one side while the other three move to the center to begin their opening variation. Then they pass off to allow the other three to dance. A section of formation dancing involving four then five of them commences. At one funny moment they flip open their legs then press them together again rapidly almost like the pages of a book being opened and shut. They bounce in place and make small kicks and then tumble.

Each of the six inhabits a private world despite their engaging unison dancing. It is a collection of insular people motivated by some inner propulsion. Suddenly they grasp their ankles and bend over with their backs to the audience. They clasp their hands to their heads and sag into a bent knee stance to waddle about, concluding the work.

Flamboyance is a quality that has little or no part in Wodynski's creative world. She is not attracted by chance or random ordering of activity but plots her pieces the way a draftsman would design a bridge. Where she differs from the scientific precision that governs such design is in her humor. There is always something slightly odd or eccentric about the completed dance, giving it a friendly quality that softens its exact construction.

CHOREOCHRONICLE
OF JAN WODYNSKI

1969

Solo Improvisation
Mood Sensations
Time Warp
Inspiration '69

1970

Phase One
Phase Two
Games
From "Goofing Off"
Aksis
*Superantics '70
In and out of Time

1971

Contours
Tudo
Incantation
Scape

1972

Gymnopédie No. 2
Interspace
Farrago

1973

Pashun Zone::Sekter Five
*Changeover
Taktiks
Freetime
Five Minutes from Now
Triad

1974

Quonsethut
Pit-Stop
Freekwensi
Koreotroniks

1975

Five Minutes More
The Gallery Event "Or How I
    Did It Way Long Time Ago"
Outing
Tudo

BATYA ZAMIR

Dancing as everyday activity is of primary concern to Zamir, who abandoned her own highly professional career as a dancer with Alwin Nikolais to create dances with people who were not primarily dancers. She is married to sculptor Richard Van Buren, and when she began to offer movement classes many friends of theirs from the world of painters and sculptors took part in them. Her teaching tends to concentrate on the simple acts of moving rather than on highly complex variations of strict dance movement. Though her own studies at the Nikolais school and her five years of performing with that company prepared her to teach at a professional level, she has chosen to return to basics. Her choreography has exploited the skills with which she has been confronted, and in its design it seems closer to life and everyday situations than it does to high art. She sets people to moving in game situations, wearing regular clothing, and allows a piece to develop from the vigorous and often ungraceful movements of her company. It is work oriented, highly energetic, sometimes skilled, sometimes humorous, and always tinglingly alive.

CARRYS

Choreography by Batya Zamir. First performed at Emmanuel Midtown YM-YWHA, New York, N.Y., December 20, 1969, by Bob Duran, Marie Frederick, Gay Glading, Al Loving, Katherine Nally, David Novros, Ed Ruda, Jan Sarkisian, Marie Savettiere, Linda Sugerman, Richard Van Buren, and James Weatherill.

In a program note to the first performance of the work Zamir extended a thanks to all those who participated in the work, and stressed the communal feeling that they had all felt while preparing for the concert. It was in a very real way a communal effort and not at all dependent on individual virtuosity. The setting was the clear, uncluttered, and athletic space of a gymnasium in Manhattan.

The dozen performers are all dressed in casual clothes; neither the men nor the women make any attempt to present the appearance of polished professionals. They enter in a long file walking normally one behind the other. Because of differences in the length of the stride the line expands and contracts like a loose but still resilient spring. A man picks up the woman nearest to him and carries her and gently places her down. Then another carry is made and another and another, in each instance by a different performer. Sometimes a man carries another man, sometimes a woman. Women carry one another and also the men. Since the performers are of widely differing sizes and strengths, the grace and ease with which each portage is accomplished vary considerably. At times it's like watching the smooth unity of a small jockey-like rider and a large, strong carrier functioning as his mount. At other times it is a comic mismatch as a tiny woman attempts to move a large man by centering his unwieldy weight on her hips. Since the design of the piece calls for each person to carry every other person at least once, the variety of moves is enormous.

The group now breaks apart like molecules and then clusters. All move to the farthest wall, and then individuals carry another person toward the audience and then run. All do a series of steps to the side and the piece concludes with a series of carrys going across the front of the area.

The piece had a healthy physicality that made the performers depend on one another, and though it was not necessary to have strict dance training to do it the performance had the healthy pulse of a dance-oriented event.

CHOREOCHRONICLE
OF BATYA ZAMIR

1969

> Releases
> *Carrys
> Prances
> Crawls
> Releases (duets)
> Shadow Slot Follows
> Slot Changes
> Laying Down Rolls
> Gravity Falls

1970

> Duet and Solo Concert

1971

> Trio Release
> Trio Exchange
> Individual Turns
> Circles to Turns
> Circle Exchange
> Slot Exchanges
> Directional Changes (group)
> Directional Changes (solo)
> Improvisational Solos and Duets

1973

> Batya Zamir Dancing Solo
> Off the Wall

1974

*Prelude to Botticelli's Revenge or
(Scar Baby and the Two
Dicks)*
*On and off the Wall and Between
the Columns*
*Saturday Morning on Sunday
Afternoon*

1975

Dance-Music Concert
(improvised collaboration of
musicians and dancers)
Botticelli's Revenge Revisited
(solo and duet form)

Chronology

OF SIGNIFICANT DATES AND EVENTS
IN MODERN DANCE DEVELOPMENT

1862 Loie Fuller, the first of the forerunners of modern dance, is born in the midst of the Civil War to a theatrical family.

1877 Ruth Dennis, who changed her name to St. Denis for the stage, is born on a farm in New Jersey.

1878 Across the continent Isadora Duncan is born in San Francisco.

1883 Maud Allan is born in Toronto, Canada, and is brought to San Francisco at an early age.

1884 Composer Louis Horst is born in Kansas City, Missouri.

1891 Edwin Meyers (Ted) Shawn is born in Kansas City, Missouri.

1894 In bustling Allegheny, Pennsylvania, Martha Graham is born the first of three daughters, two of whom make dancing a career.

1895 Doris Humphrey is born in Oak Park, Illinois.

1901 Charles Weidman is born in Lincoln, Nebraska.

1905 In New York, Helen Becker (Tamiris) is born.

1906 Lester Horton is born in Indianapolis, Indiana.

1908 José Limón is born in Mexico and is taken to the United States as a young child.

1912 Alwin Nikolais is born in Southington, Connecticut.

1914 Ruth St. Denis and Ted Shawn marry and form Denishawn, a school and company that is an amalgam of their names and talents.

Katherine Dunham is born in Chicago.

1915   Anna Sokolow is born in New York.

1916   Martha Graham takes first dance instruction at Denishawn in Los Angeles. Louis Horst accompanies her first class.

1917   Margaret H'doubler starts teaching dance in the physical education department of the University of Wisconsin.

1918   Doris Humphrey joins the Denishawn company.

1921   Charles Weidman joins Denishawn and is sent out to partner Martha Graham in her first starring role as Xochitl.

1922   Denishawn enters into its most successful years touring both at home and abroad for the rest of the decade.

1923   Martha Graham leaves Denishawn and joins the Greenwich Village Follies.

1926   The University of Wisconsin becomes the first college to have a degree program in dance at the bachelor's and master's levels.

Martha Graham forms her first company and makes her performing debut in her own choreography.

1927   Isadora Duncan dies in the South of France.

John Martin appointed as the first dance critic of the New York *Times*.

Mary Watkins appointed first dance critic for the New York *Herald-Tribune*.

1928   Loie Fuller dies.

Doris Humphrey and Charles Weidman leave Denishawn and form their own company and establish a dance studio.

1929   Martha Graham presents her all-female dance group and creates *Heretic,* her first work of special genius.

1930   José Limón joins the Humphrey-Weidman company and remains with it through the end of the decade.

Mary Wigman, German expressionist dancer, tours the United States for the first time with her company.

Paul Taylor is born.

Anna Sokolow joins the Martha Graham company.

Dance Repertory Theater is formed by Martha Graham, Doris Humphrey, Tamiris, and Charles Weidman to present a week of joint performances.

1931   Hanya Holm establishes Mary Wigman school, in New York.

Alvin Ailey is born in Rogers, Texas.

1932   Martha Graham and her company appear on the opening program of Radio City Music Hall.

Denishawn completes last tour and disbands.

Katherine Dunham establishes her school in Chicago.

1933   Ted Shawn organizes his all-male company, Ted Shawn and His Men Dancers.

John Martin publishes *The Modern Dance*.

1934   Bennington College Summer School of the Dance is established by Martha Hill and Mary Josephine Shelley at Bennington, Vermont. The faculty in the first year includes Martha Graham, Hanya Holm, Doris Humphrey and Charles Weidman.

Louis Horst founds *Dance Observer* to ensure modern dance a responsive critical journal.

YM-YWHA at Ninety-second Street and Lexington Avenue in New York offers dance instruction and a performing theater to modern dance at the urging of director William Kolodney.

1936   Doris Humphrey completes her trilogy *New Dance, Theater Piece,* and *With My Red Fires*.

1937   Dance International Festival in New York included modern dancers, Ruth St. Denis, Martha Graham, Hanya Holm, Doris Humphrey, Tamiris, and Charles Weidman as well as ballet performers.

Martha Graham becomes the first dancer to appear in the White House when she gives a performance for President and Mrs. Roosevelt.

Merle Armitage designs and edits a book of tributes to Martha Graham.

1939   First televised modern dance, Hanya Holm's *Tragic Exodus*.

Bennington College Summer School of the Dance holds its session at Mills College in Oakland, California. Martha Graham discovers Merce Cunningham and invites him to join her company.

1940   Ted Shawn disbands his men dancers at the end of its tour.

1941   Ted Shawn founds Jacobs Pillow Dance Festival.

1942   Edwin Denby appointed dance critic of the New York *Herald-Tribune* and retains post until the end of World War II.

The distinguished *Dance Index* begins publication.

Bennington College Summer School of the Dance closes.

1944   Merce Cunningham creates *Root of an Unfocus* and later dates his choreographic emergence from this time.

Doris Humphrey retires from the stage because of an arthritic hip, pursues her later career as choreographer, teacher, and artistic director of the José Limón company.

Charles Weidman forms his own company.

Katherine Dunham forms touring company.

1946   Tamiris choreographs the musical *Annie Get Your Gun*.

José Limón forms his own company.

1947   Merce Cunningham choreographs and performs *The Seasons* with Ballet Society, the precursor of the New York City Ballet.

1948   Dance Collection of the New York Public Library established.

Establishment of American Dance Festival at Connecticut College.

Charles Weidman creates *Fables for Our Times*.

Hanya Holm choreographs the musical *Kiss Me, Kate*.

Alwin Nikolais appointed director of Henry Street Settlement Playhouse.

1949   Bethsabee de Rothschild presents a series featuring modern dance companies at the New York City Center 55th Street Theater.

1951   Dance Associates founded by James Waring to present the work of experimental young choreographers.

1952   Juilliard School of Music establishes a dance department with the encouragement of its president, William Schuman.

Ann Halprin opens her experimental workshop in San Francisco.

1953   Merce Cunningham offers a full week of performances at the Off-Broadway Theater de Lys, his first entire week since founding his company.

Lester Horton dies.

1954   Paul Taylor forms his first company.

Doris Humphrey wins the Capezio Dance Award.

José Limón's company tours South America. The first modern dance company to do so under the sponsorship of the State Department.

1955   Louis Horst wins the Capezio Dance Award.

1956   Maud Allan dies.

1957   Alvin Ailey forms his first company.

Ted Shawn wins the Capezio Dance Award.

1958   Doris Humphrey dies.

Martha Graham creates her first full-evening work, *Clytemnestra*.

1959   Alwin Nikolais presents excerpts from his dances on NBC television. Eventually he works with the medium specifically designing dances made to be seen only on screen.

Doris Humphrey's *The Art of Making Dances* is published.

Martha Graham choreographs *Episodes* in collaboration with George Balanchine of the New York City Ballet.

1960   Martha Graham wins the Capezio Dance Award.

1961   The New York State Council on the Arts is founded.

Ruth St. Denis wins the Capezio Dance Award.

1962   Judson Dance Theater established at Judson Memorial Church in Manhattan to present the work of experimental choreographers. The first performance was given by graduates of musician Robert Dunn's dance composition course.

1963   Donald McKayle wins the Capezio Dance Award.

Martha Graham undertakes major foreign tour, appears triumphantly in London.

1964   Paul Taylor tours Europe.

Merce Cunningham tours Europe and Middle East.

American Dance Theater formed under the artistic direction of José Limón.

Louis Horst dies.

José Limón wins the Capezio Dance Award.

1965   Twyla Tharp forms her own company.

National Foundation of the Arts and Humanities established in Washington, D.C.

1966   Association of American Dance Companies formed.

Tamiris dies.

Twyla Tharp presents *Re-Moves,* her first dance of special achievement.

1967   Paul Taylor wins Capezio Dance Award.

1968   Ruth St. Denis dies.

Festival of Dance featuring sixteen companies co-ordinated by Charles Reinhart begins.

1969   Martha Graham retires from active performing.

John Martin wins Capezio Dance Award.

1970   An accelerating movement among companies to incorporate themselves as nonprofit corporations to receive public and private funding.

1972   José Limón dies.

Alvin Ailey establishes his company as resident modern dance company at the New York City Center 55th Street Theater.

Ted Shawn dies.

1973   Martha Graham reorganizes her company after an absence of two years.

LePercq Space opened at the Brooklyn Academy of Music for experimental dance and drama productions in a nonproscenium area.

1974 Twyla Tharp choreographs *As Time Goes By*, her second work for the City Center Joffrey Ballet.

1975 Martha Graham creates *Lucifer*, a work for international ballet stars Margot Fonteyn and Rudolf Nureyev and her company.

Charles Weidman dies.

Further Reading

BOOKS

Allan, Maud, *My Life in Dancing* (London: Everett & Co., 1908). A first-person narrative of what it was like to be a pioneer in modern dance.

Anderson, Jack, *Dance* (New York: Newsweek Books, 1974). A coherent, balanced view of dance development in Europe and the United States.

Armitage, Merle, *Accent on Life* (Ames: Iowa State University Press, 1964). Autobiographical reminiscences of musicians and dancers and others encountered during his long career as promoter, publicist, and presenter of theatrical artists.

———, *Martha Graham* (privately printed, 1937). Splendid collection of essays about Martha Graham's work and personality as seen by her contemporaries in the 1930s.

———, with Virginia Stewert. *The Modern Dance* (privately printed, 1935). Statements by choreographers themselves and contemporary critics on the emerging modern dance of the 1930s.

Cohen, Selma Jeanne, *Doris Humphrey: An Artist First* (Middletown, Connecticut: Wesleyan University Press, 1973). A portrait of the artist as reflected in her voluminous correspondence.

——— (ed.), *The Modern Dance: Seven Statements of Belief* (Middletown, Connecticut: Wesleyan University Press, 1966). Seven choreographers unburden themselves of ideas on dance in general and in particular of their reaction to a proposed theme for a dance.

Cunningham, Merce, *Changes: Notes on Choreography* (New York: Something Else Press, 1968). Set with idiosyncratic typography and difficult to read, but an utterly fascinating and revealing document about the creative impetus of a contemporary master. Just plunge in, it's rewarding.

Denby, Edwin, *Looking at the Dance* (New York: Horizon Press, 1949). Wonderfully lucid observations about works and dancers. The first collection of analytical writings by the dean of dance critics. Carefully selected by colleague B. H. Haggin.

Duncan, Isadora, *My Life* (New York: Boni and Liveright, 1927). The passionate chronicle of a life ruled by and dedicated to the art of dancing. It was considered scandalous at the time, but the value of the book lies in its detailing of her efforts to present serious concert dance to an uninformed public.

Enters, Angna, *First Person Plural* (New York: Stackpole Sons, 1937). Autobiography of the dance-mime who pursued several careers as costume designer and writer as well.

Forti, Simone, *Handbook in Motion* (Halifax, Canada: The Press of the Nova Scotia College of Art and Design, 1974). Autobiographical background and descriptions of her dances by a theorist of the sixties.

Fuller, Loie, *Fifteen Years of a Dancer's Life* (Boston: Small, Maynard & Company, 1913). The fascinating life and times of a dance innovator, who even here is reticent about discussing the incredible lighting effects that made her the talk of her day.

Graham, Martha, *The Notebooks of Martha Graham* (New York: Harcourt, Brace Jovanovich, 1973). A phantasmagoria of the choreographer's jottings and musings as she prepared librettos for her works. For full benefit a knowledge of Graham's works is recommended.

Horst, Louis, *Pre-Classic Forms* (New York: Dance Horizons, 1968). Musical analysis of the pavane, minuet, etc., with an appreciation of each and its history by the composer-accompanist who devoted a lifetime to working with modern dancers.

————, and Carroll Russell, *Modern Dance Forms in Relation to the Other Modern Arts* (San Francisco: Impulse, 1961). An instructional treatise detailing his methods of teaching dance composition.

Humphrey, Doris, *The Art of Making Dances* (New York: Grove Press, 1962). An analysis of the elements of dance making as practiced by one of the leading choreographers of her generation. Witty as well as theater wise.

Johnston, Jill, *Marmalade Me* (New York: E. P. Dutton & Company, 1971). Half diary jottings and half collected pieces from the *Village Voice* critic who wrote extensively about the early experimental work of the Judson Dance Theater at the beginning of the sixties. Perceptive and politely partisan.

Leatherman, Leroy, *Martha Graham* (New York: Alfred A. Knopf, 1966). A chatty portrait of the Graham company and its creator in the middle 1960s with lots of pictures.

Lloyd, Margaret, *The Borzoi Book of Modern Dance* (New York: Alfred A. Knopf, 1949). A clear-eyed and understanding look at modern dance up through the late 1940s. Absolutely invaluable.

Martin, John, *The Modern Dance* (New York: Dance Horizons, 1965). The first sound theoretical book about emerging modern dance written with a polemicist's enthusiasm.

——, *Introduction to the Dance* (New York: Dance Horizons, 1965). Further observations about the world of modern dance with a somewhat more softened manner of presentation.

——, *John Martin's Book of the Dance* (New York: Tudor, 1963). An illustrated guide to the world of dance, including folk and ballet as well as modern dance.

McDonagh, Don, *Martha Graham* (New York: Praeger, 1974). The first full length biography of this major American creative artist, examining the relationship between her life and her art.

——, *The Rise and Fall and Rise of Modern Dance* (New York: Outerbridge & Dienstfrey, 1970). A theoretical assessment of the 1960s and 1970s choreographers with biographical sketches of the major practitioners.

Mitchell, Jack, *American Dance Portfolio* (New York: Dodd, Mead, 1964). *Dance Scene USA* (Cleveland: The World Publishing Company, 1967). Both books combine modern dance and ballet on stage and in the studio. While the performance photos are memorable the portraits are unforgettable. Stunning!

Morgan, Barbara, *Martha Graham* (New York: Duell, Sloan and Pearce, 1941). The best book of photographs ever produced on a dancer and her work.

Percival, John, *Experimental Dance* (London: Studio Vista, 1971). A critic's eye view from England about the currents in contemporary choreography, touching on European and American companies, both ballet and modern.

Rainer, Yvonne, *Work 1961–1973* (Halifax, Canada: The Press of the Nova Scotia College of Art and Design, 1974). Autobiographical presentations of many of her works with background information about influences both personal and professional.

St. Denis, Ruth, *An Unfinished Life* (New York: Dance Horizons, 1971). Autobiography by the "first lady of American dance." Has much information about the forerunners and their progeny.

Schlundt, Christena, *The Professional Appearances of Ruth St. Denis and Ted Shawn* (New York: the New York Public Library, 1962). *The Professional Appearances of Ted Shawn and His Men Dancers* (New York: the New York Public Library, 1967). *Helen Tamiris: A Chronicle of Her Dance Career* (New York: the New York Public Library, 1970). The realities of the vaudeville and concert dancer as can be seen in the route sheets of yearly performance tours. Each section introduced with sound background information. Accurate, and fascinating if you like the real nuts and bolts.

Selden, Elizabeth, *The Dancer's Quest* (Berkeley and Los Angeles: the University of California Press, 1935). A contemporary's view of the development of the emerging modern dance of the 1920s and 1930s.

Shawn, Ted, *One Thousand and One Night Stands* (New York: Doubleday & Company, 1960). An enthusiastic autobiography of making a career in dance when the morals of women dancers were suspect and men were not supposed to dance at all.

Siegal, Marcia, *At the Vanishing Point* (New York: Saturday Review Press, 1972). A collection of critical writings, prickly with moral evaluations and aesthetic appreciations.

Sorell, Walter (ed.), *The Dance Has Many Faces*, 2nd Edition (New York: Columbia University Press, 1966). Essays and observations by leading choreographers and critics about artistic beliefs.

——, *The Dancer's Image* (New York: Columbia University Press, 1971). Long philosophical essays about dancers through the ages with most warmth expressed for the experimental work of the 1930s.

Steegmuller, Francis (ed.), *Your Isadora: the love story of Isadora Duncan and Gordon Craig* (New York: Random House & the New York Public Library, 1974). Meticulously researched and the letters speak volumes.

Terry, Walter, *The Dance in America,* Rev. Ed. (New York: Harper & Row, 1971). A lively, anecdotal look at American dancing from an enthusiastic observer.

——, *Frontiers of Dance, The Life of Martha Graham* (Thomas Y. Crowell Company, 1975). An overdue addition to the *Women of America* series.

PERODICALS

Ballet Review. A literate, opinionated journal with some of the best writing on dance extant. Don't be fooled by its name: roughly half the articles are about modern dance. Appears four times a year.

Dance Magazine. Oldest current periodical in the field and tries to touch all the bases from the most advanced to the mainstream. Appears monthly. Look for the reviews of Jack Anderson among others.

Dance News. Appears monthly and has a useful dance calendar in addition to other features and thoughtful reviewers, among whom one looks for George Jackson.

Dance Perspectives. Monographs on special subjects that range from the romantic ballet to folk dancing. Tastefully illustrated on fine printing stock. Appears quarterly.

Dance Scope. Organ of the American Dance Guild. Appears twice a year with a selection of articles geared for the most part to modern dance.

Hudson Review. Quarterly which carries a dance chronicle by Marcia Siegal.

The Nation. Reviews by clear-eyed and sensitive Nancy Goldner. Appears weekly but unfortunately Goldner is only found in every third or fourth issue.

The New York *Times* (Sunday). Regular weekly articles in Section 2 by influential Clive Barnes and also frequent second features by guest contributors. Occasional bonanza in magazine section, where long articles appear a couple of times a year on dance.

The New Yorker. Tough, provocative reviews by Arlene Croce appear in every second or third issue on average. Appears weekly.

Saturday Review. Regular reviews by Walter Terry, doyen of active critics.

The Village Voice. Weekly reviews by perceptive critic Deborah Jowitt. Covers modern dance with special sympathy.

Index